WEATHERING

Cultural Inquiry

EDITED BY CHRISTOPH F. E. HOLZHEY
AND MANUELE GRAGNOLATI

The series 'Cultural Inquiry' is dedicated to exploring how diverse cultures can be brought into fruitful rather than pernicious confrontation. Taking culture in a deliberately broad sense that also includes different discourses and disciplines, it aims to open up spaces of inquiry, experimentation, and intervention. Its emphasis lies in critical reflection and in identifying and highlighting contemporary issues and concerns, even in publications with a historical orientation. Following a decidedly cross-disciplinary approach, it seeks to enact and provoke transfers among the humanities, the natural and social sciences, and the arts. The series includes a plurality of methodologies and approaches, binding them through the tension of mutual confrontation and negotiation rather than through homogenization or exclusion.

Christoph F. E. Holzhey is the Founding Director of the ICI Berlin Institute for Cultural Inquiry. Manuele Gragnolati is Professor of Italian Literature at the Sorbonne Université in Paris and Associate Director of the ICI Berlin.

Contents

LAYERS

FLOODS

Preface

The intensifying ecological devastation of the planet is being registered across scientific disciplines and activist, artistic, or more broadly cultural endeavours in ways that rethink the temporal dimensions of a catastrophe that can no longer be considered 'looming'. In many political contexts — trying to get scientists heard, mobilizing state power and international agreements to curb the extractivist rapaciousness of global capitalism — it might still seem essential to create a sense of urgency, of a rapidly closing interval, last chance, now or never. Yet taking stock not only of the planetary sum totals of global climate change but its present local manifestations, the devastations of neo-colonial extractivism, the irreversible extinctions of countless species, destruction of ecotopes on land and in the sea, has produced a growing awareness that in many crucial senses, it is 'too late' — that the time can no longer be given as 'five minutes to midnight' but has moved a lot closer to the dead of night, whether this is being regarded primarily as a question of the cumulative loss of biodiversity as part of what is now known as the 'sixth mass extinction' or as the approach of several 'tipping points' of global climate change, such as the current ice sheet disintegrations in the polar regions, the greenhouse gas release triggered by the loss of permafrost, and irreversible desertifications. The complexion of ecology, over these last years, has turned from juicy green to dark and brittle.

The most decisive recent interventions, while acknowledging the overwhelming pessimist thrust of ecological thought, have tried to use a more complex, more differentiated account of the temporality of environmental ruination in order to reflect on the diminished possibilities for life in these ruins while avoiding familiar registers both of science fiction dystopias and self-healing planets.

Thus, while both Anna Lowenhaupt Tsing and Timothy Morton habitually invoke 'the end of the world', they try to salvage, describe, and mobilize a distinct new dimension of ecological thought — no longer extrapolating future scenarios to be averted, but vindicating different natures, enlarged and broken temporal frames, meshes of life worn, torn, and stitched.

Timothy Morton characterizes the uncanny time of 'hyperobjects', such as climate change, based not only on their temporal vastness — they stretch into an unknowable future, he says, 'like the empty streets [...] in the paintings of Giorgio de Chirico' while also predating any awareness of them — but also on their 'temporal undulation', an abyssal veiling or withdrawal:[1] 'The undulating fronds of space and time float in front of objects.'[2] If Morton's hyperobject thus has to remain uncannily out of reach, its time is 'radically different from human-scale time', approaching the present from a future beyond calculation, prognosis, projection.[3] This is the heterotemporal reservoir Morton mobilizes in the deliberately paradoxical exhortation to allow the present to be changed by the withdrawing future of hyperobjects. In his 2014 Wellek Lectures titled *Dark Ecology*, Morton will beckon even further, into what he calls 'the third darkness, the sweet one, past the second darkness, the uncanny one'.[4] The unknowable future emanating from hyperobjects, the 'ontological mystery', is supposed to be passed (or, with Morton's recoded concept, 'subscended')[5] towards an ethical 'future coexistence'.[6]

For Anna Lowenhaupt Tsing, too, the future to be mobilized by a radical ecology is one of coexistence, but she remains committed to a time-scale that contrasts starkly with Morton's temporal immensities. The temporal horizon she sketches 'at the end of the world' is not demonstratively 'posthuman' but of deliberately modest dimensions;

---

1   Timothy Morton, *Hyperobjects: Philosophy and Ecology after the End of the World* (Minneapolis: University of Minnesota Press, 2010), part i, chapter 'Temporal Undulation', pp. 55–68 (p. 55)

2   Ibid., p. 63.

3   Ibid., p. 197. The strangeness of the postulated temporality forces Morton's stylistic hand: 'The undulating temporality that hyperobjects emit bathes us in a spatiotemporal vortex that is radically different from human-scale time.' Part ii of *Hyperobjects* deals with 'The Time of Hyperobjects', pp. 99–201.

4   Timothy Morton, *Dark Ecology: For a Logic of Future Coexistence*, The Wellek Library Lectures in Critical Theory (New York: Columbia University Press, 2016), p. 5. The first darkness enumerated ('we usually don't get past the first darkness, and that's if we even care') is the nihilism and depression that comes with the realization of environmental doom.

5   Ibid., p. 116.

6   Ibid., p. 160.

the futurity brought into play is not one of mysterious withdrawal but of the surprise encounter with a matsutake mushroom: 'If we open ourselves to their fungal attraction, matsutake can catapult us into the curiosity that seems to me the first requirement of collaborative survival in precarious times.'[7] Rather than the descent into doom that Morton cultivates and that is to spawn a purgatory of ontological mystery to arrive at a paradise of bittersweet non-human coexistence, Tsing looks for a curiosity without speculative violence, a surprise thoroughly lodged in the small entanglements of gathering practices, embodied as much in her subjects as in her own writing.[8] The goal, in Tsing's words, is the preparation of an idea of a 'third nature' in contrast to both the 'first nature' of ecological relations (human and non-human alike) and the 'second nature' of 'capitalist transformations of the environment':

> My book then offers 'third nature,' that is, what manages to live despite capitalism. To even notice third nature, we must evade assumptions that the future is that singular direction ahead. Like virtual particles in a quantum field, multiple futures pop in and out of possibility; third nature emerges within such temporal polyphony.[9]

For Tsing, this temporal polyphony grows from the spore-carrying aleatorics of devastation and ruination itself, yet it is looped into the entangled unity of dispersal and discovery of repetitive, mundane, everyday gathering practices.

This modest proposal for a heterotemporal futurity 'at the end of the world' can be contrasted with Donna J. Haraway's response to the ongoingness of environmental disasters, global climate change, and extinction events — in Haraway's words: 'unnecessary killings of on-goingness'.[10] Haraway launches an audacious 'no future!', a plea against futurity as such, against fantasies of ecological securitizations or sus-

---

7   Anna Lowenhaupt Tsing, *The Mushroom at the End of the World: On the Possibility of Life in Capitalist Ruins* (Princeton, NJ: Princeton University Press, 2015), p. 2.

8   Ibid., p. viii.

9   Ibid.

10   Donna J. Haraway, *Staying with the Trouble: Making Kin in the Chthulucene* (Durham, NC: Duke University Press, 2016), p. 1.

tainabilities, but also against the deadlines of totalized environmental catastrophe:

> [M]any of us are tempted to address trouble in terms of making an imagined future safe, or stopping something from happening that looms in the future, of clearing away the present and the past in order to make futures for coming generations. Staying with the trouble does not require such a relationship to times called the future.[11]

For Haraway, the energies wasted on imagining futures dark or bright, vast or modest, would have been better spent on widening the present, rendering it diverse and messy enough so that it begins to function as a 'hot compost pile'. Indeed, a kind of generalized, or rather sprawling, tangling understanding of composting, home to an 'opportunistic, dangerous, and generative sympoiesis', provides, for Haraway, the only possibility of resurgence.[12] Yet not only is 'eschewing futurism' the precondition for present-tense composting, but the collaborative tangle of the compost heap in turn is the only way to avoid futural fixations:

> Alone, in our separate kinds of expertise and experience, we know both too much and too little, and so we succumb to despair or to hope, and neither is a sensible attitude. Neither despair nor hope is tuned to the senses, to mindful matter, to material semiotics, to mortal earthlings in thick copresence.[13]

Haraway openly embraces the circular structure of this rejection of futurity, it provides the very heat of the composting present, the pressure with which finitude, mortality, corruptibility are taken off their grand temporal scaffoldings.[14]

It seems telling that no matter how radically different these three critical responses to the current environmental catastrophe might seem, they all proceed through a reimagining of time — not an epochal break *within* time, neither dawn of a new age nor posthuman aftermath,

---

11   Ibid.
12   Ibid., pp. 4 and 168.
13   Ibid., p. 4.
14   Ibid., p. 32: 'Ecosexual artists Beth Stephens and Annie Sprinkle made a bumper sticker for me, for us, for SF: "Composting is so hot!"'.

but a non-anthropocentric reconfiguration of temporality as such, a settling into a time understood anew: whether as the extreme dilation afforded by hyperobjects, the nooks of gathering futures, or a steaming pile of compacted co-presencing.

This intense and diverse work on the temporal implications of the way in which ecological devastation is being thought also needs to be understood, of course, as a response to the headline-grabbing attempt to confront anthropogenic planetary change by inscribing it in the grander scale of geological epochs. The efforts to define and establish this epoch under the name 'Anthropocene' has taken centre stage since it was launched by the Anthropocene Working Group of the Subcommission on Quaternary Stratigraphy of the International Commission on Stratigraphy in 2009. The relative merits of this undertaking have been hotly debated over the last decade. At issue is the question of temporal scale: The assignation proffers a widening of the scope, which often translates into an elevation of the environmental impact of a global humanity past its local conflicts, 'daily squabbles', the political project-making predominant in considerations of brighter futures, and in particular the supposedly roughly equally disastrous environmental impacts of capitalist and socialist economies.[15] The convergence between certain ideas of globalization and the supposedly uniform planetary impact captured in the term Anthropocene has prompted vehement opposition. The very categories of the global and the planetary tend to obliterate the vast environmental inequities of today, insufficiently acknowledged, let alone addressed, in the NDCs (Nationally Determined Contributions) of the UNFCCC (United Nations Framework Convention on Climate Change) Paris Agreement and the carbon market it established both for ITMOs (International Transfers of Mitigation Outcomes) and emergent practices of corporate carbon offsetting.[16] Yet more importantly, they keep from

---

15   This point has been most forcefully pursued by Dipesh Chakrabarty since his seminal 'The Climate of History: Four Theses', *Critical Inquiry*, 35.2 (Winter 2009), pp. 197–222. See also Chakrabarty, 'The Human Condition in the Anthropocene', in *The Tanner Lectures on Human Values*, 35, ed. by Mark Matheson (Salt Lake City: University of Utah Press, 2016), pp. 139–88, available online: <https://tannerlectures.utah.edu/Chakrabarty%20manuscript.pdf> [accessed 1 August 2020].

16   The preamble of the Paris Agreement only half-acknowledges calls for climate justice, right alongside beliefs in a 'Mother Earth', as it 'not[es] the importance for some

view the extent to which the current situation is the outcome of centuries of colonizations and the ongoing mutations of colonial power and its ever intensifying extractivist devastations. As Kathryn Yusoff admonishes:

> Seeking to monumentalize Anthropocene history is an attempt to reclaim an 'innocence' around this geohistory. The histories of the Anthropocene unfold a brutal experience for much of the world's racialized poor and without due attention to the historicity of those events (and their eventfulness); the Anthropocene simply consolidates power via this innocence in the present to effect decisions that are made about the future and its modes of survival.[17]

For Yusoff, geohistory can acknowledge the planetary change caused by extractivism and industrialization only to the extent that it acknowledges its own involvements in these projects, that is, as long as it is willing to give up its supposed 'scientific' innocence, the 'objectivity' licensed to the natural sciences. It is indeed hard to see how the elevation of the name of humankind in the geological period assignation can help but remain complicit in the radical modes of dehumanization bound up with ecological exploitation and destruction. Yusoff's observation of the dehistoricizing implications of talk of an 'Anthropocene' exceeds the genealogy of geology through which it is filtered. She rightly insists that the temporal scale itself is not the problem. The enlarged temporal frame dehistoricizes inasmuch as it invites the sublime contemplation of an earth before (and now also after) humankind and thus still passes over into a familiar conception of 'prehistory', itself a secular heir of Christian salvation history, which justified the enslavement of non-European peoples with their presumed existence 'outside of history'.[18]

---

of the concept of "climate justice", when taking action against climate change'. See UNFCCC, Conference of the Parties, 'Adoption of the Paris Agreement. Proposal by the President' (Bonn: UNFCCC Secretariat, 2015) <https://unfccc.int/resource/docs/2015/cop21/eng/l09r01.pdf> [accessed 1 August 2020].

17   Kathryn Yusoff, *A Billion Black Anthropocenes or None* (Minneapolis: University of Minnesota Press, 2018), pp. 11–12.

18   On the cultural impact of the modern invention of 'prehistory' see *Préhistoire. Une Énigme moderne*, ed. by Cécile Debray, Rémi Labrusse, and Maria Stavrinaki (Paris: Centre Pompidou, 2019). For the anthropological division of peoples inside and

In light of these fraught attempts to address the current ecological catastrophe under the sign of an 'Anthropocene', the nature of Morton's, Tsing's, and Haraway's interventions becomes clearer: No matter how far they diverge in their conceptions, they all reject the anthropocentrist contortion and, in some sense, irony of the name 'Anthropocene', refusing to scale along the very name of a species whose exceptionalism this undertaking can only emphasize, even in its critical inflection. They all radically decentre the human and its temporal scales, insist on its entanglements, involutions, but also scatterings and dispersals. The question being negotiated among the three authors in question — but many more alongside them — concerns their search for the most effective way to breach the divide between natural history and a history of humankind, between the *anthropos* and its milieus: through composting, hyperobjects, or the errant dispersal of mushroom and gatherer.

This reconsideration of entangled, layered times, scales, durations, and the attendant turn away from evental futurity also informs the present collection and its title-giving consideration of weathering. Its authors' reflections on the diverse modalities of 'weathering' is premised on an acknowledgment of the fact that the impact of environmental catastrophes is being registered already, and disproportionately so in regions of the globe at a decisive distance from first-world hyperconsumption, a distance defined, still, by the long arm of neocolonial extractivist and exploitative schemes. To insist that environmental damage is not looming past a future horizon but is already being weathered and unevenly, injustly so, means to forgo patent illusions of sustainability or resilience and the ways in which they have amalgamated with neoliberal doctrines over the last decades. But the invocation of 'weathering' also means to emphasize a certain passivity with which cataclysmic change, often diffuse and slow (according to some time scales), is being registered and endured. There are clear affinities — yet also notable differences — to figures of vulnerability and exposure, but also resilience and endurance, around which new forms of political and ethical theorizing have emerged that distance themselves from

---

outside of history see Johannes Fabian, *Time and the Other: How Anthropology Makes its Object*, foreword by Matti Bunzl, new edn (New York: Columbia University Press, 2014).

notions of agency, sovereignty, autonomy, and self-determination and instead, often inspired by Emmanuel Levinas, produce an enriched understanding of passivity as a potential to think responsivity otherwise.[19]

In search of an extension of these explorations into an environmental ethics, Astrida Neimanis and Rachel Loewen Walker have, already in 2014, suggested the term weathering as a keyword for 'a feminist ethos of responsivity towards climatic phenomena'.[20] Providing a New Materialist expansion of 'insurgent vulnerabilities',[21] they, too, suggest a modified temporality to account for an entanglement beyond the nature-culture divide, one they term 'thick time', characterized by what they term a 'nonchronological durationality'.[22] For Neimanis and Loewen Walker, the term 'weathering' mainly signals a radical shift in the relation to global climate change as something everyone is already immersed — and implicated — in: 'We recognize our own implications in the climate conditions around us, thick with co-labored temporalities that we are also making possible.'[23] And yet Neimanis and Loewen Walker derive from this a particular 'duty' for

---

19   See, among many, *Vulnerability in Resistance*, ed. by Judith Butler, Zeynep Gambetti, and Leticia Sabsay (Durham, NC: Duke University Press, 2016). Butler acknowledges and discusses the Levinasian inspirations of this ethics of vulnerability in several texts, for example in her *Precarious Life: The Powers of Mourning and Violence* (London: Verso, 2004), chapter 5: 'Precarious Life'. But it is important to note that Levinas's resolutely anthropocentric ethics had been grafted onto ecology even earlier by, among others, John Llewelyn, *The Middle Voice of Ecological Conscience: A Chiasmic Reading of Responsibility in the Neighborhood of Levinas, Heidegger and Others* (London: Macmillan, 1992) and Silvia Benso, *The Face of Things: A Different Side of Ethics* (Albany: State University of New York Press, 2000).

20   Astrida Neimanis and Rachel Loewen Walker, 'Weathering: Climate Change and the "Thick Time" of Transcorporeality', *Hypatia*, 29.3 (2014), pp. 558–75 (p. 558).

21   Ibid., pp. 566 and 573. Like the notion of 'transcorporeality' in the subtitle, this is a reference to the work of Stacy Alaimo, in this case to: 'Insurgent Vulnerability and the Carbon Footprint of Gender', *Women, Gender, and Research* (Kvinder, Køn og Forskning, Denmark), 3–4 (2009), pp. 22–35. In her *Exposed: Environmental Politics and Pleasures in Posthuman Times* (Minneapolis: University of Minnesota Press, 2016) — which is interested in '[p]erforming exposure as an ethical and political act' and in how to 'occupy exposure as insurgent vulnerability' (p. 5) — Alaimo, in turn, suggests that '[p]erforming exposure can catalyze that very sense of weathering' (p. 82) that Neimanis and Loewen Walker are proposing.

22   Ibid., p. 561.

23   Ibid., p. 573.

'*specifically human agents* in a posthuman context [...] to direct this reponsivity in particular ways'.[24]

The present volume and its authors are more reluctant when it comes to reconstituting this kind of exceptionalist 'human guardianship', however intricately tangled or passively inflected. The emphasis, instead, lies here on the enormous richness of what the English language calls 'weathering'. Thus, for example, weathering might appear to be a surface phenomenon; or it can seem to be generally unwelcome. And yet, even the most dramatic storm or profound inner turmoil can be said to have been weathered; and weathering also denotes a host of cultural techniques that makes use of the elements in drying fruit or varnishing artefacts. It seemed imperative to the participants of this project to explore the semantic richness of the term that refuses all symmetries, deranges etymological sequencing, and can hardly be divvied up into literal and figurative uses. Its semantic spread seems at times as diffuse as the phenomena it describes, its impact deeply ambivalent, to say the least.

Yet if the diverse considerations and interventions presented in this volume engage with one another and tangle in often unforeseen ways, this is a result of a longer process and exchange: The authors of this volume had convened as the primary researchers of the two-year research project 'ERRANS environ/s' in 2018, under the auspices of the ICI Berlin. The project, concluding part of the six-year ERRANS cycle of the Institute, followed the research project 'ERRANS, in Time' and indeed emerged from the latter, inheriting many of its engagements with non-linear temporalities, questions of temporal scales, standstills, and reversals. ERRANS environ/s had been devised to track the wider scientific and cultural impact of ecology, of notions such as milieu and environment, as one of diffusion, scatter, dispersion, and blurring rather than totalization. Over the course of the first year of research, the group chose the term 'weathering' to focus its reflections, which were presented in a workshop in the Fall of 2019. The individual contributions were elaborated and expanded under difficult circumstances, the COVID-19 outbreak becoming a 'Public

---

24   Ibid.; emphasis in original. The imperative continues: 'Our call is [...] for those of us living in privileged, high-consumption situations to direct our responsivity more consciously, in a way more closely attuned to that which we are affecting.'

Health Emergency of International Concern' in January 2020 and a 'Pandemic' by March, effecting a dispersal of the research group, which continued and concluded its work under distancing provisions.

While the contributions appear clustered in the table of contents, this certainly does not suggest that the plurality of disciplines, approaches, theoretical interventions, choices of subject matter allow for any kind of systematization whatsoever. Quite on the contrary, the section headings (Elements, Traces, Layers, and Floods) seek to effect a refractive multiplication rather than any logic of subsumption. The first contributions, gathered as 'Elements', seek to show the expanse of weathering, semantically, logically, but also historically. The second cluster, 'Traces', considers the interaction between weathering and the particular figure of the trace, its degradation, but also the idiom — including the linguistic boundaries of the idiomatic idiosyncracies with no exact parallel outside of the English language. The essays gathered under 'Layers' show that an attention to weathering might start on a surface but ultimately invites a model of layered complexity, whether this applies to environmental policy, the violence of border regimes, or the role of revolutionary contingencies. And the final grouping, 'Floods', quite directly engages with an elemental dimension, water, which has been figuratively tied to forgetting and erasure.

Weathering becomes a principle of this presentation insofar as its collection implies an exposure and inasmuch as the authors were aware of the fact that the resulting process should not be considered arrested and preserved in print (and digital object identification) but invites a mutability that, ultimately, remains incalculable.

*

The section 'Elements' begins with a chapter by Christoph F. E. Holzhey, who engages the nature–culture divide with the generative ambivalences of weathering in both language and physics. Taking the different uses of the enantiosemic and ambitransitive verb as indicative of the human's fraught relationship with its environment and itself, the chapter analyses multiple ways in which 'weathering' can involve subject–object relations, objectless subject–predicate relations, or even subjectless processes, and proposes to think them with mechanics, thermodynamics, and chaos theory.

The brief explorations of radiation exposures that Alison Sperling presents within the second chapter draw primarily from nuclear art and culture and contribute to the field of nuclear aesthetics, which has long been fixated on the problem of visibility and the representation of nuclear residues. The examples draw primarily from photographic technologies and other aesthetic registers that capture visual residues of radiation. The challenges of nuclear aesthetics are also political and social. This constellation of objects and inquiries is meant to explore the fraught political, environmental, and social relations between radiation, visibility, toxicity, through the concept of *exposure*. They offer feminist glimpses into other ways of thinking exposure, as it develops in relation to (often imperceptible) toxicity that is not inscribed into a logic that partitions the passive victim of suffering from some pure or unaffected subject. They are examples that are both forms of exposure specific to the nuclear while also, perhaps, helping to expose more nuanced and complex ways of understanding forms of exposure that extend beyond nuclearity.

In 'Weathering the Afterlife', Nicolò Crisafi and Manuele Gragnolati investigate the meteorological phenomena represented in Dante Alighieri's *Commedia* and their interrelation with the subjectivity of the dead in Hell, Purgatory, and Heaven. Examining how the dead weather the afterlife and how the elements affect them, in turn, the essay takes the complex enantiosemy of the word 'weathering' as a conceptual guiding thread for the exploration of dynamics of exposure (*Inferno*), vulnerability (*Purgatorio*), and receptivity (*Paradiso*).

Daniel Liu addresses 'Scaling from Weather to Climate'. One of the theoretical tensions that has arisen from Anthropocene studies is what Dipesh Chakrabarty has called the 'two figures of the human', and the question of which of these two figures of the human inheres in the concept of the Anthropocene more. On the one hand, the Human is conceived as the universal reasoning subject upon whom political rights and equality are based, and on the other hand, humankind is the collection of all individuals of our species, with all of the inequalities, differences, and variability inherent in any species category. This chapter takes up Deborah Coen's argument that Chakrabarty's claim of the 'incommensurability' of these two figures of the human ignores the way both were constructed within debates over how to relate local geophysical specificities to theoretical generalities. It examines two cases in the history of science: Martin Rudwick's exploration of how geologists slowly gained the ability to reconstruct the history of the Earth in deep time, and Coen's own history of Austrian climate science, a case where early assumptions about the capriciousness of the weather gave way to theories of climate informed by thermodynamics and large-scale data collection.

The section 'Traces' opens with an essay about rust co-authored by Amelia Groom and M. Ty. Iron usually plays the part of strength, stubbornness, and impenetrability, but rust registers the dimension of time in the material, reminding us that it always carries the potential for its own decomposition. While great expense is incurred to stave off iron's oxidization, Groom and Ty read the uselessness that rust precipitates as an interruption of the instrumental logics that sustain racial capitalism. Looking to the rusted ring that became Elsa von Freytag-Loringhoven's *Enduring Ornament* (1913), they consider how the discarded and defunctionalized lend themselves to ornamental redeployment. The essay then turns to works by the contemporary American artists David Hammons and Andrea Fraser, both of which turn Richard Serra's rusty steel sculptures into a backdrop for fleeting gestures of impromptu reclamation. Attending to questions of susceptibility and monumental weathering, these reflections look to rusty leakages that play out the impossibility of refusing the environment. Rust, the authors suggest, is a material archive of exposure that does not keep itself, but flakes apart and seeps away.

Damiano Sacco's chapter addresses the question of weathering by considering its excess to the conceptual dimension and relating it to what Jacques Derrida names (the) 'trace'. The study of the 'logic' of weathering/the trace is confronted with Giorgio Agamben's critique of Derrida's project. Their two different conceptions of language, of its presuppositional structure, and of its order of 'metaphysical presence' are considered, in particular by turning to Werner Hamacher's work on these and related matters.

'Glaze: Or Formulas to Get through Bad Weather' is a short story by Umut Yıldırım set during the military junta of 1980 in Istanbul.

On the run and underground with her family, Ö searches for ways to bestow meaning on numerous encounters her father had with thieves.

The section 'Layers' starts out with the chapter 'Weathering Weather: Atmospheric Geographies of the Guiana Shield' by Yolanda Ariadne Collins. It argues that paying attention to the weather and its associated processes of geological, biological, and social weathering can destabilize knowledge traditions that insist on dichotomies. Looking to specific histories and current conditions in Guyana and Suriname, this chapter shows how notions of weathering can accommodate a wide range of referents, ranging from the weathering of rock to socio-political and historical afterlives of violent colonial displacements.

Following Hannah Arendt's remarks on refugee camps as spaces of 'worldlessness', Anja Sunhyun Michaelsen examines how, in films on European asylum facilities, systemic violence 'makes itself known' in images of nature. The chapter "'Locked out in nature'" shows how nature separates and isolates (*La Forteresse, Forst*), constitutes a sphere of domination and control (*View from Above*), and functions directly as a murder weapon (*Purple Sea*). Nature, in these films, indicates the Outside within, haunted by the latent and ghostly presence of systemic violence.

Entitled 'On Bad Weather: Heidegger, Arendt, and Political Beginnings', Facundo Vega's chapter restages Hannah Arendt's *Auseinandersetzung* with Martin Heidegger regarding 'political beginnings'. Sketching Heidegger's exceptionalist account of 'new beginnings' and Arendt's dispute with him in relation to the tension between the spheres of 'philosophy' and 'politics', Vega traces her position about 'political founding'. According to Vega, Arendt invites us to recognize the 'principle of an-archy' innate to 'political beginnings', which cannot be absorbed by exceptionalist invocations of the 'history of Being'.

The final section 'Floods' begins with Marlon Miguel's chapter 'Representing the World, Weathering its End: Arthur Bispo do Rosário's Ecology of the Ship'. The chapter explores the intrinsic relationship between weather/weathering and the imaginary of the sea, which features in the work of artist Arthur Bispo do Rosário. Bispo was a black man who spent most of his life in psychiatric institutions. There is an important interplay between his psychotic deliriums and the production of hundreds of objects, many of them ships or forms that relate to the sea. These objects open up a discussion on decoloniality as they are embedded with marks left by the transatlantic slave trade.

Claudia Peppel's chapter is entitled 'Enduring Rain'. Over the six months in which Vajiko Chachkhiani's *Living Dog Among Dead Lions* was exhibited at the Georgian Pavilion at the 57th Venice Biennale in 2017, heavy rain was pouring inside the installation. This artificially generated process provokes thoughts on the nature of the here and now as well as of the afterlife and of the future appearance of the hut's water-sensitive insides. Eventually, the spaces and furniture exposed to rain and water stagnation will begin to rot and disintegrate, and mould and moss might grow over them. Its viewers feel caught between what they see and what they hope to see; between their perceptions and expectations, in an exceptional time zone where 'natural' weathering is being performed as a subject of meditative observation. The chapter is followed by a conversation between Vajiko Chachkhiani and Claudia Peppel. Entitled 'Life Never Stops Being Violent', it focuses on the role of extreme weather conditions and the vulnerability to weathering in Vajiko Chachkhiani's work, especially in the piece *Living Dog Among Dead Lions*.

In 'Confined Weathers: Graciela Iturbide and Mario Bellatin's *The Bathroom of Frida Kahlo/Demerol without Expiration Date*', Delfina Cabrera asks: What is the work of weathering in an enclosed space? What if that space was the bathroom of the famous Mexican painter Frida Kahlo? Defying prudeness and asepsis, writer Mario Bellatin and photographer Graciela Iturbide enter that intimate room and through a series of artistic interventions give Kahlo's weathered legacy a new afterlife. The logic of the archive is their guiding principle: in order to protect what has been locked inside, they must expose it and return it to common use.

ARND WEDEMEYER
CHRISTOPH F. E. HOLZHEY

ELEMENTS

Weathering Ambivalences
Between Language and Physics

CHRISTOPH F. E. HOLZHEY

INTRODUCTION

Proverbially unpredictable, the weather presents many challenges and ambivalences both on the level of (human) language and of (natural) science. Many languages have a particular, rather peculiar class of 'weather verbs', which are arguably as 'ill-behaved' as the weather itself. Nothing seems more banal than to speak about the weather, wondering whether it will be warm or cool today, whether it will rain or storm. Yet, linguists still discuss the '*it* that does the raining in English and many other languages'.[1] They ask, for instance, whether 'it' is a dummy, expletive pronoun or whether 'it' refers rather to an 'all-encompassing', 'total environment'.[2] Perhaps this wavering between

---

1   Ronald W. Langacker, *Foundations of Cognitive Grammar*, 2 vols (Stanford, CA: Stanford University Press, 1991), II: *Descriptive Application*, p. 365, quoted by Beth Levin and Bonnie Krejci, 'Talking about the Weather: Two Construals of Precipitation Events in English', *Glossa: A Journal of General Linguistics*, 4.1 (2019), Art. 58, pp. 1–29 (p. 1) <https://doi.org/10.5334/gjgl.794>.

2   Dwight Bolinger, *Meaning and Form*, English Language Series, 11 (London: Longman, 1977), pp. 78, Dwight Bolinger, 'Ambient *It* Is Meaningful Too', *Journal of Linguistics*, 9.2 (1973), pp. 261–70 (p. 261) <https://doi.org/10.1017/S0022226700003789>, and Wallace L. Chafe, *Meaning and the Structure of Language* (Chicago: University of Chicago Press, 1970), pp. 101–02.

all and nothing should be taken as an indication that the subject of the weather is an ill-posed question. Indeed, what Noam Chomsky calls the 'weathering-*it*' conjures up the kind of 'grammatical habit' and 'seduction of language' that Friedrich Nietzsche insistently considered as the source of misguided beliefs.[3] Following Nietzsche's reasoning, the question of the (grammatical) subject of weather verbs can indeed be said to transport an erroneous and detrimental dualism that takes all change, alteration, and becoming to be conditioned and caused by a radically different, separate subject — essentially the Cartesian ego conceived as substance, being, and free will.

Correcting the *Cogito* by an 'it thinks' is insufficient for Nietzsche, insofar as the doing remains doubled by a fictive doer — leading to

---

3   Noam Chomsky, *Lectures on Government and Binding*, Studies in Generative Grammar, 9 (Dordrecht: Foris Publications, 1981), pp. 324–25; Friedrich Wilhelm Nietzsche, *Beyond Good and Evil / On the Genealogy of Morality*, trans. by Adrian Del Caro, The Complete Works of Friedrich Nietzsche, 8 (Stanford, CA: Stanford University Press, 2014), *Beyond Good and Evil*, §17, p. 19 and *Genealogy of Morality*, I-13, p. 236. To quote the passages to which I will return more fully, Nietzsche writes in *Beyond Good and Evil* (1886): 'it is a *falsification* of the facts to say: the subject "I" is the condition of the predicate "think." It thinks: but that this "it" is precisely that old famous "ego" is only an assumption, an assertion, to put it mildly, and by no means an "immediate certainty." In fact too much is already claimed with this "it thinks": even this "it" contains an *interpretation* of the process and doesn't belong to the process itself. Here the concluding is done according to grammatical habit, namely "thinking is an activity, to every activity belongs something that is active, therefore— ." Following basically the same scheme, the older atomism looked at every effective "force" for that little particle of matter in which it resides, and from which it produces effects, that is, the atom; more rigorous minds finally learned to do without this "earth residuum," and perhaps someday we will even accustom ourselves, logicians included, to doing without this little "it" (into which the honest old ego has vanished)' (§17, p. 19). In *On Genealogy of Morality* (1887), Nietzsche further expands on this 'grammatical habit', referring to the 'seduction of language (and the basic errors of reason petrified in it), which understands and misunderstands all effecting as conditioned by something that effects, by a "subject." For instance, just as ordinary people separate lightning from its flashing and take the latter as its *doing*, as the effect of a subject that is called lightning, so too popular morality separates strength from the expressions of strength, as if behind the strong one there were an indifferent substratum *free to* express strength or not to. But there is no such substratum; there is no "being" behind the doing, effecting, becoming; the "doer" is merely tacked on as a fiction to the doing — the doing is everything. The people basically double the doing when they have the lightning flashing; this is a doing-doing: it posits the same occurrence once as cause and then once more as its effect. Natural scientists do no better when they say "force moves, force causes" and so on — despite all its coolness, its freedom from affect, our entire science still stands under the seduction of language and has not gotten rid of the false changelings foisted upon it, the "subjects" (the atom for instance is such a changeling, likewise the Kantian "thing in itself")' (pp. 236–37).

a redundant 'doing-doing' as he notes in a related text, which takes the common separation of 'lightning from its flashing' as example for language foisting in subjects everywhere. Suggesting that the natural sciences succumb to the same seduction when they speak of forces that move and are to be localized in matter, Nietzsche claims that 'more rigorous minds finally learned to do without this "earth-residuum"', and looks forward to the day when we 'accustom ourselves, logicians included, to doing without this little "it" (into which the honest old ego has vanished [zu dem sich das ehrliche alte Ich verflüchtigt hat])'.[4]

However, such attempts at overcoming the last anthropomorphism — even in impersonal weather verbs with expletive or all-encompassing subjects — risk reinforcing anthropocentric oppositions and generating new human, or indeed overhuman, figures. If talking about the weather is a well-tried manner of establishing sociality, the unpredictable power of the elements, weather conditions, or atmospheric agencies conjure up an abyss of chaos as the sublime ground for (re)newed constitutions of the human.

As I shall suggest, such an anthropogenic function of the weather is sedimented in the verb 'to weather' insofar as this verb seems to be the precise obverse of impersonal weather verbs: in its manifold and multivalent uses, it takes for granted the activity and effects of the elements and considers them as implicit, impersonal background for subjects that are always human or, at least, anthropocentric.

At the same time, I will argue that if weathering has a semantic history that is anthropocentric, its multivalent grammar also points to a process of weathering that not only precedes oppositions of subject and object, culture and nature, or language and science but that can also be understood as the ground from which such oppositions emerge. And while language may not be able to do without the subject, reading the ambivalences of linguistic weathering with those of scientific weathering opens the possibility of re-working time-honoured

---

4   Ibid., p. 19. Walter Kaufmann's translates the bracket as 'which is all that is left of the honest little old ego', which suggests to my mind more accurately that the ego is still present in this 'it'. See Friedrich Wilhelm Nietzsche, *Beyond Good and Evil: Prelude to a Philosophy of the Future*, trans. by Walter Arnold Kaufmann (New York: Vintage Books, 1989), §17, p. 24.

dualistic oppositions so that they come to matter otherwise, that is, in a less anthropocentric manner. The idea here is not that science can avoid the linguistic predicate-subject separation, which tends to substantialize the subject even before it is opposed to an object, but rather that physics, for instance, in seeking to model unpredictable phenomena on the basis of natural laws, conjures up other kinds of 'subjects', which may help keep the grammatical subject from default-ing into an emphatic human subject.[5]

CO-CONSTITUTIVE WEATHERING

In their 2014 article '*Weathering*: Climate Change and the "Thick Time" of Transcorporeality', Astrida Neimanis and Rachel Loewen Walker propose to create 'weathering' as a concept 'to counter the fallacy of a bifurcated understanding of "nature" and "culture" — or of weather and humans'.[6] They draw on feminist new materialist and posthumanist approaches that highlight the fundamental entangle-ment, mutual imbrication, and inseparability of 'human and nonhu-man natures'.[7] In particular, they invoke Stacy Alaimo's notion of 'transcorporeality', which stresses 'the extent to which the substance of the human is ultimately inseparable from "the environment"',[8] and propose an 'understanding of ourselves as weather bodies':[9]

> We seek to cultivate a sensibility that attunes us […] toward ourselves and the world as weather bodies, mutually caught up in the whirlwind of a weather-world, in the thickness of climate-time. In short, as *weathering*.[10]

---

5   In other words, the general strategy could be described as countering a dualism of substance, which would oppose the human to the nonhuman, by a dualism of method — or more precisely a complementary of methods, which takes the risk of universalizing both anthropomorphism (or vitalism) and mechanism in order to attend in either case to the emergence of differences that have not been pre-supposed.

6   Astrida Neimanis and Rachel Loewen Walker, 'Weathering: Climate Change and the "Thick Time" of Transcorporeality', *Hypatia*, 29.3 (2014), pp. 558–75 (p. 560) <https://doi.org/10.1111/hypa.12064>.

7   Ibid., p. 563

8   Stacy Alaimo, *Bodily Natures: Science, Environment, and the Material Self* (Blooming-ton: Indiana University Press, 2010), p. 2 cited by Neimanis and Loewen Walker, 'Weathering', p. 563.

9   Neimanis and Loewen Walker, 'Weathering', p. 560.

10 Ibid., p. 561.

Neimanis and Loewen Walker seek to radicalize their notion of weathering further by drawing on Karen Barad's theory of 'intra-action', according to which separable entities (onto)logically do not precede their relations but co-emerge through them. While Alaimo's transcorporeality allows for relations of contiguity, continuity, or immersion, they maintain that intra-action clarifies the claim that 'humans and nonhuman climate and weather phenomena are co-constitutive. We are mutually emergent, coextensive. Together, we *weather* the world.'[11]

Moving from 'Transcorporeal Weather' to 'Transcorporeal Temporalities', Neimanis and Loewen Walker enlist the notion of intra-action to radicalize the collapse and co-constitution of distinctions even further and extend them to space, time, and matter. The principal target remains the belief that human bodies can be separated from their environment. They had already made the intriguing and subtle suggestion that it is not enough to speak of immersion: 'the weather and the climate are not phenomena "in" which we live [...] but are rather of us, in us, through us.'[12] Referring to Claire Colebrook's observation that 'our attempts to externalize climate deny the fact that we are already entangled in its forces and flows', they now move to a critique of the 'exteriorization' and 'spatialization of time'. In particular, they object to narratives of sustainability, progress, or apocalypse that 'rely on a linear earth time where past, present, and future make up a time-line of human progression.'[13] It is in order to counter such an exteriorization and spatialization of time that Neimanis and Loewen Walker turn again to Barad's notion of intra-action to consider 'the co-constitutive functionings of matter and meaning that collapse any notion of distinct space and time into an "iterative becoming of spacetimemattering"'.[14] Shifting attention towards non-spatialized temporalities thus ends up involving the collapse of all distinctions — of and within space and time as well as matter and meaning into what one might well call space-

---

11   Ibid., p. 564.

12   Ibid., p. 559.

13   Ibid., pp. 569 and 567.

14   Ibid., p. 569, quoting Karen Barad, *Meeting the Universe Halfway: Quantum Physics and the Entanglement of Matter and Meaning* (Durham, NC: Duke University Press, 2007), p. 234.

timematteringsemiosis[15] — so as to be able to think their intra-active co-emergent co-constitution.

The move from 'Transcorporeal Weather' to 'Transcorporeal Temporalities' does not imply that Neimanis and Loewen Walker abandon weathering. On the contrary, it is meant to lead them deeper into weathering as 'the intra-active process of a mutual becoming' through which 'humans and climate change come to matter'. Thus, they make the striking claim that 'matter is *weathering* in its making of temporality'.[16] Such a concept of weathering 'means to think of bodies as part and parcel of the making of time [...]. Our very bodies, thoughts, actions, and behaviors make the present, past, and future'.[17] Understood as a 'making of temporality', weathering leads them to the provocative 'claim that we *are* time' — or at least to the notion of 'a time that we weather together'.[18]

Time, here, has taken the place of the world in the rallying cry 'Together we *weather* the world'. Such formulae are intriguing and highly suggestive, but upon closer inspection, the sense of weathering emerging from them is quite ambivalent, difficult to ascertain, and hard to retain. Indeed, they may serve rather as examples for the difficulty of fully grasping the 'profound conceptual shift' that the notion of intra-action represents in Barad's own words. Whereas the more common idea of 'interaction' presumes the 'prior existence of independent entities or relata', the notion of 'intra-action' insists that 'relata do not preexist relations' and claims instead that they 'emerge through specific intra-actions'.[19] Such a definition of intra-action is both compelling and easily repeated. However, articulating or even just thinking relations without preexisting relata — or, for that matter, the very notions of 'preexisting', 'preceding', or processes of co-emergence without a linear (temporal or logical) order — remains hard without getting seduced by the duplications, separations, and reifications of language.

---

15   Other than 'spacetimemattering', Barad often uses 'ontoepistemological' and occasionally 'ethico-onto-epistemology' (Barad, *Meeting the Universe Halfway*, p. 409n10).

16   Neimanis and Loewen Walker, 'Weathering', pp. 560 and 569.

17   Ibid., p. 569.

18   Ibid., p. 570.

19   Barad, *Meeting the Universe Halfway*, pp. 139–40.

A sentence such as 'Together, we weather the world' no doubt describes a relational process, but insofar as it has a clear subject-predicate-object structure, it invariably conveys the sense that these identifiable, distinct elements precede their relation in the sentence. As Neimanis and Loewen Walker had previously defined 'weathering' as 'mutual worlding', the sentence should be read as 'Together, we mutually world the world', which becomes even more redundant and tautological if one remembers that 'we are the world' insofar as 'humans and nonhuman climate and weather phenomena are co-constitutive' and 'we are mutually emergent, coextensive'. In other words, by identifying the relata preceding the relation, one arrives at a triplicating but also manifestly circular 'The world worlds the world', while what emerges from the original formulation is not only the separation of 'we' from the 'world', but also a subject-object relation with a defiant predicate resonating well with how weathering is commonly used as a transitive verb when one says, for instance, 'the crew weathered the storm'.

My point here is not to criticize some particular, perhaps unfortunate formulations, but rather to note that when invoking intra-action to emphasize the ontological indeterminacy of anything preceding relations, one should not forget that this is only the premise for the claim that intra-action is meant to account for the co-constitution of separable entities. Such co-constituted entities seem to acquire strong, separable identities — stronger than what is suggested by contiguity, continuity, or immersion, which intra-action supposedly radicalizes. Indeed, the process of intra-active co-constitution is often referred to as a 'coming to matter',[20] but what is remarkable is that the co-constitution happens here in and through common language. If 'Together, we weather the world' has any referent and describes anything, it is the imaginary of a 'we', of a 'world', and of their mutual constitution that the sentence performatively produces. While the notion of intra-

---

20   Neimanis and Loewen Walker, 'Weathering', adopt this pervasive language of mattering in another formulation that works to equate weathering with intra-active processes: 'it is through weathering — the intra-active process of a mutual becoming — that humans and climate change come to matter' (p. 560). However, the premise and claim of intra-action that relata come to matter through the relation rather than preexisting it, is immediately contradicted by the subsequent sentence offering an alternative definition by way of conclusion: 'Weathering, then, is a logic, a way of being/becoming, or a mode of affecting and differentiating that brings humans into relation with more-than-human weather' (p. 560).

action may well succeed in dispelling the belief in separate entities being ontologically pre-given, it is far less clear to what extent new-materialist talk of mattering through intra-active, agential separation does not yield to the seduction of language of foiling subjects into everything and doubling or even tripling processes into a doing-doing or world-worlding world.

Again, there is much to be said for taking the risk of anthropomorphizing in order to help balance the alternative risk of anthropocentrism, but it requires critical, methodological self-reflection if the twin risks are to be avoided. The problem with the way in which Neimanis and Loewen Walker create the concept of weathering is not so much that it involves a performative contradiction, which as such may well be unavoidable if language is always performative and enacts divisions into separable entities that appear to have pre-existed their (linguistic) relation.[21] Such a temporal entanglement, whereby language produces what it presupposes, could well be considered part of their critique of 'linear time' and correspond to the 'cultivation of the sensibility of thick time' they propose and describe. However, what would warrant critical reflection is the deliberate gesture of 'concept-creation',[22] which implies sovereign, anthropocentric subjects that can create a concept such as 'weathering' *ex nihilo* (even as it explicitly draws on theoretical sources) and disregard the multiple significations that centuries of language use have sedimented into that signifier.

Disclaimers here seem insufficient and function rather as disavowals, denials, or negations in Sigmund Freud's sense of *Verneinung*,[23] as when the authors distance themselves from both anthropomorphism and human exceptionalism,[24] but otherwise quite consistently seek to reduce distances and deny the relevance of scale, thereby suggesting a

---

21   For an attempt to move beyond this logic of presupposition arguably characterizing the experience of language from Aristotle to Derrida, see Damiano Sacco's chapter 'The Weathering of the Trace: Agamben's Presupposition of Derrida' in this volume.

22   Neimanis and Loewen Walker, 'Weathering', p. 560.

23   Highlighting the difficulty of retain the ambiguity of this term in translation, Jean Laplanche and Jean-Bertrand Pontalis, *The Language of Psycho-Analysis* (London: Hogarth, 1973) conclude their entry on negation, Verneinung, (dé)négation by highlighting three closely related assertions in Freud's analysis: 'taking cognizance of what is repressed' and engaging in 'a kind of intellectual acceptance of the repressed', and 'thinking frees itself from the restrictions of repression' (p. 263).

24   Neimanis and Loewen Walker, 'Weathering', pp. 563–64.

strict symmetry and even equivalence in relations of mutuality and in figures such as 'weather bodies'. In particular, they explicitly question common distinctions between climate and weather based on different time-scales and aim 'to reduce the distance between the enormity of climate change and the immediacy of our own flesh', or again they propose to 'bridge the distance of abstraction [which they criticize in climate discourse] by bringing climate change home'.[25]

Similarly, Barad's disclaimer that she does not intend to 'make general statements [...] about all entanglements, nor to encourage analogical extrapolation from [her] examples to others'[26] sits uneasily with the far-reaching consequences she and others draw from the notion of intra-action as 'mutual constitution of entangled agencies'. After all, Barad's neologism is only spelled out and specified in a precise, technical sense for the example of quantum diffraction experiments and their interpretation in terms of Niels Bohr's particle-wave complementarity. Barad's point that quantum entanglement is not limited to microscopic scales and can therefore apply also on macroscopic scales in a literal rather than analogical manner, is well taken, but in practice, when entanglement is invoked to deny the relevance of scale, literality seems to be a question of language rather than physics.[27]

Seeking to negotiate between conflicting risks perhaps always runs the worse risk of disavowal, that is, of glossing over internal tensions, while reproducing what is to be avoided. Immunizing itself against critique, disavowal fosters a voluntarist decisionism concerning, for instance, the question of when separability is to be rejected in favour of

---

25   Ibid., pp. 562 and 559. The formulation 'bringing home' is introduced indirectly through the initial reference to Rachel Slocum, 'Polar Bears and Energy-Efficient Lightbulbs: Strategies to Bring Climate Change Home', Environment and Planning D: Society and Space, 22 (2004), pp. 1–26.

26   Barad, *Meeting the Universe Halfway*, p. 74.

27   In addition to the 'caveat' on using weather and climate interchangeably — justified by suggesting that distinguishing time scales means to 'promote a spatialized view of climate time' — there are further examples of disclaimers that I would read as disavowals, that is, as acknowledging that there is something to what is explicitly denied. For instance, there are the caveats that the 'shift away from the "stop climate change" temporal narrative is not for us a weakening of possibilities for ethico-political engagement' and that their proposal does not seek to 'denigrate other feminist analyses of climate change that underline the gendered, racialized, and colonial power politics at play' ('Weathering', p. 561), or the 'clarifications' in which Neimanis and Loewen Walker distance themselves from holism and from a perspective on processes 'bound to the human mind' (ibid., pp. 570–71).

inseparable entanglements and when it is to be embraced as the mode in which anything 'comes to matter'. In order to negotiate conflicting risks, it may be better to focus on the opportunities that are in apparent conflict and envisage the possibility of fully endorsing heterogeneous accounts, even if they are mutually incompatible and cannot be pictured together. Such a possibility is envisaged by Bohr's principle of complementarity, which plays a decisive role in Barad's inspiring advancement of the diffractive methodology that Donna J. Haraway had proposed as alternative to 'reflection'. While I find the development of an ontology of indeterminate matter through a method of complementary diffraction compelling, I would highlight that this approach crucially relies on disparate scales and insist on retaining the *method* across different scales and fields rather than extrapolate the *ontology* linearly or even simply unchanged. In particular, it may be productive to think of the relation between the weather and human bodies, nature and culture, physics and language as entangled and perhaps even in some sense as intra-active, but not in the same sense in which electrons are entangled and materialize through the measurement process: unlike entangled electrons, each side of the relation has already come to matter — if anything ever does.

The weathering article by Neimanis and Loewen Walker makes it admirably transparent that the appeal of new-materialist theories and notions such as intra-action often lies in opening up possibilities by enabling a 'new imaginary' — a way to 'reimagine our bodies', 'reimagine climate change', and 'reimagining our literal inextricability from that towards which we are called to respond' — rather than in providing a less human-centred, somehow more direct account of matter. No doubt, the 'reimagination of ourselves as weather bodies [...] is *already a politics*'.[28] However, it is more difficult to see how a politics of reimagination and intensive feeling can be reconciled as such with the declared premises and aims of new-materialist and posthumanist approaches, such as the explicit critique of human exceptionalism and of the bifurcation of nature and culture. At least in its general outline, it ultimately seems rather to be a fully anthropocentric, humanist, even idealist politics. Perhaps in response to such reservations, the 2018

---

28   Neimanis and Loewen Walker, 'Weathering', p. 572.

article 'Weathering', which Neimanis co-authored with Jennifer Mae Hamilton, appears more anchored and explicit in associating weathering with 'specific feminist, antiracist and decolonial intersectional attentiveness'.[29] For instance, it exemplifies its expanded, 'naturalcultural' understanding of the weather by making contact with Christina Sharpe's notion of weather as 'totality of our environments' and 'total climate' characterized as 'antiblack', and helpfully situates weathering 'between the neo-liberal heroics of resilience and the victim politics of vulnerability'.[30] In these contexts, the image of intra-active, co-constitutive weathering is particularly provocative, and while probing its specific political potential falls beyond the purview of this chapter, I will concentrate on exploring its logic both on the level of language and on the level of physical reality to which Barad's argument lays claim.

WEATHERING THE DICTIONARY

Creating weathering as a concept of co-constitutive worlding is provocatively counter-intuitive insofar as both 'co-constitution' and 'worlding' suggest constructive processes. Even if one takes these processes also as undermining the autonomy of the subject, the most common use of the noun 'weathering' is rather more destructive: The Oxford English Dictionary (OED) defines the noun as the 'action of the atmospheric agencies or elements on substances exposed to its influence; the discoloration, disintegration, etc. resulting from this action'.[31] However, especially the verb 'to weather' is actually remarkably ambivalent. Now usually associated with disintegration, deterioration, and decay — or at least the risk thereof — its first meaning was '1. to subject to the beneficial action of the wind and sun; to air'.[32] The subentries in the OED indicate that 'weathering'

---

29   Astrida Neimanis and Jennifer Mae Hamilton, 'Open Space Weathering [sic, according to the journal's citation recommendation]', *Feminist Review*, 118.1 (2018), pp. 80–84 (p. 83) <https://doi.org/10.1057/s41305-018-0097-8>.

30   Neimanis and Hamilton, 'Weathering', pp. 81 and 83, Christina Sharpe, *In the Wake: On Blackness and Being* (Durham, NC: Duke University Press, 2016), p. 104.

31   'weathering, n.', in *OED Online* (Oxford: Oxford University Press, 2020) <https://www.oed.com/view/Entry/226660> [accessed 10 May 2020].

32   'weather, v.', in *OED Online* (Oxford: Oxford University Press, 2020) <https://www.oed.com/view/Entry/226641> [accessed 22 February 2020].

was initially understood as a cultural technique encountered in such diverse contexts as hawking (the 'sport or practice of chasing birds or small animals by means of trained hawks'), house- and farm-work (airing linen, drying harvested crop), or handicraft (exposing clay for brick- or tile-making).[33]

While the second meaning is formulated quite neutrally in terms of a change through exposure, the several sub-entries indicate that a complete reversal to the weather's detrimental effects has taken place:

> 2. To change by exposure to the weather
> a. *transitive.* To wear away, disintegrate, or discolour by atmospheric action. [...]
> b. *intransitive.* To become worn, disintegrated, or discoloured under atmospheric influences. [...]
> c. In passive, esp. of a crop: To be deteriorated by too long exposure to bad weather.
> d. *intransitive.* To wear (well or ill) under atmospheric influences.

The final sub-entry (2d), which could suggest a return to a neutral sense of change, only serves to confirm the full reversal in relation to the beneficial weathering of hawking and other cultural techniques. Indeed, 'wearing well' merely seems to mean 'wearing less badly', and the only sample phrase is: 'For outside work, boiled oil is used, because it weathers better than raw oil.'

Subsequent entries, which often invoke a nautical context, entail another kind of reversal without entirely restoring the initial, beneficial meaning.[34] Weathering here refers to the ability to resist or escape detrimental, even disastrous effects: 'to get safely round' (3b), 'to withstand and come safely through (a storm)' (4a), 'to sustain without disaster' (4b), or 'to pass through and survive (severe weather)' (4c). The previous meaning of weathering as a deteriorating change is implied here as a threat or risk, but the verb is now used in an opposite sense, namely as successful opposition to such a change.

---

33   'hawking, n.1', in *OED Online* (Oxford: Oxford University Press, 2020) <https:// www.oed.com/view/Entry/84775> [accessed 6 June 2020].

34   The nautical associations of weathering are emphasized by the Marlon Miguel's chapter 'Representing the World, Weathering its End: Arthur Bispo do Rosário's Ecology of the Ship' in this volume.

The final, rather specialized meanings listed in the OED return to specific cultural techniques. One of them is directly beneficial, namely '6. To set (the sails of a windmill) at the proper angle to obtain the maximum effect of the wind-force'; while the other one consists again rather in avoiding detrimental effects, namely the technique in architecture 'to slope or bevel (a surface) so as to throw off the rain' (7).

Of course, many words are polysemic, but the OED definitions suggest that the verb 'to weather' may be regarded, more radically, as enantiosemic, that is, as having mutually opposite meanings. Such words, which are their own antonyms, are more common than one might expect, and include in English, for instance, 'to cleave' (to adhere or separate), 'to sanction' (to approve or penalize/boycott), or 'to rent' (to purchase use of something or sell it).[35] The verb 'to weather' is even more peculiar insofar as it can be said to be doubly enantiosemic and confound oppositions both of activity and quality: Usually signifying a deteriorating change, it can also mean, on the one hand, successfully opposing such a change and, on the other hand, undergoing a beneficial change.

While context often clarifies the intended meaning, the coincidence of opposites in a single word remains highly unstable. Sometimes, enantionyms are true homonyms, that is, words that have different etymological origins and just happened to have become homographs and homophones in the course of linguistic evolution.[36] But the possibility of opposite meanings coming together in a word through condensation, contraction, reduction, or equivocation can also be indicative or evocative of a generative kernel from which such oppositions have emerged in the first place and from which diverse meanings continue to emerge. The puzzling, vertiginous implications of such productivity appears reflected in the ongoing proliferation of terms proposed to name this category of words: from 'Janus word', which seems to be the only one to have found its way into the OED, to 'self-antonym', 'auto-antonym' or 'autantonym', 'con-

---

35 Mark Nichol, '75 Contronyms (Words with Contradictory Meanings)' <https://www.dailywritingtips.com/75-contronyms-words-with-contradictory-meanings/> [accessed 15 June 2020]. The list includes 'Weather: To withstand, or to wear away'.

36 See 'Janus Words', Online Etymology Dictionary (2019) <https://www.etymonline.com/columns/post/janus-words> [accessed 15 June 2020]. An often-cited example is 'to cleave'.

tronym' or 'contranym', as well as 'enantionym', 'enantiadrome', and 'antagonym'.[37] Going further back, there is the notion of 'primal words [Urworte]', Carl Abel's thesis of their 'antithetical meaning [Gegensinn]', and the analogy that Sigmund Freud establishes with the logic and language of dreams.[38] Highlighting that a 'no' does not seem to exist for dreams, which 'feel themselves at liberty, [...] to represent any element by its wishful contrary', Freud notes:

> [T]he most ancient languages behave exactly like dreams in this respect. In the first instance they have only a single word to describe the two contraries at the extreme ends of a series of qualities or activities [...]; they only form distinct terms for the two contraries by a secondary process of making small modifications in the common word [Urwort].[39]

Without necessarily endorsing Abel's and Freud's claims concerning the historical evolution of languages and acknowledging that many enantiosemic words have separate etymologies that only happened to converge into single words, I maintain that the double enantiosemy of 'to weather' is more than a contingent, historical accident. Instead, my suggestion is that it is indicative of an undecidability that lies at the heart of the fraught relationship humans entertain with their environment and allows for manifold articulations. While such an understanding of weathering resonates with the concept Neimanis and Loewen Walker develop by drawing on contemporary theories of transcorporeality and intra-action, I consider it as a case less of 'concept-creation' than of learning from the experience and peculiar logic sedimented and implied in the word's enantiosemic uses. If the appeal of weathering lies in its generativity and beneficial potentials,

---

37   Cf. Burcu I. Karaman, 'On Contronymy', *International Journal of Lexicography*, 21.2 (2008), pp. 173–92 <https://doi.org/10.1093/ijl/ecn011>, David-Antoine Williams, 'Poetic Antagonyms', *The Comparatist*, 37.1 (2013), pp. 169–85 <https://doi.org/10. 1353/com.2013.0009>.

38   Carl Abel, *Über den Gegensinn der Urworte* (Leipzig: Verlag von Wilhelm Friedrich, 1884) and Sigmund Freud, *The Standard Edition of the Complete Psychological Works of Sigmund Freud*, 24 vols (London: Hogarth, 1953–74), IV: *The Interpretation of Dreams (1900)* (1953), p. 318.

39   Freud, *Interpretation of Dreams*, pp. 318–19. Concerning primal words, Freud also suggests that what is today symbolically related was 'probably united in prehistoric times by conceptual and linguistic identity' and draws on Hans Sperber's thesis on the sexual reference of all primal words (p. 352).

a critical question is understanding the conditions under which the effects of weathering may reverse from detrimental to beneficial and may open possibilities beyond such cultural techniques as hawking and setting sails. The weather sciences and ultimately physics are no doubt indispensable for understanding the conditions of beneficial weathering, but the conditions are also a matter of politics, of socio-economic and cultural values, of psychology, and ultimately of language, which structures thought and experience. While this chapter remains focused on weathering's language, I seek to develop it in ways that may resonate and interfere with its physics.

ANTHROPOCENTRIC GRAMMAR OF WEATHERING

Whereas the OED traces the historical development of word use, the Merriam-Webster dictionary (MWD) takes a more systematic, grammatical approach. It distinguishes on a first, hierarchical level between transitive and intransitive uses of the verb, and then, on a second level, between two transitive meanings:

> transitive verb
> 1: to expose to the open air: subject to the action of the
>   elements
> 2: to bear up against and come safely through
> //weather a storm
> //weather a crisis
>
> [3] intransitive verb
> : to undergo or endure the action of the elements.[40]

This scheme can help clarify the grammar of weathering by being more consistent than the OED, which likewise organizes different meanings on two levels and foregrounds the transitive/intransitive distinction, but uses this distinction on both levels and entangles it with other categories such as 'passive' or even 'figurative', 'nautical', and 'architecture'. For example, the OED entries one and four have the heading 'transitive' and five is entitled 'intransitive', while three is entitled 'nautical'

---

40   'Weather', in *Merriam-Webster.com Dictionary* (Springfield, MA: Merriam-Webster, 2020) <https://www.merriam-webster.com/> [accessed 20 February 2020].

and has subheadings '3.a. transitive', '3.d. intransitive', and '3.b. figurative'.[41] Clearly, 'figurative' or 'nautical' exclude neither each other nor the categories of 'transitive' or 'intransitive'. Indeed, in this case the figurative use 'to get safely round' is not just transitive but corresponds well to Merriam-Webster's second transitive meaning of 'to bear up against and come safely through'.

The simplicity of the MWD scheme is deceptive and would require considerable commentary to unfold all its implications. No doubt, the historical use of weathering is richer and more nuanced, but I would like to give some indications of how the MWD's compact grammatical scheme suggests another story, one that is less historical than logical, reductive, but also constructive, ultimately leading to a generative kernel of indistinction and the possibility of as yet uncommon uses.

The compact three-fold definition formalizes well the double reversal from beneficial to detrimental exposure via successful resistance on which I have already remarked. However, what is perhaps most significant is that the MWD definitions conjure up an anthropocentric division of nature and culture. The grammatical subject of weathering indeed always seems to be human or an object of human interest, such as ships that have weathered storms. It is true that one can also speak of rocks that weather even if they have no specific human interest. But although there is a sense in which the activity of the weather or, more generally, 'the action of the elements' are always implied, the possibility of the elements becoming the subject of weathering is not envisaged. In other words, weathering is an anthropocentric predicate insofar as it excludes the weather or the elements as core argument in the subject function.

One might say that weathering denies the agency of the elements by excluding them from the subject position, but my claim concerning the anthropocentric bias of weathering needs to be articulated more carefully. After all, one could say that the elements are excluded as subjects only because their action is taken for granted and already implied in the predicate 'to weather'. Yet, as already mentioned, a characteristically anthropocentric mode of relating to nature is precisely to take

---

41 Altogether, the OED has seven headings on the first level and fifteen subheadings on the second level. Some first level entries have no subdivision and others as many as four.

nature for granted as a (back)ground for the figure of the human and their actions.[42] This also means that emphasizing the activity or even agency of nature is insufficient to counter anthropocentrism. There is indeed good reason to maintain that the elements are the primary source of all weathering activities, while humans are at best reactive if not entirely passive. But such a simple reversal of activity and passivity merely re-affirms the anthropocentric nature-culture divide as long as it involves predicates that enforce that divide. In other words, weathering is anthropocentric not because it denies agency of the weather as such — it does not preclude the existence of other predicates taking the weather as active subject — but insofar as it is premised upon a divide such that the weather is contained in the predicate (and possibly other arguments the predicate controls), but excluded as subject.

This analysis of weathering's anthropocentric bias indicates a possible strategy for countering it, namely to insist that there is no pre-given divide that would preclude the weather as subject of different forms of weathering; to expand accordingly the use of weathering at the risk of anthropomorphism; and thereby to allow for an exploration of how nature and culture may be understood as more entangled and/or became separated through weathering.

The OED actually allows for such an expanded use of weathering with some qualifications. As already mentioned, it includes the transitive use 2a 'to wear away, disintegrate, or discolour' and gives a couple of examples in which atmospheric phenomena or processes such as clouds, smoke, or percolation do the weathering.[43] At the same time it notes that the verb is then 'chiefly in *passive*', meaning that the agent

---

42   Cf. Neimanis and Loewen Walker, 'Weathering', which repeatedly opposes the tendency to externalize weather or climate: 'When we hold onto the belief that we can separate our human bodies from climate (close our doors, resist the winds), we maintain a worldview of relating *to* the earth, rather than worlding *with* it. As Colebrook has argued, our attempts to externalize climate deny the fact that we are already entangled in its forces and flows' (p. 567, emphasis in the original); 'The consequence of time's exteriorization is that, we, as bodies, are conceived as only ever in time, subject to forces that carry on beyond and outside of us. The weather/environment serves only as background, thus making for a particular mode of relating to the earth, as though human beings are somehow separate from the natural elements' (p. 568).

43   The sample phrases are: 'The rain-cloud hangs low..overhead; the smoke hovers around; and they weather the fines sculptured surface' and 'It [sc. percolation] acts also very powerfully in weathering the rocks through which the water passes' ('weather, v.', in *OED Online*; ellipsis and square bracket in the original).

is in a peripheral function or omitted entirely: the rock is weathered
by persistent rain or it is weathered *tout court*.[44] While one sees here
how the agency of the weather is at once presumed and pushed into
the background, this is only the beginning of what becomes visible
and available to analysis when this less common use of weathering is
included. In particular, I would like to ask to what extent this use of
weathering is distinct from the other uses or can be related to them,
and ultimately what the different weathering verbs have in common
other than their name.

AMBIVALENT WEATHERING OF A STORM

I propose to augment the three-fold scheme of the Merriam-Webster
dictionary by explicitly adding the missing transitive use of weathering,
which takes the weather or the elements as subject, and place it alongside the second transitive meaning of weathering (see Table 1 below).
Sample sentences of these two uses have the same basic subject-
predicate-object structure and differ only insofar as the weather is,
in one case, the object and, in the other, the subject. Corresponding
formally to a simple interchange of subject and object, they can be
combined into a single, seductively simple sentence, such as: 'I weather
the storm as the storm weathers me.'[45] This sentence could well be
taken as paradigmatic for a transitive sense of weathering that relates
nature and culture without being anthropocentric. Indeed, the sentence suggests symmetry, relationality, mutuality, perhaps even a form
of co-constitution.

---

44   Of the seven examples for this entry 2a, only the two quoted in the previous footnote
      are in the active voice. Curiously, the transitive definition 2a itself already has the
      'atmospheric action' in a peripheral position: 'to wear away [...] by atmospheric action'
      or indeed 'to change by exposure to the weather'. It is as if the transitive subject were
      here not atmospheric action or the weather but once again human beings, that is, as
      if the whole second definition were ultimately just the malignant counter-part to the
      first definition of 'subjecting to the beneficial action of the wind and sun'.

45   Note that dictionaries tend to define verbs without specifying the subject, as if the
      verbs could be universally used for any subject, while they do often specify the kind
      of object that comes with certain uses: 'to air (linen, etc.)', 'to expose (land, clay for
      brick- or tile-making)', 'To set (the sails of a windmill)', 'to slope or bevel (a surface)',
      etc. In order to mark the anthropocentrism veiled by the universalism of the subject,
      I find it necessary to specify not only the object but also the implied subject, using in
      this case 'I' and 'the storm'.

However, there is something instructively wrong here — not in the introduction of posthumanist weathering nor in the sentence combining it with the more common, anthropocentric transitive use, but in being led astray by the polysemy of both the predicate 'weathering' and the conjunction 'as', which here should be read temporally or causally rather than as establishing an equivalence. I may manage to weather the storm while it weathers me, but I do not weather it 'just as' it weathers me.

The suggestion of symmetrical co-constitutional relations is actually plausible for similar sentences with predicates such as fighting or attracting: A arguably cannot fight, attract, or repel B if B does not also fight, attract, or repel A — at least not if one understands such verbs in a mechanical sense cohering with Isaac Newton's third law 'actio=reactio': every action not only elicits a reaction but is precisely equal (and opposite) to it, which means, among other things, that neither comes first, and it is arbitrary which one is called action and which reaction. A simple example would be the mutual gravitational attraction between earth and moon, or the (electromagnetic) repulsion preventing a building from falling to the centre of the earth and keeping it on the ground.

However, applying Newton's third law can be tricky. The law resonates strangely with Michel Foucault's dictum '[w]here there is power, there is resistance' and with his relational understanding of force and power that views resistance as a condition for power relations rather than a passive reaction to a power that that would precede it.[46] Yet, a balance of attractive and repulsive forces between two bodies by no means implies that a building could not collapse under its own weight. Two different kinds of forces, such as gravity and electromagnetism (ensuring rigidity), are at work here, and there is no law of equality or reciprocity for their relationship. Instead, they are quite independent from one another, each action eliciting a reaction in the other body, and there is equilibrium only if and when they balance each other out.

---

46   Cf. Michel Foucault, *The History of Sexuality* (New York: Pantheon, 1978), i: *An Introduction*, pp. 92–97.

I may weather the storm while it weathers me, but there is no guarantee that I will succeed: although the two instances of weathering in this sentence are equally transitive, they do not only exchange subject and object but also have no necessary relationship between them. [To this extent we are far from being coextensive, let alone co-constitutive.] The deceptive symmetry can be grasped even more compactly through the ambivalent formulation of 'the weathering of a storm'. Grammatically, the genitive can be subjective or objective, that is, it can be the agent or the patient to yield a storm that weathers things or a storm that is being weathered. There may be symmetry in grammar but there is none in the action. The difference here is not so much in scale — a storm is generally much larger than anything that may weather it — but in kind: a storm threatens everything within its scope with death and destruction, whereas that which weathers the storm only saves itself and need have no effect on the storm.

Transitive weathering thus splits into two meanings that are quite independent from one another even if they are equally relational and mutually opposed. To make this explicit, one could write as defining phrase '2α I weather the storm while 2β the storm weathers me'. The grammatical reversibility of weathering — the possibility of interchanging subject and object in its transitive use — therefore does not imply relations of symmetry, mutuality, and co-constitution, as it does with verbs for fighting or mutual attraction and repulsion. Instead it is the result of weathering's specific enantiosemy that makes it appear as its own reciprocal complement. What I mean by this is that transitive weathering behaves in many ways like predicates that change into a contrary, reciprocal predicate when their subject is interchanged with another argument and that form couples such as 'attack–defend', 'inflict–suffer', or 'show–watch', except that it takes the same word for both meanings. In other words, the grammatical reversibility of weathering implies the couple '2αweathering–2βweathering', where 2αweathering involves self-preservation, sustained identity, and survival, and 2βweathering denotes destruction, disintegration, and death. Reducing even further, an equation of life and death could be said to lie at the core of weathering's enantiosemy.

FANTASY AND WEATHERING WEATHERING

Insisting on transitive weathering as enantiosemic and split into two different meanings is ambivalent insofar as it can both re-enforce ontological divisions and suggest different strategies of countering them. The division is reproduced if the contrary meanings are understood to be uniquely determined by the subject, that is, if a human(-centred) subject implies self-preserving [2α]weathering and an atmospheric subject implies destructive [2β]weathering. However, the division is undermined by insisting not merely on the atmosphere's agency, but on the possibility of human and non-human agents each being capable of being the subject of both [2α]weathering and [2β]weathering.

The enantiosemy of weathering — joint by common use and experience — makes it rather difficult to imagine and convey the possibility that I could weather the storm just as it weathers me, that is, that I [2β]weather it, wear it out, and make it decay; or that the storm could weather me just as I weather it, that is, that it [2α]weathers me, resists being worn out, and safely comes through all my attempts to annihilate it.

At the same time, the enantiosemy of weathering may be suggestive in indicating that such exercises in logical permutations and pedantic differentiations may be unnecessary and that there actually is a continuity between contrary meanings, that is, that some common, perhaps non-differentiated, ground exists from which they emerge. While such a continuity goes counter a logic of non-contradiction and is therefore hard to think, it can be dreamt and, in some languages, also said.

What I am proposing here is that the enantiosemy of weathering, its multiple reversals, and grammar can be read with Freud's remarks on antithetical primal words in his *Interpretation of Dreams* and his analysis of the vicissitudes of drives, which he tightly links to 'grammatical transformations'.[47] At one point, he derives masochism from sadism, which he considers as a 'pair of opposites', through a change from active to passive aim, which he calls 'reversal into its opposite', and through an interchange of subject and object, which he describes

---

47   Jean Laplanche, *Life and Death in Psychoanalysis*, trans. by Jeffrey Mehlman (Baltimore, MD: Johns Hopkins University Press, 1976), p. 143n7.

in two steps: first, the object of sadism is given up through a 'turning round upon the subject's own self' and secondly, another person is sought to take over the role of the subject. Noting that only the final stage corresponds to what is commonly called masochism, Freud also highlights the necessity of assuming the existence of the intermediate stage, which he explicitly describes in grammatical terms as a change from the 'active voice [...] not into the passive, but into the reflexive, middle voice'.[48]

Jean Laplanche scolds Freud here for clouding his remarkable grammatical analysis by confusing the reflexive voice (e.g., to hit oneself) and the middle voice, which is somehow between or beyond the active and the passive. Unlike Ancient Greek, English and most other modern language have no verb form for the middle voice, but Romance languages, for instance, often approximate it through a particular use of the reflexive. Laplanche invokes the French example 'se cogner [to knock oneself]' and distinguishes between an accidental knocking oneself against a chair in the dark (corresponding to the middle voice) and an intentional knocking of one's head against the walls (which is more properly reflexive).

While Laplanche privileges the properly reflexive form for its clear distinction of subject and object over the middle form, where the terms 'remain in something of a state of coalescence',[49] in the context of my chapter, the intermediate stage between opposites is most promising precisely when it coalesces rather than distinguishes subject and object, activity and passivity. An intermediate stage characterized by a 'reflexive, middle voice' plays a pivotal role also in Freud's discussion of the pair of opposites 'scopophilia [voyeurism]—exhibitionism', where he links this stage to a much earlier, autoerotic stage, which he understands as the 'source of *both* the situations represented in the resulting pair of opposites'.[50]

Questions of original autoeroticism and of a primary, reflexive masochism have been much debated as Freud remains notoriously

---

48 Freud, 'Instincts and Their Vicissitudes', in *The Standard Edition of the Complete Psychological Works of Sigmund Freud*, ed. and trans. by James Strachey, 24 vols (London: Hogarth, 1953–74), XIV: *On the History of the Psycho-Analytic Movement, Papers on Metapsychology, and Other Works (1914–1916)* (1957), pp. 109–40 (pp. 126–28).

49 Laplanche, *Life and Death*, p. 143n7.

50 Freud, 'Instincts and Their Vicissitudes', p. 130; emphasis in the original.

— but also overtly — ambiguous, contradictory, or undecided about them.[51] In a beautiful essay on original fantasies, fantasies of origin, and origins of fantasy, Jean Laplanche and Jean-Betrand Pontalis have insisted on this question for an understanding of the origin of sexuality in the properly psychoanalytic sense as a deviation from biological needs 'into the field of fantasy' and/or through a 'breaking in of fantasy'.[52]

Rather than speculating further on the onto- or phylogenetic origin of an emergent splitting off of a specifically psychoanalytical — and human — order from the order of nature, I will return to the MWD's three-fold anthropocentric definition of weathering and my pairing of the central transitive definition with a weathering that — at the risk of anthropomorphizing — takes the elements as subject. Perhaps even more speculatively, I would like to propose that this scheme can tell another story, which, rather than by emergent splittings, proceeds by a progressive reduction that may well end up turning weathering into a primal weather verb that does not even have a subject.

PROGRESSIVE VALENCY REDUCTION

The story I propose progresses by reducing what linguists call a verb's 'valency'. This notion is taken from chemistry, where it indicates the number of bonds an atom can establish with other atoms such as hydrogen, and refers to the number of arguments controlled by a predicate. Transitive verbs are typically divalent — taking a subject and an object — or trivalent, when they also take an indirect object, while intransitive verbs are typically monovalent. Most languages have valency-lowering and valency-raising mechanisms, such as the passive

---

51   In a footnote added nine years later, in 1924, Freud just comments his rejection of the existence of primary masochism by saying: 'In later works [...] I have expressed an opposite view' (p. 128n2).

52   Jean Laplanche and Jean-Bertrand Pontalis, 'Fantasy and the Origins of Sexuality', in *Formations of Fantasy*, ed. by Victor Burgin, James Donald, and Cora Kaplan (London: Routledge, 1989), pp. 5–34 (p. 25). The original title, which I paraphrased, is 'Fantasme originaire, fantasmes de origines, origines du fantasme', *Les Temps Modernes*, 19.215 (1964).

1	I weather a hawk	3
2	α) I weather the storm as β) the storm weathers me	2
3	I weather	1
4	[It] weathers	0

Table 1. Definition of weathering on the basis of the MWD, making the implied subject explicit, splitting the second definition by adding 2β (see above), and adding an understanding of weathering as an avalent weather verb (see below). The number at the end of the lines indicate the verb's valency.

or reflexive, which lower the valency, or the causative, which raises it: 'to make someone do something'.[53]

Like the historically oriented OED, the MWD begins with weathering as a cultural technique. Grammatically, this transitive use of weathering is divalent: in weathering a hawk or weathering linen there are two arguments: subject and object. Yet, as the definition 'to subject to the action of the elements' suggests, the verb's valency is effectively increased to three. Two agents indeed seem to be present, not only the grammatical, usually human, subject of the sentence, but also the weather, the air, the sun, or other atmospheric elements. Although grammatically divalent, the historically first use of weathering thus involves a triangulation: to weather hawks or linen means that one has the weather weather them.

On this view, the second transitive use of weathering involves a reduction of the number of predicate arguments, leading to a semantically as well as grammatically binary subject-object relation: to weather a storm or crisis. However, upon closer inspection, it is hard to see how this transitive use could be obtained from the first one through valency-reduction, which points rather to its opposite 2β: I weather a hawk = I have the elements weather a hawk → the elements weather a hawk.

---

53   For an overview of the wide range of valency changing mechanisms and case studies in different languages, see *Changing Valency: Case Studies in Transitivity*, ed. by Robert M. W. Dixon and Alexandra Y. Aikhenvald (Cambridge: Cambridge University Press, 2000).

Proceeding to the third meaning in the MWD involves a further reduction of valency. In rocks that weather, there is a subject but no object and weathering as an intransitive verb is monovalent. Verbs that can be both transitive and intransitive are sometimes called 'ambitransitive' or 'labile' verbs.[54] But here, too, it is hard to see how such a use could be derived from the original transitive use 2α, whereas it comes rather easily from 2β: The storm weathers me = I am weathered by the storm ≈ I am weathered → I weather. There is something quite remarkable in the last step from the passive (which is already monovalent) to the intransitive insofar as grammatically it involves a reversal from the passive to the active. Yet, it is linguistically not that unusual and is the mode of valency reduction of so-called 'patientive ambitransitives'. A standard example in English is the verb 'to break': I break the cup = The cup is broken by me ≈ The cup is broken → The cup breaks.

Adding the use 2β thus facilitates an understanding of the three-fold MWD scheme in terms of a progressive reduction of valency. In a way, this is just the result of 2β making explicit the 'action of the elements', which 1 and 3 take for granted but place in the background. One might indeed object that if one considered the first use (i.e., weathering hawks) as trivalent, one should now also say that the intransitive verb is effectively divalent insofar as the weather remains implied as agent. In other words, one might say that the use 2β was not entirely absent in the MWD but effectively contained in 3. If this observation can further the strategy of countering the anthropocentric nature-culture divide by insisting on the agency of the elements, I would now like to suggest that there is also something to be said for taking the grammatical reduction of valency from 2β to 3 more seriously.

While transitivity is premised upon a separation of subject and object, which easily aligns with nature and culture — regardless of whether one says 'I weather the elements' or 'the elements weather me' — intransitivity can do without a system–environment distinction and makes no reference to the environment. Is there not indeed a sense in which everyone and everything weathers and does so 'by itself', without any particular external influence? This would mean understanding intransitive weathering not as an implicit or 'agentless'

---

54   Ibid., p. 4.

passive that disavows the 'action of the elements', taking it for granted and placing it in the background, but rather as a kind of reflexive or middle voice, perhaps as an activity that turns against itself when it finds no object, or, vice versa and more radically, as an 'anticausative' verb from which a subject-object distinction co-emerges without being implied.[55] It could even mean understanding intransitive weathering as a form of reflexive masochism or, with Freud's re-articulation of primary masochism in *Beyond the Pleasure Principle*, as a manifestation of the death drive.

Weathering in this sense is a correlate of ageing or the passage of time, as Romance languages using the same word for 'weather' and 'time' suggest.[56] Even though some things age well and growing up and maturing are often welcomed, and even though some storms and crises may be weathered, deterioration, decay, and death appears as ineluctable fate of all temporal existence. In other words, 'the action of the elements' undergone or endured in intransitive weathering may well be just a way of speaking of a law of nature. A famous law quickly comes to mind: the second law of thermodynamics, the law of increasing entropy, which is often invoked to define the arrow of time.

Perhaps there is a good reason, then, that using weathering for 'the action of the elements' is uncommon and that this action is taken for granted or even dismissed. Not only would it be a pleonasm to say that 'the weather weathers', but following Nietzsche one could insist that the process of weathering is all there is and that a subject is added only out of grammatical habit producing a 'doing doing'. 'The weather' and 'the elements' would then only be abstract fictions without real existence. All there is then is the process of weathering

---

55   Cf. Dixon and Aikhenvald on the distinction between the 'prototypical passive', where the agent is named, the 'agentless passive', where the agent is implied — 'the glass is broken (implied: by someone)' — and the 'anticausative', where an agent is neither stated nor implied: 'the glass broke' (p. 7). (In this case, the object is explicitly assumed as grammatical subject, and my suggestion of co-emergence gestures already further towards an avalent 'it weathers'.) Concerning the term 'middle', the authors warn that it is used with a 'frightening variety of meanings' — including the anticausative and reflexive — lacks in 'typological clarity', and often amounts to a '(general) intransitivizer' (p. 11–12).

56   On the association of weather and time, or weathering and change, see Niccolò Crisafi and Manuele Gragnolati's chapter 'Weathering the Afterlife: The Meteorological Psychology of Dante's *Commedia*' in this volume.

that takes place in everything — in the elements themselves — without the intervention of some subject or agent. In other words, weathering would be an avalent weather verb after all: 'it weathers', and even speaking of an 'it' may be already saying too much.

But what about the more positive meanings of weathering: the possibility of weathering storms and crises, or even the beneficial actions of the weather? Do they have an intransitive, even avalent correlate or substrate from which they can be imagined to emerge, or are they in inherently bound to human subjects?

No doubt the positive evaluation of weathering is to a large extent anthropocentric. The outright beneficial character of the elements in the first use indeed seems due to cultural mediation — be it because we channel the actions of the elements, because the weathering is good for us but not the hawk (not to speak of sun-dried tomatoes or raisins), or because weathering hawks means temporarily lifting their confinement and putting them back in their element. Most strikingly, the OED counts the meaning 'to expose [...] to the pulverizing action of the elements' under the rubric 'to subject to the beneficial action of the wind and sun', which sounds violent and could even appear sadistic if the utility for 'brick- or tile-making' were not mentioned in my ellipsis.

However, there is also a sense in which beneficial weathering can be understood with respect to an entity's identity, self, or unity as a system rather than human utility. Garments that are being weathered lose their odour and other contaminations, making them less susceptible to moths, for instance. Weathering here purifies; it takes off what is not essential, making the object more durable. Clothes that are dried in the open air do not rot, nor will grapes and tomatoes, for instance. Perhaps this weathering takes out some life — or the potential for unwanted life, like mould — but even disregarding human utility, it seems distinguishable from entropic processes of disintegration and dissipation that involve homogenization and a loss of structure and order. Indeed, it lays bare what persists, such as an underlying structure otherwise hidden under a superficial, perhaps only ornamental layer (as it is in plastered buildings or artworks).

In other words, weathering can accentuate a thing's identity in its constitutive difference from the environment by enacting the differentiation of that which in it weathers and that which does not. Or, more suggestively, weathering constitutes identity by enacting a differentiation between two kinds of weathering, between 'what ^{3}weathers' and 'what $^{2\alpha}$weathers the elements'.

Again, one could insist that intransitive ^{3}weathering is really a passive form that implies the environment as agent and therefore presupposes a self that is distinguished from the environment. But one might also take the valency reduction more seriously and extend instead the intransitive meanings of weathering. In this way, if I argued that the ordinary intransitive use of weathering forms with $^{2\beta}$weathering a patientive ambitransitive pair, $^{2\alpha}$weathering could well be considered part of an agentive ambitransitive pair, where the intransitive simply omits the transitive object. Examples in English include eating but also winning. Not only does 'to come safely through' — the MWD definition for $^{2\alpha}$weathering — resonate with winning, but it is also itself intransitive, and perhaps one can hear in intransitive weathering not just resignation but also defiance: 'I weather!'.[57]

With such a doubling of intransitive weathering, a sense of identity becomes conceivable that relies not on a pre-given distinction from the environment — the subject-object opposition of transitive verbs — but that is instead constituted through the internal differentiation of 'what $^{\alpha a}$weathers' and 'what $^{\beta p}$weathers'. The additional superscript is necessary because one can also imagine another permutation of having the two transitive meanings of weathering enter the two varieties of ambitransitivity, arriving at both a $^{\beta a}$weathering and a $^{\alpha p}$weathering of the elements (subjective genitive).[58] For a full account of self-constituted identity that does not rely on ontological divisions, the intransitive weatherings must not, of course, predetermine their

---

57   While defiant weathering may provide a (politically) unattractive model insofar as it approaches 'neoliberal resilience' (Neimanis and Hamilton, 'Weathering', p. 83) or a 'macho model' of subjectivity, which Crisafi and Gragnolati exemplify with Capaneus in Dante's *Comedy* ('Weathering the Afterlife', p. 74), one can also think of the gay anthem during the AIDS pandemic 'I will survive', which its singer Gloria Gaynor adapted in 2017 for hurricane victims into 'Texas Will Survive', Twitter, 31 August 2017 <https://twitter.com/gloriagaynor/status/903027825443254273> [accessed 5 July 2020]).

58   If 'I $^{\alpha a}$weather' comes from dropping the object in 'I $^{\alpha}$weather the storm' and 'I am being $^{\beta}$weathered [by the storm]' leads to 'I $^{\beta p}$weather', the storm can $^{\beta a}$weather by dropping the object in 'The storm $^{\beta}$weathers me' or by turning the passive 'The storm is $^{\alpha}$weathered [by me]' into an intransitive 'the storm $^{\alpha p}$weathers'.

possible subjects. That is, in principle, one would have to allow for a fourfold intransitive weathering for both 'the elements' and other, in particular human, subjects, or ultimately just an avalent four-fold 'it weathers'.

TOWARDS A PHYSICS OF FOUR-FOLD WEATHERING

No doubt, we have long left behind even less common uses of weathering, and there is also no reason to assume that every verb should be doubly ambitransitive. However, the combinatorics of valency reduction on the one hand raises critical questions worth exploring further. What would it mean if attempts at going beyond fixed subject-object binaries led to a proliferation of monovalent or eventually avalent weatherings? Does it suggest that the problem of binaries repeats itself in a different guise? Or could one take weathering's enantiosemy — the use of the same word 'weathering' for all the different meanings that can be kept separate only with considerable analytical effort — as a hint that weathering defies language, logic, and reason, that one can only attempt to get to a fuller account by bringing together all these different, contrary meanings even though they cannot be pictured together, and that it forms an ultimately ungraspable kernel from which all the distinctions emerge that are retroactively used to project out complementary aspects?

On the other hand, I would maintain that the linguistic combinatorics can be productively related to different material phenomena and some thorny questions in the history and philosophy of physics. I have already suggested that thermodynamics and its second law of irreversible entropy production and dissipation strongly resonates with ubiquitous intransitive weathering, which now should be specified as $^{\beta P}$weathering. However, the second law continues to raise profound questions and elicit much debate. Insofar as it defines an arrow of time — an irreversible tendency towards larger entropy, disorder, equilibrium, and homogeneity — it confirms the intimate connection between weather and time suggested by Romance languages. As such, it is arguably necessary for any kind of phenomenal experience.

Yet while often regarded as the most fundamental law, the second law is alternatively, sometimes even simultaneously, considered as re-

1	**I weather a hawk**	
2	**I $^{\alpha}$weather the storm**	The storm $^{\beta}$weathers me
3	I $^{\alpha\alpha}$weather [the storm]	**I $^{\beta p}$weather /** am $^{\beta}$weathered [by the storm]
	The storm $^{\alpha p}$weathers / is $^{\alpha}$weathered [by me]	The storm $^{\beta a}$weathers [me]
4 [it]	$^{\alpha\alpha}$weathers $^{\alpha p}$weathers	$^{\beta p}$weathers $^{\beta a}$weathers

Table 2. Completing the three MWD definitions of weathering (in bold) by allowing the storm to be the subject and considering both αweathering and βweathering as both agentive ambitransitives and patientive ambitransitives.

ducible to more fundamental laws at lower scales and/or in profound conceptual conflict with these laws.[59] The basic reason for the conflict is that physics tends to theorize fundamental laws as reversible and conservative rather than dissipative, that is, despite its early twentieth-century revolutions, it continues to follow the paradigm of Newtonian mechanics and its laws of inertia and conservation, which it extends from energy and momentum to other quantities and information. The basic conflict between classical mechanics and thermodynamics can be aligned with the difference between α-weathering connoting persistence and β-weathering connoting decay, deterioration, and loss. More precisely, the conflict here corresponds to the difference between $^{\alpha\alpha}$weathering (a persisting obtained from the active 'I $^{\alpha}$weather [the storm]') and $^{\beta p}$weathering (a decaying obtained from the passive 'I am being $^{\beta}$weathered [by the storm]').

Furthermore, there is the counter-intuitive claim — forcefully advanced especially by Ilya Prigogine, the 1977 Chemistry Nobel Prize winner for his work on dissipative structures — that it is the second

---

59 While the literature on this topic is vast, a helpful point of entry may be Craig Callender, 'Taking Thermodynamics Too Seriously', *Studies in History and Philosophy of Science Part B*, 32.4 (2001), pp. 539–53.

law that accounts for the emergence of order and structure.[60] Prigogine's claim is remarkably hard to grasp in its provocatively general
ramifications. It is often emphasized, for good reasons, that a key point
for making the self-organized order and growth of living organisms
consistent with the second law is to consider them as open systems
that exchange energy with their environment and, more specifically,
discharge more entropy into their surroundings than they ingest.[61] To
this extent, one could say that the key insight is that organisms behave
like little storms that [βa]weather in the form of exhaling, sweating, defe-
cating, and urinating.

However, Prigogine goes further to suggest that self-organization
is not merely compatible with the second law but follows from it, that
is, that a system's identity and organization emerge and persist thanks
to dissipation. It is as if α-weathering of mechanical persistence were
subsumed under thermodynamic β-weathering and pushed towards
an ambiguous vitalism. Such a move can already be found in Spinoza's
notion of conatus as a 'striving to persevere in one's being', which is
modelled upon mechanical inertia but tends to retain sense of desire
and teleology of upward progression.[62]

The basic issue remains how anything can emerge to grow in
the first place. Although the [βa]weathering verbs of excretion are all
intransitive, they — and the very notion of an open system — all
presuppose a distinction between system and environment. I would
argue that it is therefore misleading to say that a system's identity and
organization can emerge through dissipation as such, and maintain
instead, as already indicated, that a differentiation between different
modalities of intransitive weathering is required, which can now be

---

60   Ilya Prigogine and Isabelle Stengers, *Order Out of Chaos: Man's New Dialogue with Nature* (London: Heinemann, 1984).

61   In *What Is Life?* from 1944, Erwin Schrödinger highlights that 'an organism feeds on negative entropy'. While the related notion of 'negentropy' remains controversial, the basic idea is clear: for a self-organizing organism to respect the second law of global entropy increase, 'the essential thing in metabolism is that the organism succeeds in freeing itself from all the entropy it cannot help producing while alive' (Erwin Schrödinger, *What Is Life? The Physical Aspect of the Living Cell with Mind and Matter and Autobiographical Sketches* (Cambridge: Cambridge University Press, 2013), p. 71).

62   Cf. Christoph F. E. Holzhey, 'Conatus Errans: Paradoxe Lust zwischen Teleologie und Mechanik', in *Conatus und Lebensnot: Schlüsselbegriffe der Medienanthropologie*, ed. by Astrid Deuber-Mankowsky and Anna Tuschling, Cultural Inquiry, 12 (Vienna: Turia + Kant, 2017), pp. 66–123.

specified as a differentiation of persisting $^{\alpha a}$weathering and dissipative $^{\beta a}$weathering.

Among the most familiar and deceptively simple examples from physics with which to test out these ideas is the formation of crystals in a super-cooled liquid. The process depends as much on the formation of persistent bonds in the emergent solid as on the flow of energy into the surrounding liquid, where it dissipates to increase the overall entropy. Furthermore, the liquid keeps threatening to dissolve the nascent crystal again, and it would quickly do so if its relative volume were not so large that it can easily absorb and dissipate the crystallization energy without being significantly affected by it. One could well speak here of a mutual weathering and even of the co-emergence and co-constitution of 'things' and their environment. Indeed, crystallization provides a model with which to think through the intriguing but hard to grasp notion of intra-action as process through which separable entities emerge and materialize in relations without preexisting relata. The model of crystallization helps understand, for instance, that mutuality, co-extensiveness, and co-constitution need not imply symmetry or similarity between the emergent entities, nor do they question the solidity and durable persistence of what emerges. It is helpful in clarifying the roles of indeterminacy, virtuality, and contingency, but also predictability. A closer analysis could thereby help sharpen the larger claims and expectations attached to such notions as intra-action, co-emergence, and co-constitution, even if — or rather precisely as — it may disappoint insofar as the general trajectory is quite predictable and progresses linearly from homogeneous liquid to immersed crystals, leaving only — though, to be sure, significantly — their actual location and shape open to a range of variation.

Much the same could be said about the more dynamic phenomenon to which Prigogine repeatedly refers as paradigm for dissipative structures, namely the spontaneous emergence of so-called Bénard convection cells in a homogeneous layer of liquid that is heated from below. This model relates in several ways to the multiple, ambivalent meanings of weathering. Above all, it provides the basic mechanism for the formation of wind patterns in the earth's atmosphere under the effect of the sun's influx of heat, which eventually gets radiated in a more isotropic and entropic form into outer space. But its closer analysis also gives an indication of what could be meant by [αP]weathering, which in my analysis of the grammatical possibilities of weathering remained perhaps most obscure: what does it mean to consider [α]weathering as a patientive ambitransitive, that is, to say that the storm [αP]weathers insofar as it is weathered by me? How could a storm possibly be affected by my weathering it?

The attempt to model the weather through numerical calculations of the equations governing atmospheric convection made meteorologist Edward Lorenz a pioneer of so-called chaos theory. Repeating his computer simulations, Lorenz discovered that the sequence of convection patterns is extremely sensitive to initial conditions, making the weather unpredictable for all practical purposes even when it is assumed to be governed by fully deterministic and reversible equations.[63] This defining characteristic of chaos as understood in mathematics and physics — the appearance of randomness and chance in fully deterministic systems due to sensitivity to initial conditions — is at the heart of the famous 'butterfly effect'. As Lorenz himself highlights in retrospect, this expression has a 'cloudy history'.[64] Often traced to his 1972 paper entitled 'Predictability: Does the Flap of a Butterfly's Wings in Brazil Set off a Tornado in Texas?', it refers to the possibility of small causes having large effects.[65] It suggests, in particular, that what an organism does to persist can have far-reaching effects — it can even set off a storm somewhere on the globe, or also prevent it.

As Lorenz notes, 'Perhaps the butterfly, with its seeming frailty and lack of power, is a natural symbol of the small that can produce the great.'[66] However, the agency that the butterfly effect attributes to everything, including the small and meek, is ultimately deeply ambivalent: its potentially enormous effects could seem to show the

---

63   See Edward N. Lorenz, 'Encounter with Chaos', in Edward N. Lorenz, *The Essence of Chaos* (London: UCL Press, 1995), pp. 111–60, especially 'Searching', pp. 130–35. Lorenz's chance discovery is dramatized in the opening chapter 'The Butterfly Effect' of the best-selling book James Gleick, *Chaos: Making a New Science* (London: Cardinal, 1988), which Lorenz credits for having established the butterfly effect as the 'symbol for chaos' (p. 13).

64   Lorenz, *Essence of Chaos*, p. 14.

65   The talk given in 1972 is published in ibid., pp. 179–82.

66   Ibid. p. 15.

irrelevance of scale, make everything possible, and even feed fantasies of omnipotence, but they are utterly unpredictable and knowable only retroactively. Furthermore, even if an agent knew what it was doing, any intention, plan, or strategy would be foiled by myriads of equally powerful and unpredictable agents. Whatever happens ultimately depends on the constellation and behaviour of all agents, which are so thoroughly entangled as to make the very notion of agency meaningless.

If anything, it is the weather that gains agency through the entanglement of zillions of effective butterflies. As everything weathers the weather, the weather is weathered and therefore could be said to [αP]weather in an entirely unpredictable manner, behaving, for all practical purposes, as if it had a mind of its own. Furthermore, if [αa]weathering is above all about self-preservation, survival, and persisting self-identity — the storm figuring only as a grammatical object but not as the object towards which one's action is directed — the point of chaos theory could be said to assert much the same of [αP]weathering.

Chaos as understood by mathematics and physics is not pure randomness. Instead, it is defined in terms of a causally fully determined dynamic and involves a peculiar and ambivalent kind of unpredictability. If the figure of the butterfly ultimately established itself for chaos theory, it is arguably because it symbolizes not only the 'small that can produce the great', but also another defining aspect of chaos, namely the presence of so-called 'strange attractors', which constrain and govern the apparently random behaviour of chaotic systems. An attractor represents a small subset of possible configurations or dynamic patterns towards which a dynamic system is 'attracted' no matter where it begins. In the simplest case, the attractor is a point, such as the bottom of a well where a ball will end up whichever way it is thrown in. The attractors of chaotic systems are 'strange' insofar as they have a very complicated, so-called fractal geometry (Figure 1 shows an example). This strangeness accounts for the appearance of randomness as a system will be attracted to a different part of its attractor when the initial conditions are slightly different. Yet the attractor itself can be understood as a system's signature, that is, as a robust, intrinsic telos towards which the system will evolve and to which it will return when disturbed.

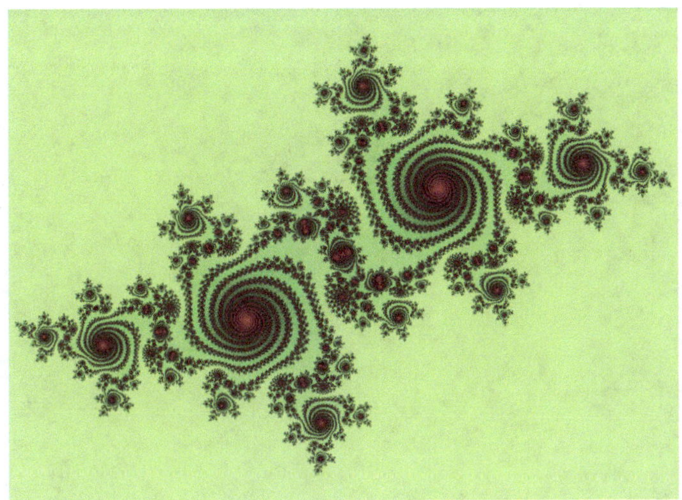

Figure 1. A Julia Set <https://commons.wikimedia.org/wiki/File:
Julia_set_(chartreuse).png>.

Among the earliest and most famous attractors is the one that
Lorenz found while modelling some aspects of atmospheric convection. In its by now customary representation, it happens to resemble a
butterfly (see Figure 2), which provides another genealogy and meaning of the butterfly effect.[67] In this case, the butterfly would be the
symbol less of small external causes having large effects in systems
that are very sensitive to initial conditions and therefore effectively
random than of the robust identity of the system itself, which is drawn
to sets of patterns in a way that is no doubt highly irregular, but still
characteristic and recognizable like the dazzling colours of a butterfly's
wings.

Combining the two genealogies, the butterfly can symbolize a profound ambivalence of chaotic systems like the global weather system.
On the one hand, it highlights their frailty and instability if even the
flap of a single, frail butterfly can cause or prevent the occurrence of

---

67   See Robert C. Hilborn, 'Sea Gulls, Butterflies, and Grasshoppers: A Brief History of
      the Butterfly Effect in Nonlinear Dynamics', *American Journal of Physics*, 72.4 (2004),
      pp. 425–27 (p. 425) <https://doi.org/10.1119/1.1636492>. Lorenz himself remains
      agnostic: 'A number of people with whom I have talked have assumed that the butterfly
      effect was named after this attractor. Perhaps it was' (Lorenz, *Essence of Chaos*, p. 11).

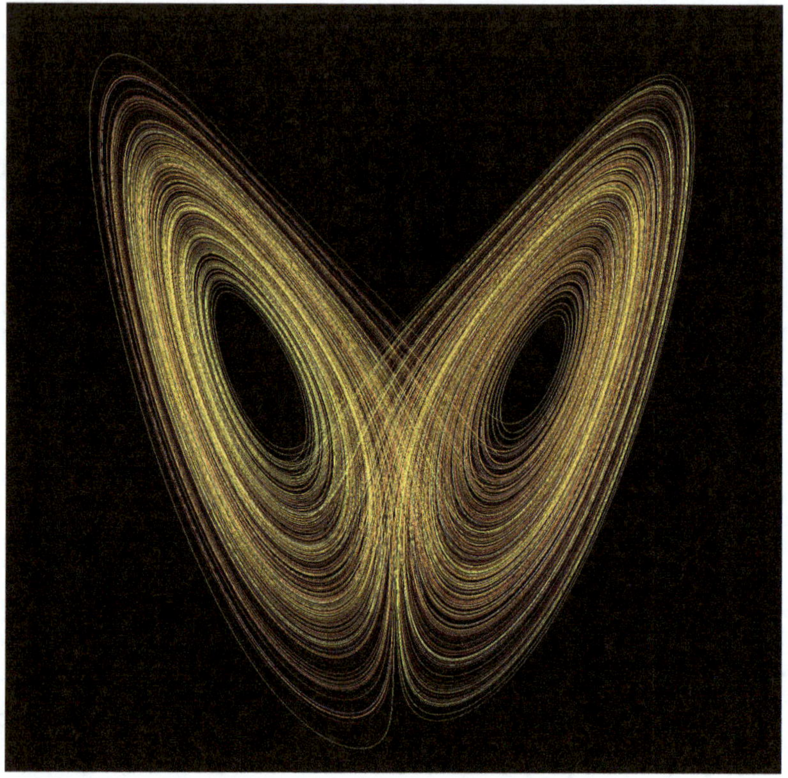

Figure 2. The Lorenz Attractor aka Butterfly Attractor
<https://commons.wikimedia.org/wiki/File:
Lorenz_system_r28_s10_b2-6666.png>.

a storm. But the utter unpredictability resulting from this sensitivity, which leads to an inextricable entanglement with all elements, is only half the reason of why the weather behaves as if it had a mind of its own. Just as importantly, the weather behaves on the other hand in a manner that is not random but indeed of its own, always moving towards and along the intricately folded lines of its strange attractor, which characterizes the weather system and endows it with its own robust autonomous identity and idiosyncratic dynamic.

According to Lorenz, the strange attractor of the global weather system is 'simply the climate',[68] and it imposes an indeed remarkably

---

68 Lorenz, *Essence of Chaos*, p. 48.

stable identity on the weather. While explaining a difficulty in numerical weather simulations, he asks his readers to 'imagine an enormous creature from outer space that swoops down close to the earth, reaches out with a giant paddle, and stirs the atmosphere for a short while before disappearing'.[69] Such a drastic intervention will have violent effects, of course, but Lorenz maintains that they will quickly dissipate; the perturbation of the weather will then be 'hardly detectable and the weather will be back to normal, although the particular sequence of weather patterns will undoubtedly not be the one that would have developed without the disturbance.'[70] Clearly, Lorenz was not thinking of climate change here, but his argument does not deny its possibility and remains instructive in understanding how one can insist both on the weather's resilient autonomy and on its instability, unpredictability, and sensitivity: Even after an enormously powerful intervention from outer space, the weather system quickly returns to 'normal' (that is, to its strange attractor), but at the same time the particular sequence of weather patterns (where and when a tornado forms, for instance) remains susceptible to even the most minute interventions.

While much more could be said about chaos theory, its premises, and consequences, I will conclude by proposing that it can provide useful models with which to think some of the ambivalences of weathering that the enantiosemic uses of the word have revealed. In particular, by engaging with profound ambivalences of un/predictability, im/potency, and dis/entanglement it may help grasp the peculiar kind of subject evoked when one uses weather verbs and says 'it storms', 'it rains', 'it is hot', or 'it is cold'. What remains perhaps necessarily ambivalent is the question of whether the weather as subject anthropomorphizes the weather or deflates the notion of a subject. As noted at the outset, it may be preferable to err on the side of anthropomorphism and exclude an anthropocentric dualism in which the human (subject) constitutes itself in opposition to the (nonhuman) elements. Yet blurring all distinctions runs the risk of re-asserting through disavowal an emphatic autonomous subject with a vengeance, making the subject omnipotent by considering everything inseparably entangled, denying

---

69   Ibid., p. 96.
70   Ibid., pp. 96–97.

the relevance of scale, and allowing for decisionist agential cuts that determine what comes to matter and what is left to draw on. What I am suggesting instead is to trouble human exceptionalism through the peculiar subject of weathering that transpires when weathering is methodologically situated in both language and physics and grasped in its generative enantiosemy and ambivalence.

Radiating Exposures

ALISON SPERLING

1

On an overcast afternoon in Paris in 1896, Henri Becquerel opened a dark drawer and accidentally discovered spontaneous radioactivity. He had been studying the absorption of sunlight by phosphorescent uranium salts, hypothesizing that they might re-emit the sunlight as X-rays. But the weather in Paris in late February was not so agreeable to his experiments, and Becquerel, waiting for the next sunny day to test his theory, placed the wrapped photographic plates and uranium salts in his desk drawer. On 1 March, he opened the drawer and developed the plates to find that the image of the salt crystals on the plate was actually amazingly clear. He had discovered that uranium emitted radiation without any sunlight, a phenomenon that his student Marie Curie would later coin 'radioactivity'.

This well-rehearsed historical moment of the chance discovery of radioactivity is one marked by a process of exposure without light. Indeed, Becquerel would later learn that non-phosphorescent uranium compounds also had the same effect on the photographic plate, confirming that the radiation from non-luminescent uranium compounds had the identical effect of rendering an image visible without the presence of light. This moment of chance marks a profound shift in visibility. Thus, early nuclear physics paired with early photographic technologies contributed to an unseating of (unassisted) vision as the epistemic centre of human experience. As John O'Brian writes in the introduction to *Camera Atomica*, 'Wherever nuclear events occur, photographers are present. They are not there only to record what happens, but also to assist in the production of what happens.'[1] The photographic image, with or without the use of light, is not (only, if at all) a representation or a reproduction of the nuclear event, but actively participates in the construction of the nuclear regime.

In 'La Nucléarisation de monde', Jaime Semprun writes that '[b]ecause nuclear fission acts on the very structure of inorganic matter [...], from now on there is no longer anything to see'.[2] Sven Lütticken likewise identifies the emergence of the nuclear regime as 'exacerbat[ing] a certain modern crisis of the aesthetic', one that 'confirms that the aesthetic is a practice and theory of crisis'.[3] This early non-luminescent exposure, rendering visible an image of otherwise imperceptible radiation, remains a touchstone of nuclear aesthetics, as well as of the broader crisis of representation that the discovery of the nuclear sciences participated in ushering in. This crisis identified by both Lütticken and Semprun manifests itself in the sciences, as physicist and philosopher Karen Barad's account[4] of microscopic technologies that render the atom 'visible' has demonstrated,[5] as well as in art and culture more broadly as 'reality' recedes from the visual field. With scientific technologies, the crisis of representation is a crisis

---

1   John O'Brian, 'Introduction: Through a Radioactive Lens', in *Camera Atomica*, ed. by John O'Brian, Art Gallery of Toronto (London: Black Dog Publishing, 2014), pp. 11–29 (p. 11).

2   Jamie Semprun, *La Nucléarisation du monde* (France: IVREA Press, 1986). English translation accessed via *Libcom.org*: <https://libcom.org/library/nuclearization-world-jaime-semprun> [accessed 3 July 2020], p. 30.

3   Sven Lütticken, 'Nuclear Aesthetics: Beyond Big Bangs', *kunstlicht: Journal for Visual Art, Visual Culture, and Architecture*, 39.3–4 (2018), pp. 13–19 (p. 14).

4   Karen Barad, *Meeting the Universe Halfway: Quantum Physics and the Entanglement of Matter and Meaning* (Durham, NC: Duke University Press, 2007) <https://doi.org/10.1215/9780822388128>. She details, for example, the way in which scanning tunnelling microscopes (STM) are not operating as magnifying tools but rather as 'an encounter that engages the sense of touch rather than sight' (p. 52). In this way, realism, following Ian Hacking, is without representation, it is intervening rather than representing.

5   Barad troubles the idea of sight through Ian Hacking, arguing that 'seeing' the microscopic is not the same as merely 'looking' — the latter being passive and the former active, an intervention (see previous footnote).

precisely because where one feels as though these technologies should render 'reality' more visible, when in fact they have the opposite effect.

Writing of the atomic radiation unleashed in the U.S. bombings of Hiroshima and Nagasaki at the end of World War II, Akira Mizuta Lippit describes a related crisis, one of the constitution of the human body.[6] Lippit claims a sudden 'excess of visuality' that 'threatened the material and conceptual dimensions of human interiority and exteriority'.[7] He also connects this crisis to technologies of interiority developed fifty years earlier, namely psychoanalysis, the X-ray, and cinema. Here the excess of the visible following penetrating radiation is the fragility of the body, its interiority made violently external. The X-ray, and later, the atomic bombs, caused a 'destructive visuality, a visibility born from annihilation'.[8] Of X-Ray technology he writes that it is a 'method of dissecting the human body into minute planes'.[9] He continues by likening the consequences of the X-ray for the visuality of the human to those of the atomic bomb: 'Like the X-ray, total visibility brought total destruction [...] the body reduced to sawdust. An atomic body, avisual.'[10] To return to the provocative claim by Semprun, rather than gaining further access to 'the real' or generating *excessive* visibility, the mediation of knowledge about sub-atomic particles through technological means actually demands that representation must move beyond the threshold of the visible, perhaps to point to its own destruction — 'there is no longer anything left to see'.

The brief explorations of nuclear exposures I offer in what follows draw primarily from nuclear art and culture or nuclear aesthetics, which have long been fixated on the problem of visibility and the representation of nuclear residues. As Lütticken has argued, the challenges of nuclear aesthetics are also political and social. Following

---

6   Akira Mizuta Lippit, *Atomic Light (Shadow Optics)* (Minneapolis: University of Minnesota Press 2005), p. 4. Thanks to Arnd Wedemeyer for this reference, and to pushing me here on whether the crisis is excessive visuality or, conversely, the annihilation of the visual, which is not solved here but hopefully better points to a relation where they are not such easily distinguishable conditions from one another.

7   Ibid., p. 4.

8   Ibid., p. 48.

9   Ibid. Lippit here is drawing from Catherine Waldby's work on The Visible Human Project (2000), where she traces the VHP back to X-ray technology.

10   Ibid.

Joseph Masco,[11] Lütticken points to the ways in which the 'poverty of human perception', which according to him became evident in the late nineteenth century with the revelations of film and photographic technologies, has only 'continued to widen in the post-war nuclear regime'.[12] These explorations do not mean to undermine the ongoing violence of the nuclear regime, the many lives that exposure to radiation through militarism and colonialism, extractivist projects, or the disposal of toxic waste has taken, and continues to put at risk around the world. Instead, they are meant to explore the fraught concept of *exposure* in ways specific to nuclearity and to radiation, while recognizing that: 'Nuclearity is not the same everywhere […]. Nuclearity is not the same for everyone […]. Nuclearity is not the same at all moments in time.'[13] They offer glimpses into other ways of thinking exposure, as it develops in relation to a (in varying ways, imperceptible) toxicity that is not inscribed into logics that partition the passive victim of suffering from some pure or unaffected subject.[14] They are examples that are both forms of exposure specific to the nuclear while also, perhaps, helping to expose more nuanced and complex ways of understanding forms of exposure that extend beyond nuclearity.

The effects of long-term radiation are impossible to quantify or to know conclusively through scientific techniques, as countless scientific studies of irradiated ecologies and biological populations continue to demonstrate. There are no scientific tools that can separate natural from artificial radiation, no confirmed method of tracing cellular or genetic degradation with full certainty back to a specific nuclear event or catastrophe. While there are clear correlatations between, for example, elevated thyroid cancer in children following Chernobyl, there is no 'data' that can clearly make the connection. This is why environmental justice scholar and advocate Michelle Murphy, following

---

11   Joseph Masco, *The Nuclear Borderlands: The Manhattan Project in Post Cold-War New Mexico* (Princeton, NJ: Princeton University Press, 2006) <https://doi.org/10.1515/9781400849680>.

12   Lütticken, 'Nuclear Aesthetics', p. 13.

13   Gabrielle Hecht, *Being Nuclear: Africans and the Global Uranium Trade* (Cambridge, MA: MIT Press, 2012), p. 15. I encountered this passage in part of an epigraph that opens Kyveli Mavrokordopoulou and Ruby de Vos' introduction to the issue 'Nuclear Aesthetics', *kunstlicht: Journal for Visual Art, Visual Culture, and Architecture*, 39.3–4 (2018), pp. 6–12 (p. 6).

14   Thanks to M. Ty for helping me to clarify this point.

Eve Tuck, calls for taking stock of environmental toxicity outside of what she calls a 'data of damage'.[15] Murphy demonstrates the ways in which toxic chemicals are often treated as if they are discrete entities or molecules, and how, '[a]s a result, the infrastructure of chemical relations that surround and make us largely resides in the realm of the imperceptible.' In other words, the 'fullness of our chemical relations ends up being largely conjectural'. She argues that 'technoscientific research […] tends to proceed by measuring the damage chemicals do to bodies' which tends to 'amplify the burdens of settler-colonial and racist violence'.[16] Instead, she argues that we must think against a data of damage, an approach especially relevant in the realm of radiotoxicity. Origin as contaminant is so dispersed, and so imperceptible, that it is impossible to trace a singular moment of object of contamination. Murphy and Tuck's argument is important because radiation exposure presents particular problems to those affected by it and in need of care or reparations; its damage is neither quantifiable nor verifiable in scientific terms. Forms of radiation exposure, thus, draw attention to immeasurable consequences of vulnerability and forms of embodied knowing that are often rejected under regimes of knowledge that rely solely on scientific verification.

The condition of being exposed can mean one is or has been particularly vulnerable or in a state of heightened risk. But it's not always true that the result of exposure is thought only in negative terms. One can be purposely exposed to a virus in the form of a vaccine in order to safeguard against infection; one can find oneself exposed to new ideas for the first time, to feel liberated or opened up in new ways. One might describe feeling exposed after a secret about them is revealed, turned inside-out, made vulnerable. The notion of exposure is often temporally, relationally, and sometimes spatially situated. It can require duration, pliability, resilience. Exposure, in colloquial uses, seems to imply a kind of porosity or laying bare but also captures an indeterminacy that helps to ask larger questions of weathering the nuclear. How might exposure to radiation resist being marked or measured, and in the spirit of this collection, how might these forms of exposure help us

---

15   Michelle Murphy, 'Alterlife and Decolonial Chemical Relations', *Cultural Anthropology*, 32.4 (2017), pp. 494–503 <https://doi.org/10.14506/ca32.4.02>.

16   Ibid., p. 496.

to think through unperceivable weathering that resists its registration by the human sensorium?

In *Exposed: Environmental Politics & Pleasures in Posthuman Times*, Stacy Alaimo describes exposure as a kind of political act by way of nuclear catastrophe:

> Performing exposure as an ethical and political act means to reckon with — rather than disavow — such horrific events and to grapple with the particular entanglements of vulnerability and complicity that radiate from disasters and their terribly disjunctive connection to everyday life in the industrialized world. To occupy exposure as insurgent vulnerability is to perform material rather than abstract alliances, and to inhabit a fraught sense of political agency that emerges from the perceived loss of boundaries and sovereignty.[17]

For Alaimo, exposure is performed, reckoned with, occupied, and inhabited. The 'horrific event' Alaimo references here is the Chernobyl catastrophe of 1986 and the 'total unprotectedness' that suddenly came to define biopolitical subjectivity with regard to the claims and actions of the state, especially in Ukraine and Belarus.[18] What the Chernobyl explosion and the subsequent massive dispersal of radioactive particles into the atmosphere demonstrate is that the nuclear Anthropocene ushers in forms of exposure that rapidly and dramatically undermine the sovereignty of the embodied self. If the Anthropocene has revealed existence itself as already a state of exposure, thinking radiation exposure troubles the distinction between a supposedly passive state of absorption and the fraught occupation of vulnerability as forms of biopolitical agency.

2

Michael Marder and Anaïs Tondeur's collaborative project *The Chernobyl Herbarium* is a 2016 rayogram-essay of 30 fragments,

---

17   Stacy Alaimo, *Exposed: Environmental Politics and Pleasures in Posthuman Times* (Minneapolis: University of Minnesota Press, 2016), p. 5 <https://doi.org/10.5749/minnesota/9780816621958.001.0001>.

18   Adriana Petryna, *Life Exposed: Biological Citizens After Chernobyl* (Princeton, NJ: Princeton University Press, 2013), p. 216 <https://doi.org/10.1515/9781400845095>.

one for each year since Chernobyl in 1986.[19] On alternating pages
with short texts written by Marder are pages depicting Tondeur's
herbarium specimens, grown in the radioactive soil of the Chernobyl
exclusion zone and arranged on photosensitive paper. The result is a
luminescence of the vegetal object surrounded by a darkness, awash
only with spots of light and indiscernible, sweeping markings. These
images are 'the visible record of an invisible calamity' as Tondeur
'liberates luminescent traces without violence, avoiding the repetition
of the first, invisible event of Chernobyl and, at the same time,
capturing something of it'.[20] Radioactive soil, out of which the plant
is nourished and sustained, is registered in the plant and then on
the paper as a brightness, an outline, a 'shimmer behind [a] shining'.
Marder writes that the plants which 'assimilated the imperceptible
and the inconceivable' are '[i]n the thick of infinite openness and
exposure'.[21]

Structuring the text is a story that Marder relates from his boy-
hood. Travelling on a train to Anapa on 26 April 1986, neither Marder
nor anyone on board one is yet aware of what has happened 1200 kilometres northwest. By May — Marder would be in Anapa all Summer
that year — radiation readings would reach 60 mR/hr (milliRoentgens
per hour), a value some 300 times higher than the 'normal' levels of
0.2 mR/hr.[22] Marder asks: 'How many layers or levels of exposure are
there before us? Who is the exposing and who or what the exposed?'.[23]
The text is entirely occupied with the boundaries and mediations of
the detectable, the rayograms serving as imprints of the assimilation of
invisible radioactivity transferred as a form of light onto the page. Are
these images of 'excess' as Marder describes them, or put differently,
of a trace?

The Chernobyl Herbarium has one fragment titled 'Exposure', but
the entire project might be understood as a meditation on the concept.

---

19   Michael Marder and Anaïs Tondeur, *The Chernobyl Herbarium: Fragments of an Ex-
      ploded Consciousness* (London: Open Humanities Press, 2016) <https://doi.org/10.
      26530/OAPEN_606220>.

20   Ibid., p. 14.

21   Ibid., p. 20.

22   Ibid., p. 18.

23   Ibid., p. 22.

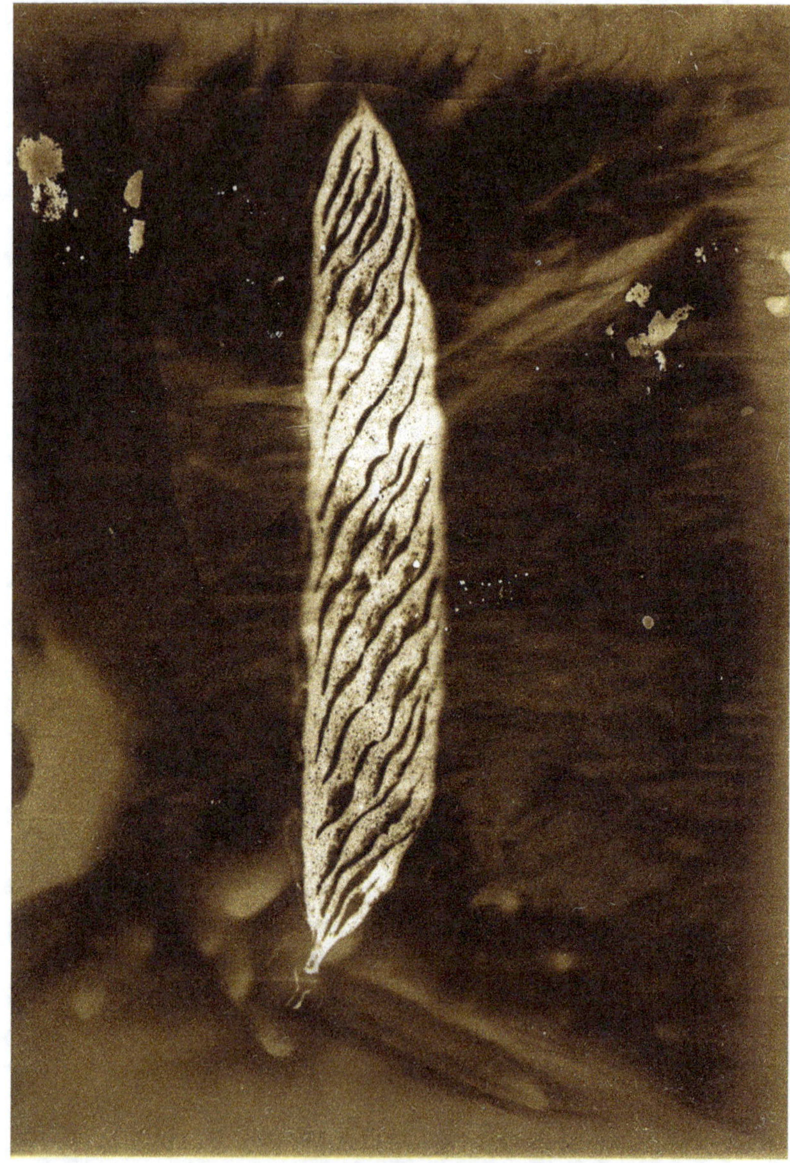

Figure 1. Anaïs Tondeur, *Phaseolea, Exclusion Zone, Chernobyl.*
Radiation level: 1.7 Microsieverts/hr. Rayogram on Rag paper, 24x36
cm, 2016, ongoing, courtesy of the artist.

Exposure is thus differentiated and theorized along various planes and scales of vulnerability, adaptability, and resilience:

> This openness spelled out unfathomable vulnerability, the incapacity to defend oneself from a threat that was unknown and undetectable by the sensorium. One is ineluctably passive in the face of radio*activity* [...]. [Plants] are more adaptable: soybeans experimentally grown in Chernobyl's radioactive environment have displayed drastic changes in their protein makeup, enabling them to improve their resistance to heavy metals and to modify their carbon metabolism [...]. Their exposure *to* the world is one of piece with learning *from* the world and giving plenty of things *back* to it. Only our, human, exposure betokens pure vulnerability, passivity, helplessness.[24]

If the exposed human is objectified, made passive ('Those of us who have been [in radiation's] eerie neighbourhood have resembled objects'), vegetal exposure is agential responsiveness that resists, that pushes *back*. Marder: 'Vegetal life is not merely exposed; it *is* exposure, exteriority, outwardness.'[25]

Tondeur's images do produce a sense of exteriority, a vibrancy particular to plant-life in the exclusion zone or other irradiated spaces. Marder seems to want to ontologically split vegetal and human life, to distinguish between forms of exposure that are 'pure vulnerability, passivity' for the human and, in a kind of metaphysical slide, deem vegetal life as *itself* exposure. In one sense, Marder's idea that 'the human' can only experience exposure as something that happens *to* oneself, that delimits agential capacity and renders the subject helpless, is one interpretation of exposure that I am attempting to question in this paper. Marder points to the *ex* in human *ex*perience in order to say that only in 'limit circumstances' can the human *ex*perience *ex*posure 'on our skin', as a kind of *ex*ternality embodied by the vegetal or as a life-form as itself exposure. *Ex*, from Latin for 'out', is drawn out in Marder's account in order to claim that plants are always outside of themselves, always moving outward, growing. But the skin is perhaps more of an externality in the vegetal sense than in the sense that it bounds or

---

24   Ibid.
25   Ibid.

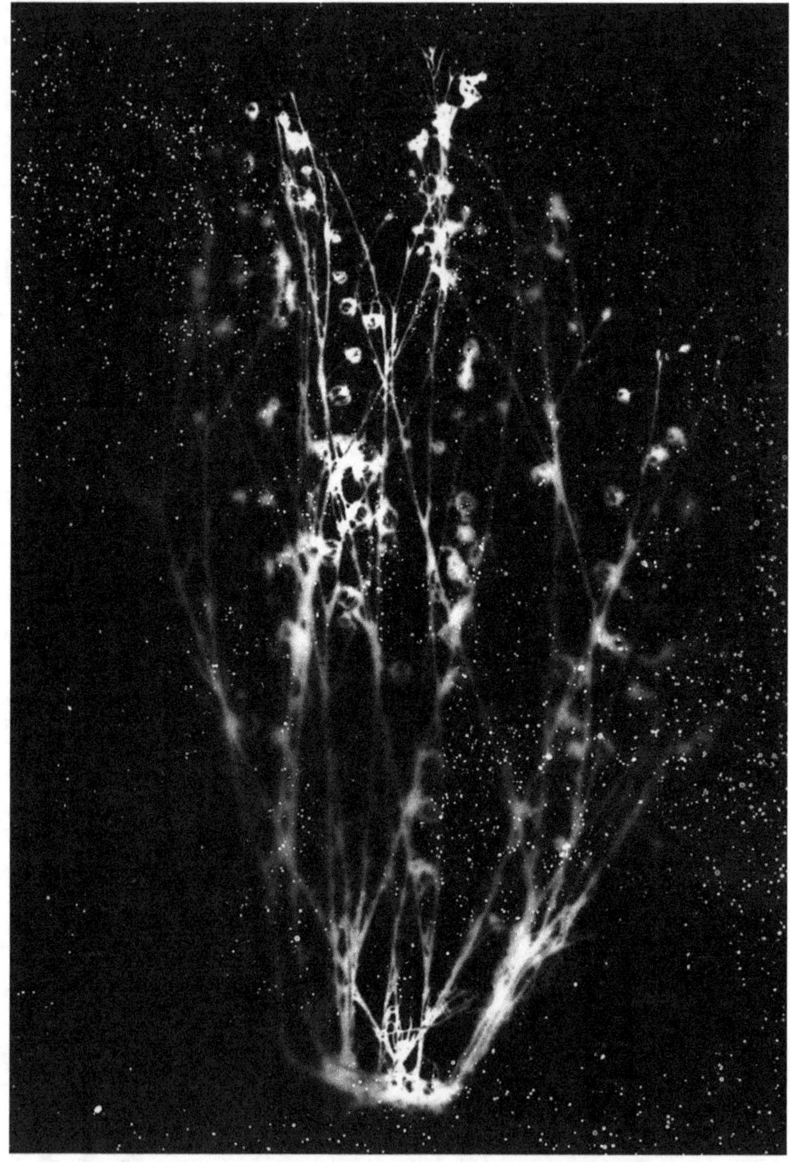

Figure 2. Anaïs Tondeur, *Linum usitatissimum, Exclusion Zone, Chernobyl*. Radiation level: 1.7 Microsieverts. Rayogram on Rag paper, 24x36 cm, 2016, ongoing, courtesy of the artist.

bars the human from performing exposures in a more vegetal mode. In feminist science studies, especially in the work of Murphy, Alaimo, and Nancy Tuana, they have reminded us of the porosity of the skin and indeed the ways in which the human body is itself always passing materials both into and outside of itself. Rather than a closed bounded subject, the human is in a constant relation with the world and with others that is perhaps much more exposed and external than Marder seems to grant here. The danger of such a distinct splitting of the vegetal and the human may reinstate the bounded human subject that posthumanism has worked to undo. And yet, at the end of the section, Marder points to the provocative notion that exposure might also unite the human and the vegetal: 'What did our [human?] exposure amount to? Did it prepare the grounds for a trans-human solidarity?', suggesting that exposure may also provide an opening for a kind of trans-species alliance.

3

In August of 1945, Julian H. Webb, a physicist in the research department of Eastman Kodak in Rochester, New York, took it upon himself to investigate a sudden flurry of complaints from customers of Kodak X-ray film. The film was reported by consumers to be 'fogged' by black spots that Kodak then attributed to a contamination of the cardboard, which encased that batch of film. Webb was able to trace the paper from the packaging back to a mill in Vincennes, Indiana, situated on the Wabash River. Testing the run of paper produced on 6 August, Webb discovered a new artificially radioactive particle with strong beta-activity and a half-life of approximately thirty days, Cerium-141, and in doing so, also happened upon the discovery of a confidential nuclear weapons test detonation that had occurred on 16 July nearly 2000 miles away.[26]

Indeed, Kodak film in Indiana had registered the world's first nuclear explosion; the now infamous Trinity Test had taken place without public knowledge two weeks earlier in Alamogordo, New Mexico.

---

26   Julian H. Webb, 'The Fogging of Photographic Film by Radioactive Contaminants in Cardboard Packaging Materials', *Physical Review*, 76.3 (1949), pp. 375–80 <https://doi.org/10.1103/PhysRev.76.375>.

Radioactive fallout had blown thousands of miles, and found its way into the paper mill through the river water, causing the disturbance in any film that was packaged with the paper produced on 6 August. It would take Webb four years to publish his highly sensitive findings. He finally did in 1949, writing with a certain clarity: 'The most likely explanation of the source of this radioactive contaminant appears to be that it consisted of wind-borne radioactive fission products derived from the atom-bomb detonation in New Mexico on July 16, 1945.' It would seem that what was exposed on film in turn exposed an entirely new and covert industry that could neither hide nor control the planetary effects of nuclear weapons tests that have since come to define the start of the 'nuclear Anthropocene'.[27]

In 1951, having been through something like this six years prior, Kodak again registered high levels of radiation in snowfall, this time along the shores of Lake Ontario. They registered a complaint with the National Association of Photographic Manufacturers, who then telegrammed the Atomic Energy Commission. The AEC replied that a major test, what would later be revealed as test 'Able', had in fact taken place, but that the situation was not of any threat to public health. But Kodak's general manager threatened to sue the government should the company or its film stock suffer serious damage as a result of testing, and the AEC responded with an offer. Presumably in an effort to avoid a major lawsuit, the AEC would provide Kodak with maps of all weapons tests prior to their occurrence that would detail areas of potentially heavy fallout and adjust their operations and manu-

---

27   It is outside of the scope of this short paper to detail the discussion about when the Anthropocene begins and the Holocene ends. As the previous footnote shows, scientists have in recent years have claimed that the Anthropocene is set in motion at the beginning of the atomic era. But in the humanities, scholarship on the Anthropocene tends to mark it with a much deeper history, one inherently tied to the transatlantic slave trade or to early agriculture practices. But in the sciences, see as examples of studies that mark the Anthropocene as beginning in the Nuclear Age: Colin N. Waters and others, 'Can Nuclear Weapons Fallout Mark the Beginning of the Anthropocene Epoch?', *Bulletin of the Atomic Scientists*, 71.3 (2015), pp. 46–57 <https://doi.org/10.1177/0096340215581357>, Jan Zalasiewicz and others, 'When Did the Anthropocene Begin? A Mid-Twentieth Century Boundary Level Is Stratigraphically Optimal', *Quaternary International* 383 (2015), pp. 196–203, and Gary J. Hancock, Stephen G. Tims, L. Keith Fifield, and Ian T. Webster, 'The Release and Persistence of Radioactive Anthropogenic Nuclides', *Geological Society, London, Special Publications*, 395.1 (2014), pp. 265–81 <https://doi.org/10.1144/SP395.15>.

facturing accordingly, solidifying a decade-long relationship between the largest photographic film manufacturer and the U.S. industry of nuclear militarism, a double exposure (at least).

4

An elaborate, golden, three-tiered chain necklace with deep-blue jewels sits in a glass case. *Inheritance*, as this work is titled, is part of the exhibition 'Invisible Forces' at ArtLaboratory Berlin featuring works by artists Erich Berger, Mari Keto, and Martin Howse.[28] The necklace is displayed in a row of deconstructed parts of a concrete box that has housed it in order to keep handlers from being exposed to its radioactivity. Next to the parts read the following instructions, engraved on a copper plate:

> This jewelry box contains your inheritance: a necklace and earrings crafted from gold, silver, thorite, thorianite, and uraninite; an electroscope with spare leaves for detecting the jewelry's radiation, a glass rod with a piece of fur to electrostatically charge the electroscope; a timer for recording the time and these instructions for the ritual of measurement. A generation ago when the box was last opened, the jewelry proved unready for wear and was locked away. Today you will perform the ritual of measurement with your elder to find out if you can wear the jewelry, or it you need to lock it away again for another generation.

The display instructions continue with detailed instructions about how to proceed with the ritual of testing the jewellery every hundred years for its eventual wear-ability. Thus, the inheritance is the legacy of atomic science (including, among other things, nuclear weapons testing and deployment, mining projects, nuclear energy, nuclear waste disposal) transposed onto a family heirloom, passed down for innumerable generations.

The artists, Berger and Keto, write in the exhibition text that the piece 'attempts to address the long time component of nuclear waste

---

28   'Invisible Forces' ran from 19 October to 8 December 2019 at ArtLaboratory Berlin, Prinzenallee 34, 13359 Berlin, curated by Regine Rapp and Christian de Lutz. The necklace is part of the artists' ongoing work, 'The Inheritance Project' <http://inheritance-project.net/index.php/page-2/> [accessed 3 July 2020].

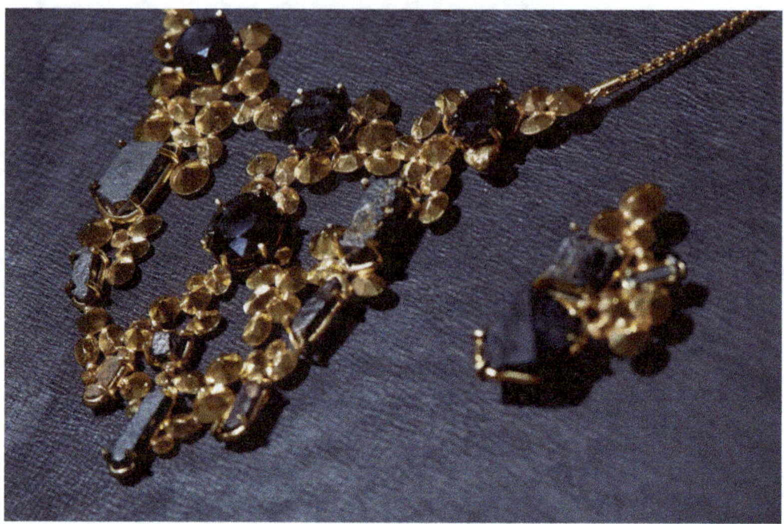

Figure 3. Erich Berger and Mari Keto, *INHERITANCE*, 2016, jewellery close-up, gold, silver, uraninite, thorite, thorianite, courtesy of the artists.

by transferring it into the intimate and caring concept of a family without compromising the deep time aspect'. The work invites contemplation about the nature of inheritance by way of multiple vectors, including the ways in which nuclear waste is an inheritance that operates on a vastly different timescale than that of the human lifespan — the jewelry can only be tested every hundred years. By imbuing the family heirloom with the deep toxic time of nuclear waste, perhaps it is easier to conceive of just how long this waste lives on past the finite temporality of human life. But the piece also suggests something desirable about radioactivity, jewels behind a casing that cannot be touched for entire lifetimes.

Naturally, there are other temporalities at play here, too, that of a certain class and economic status, of aesthetics and materials of a certain historical moment or place; its very status as an heirloom suggests a moment of importance in the act of passing down, and of transmission. But the piece is challenging in that it is difficult to think of nuclear inheritance as a tender or intimate act, or as existing within normative family structures within which acts of inheritance such as this would be located. In a way similar to that of *Inheritance*, atomic artwork installations often exhibit items that emit radioactivity, or that claim to — gallery goers threatened (though perhaps largely fabricated or imagined) with exposure to low-levels of radiation. Suggesting the risk of exposure, however fabricated or exaggerated it might be, can indeed expose fears of that which one cannot simply perceive. But it can also expose a kind of privilege that does not contemplate or alleviate the violence of the nuclear regime, but rather contributes to its dangerous seduction.

5

'Dark tourism', a term introduced by John Lennon and Malcolm Foley in 1996, describes recreational travel to places marked by death and suffering. While scholars of 'dark' or 'disaster' tourism have come up with a number of reasons for why people flock to these kinds of sites, most will agree that it's often too difficult to parse. Some have recently argued, for example, that visitors to dark sites gain satisfaction from observing the sites of violence and conflict (Debbie Lisle), or that they seek commemoration of a tragedy (Lennon and Foley).[29] Dark tourism, a fairly recent field of research,[30] remains therefore a controversial ethical enterprise.

As a site often considered, alongside the Nazi Death Camps, to define the enterprise of disaster tourism, the Chernobyl 2600 square km exclusion zone in Ukraine attracts an estimated 10,000 tourists every day.[31] On the *Chernobyl Welcome Tour* website, one of the more popularly booked tours of the zone, they promise that radiation exposure during the excursion will not exceed 3-4 microsieverts, 'which

---

29   For a brief summary of tourism studies and dark tourism that I turn to in this section, see these citations and others in Ganna Yankovska and Kevin Hannam, 'Dark and Toxic Tourism in the Chernobyl Exclusion Zone', *Current Issues in Tourism*, 17.10 (2014), pp. 929–39 <https://doi.org/10.1080/13683500.2013.820260>.

30   See Philip Stone, 'Dark Tourism — an Old Concept in a New World', *The Tourism Society Journal*, 125 (2005), p. 20 <http://clok.uclan.ac.uk/29705/>.

31   See Nicholas Hryhorczuk, 'Radioactive Heritage: The Universal Value of Chernobyl as a Dark Heritage Site', *Qualitative Inquiry*, 25.9–10 (2019), pp. 1047–55 <https://doi.org/10.1177/1077800418787553>.

is the equivalent to around 4 hours on an intercontinental flight'.[32] For one hundred and nineteen euros, visitors are bussed from Kiev to Chernobyl and escorted around parts of the zone, including walking right up to the protective sarcophagus of the blown reactor. Each person also receives a portable dosimeter — a small Geiger counter — to measure radiation levels throughout the tour. The tours paradoxically promise both risk and safety; they are extreme and dangerous but supply tourists with the necessary technologies to measure their risk along the way.

In their study of tourism in Chernobyl, Ganna Yankovska and Kevin Hannam suggest thinking about the phenomenon not only as dark tourism but as 'toxic tourism', a term developed by Phaedra C. Pezzullo to describe tours to sites of environmental degradation in the United States.[33] Interested in the ways in which toxic tourism might open up possibilities for building solidarity by focusing on the relationship between environmental and social degradation, Yankovska and Hannam also point to the strangeness that inheres in people's desire to visit (still) toxic sites. As one of the tour guides they interviewed describes critically, 'People [that visit Chernobyl] [...] are not interested in real history and valid information anymore. What is more, they want to risk their lives and find adrenalin instead of appreciation and memorialization of the past.'[34] Exposure, in this context, is sought out in a way that some of the tour guides reported as an unethical response to historical tragedy. Although an individual dosimeter can pick up levels of atmospheric radiation, the ways in which low-level radiation affects biological life over generations remains, of course, largely speculative. Countless studies of life in the zone have been done and though many have found significant changes to specific species under study as well as to the larger ecological relations within the zone, nearly all studies conclude that there is still too little known about the effects of radiation poisoning that will last at least 20,000 years more into the future.

---

32   See 'Chernobyl 1 Day Tour', Chernobylwel.come (Bratislava: radioPROactive, 2018) <https://www.chernobylwel.com/tour/7/chernobyl-1-day-tour> [accessed 29 July 2020].

33   Phaedra C. Pezzullo, *Toxic Tourism: Rhetorics of Pollution, Travel, and Environmental Justice* (Tuscaloosa: University of Alabama Press, 2007).

34   Quoted in Yankovska and Hannam, 'Dark and Toxic Tourism', p. 936.

There are scholars of dark tourism that claim that the draw to post-disaster or toxic sites is the fixation on death or suffering, or the desire to contemplate one's own mortality. Focused primarily on tourist responses to the fatalities of historical catastrophes, rarely do these studies think deeply about the specificity of tourism in irradiated zones, where tourists decidedly put themselves at some level of radiation risk, however slight or downplayed by local authorities. What marginal, perverse, conscious, or unconscious desires draw people to these kinds of sites of exposure? Somehow the dual but conflicting assurance of both high risk and personal safety that provides tour-goers to assure themselves of either one at any given time, an experience that plays out as a kind of seeking of exposure while also requiring the promise of protection.

5.5

Bionerd23, a Youtube-er with 157,000 followers, has published/posted over seventy self-made videos from within the Chernobyl exclusion zone since 2013. The videos show bionerd23 walking freely around Chernobyl, filming a nearby rabid fox, getting bitten by ants, and picking up radioactive glass shards with her bare hands. Wearing an army-patterned jacket and a closely shorn buzz-cut, she takes samples and tests them in the videos in order to dispel supposed myths about the levels of toxicity that are said to exist in the zone. In one of her most-watched videos, she picks an apple near the iconic Ferris wheel inside the zone and eats it on camera.[35]

6

Aldona, a quiet, twelve minute film by Lithuanian artist Emilija Škarnulytė, follows Aldona, the artist's grandmother, around her

---

35   See 'Chernobyl Wild Zone: Radioactive Rabies, Autumn Fruit and Foxes', online video recording, YouTube, 30 September 2014 <https://www.youtube.com/watch?v=u_ZvHMGXdbE> [accessed 24 February 2020], and Dan Nosowitz, 'The Woman Who Ate Chernobyl's Apples', online video recording, Atlas Obscura, 15 April 2015 <https://www.atlasobscura.com/articles/the-woman-who-ate-chernobyl-s-apples> [accessed 4 March 2020].

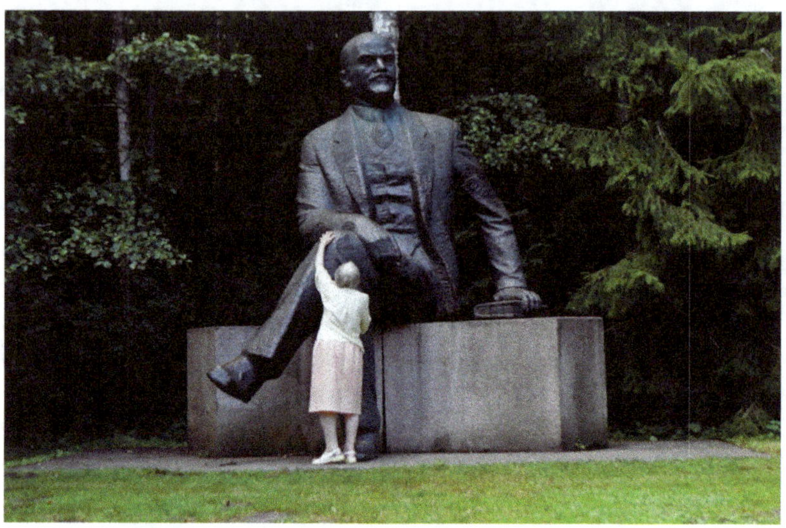

Figure 4. Film Still from *Aldona*, dir. by Emilija Škarnulytė, 2013,
courtesy of the artist.

property and through Grūtas Park in southeastern Lithuania.[36] The
park, an open-air museum, was opened in April 2001 by businessman
Viliumas Malinauskas on his private property, without taxpayer
money. The park is an odd tourist destination with a complicated
relationship with Lithuanian's Soviet heritage; it displays recuperated
Soviet-era sculptures and large-scale stone monuments of Marx,
Lenin, and Stalin.[37] Aside from the ways in which the park has caused
debate amongst Lithuanians for its unclear relation to the past, the
museum site itself is located nearby to the Grūtas Forest, where
Lithuanian partisans lost a bloody war against the Communist Red
Army.[38]

---

36   *Aldona* was part of the exhibition 'Presence in the Absence', 18 January – 21 February
     2020, which I visited at the Alexander Levy Gallery Berlin, Germany.

37   For a discussion of Grūtas Park and dark or what the authors call 'thanatourism,'
     see Rami K. Isaac & Laurencija Budryte-Ausiejiene, 'Interpreting the Emotions of
     Visitors: A Study of Visitor Comment Books at the Grūtas Park Museum, Lithuania',
     Scandinavian Journal of Hospitality and Tourism, 15.4 (2015), pp. 400–24 <https:
     //doi.org/10.1080/15022250.2015.1024818>.

38   Ibid., p. 406.

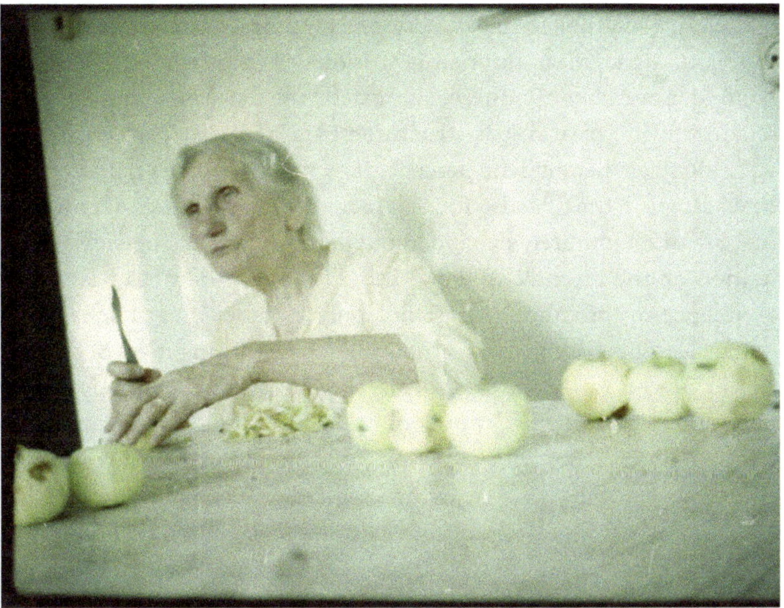

Figure 5. Emilija Škarnulytė, photograph from the shooting of *Aldona*, 2013, courtesy of the artist.

In the film, Aldona makes her way through the park without the use of sight; the exhibition catalogue tells us that she has been blind since Spring of 1986, a likely result of the Chernobyl explosion in April of that year. Walking through the park, we watch as she runs her hands along the gigantic stone bodies of (once-memorialized, then discarded, now somewhat revived) Soviet figures now confined in what has been called a kind of enactment of imprisonment: a network of wire fences and canals surround the park, and several watch towers circle the park's territory. In other scenes, we watch Aldona's solitary domestic activities: she peels apples, listens to the radio, rinses the dishes. The only sounds are those of birds and the wind blowing through the trees.

The film is part of a larger body of work that has established Škarnulytė as a significant artist within nuclear art and culture. Here, she invokes the nuclear past of Lithuanians in the Soviet-era, channelled through the familial.[39] Aldona's blindness may be the result of exposure to radiation. But neither Aldona nor the framing of the film seem to mourn her blindness, but instead the piece imagines Aldona's relation to the past as it is structured by a non-visual sensorium. In addition to challenging the perceptual registers on which radiation can be catalogued, the film also focuses in on the temporalities of radiation that are often infinitely expanded outwards by refocusing viewers' attention on the intimate, the domestic. Fallout of decades past is not a violence in this film, at least not only violence, but attached to a tenderness that Aldona has learned and which the quietness of the film allows viewers to see and hear — the flies buzzing on delicately peeled fruits, the old radio, the lapping of water in Aldona's coffee mug. The temporality of living with radiation, or more precisely not really ever being *sure* if and how one is living with radiation, is diffused through (nuclear) history, as well through a domestication of radiation that is rendered not (only, or merely) traumatic, but tender and soft.

7

Since around 2015, a wave of very particular journalistic stories have been revisit aging, still-radioactive exclusion zones.[40] The phenomenon emerged perhaps in response to commemorations of the fifth anniversary of the disaster at the Fukushima Daiichi Nuclear Power Plant in Japan, 2011. Focused largely on Fukushima and Chernobyl but including Three Mile Island, Bikini Atoll, areas around the Nevada Test Site, and the Semipalatinsk site, what I

---

39   Soviets sent an estimated 7,000 Lithuanians to labour camps and into other services providing cleanup efforts for Chernobyl, performing work like dousing flames or building dams to filter radiation from nearby rivers. Lithuanian borders are about 450 kilometres from Chernobyl. See Andrius Sytas, 'New Tours, Painful Reminders in Lithuania After Hit Chernobyl Show', *Reuters*, 31 July 2019 <https://www.reuters.com/article/us-lithuania-chernobyl/new-tours-painful-reminders-in-lithuania-after-hit-chernobyl-show-idUSKCN1UQ1WF> [accessed 19 July 2020].

40   As part of my project as a Fellow at ICI Berlin, I have been working on questions of radioactive wildernesses and irradiated natures. I've collected over fifty articles from popular media sources such as *Grist*, *The Guardian*, *The Atlantic*, *The Independent*, *Huffington Post*, *The New York Times* and others of varying levels of credibility. The headlines declare that the flora and fauna are flourishing and proliferating wildly since (and in fact because of) nuclear catastrophe and radiation exposure.

identify as a surge in 'popular' interest in irradiated zones seems to have become quite suddenly fixated on the question of how these exposed areas have fared over time. Implicit in this fascination is the understanding that (low-level) radiation exposures are not singular in their temporality or moment, but rather are forms of exposure that develop more so over impossibly long periods of time and about which there is still very little conclusive data. Evacuated of the human, zones of alienation are the new test sites of the nuclear age. As dozens of articles pronounce almost unanimously — Nature has reclaimed its space, overgrown and rampant, feral and unyielding — it may be toxic, but it flourishes nonetheless in the absence of human polluters, hunters, and settlers. As *National Geographic* proclaims in a Youtube video to their 14.5 million subscribers: '30 Years After Chernobyl: Nature Is Thriving'.[41]

I conclude with these 'reports from the zone' in order to return to the questions with which I opened this incomplete archive of things. What is exposure when taken from the frame of victimhood, passivity, and vulnerability. How can exclusion zones, like those I've referenced above, be both toxic and a site of flourishing at once; to go even further, what is exposure when it is celebrated, sought out, empowering — something one can be resilient in the face of, or feel queerly intimate towards?[42] This paper hopes to raise these questions through exposures that resist weathering as either an absorption/projection of experience, or as a form of resilience. I have also pointed to the ways in which exposure is often understood as a process made legible primarily through the register of visuality, whereas radiation forces a different set of questions around what it is to weather imperceptibly, even unknowingly. Indeed, to think radiation, to radiate exposures outward (as well as countless forms of imperceptible toxicities in the Anthropocene, in different ways), not only grapples with the unknowable, it necessitates

---

41   National Geographic, '30 Years After Chernobyl: Nature Is Thriving', online video recording, YouTube, 20 April 2016 <https://www.youtube.com/watch?v=E-h1SwX14po> [accessed 4 July 2020].

42   Disability studies and crip theory have done a lot of important work on the question of toxic intimacies, which lie outside of the scope of this short paper, but which I have explored elsewhere. For an excellent example of this scholarship which has deeply informed my thinking here, see Mel Y. Chen, *Animacies: Biopolitics, Racial Mattering, and Queer Affect* (Durham, NC: Duke University Press, 2012).

forms of not-knowing. To weather exposures of these sorts is, thus, crucially a speculative practice, a challenge to ways of tending to a profoundly contaminated world, and a confrontation with impossibly deep, nonhuman temporalities.[43]

43 I am indebted to the editors, Arnd Wedemeyer and Christoph Holzhey for their attentive and thorough comments on an earlier draft, which I could only partially attend to here. I also extend gratitude to the fellows at ICI Berlin who workshopped the idea of weathering together for months and who helped my thinking along for this paper. A special thanks to Anja Sunhyun Michaelsen and M. Ty for their invaluable comments on the first draft.

Weathering the Afterlife
The Meteorological Psychology of Dante's *Commedia*

NICOLÒ CRISAFI AND MANUELE GRAGNOLATI

In this essay, we investigate the meteorological psychology of Dante's *Commedia*, which we define as the way in which human subjectivity is expressed and constituted in its exposure to weather phenomena.[1] Weathering provides us with a guiding thread to study this relation in a twofold way. First, we take weathering in the strict etymological sense of the word, as an action associated with the weather, such as rain, wind, and snow. In Dante's representation of Hell, Purgatory, and Heaven, these weather phenomena affect the dead exposed to the elements, for example, with the aim of punishing them, transforming them spiritually, or rewarding them. The second meaning of weathering that we bring to this analysis is more conceptual, as a notion belonging to a special class of words called enantiosemic. Enantiosemic words, sometimes called Janus words and named for their ability to look in two directions at once, bind together opposite connotations. As Christoph Holzhey explains in his chapter in this volume, the term 'weathering' is a complex case of enantiosemy. On the one hand, it can be used to express the action of wearing something

---

1   We are especially grateful to Y. Ariadne Collins, Vittoria Fallanca, Elena Lombardi, Francesca Southerden, and Alison Sperling for their insight and feedback on an early draft of this paper; and to the editors of this volume Christoph F. E. Holzhey and Arnd Wedemeyer for their comments and revisions on the last one.

down, as well as the opposite action of resisting wear. On the other hand, the word can be used to describe processes that are detrimental but also for those that are beneficial.[2] In what follows, we interrogate the different dimensions of the concept of weathering and trace and track their relations to the meteorological psychology of the *Commedia*. As we will see, in the three realms of Dante's afterlife, the dead weather in different ways: the damned of the *Inferno* experience their punishments with helplessness and sometimes defiance; the purging souls of *Purgatorio* are shielded from adverse weather and progressively learn to embrace their vulnerability; and the blessed of *Paradiso* are exposed to an unexpectedly extreme environment but fully open to it.

A NOTE ON WEATHERING AND MEDIEVAL METEOROLOGY

Any discussion of weathering that occurs outside of the English language must contend with the fact that the word is arguably untranslatable: no direct translation of the term 'weathering', in a Romance language, does justice to the distinctive enantiosemy of wearing down and resisting wear that we have highlighted above. Moreover, Italian does not have a word exclusively dedicated to the weather but must make do with the polysemous word 'tempo'. It is a fascinating word in its own right. Similarly to the French 'temps', the Spanish 'tiempo', and the Portuguese 'tempo', Italian 'tempo' accommodates three main meanings into one term: firstly, it refers to 'il tempo che fa', the weather; secondly, it connotes 'il tempo che passa', time; and thirdly, 'il tempo dei verbi', the tense of verbs, the temporality of an action.[3] It is perhaps by attending to these three meanings simultaneously that one can access the connotations of the English term, 'weathering', as the action

---

2   On the enantiosemy of 'weathering' see Christoph F. E. Holzhey's chapter in this volume. For the analysis of how enantiosemy plays in the poetic language of Dante's *Paradiso*, see Sara Fortuna and Manuele Gragnolati, 'Dante after Wittgenstein: "Aspetto", Language, and Subjectivity from *Convivio* to *Paradiso*', in *Dante's Plurilingualism: Authority, Knowledge, Subjectivity*, ed. by Sara Fortuna, Manuele Gragnolati, and Jürgen Trabant (Oxford: Legenda, 2010), pp. 223–48.

3   For this distinction and its untranslatability in another Romance language, French, see 'Temps', in *Dictionary of Untranslatables: A Philosophical Lexicon*, ed. by Barbara Cassin, Emily Apter, Jacques Lezra, and Michael Wood (Princeton, NJ: Princeton University Press, 2014).

or process by which the weather wears something down and affects it with change over time.

The definition of weather as that which produces change was central to medieval meteorology. In Dante's time, the discipline was largely informed by Aristotle's *Meteorology*, a treatise that Dante mentions twice in the *Quaestio de aqua et terra* (14 and 83) and that circulated in two Latin translations as well as through the mediation of influential scholastic commentaries such as those by Albert the Great (c. 1200–1280) and Thomas Aquinas (1225–1274).[4] Meteorology was understood as part of natural philosophy, the branch of knowledge that studied 'things of Nature', which are characterized by the fact that they 'move and change'.[5] Aristotle's *Meteorology* followed his other works on change in general (*Physics*), the movements of the stars and heavens (*On the Heavens*), and change undergone by matter on Earth (*Generation and Corruption*). The area of Aristotelian meteorology in the Middle Ages included 'all the transient phenomena which are caused by the action of Heat and Cold and which involve [...] the transformation of the "simple bodies" [i.e., the elements earth, water, air, and fire] one into another'.[6] Aristotle and his medieval commentators studied a wider range of phenomena than modern meteorology, focussing on the so-called 'sublunary' world in its entirety, from the

---

4   Dante Alighieri, *Quaestio de Aqua et Terra*, ed. by Francesco Mazzoni, in *Opere*, dir. by Marco Santagata, 2 vols (Milan: Mondadori, 2011–14), pp. 693–880. See Enrico Berti, 'De Meteoris (Meteorologica)', in *Enciclopedia Dantesca Italiana* (1970), <http:// www.treccani.it/enciclopedia/de-meteoris_(Enciclopedia-Dantesca)> [accessed 18 March 2020]; Patrick Boyde, *Dante Philomythes and Philosopher: Man in the Cosmos* (Cambridge: Cambridge University Press, 1981), chapter 3: 'Meteorology', pp. 74–95; also Alison Cornish, 'The Vulgarization of Science: Dante's Meteorology in Context', in *Science and Literature in Italian Culture from Dante to Calvino: A Festschrift for Patrick Boyde*, ed. by Pierpaolo Antonello and Simon A. Gilson (Oxford: Legenda, 2004), pp. 53–71.

5   Aristotle, *Physics*, ed. by Francis Macdonald Cornford and trans. by Philip H. Wicksteed, rev. edn, 2 vols, Loeb Classical Library, 228 and 255 (Cambridge, MA: Harvard University Press, 1934–57), I, pp. 16–17 (I. xii. 185a12–13) (cf. Dante Alighieri, *Dante's 'Il Convivio'*, trans. by Richard H. Lansing, Garland Library of Medieval Literature, 65 (New York: Garland, 1990): II. xiv. 8–11). As Alison Cornish notes, 'Meteorology is technically absent and poetically present in the *Commedia* for one thing because it deals with change, which is the fundamental advantage the living have over the dead. The mutation of vapour into water, wind, frost, comet or earthquake serves as an analogue for the spiritual transformation that the poem's characters have already undergone' ('The Vulgarization of Science', p. 54).

6   Boyde, *Dante Philomythes*, p. 74.

surface of the Earth and its atmosphere to the sphere of the Moon. As such, meteorology investigated celestial bodies that are now considered part of astronomy (such as the Milky Way, comets, shooting stars and meteors) as well as the weather phenomena of the lower atmosphere that are more readily associated with modern meteorology (such as the formation and transformation of clouds, rain, mist, dew, frost, snow, and hail through such processes as evaporation and condensation). Most importantly for our purposes, meteorology was concerned with weather as an agent of environmental change. It discussed, for instance, the ways in which the formation of rivers and their exsiccation can gradually transform the geological configuration of their environment through phenomena that modern geology identifies with erosion, rising sea levels, desertification, and emersion of land masses.[7] This corruptibility of the Earth, its inherent exposure to wear and tear, was the defining characteristic of the entire 'sublunary' world. For Aristotle and his medieval commentators, then, weather was always already weather*ing*: a process whereby atmospheric phenomena arise and affect the world.

A FROZEN *INFERNO*

Writing within this framework, Dante is interested in the weather mainly insofar as it affects human beings. Whereas in his other works such as *Convivio*, *De vulgari eloquentia*, and *Monarchia* this anthropocentric interest focuses primarily on the effects of local climates and earthly temporality on laws, customs, and language,[8] the *Commedia* — in line with its existential and moral focus — delves deeper into the relation between the elements and human subjectivity. Dante's

---

7   Aristotle, *Meteorologica*, ed. and trans. by Henry D. P. Lee, rev. edn, Loeb Classical Library, 397 (Cambridge, MA: Harvard University Press, 1952), p. 105 (ɪ. xiv. 351a19–353a28).

8   For Dante's references to how local climates affect customs and laws see Dante Alighieri, *Monarchia*, trans. by Prue Shaw (Cambridge: Cambridge University Press, 1996): ɪ. xiv. 6; for the ways sublunary temporality ('tempo'/'tempus') wears down (and renews) language, see Dante Alighieri, *De vulgari eloquentia*, trans. by Steven Botterill (Cambridge: Cambridge University Press, 1996): ɪ. ix. 6; *Convivio* ɪ. v. 9; and *Paradiso* xxvɪ, 124–38. For a discussion of the latter three passages, see Elena Lombardi, *The Syntax of Desire: Love and Language in Augustine, the Modistae, Dante* (Toronto: University of Toronto Press, 2007), pp. 129–40.

eschatological poem does so by dramatizing different modes in which the shades of the dead relate to the atmospheric phenomena, affecting them in the three very different realms of the afterlife. How do the souls relate to this force? Do they defy it, avoid it, or embrace it? Can their exposure be perilous and beneficial at the same time?[9]

In Hell, the realm of the afterlife represented in the first part of Dante's poem, brutal exposure to the elements characterizes the experience of many damned. Here we find a harsh, bare exposure to weather. In Hell, atmospheric phenomena are the means to inflict physical suffering on the damned (what contemporary theologians called *poena sensus*) and are designed to play a role in the divine punishments precisely for their concrete capacity to hurt, strike, scald, deform, consume, freeze, blind the dead through the aerial bodies that the separated souls can create in the Afterlife.[10] One is tempted to relate this insistence on weather as punishment to the Biblical story of the Flood in Genesis 6. In *Inferno*, extreme weather announces itself even before Dante sees it first-hand, when the ferryman of the dead, Charon, defines the infernal realm in terms of 'eternal darkness, [...] heat and chill' (*Inferno* III, 85).[11] *Inferno* displays some of the most extreme weather of the entire *Commedia*: tempestuous winds, putrid precipitations, a rain of fire, icy winds, hailstorms. The damned are completely exposed to the violence of the elements and helpless to them. In the second circle of Hell, for instance, 'a hellish [storm], that never rests' (*Inferno* v, 31) buffets the lustful, the first damned affected by physical pain that Dante meets on his journey (Figures 1 and 2).

---

9   On some positive aspects of 'exposure', see Alison Sperling's chapter in this volume.

10   Medieval theologians insisted that fire of Hell and Purgatory is physical and struggled to justify how a soul separated from its body could feel corporeal pain. Dante imagines that when the soul separates from its body at physical death and gets to the afterlife, it can create a body of air that allows it to have a shape and continue to express sensorial faculties. See Manuele Gragnolati, *Experiencing the Afterlife: Soul and Body in Dante and Medieval Culture* (South Bend, IN: Notre Dame University Press, 2005), pp. 67–87.

11   Quotations from Dante's poems are taken from *La Commedia secondo l'antica vulgata*, ed. by Giorgio Petrocchi, 2nd edn, 4 vols (Florence: Le Lettere, 1994). All translations from the *Commedia* are taken from Robert and Jean Hollander's three-volume edition of *Inferno* (New York: Doubleday/Anchor, 2000), *Purgatorio* (2003) and *Paradiso* (2007). The notable expression 'aere sanza tempo' (timeless air; *Inferno* III, 29) is generally taken to refer to the absence of any succession of day and night in Hell but could also be read as a pun on the other connotation of the Italian 'tempo': the atmosphere of Hell might be 'timeless' yet it is anything but 'weatherless'.

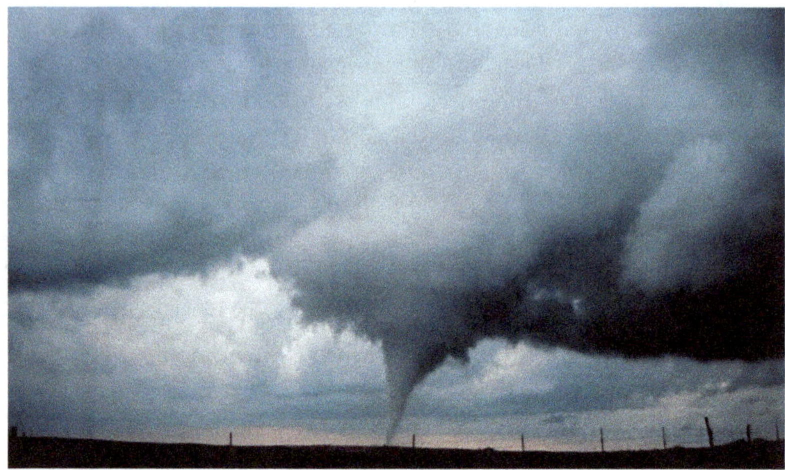

Figure 1. 'The hellish storm, which never rests...' (*Inferno* v, 31). Project
VORTEX-99, *Occluded Mesocyclone Tornado*, 3 May 1999, Anadarko,
Oklahoma. Credit: OAR/ERL/National Severe Storms
Laboratory/Wikimedia Commons.

Their punishment is an early example of an important structuring
principle of Dante's afterlife — called *contrapasso* in *Inferno* XXVIII, 142
— whereby the form of the punishments in Hell and Purgatory fits, by
analogy or contrast, the sin that has been committed on Earth. Thus,
as the lustful were buffeted by the passions in life, in Hell a real wind
now 'sweeps [the] spirits in its headlong rush, | tormenting, whirls and
strikes them' (*Inferno* v, 32–33); 'propel[s] the wicked spirits. | Here
and there, down and up, it drives them' (42–43). The storm carries
them away in a manner that matches the lack of control over their
desire on Earth. Among the yells, cries, and laments, the lustful are
also heard swearing against the action of the elements and the divine
power that regulates them (35–36), manifesting that hatred is the only
form of protest available to them against the punishment that afflicts
them.[12]

12　The dead that are waiting to cross the Acheron river 'Bestemmiavano Dio e lor parenti'
(*Inferno* III, 103). Blasphemy as an act of defiance against the punishment is also ex-
pressed by Vanni Fucci (*Inferno* XXV, 1–3) and of course, the emblematic blasphemer,
Capaneus in *Inferno* XIV, discussed below.

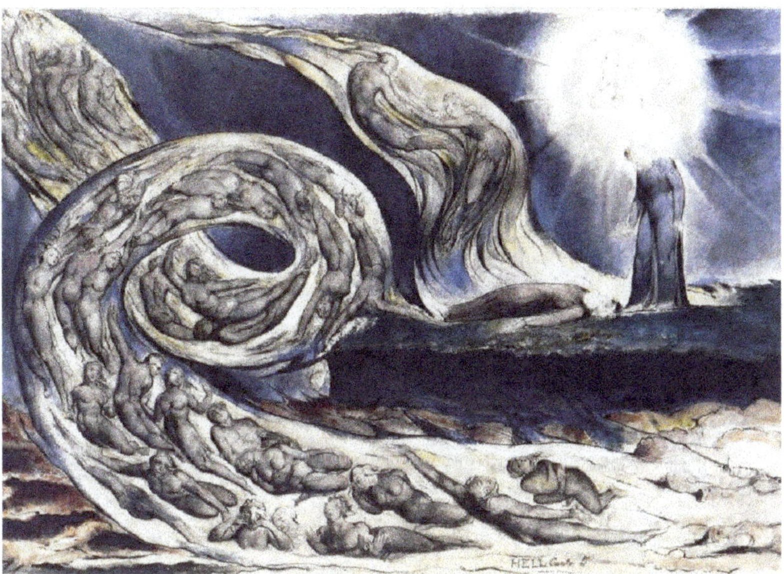

Figure 2. '[S]weeps [the] spirits in its headlong rush, | tormenting,
whirls and strikes them': the torment of the lustful (*Inferno* v, 32–33).
William Blake, *HELL canto* 5, 1824–27, pen, ink and watercolour,
Birmingham Museum and Art Gallery. Credit: Wikimedia Commons.

If the lustful lose autonomy of movement yet seem to maintain
their physiognomy, the gluttons of the next circle are also cruelly
disfigured in their appearance. As '[h]eavy hailstones, filthy water, and
snow | pour down through the gloomy air' (*Inferno* vi, 10–11) and
drown them into a malodorous mud, their anguish consumes them to
the point that they are almost unrecognizable (41, 43–45).[13] As in the
case of the lustful, the punishment of the gluttons functions in analogy
with their sin and the filthy rain tormenting them replicates the effects
that excessive eating and drinking has on the body.

It is among the dead of *Inferno* xiv–xvii that the 'logic' informing
the damned's brutal exposure to the infernal punishment is laid bare. A
fiery rain batters and burns those that have been violent against God —
blasphemers, sodomites, and usurers: 'in slow descent, | broad flakes of

---

13   See the 'piova | etterna, maladetta, fredda e greve' (*Inferno* vi, 8–9); '[g]randine
grossa, acqua tinta e neve | per l'aere tenebroso si riversa; | puta la terra che questo
riceve' (10–12); 'le ombre che adona | la greve pioggia' (32–33).

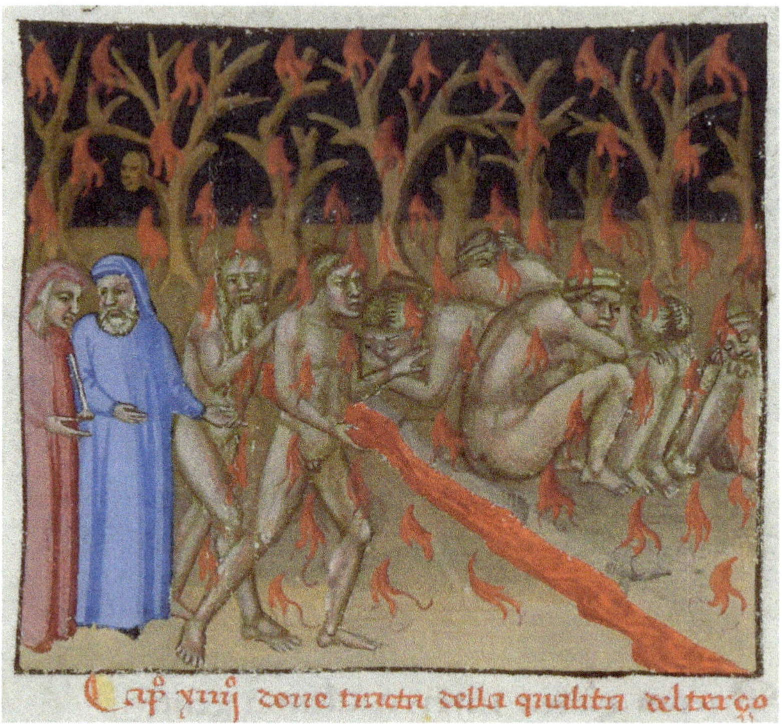

Figure 3. '[I]n slow descent, | broad flakes of fire showered down'
tormenting the violent (*Inferno* XIV, 28–29). Detail of a miniature by
Bartolomeo di Fruosino, *Inferno* XIV, 14th century, MS It. 74, f. 42,
Bibliothèque Nationale de France, Paris. Credit: gallica.bnf.fr / BnF.

fire showered down | as snow falls in the hills on windless days' (*Inferno*
XIV, 28–30) (Figure 3).

These shades struggle to pat themselves down to ease the pain
from the rain of fire (XIV, 40–42; XVII, 46–51), and are excoriated,
blackened, and disfigured by their punishment (XV, 26–28; XVI, 30
and 35). The case of Capaneus is the most emblematic here: he was
one of the mythical seven kings that assaulted the Greek city of Thebes
and is encountered by Dante under the rain of fire that torments the
blasphemers. Dante inquires about him:

> chi è quel grande che non par che curi
> lo 'ncendio e giace dispettoso e torto,
> sì che la pioggia non par che 'l maturi?

> (Who is that hero who seems to scorn the fire
> and lies there grim and scowling
> so that the rain seems not to ripen him?)
> (*Inferno* XIV, 46–48)

In a paradoxical way, Capaneus is both utterly helpless and proudly weather-resistant. On the one hand, he is prostrated by the rain of fire ('lies there', 47) which, according to one interpretation of the adjective 'torto' (47), contorts him under the pain of his torment. On the other hand, he compensates for this helplessness with 'scorn' (46), remaining defiant and resistant to any change.[14]

One could think that Capaneus's ability to face the extreme weather of Hell without it annihilating his body or bending his will and desires represents a successful form of 'weathering the storm'. However, the rest of the episode reframes Capaneus's resistance as his own major limit. As will become apparent in the *Purgatorio*, what is missing in Capaneus according to the conceptual framework of the poem — and what is impossible in Hell — is the leap from the exposure to pain to the realization of its beneficial potential. In this attitude, he is emblematic of the kind of weathering that is specific to the atmospheric phenomena of Hell as a place of hopeless damnation, where 'one of the features of [...] punishment is the incapacity of the damned to perceive their own damnation in any way beyond the brutality of their physical torment'.[15] Capaneus remains fixed in his rage, arrogance, and hatred, which the punishment does not wear down. When Capaneus proudly claims that Hell does not change him ('What I was alive, I am in death', 51) and continues blasphemously to challenge God in

---

14 The *Commedia*'s authoritative editor Giorgio Petrocchi prefers to amend the text of line 48 to 'non par che 'l marturi' ('seems not to *torture* him', as translated by Hollander), meaning that Capaneus appears psychologically unaffected or physically unhurt by the torment of the rain of fire; but if we follow the manuscript tradition, the reading 'maturi' ('seems not to *ripen* him') places the emphasis on Capaneus resisting the opportunity to be ripened by the experience of torment, i.e., by developing some insight into his sinful past. See Gragnolati, *Experiencing the Afterlife*, pp. 115–16; and 'Gluttony and the Anthropology of Pain in Dante's *Inferno* and *Purgatorio*', in *History in the Comic Mode: Medieval Communities and the Matter of Person*, ed. by Rachel Fulton and Bruce W. Holsinger (New York: Columbia University Press, 2007), pp. 238–50 (pp. 244–45).

15 Elena Lombardi, *The Wings of the Doves: Love and Desire in Dante and Medieval Culture* (Montreal: McGill-Queen's University Press, 2012), p. 48.

the same way as he did on Earth (52–60), Virgil — Dante's guide through the afterlife — explains that the identity boasted by Capaneus is actually part of the infernal punishment itself, which consists in the dull and never-ending repetition of sin: 'O, Capaneus, | because your pride remains unquenched | you suffer greater punishment. | In your anger lies your agony' (62–65).[16] Indeed, as Mark Cogan explains, the fiery rain and the heat tormenting the damned in the seventh circle of Hell are 'an exact replica of his sin itself' and reflect the passionate wrath and unjustified irascibility of the sin of violence, and blasphemy in particular.[17]

This paradigm of weather-resistance, of exposure without change, can be read as a hallmark in the subjectivity of the *Inferno* as a whole. One critic has termed this condition as the 'tragedy of rigidity',[18] whereby the aerial bodies of the damned are constantly exposed to the elements while the souls continue to be stuck in their Earthly sin and to experience its devastating effects. This experience of fixation, entrapment, and spiritual impermeability is most poignantly expressed in the climate of the last zone of *Inferno*, at the very bottom of Hell. There the condition of utmost desolation is symbolized by a freezing cold, a negative weather made of the absence of light, warmth, and any possibility of change of state. The traitors, who for Dante have enacted the worst perversion of humanity, lie icebound in the frozen lake Cocytus (Figure 4) and are tormented by a glacial wind produced by the wings of Lucifer, himself stuck in the ice (*Inferno* XXXIV, 46–52).[19]

These extreme conditions constitute a limit case of what 'weathering' can mean. Glacial temperatures are a kind of weather whose action

---

16   Ironically, Capaneus expresses his defiance through meteorological imagery (*Inferno* XIV, 52–60): 'the pagan Capaneus still defies Jupiter to take his vengeance by hurling thunderbolts until the arms of his giant smiths will be weary from forging them' (Boyde, *Dante Philomythes*, p. 81).

17   Marc Cogan, *The Design in the Wax: The Structure of the 'Divine Comedy' and its Meaning* (South Bend, IN: Notre Dame University Press, 1999), pp. 53–58, quotation on p. 58.

18   Thomas M. Greene, 'Dramas of Selfhood in the *Comedy*', in *From Time to Eternity: Essays on Dante's 'Divine Comedy'*, ed. by Thomas G. Bergin (New Haven, CT: Yale University Press, 1967), pp. 103–36 (p. 107).

19   The atmospheric conditions of the pit of Hell are also described directly or indirectly in *Inferno* XXXII, 22–75; XXXIII, 94–128; XXXIV, 4–9, 22.

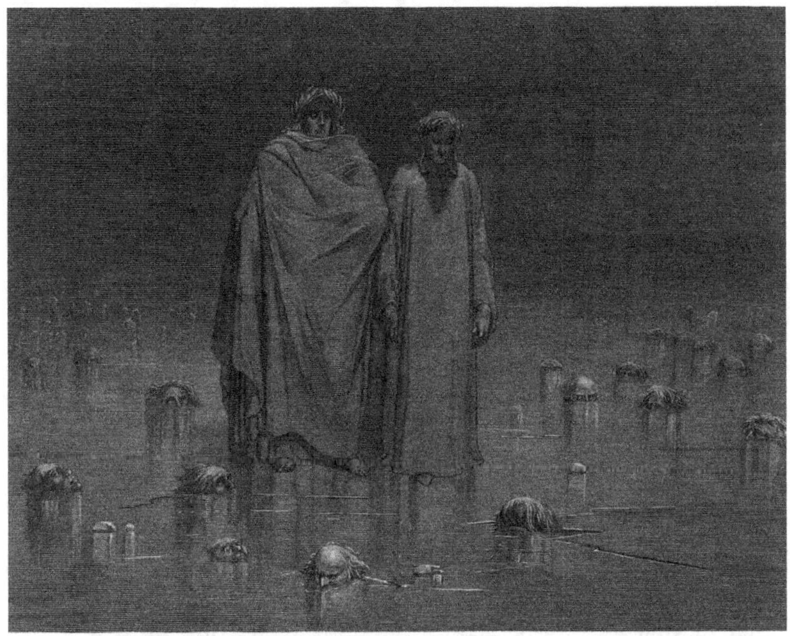

Figure 4. 'I saw a thousand faces purple | with the cold': the traitors
frozen in Lake Cocytus (*Inferno* XXXII, 70–71). Gustave Doré, *Inferno*
XXXII, 1861, wood engraving. Credit: gallica.bnf.fr / BnF.

expressly consists, not in gradually wearing down or consuming, but
in congealing into a fixed state. The *Commedia* takes ice as the ultimate
symbol of infernal subjectivity:[20] exposed to the punishment tormenting their body without spiritually softening their soul, the damned are
petrified, trapped in their sin, and unable to change or improve.[21]

---

20 Hegel takes freezing as emblematic of the individuals as depicted in the *Commedia*.
    Although the passage concerns all three realms, we think that his description perfectly
    captures the specificity of infernal weathering: 'For as individuals *were* in their passions
    and sufferings, in their intentions and their accomplishments, so now here they are
    presented for ever, solidified into images of bronze. [...] [O]n this indestructible foun-
    dation the figures of the real world move in their particular character, or rather they
    have moved and now in their being and action are frozen and are eternal themselves
    in the arms of eternal justice' (G. W. F. Hegel, *Hegel's Aesthetics: Lectures on Fine Art*,
    ed. and trans. by Thomas Malcolm Knox, 2 vols (Oxford: Clarendon Press, 1975), II,
    p. 1104 (part III. section 3. chapter. C. A. 3. ββ). For a reflection on this passage, see
    Erich Auerbach, 'Dante and the Romantics', in *Time, History, and Literature: Selected
    Essays of Erich Auerbach*, ed. by James I. Porter, trans. by Jane O. Newman (Princeton,
    NJ: Princeton University Press, 2014), pp. 141–42.
21 See Manuele Gragnolati, *Amor che move: Linguaggio del corpo e forma del desiderio in
    Dante, Pasolini e Morante* (Milan: Il Saggiatore, 2013), pp. 79–83.

THE REGULATED ATMOSPHERE OF *PURGATORIO*

With its macho model of defiance against the weather and disavowal of his own vulnerability, Capaneus can be read as a version of the autonomous, closed, self-righteous subject that has been associated with Western modernity and 'the violent practices of domination, exclusion, and devastation of which the subject itself is an accomplice'.[22] While this subject has been the object of critique and deconstruction for over a century, recently, feminist scholar Adriana Cavarero, in the wake of Judith Butler, has 'concentrate[d] on the category of relation to rethink a subjectivity marked by exposure, vulnerability, and dependence'.[23] Moving now to *Purgatorio*, we are interested in exploring how it presents a model of subjectivity that resonates with this appreciation of vulnerability and suggests possibilities and conditions for its productivity. In particular, we will show how Dante's Purgatory provides a regulated environment in which vulnerability can flourish and allow for the souls' spiritual improvement and for the gradual weathering down of their disorderly dispositions and past fixations.

The Church's official recognition of the otherworldly realm of Purgatory in the late thirteenth century was relatively recent in Dante's time and had nothing like the extensive literary and iconographic tradition of Hell and Heaven to support it.[24] Unfettered by tradition, Dante had free rein in representing Purgatory as he pleased, and he devised it as a mountain lying in the Southern Hemisphere of the Earth, yet free from earthly weather. Earthly meteorology plays no role in the punishments that take place in its seven terraces. If, on this count, *Purgatorio* is deliberately set apart from the atmospheric torments of *Inferno*, its suspension of adverse weather would seem to

---

22   See Adriana Cavarero, *Inclinations: A Critique of Rectitude*, trans. by Amanda Minervini and Adam Sitze (Stanford, CA: Stanford University Press, 2016), p. 12.

23   Cavarero, *Inclinations*, p. 11. Judith Butler's work to which Cavarero is referring is *Precarious Life: The Powers of Mourning and Violence* (London: Verso, 2004). For a more recent discussion of the political value of vulnerability, see *Vulnerability in Resistance*, ed. by Judith Butler, Zeynep Gambetti, and Leticia Sabsay (Durham, NC: Duke University Press, 2016), especially the 'Introduction' by Butler, Gambetti, and Sabsay, pp. 1–11, and the essay by Judith Butler, 'Rethinking Vulnerability and Resistance', pp. 12–27.

24   Jacques Le Goff, *The Birth of Purgatory*, trans. by Arthur Goldhammer (Chicago, IL: University of Chicago Press, 1984).

share the assumption that exposure is inextricable from harm. The early cantos open on beautiful clear skies (*Purgatorio* I, 13) and breezy (117, 123), sunlit (122) landscapes that will characterize the mountain as a whole, yet, as we will now see, they are also haunted by flashbacks and reminders of weather as a harmful force.

A first reminder is offered by Dante's guide Virgil who explains that in the afterlife the souls are given a body of air precisely for its capacity to suffer pain.[25] Extreme heat and freezing colds are central to Virgil's definition of the body of air as capable of being affected by physical torment:

> A sofferir tormenti, caldi e geli
> simili corpi la Virtù dispone
> che, come fa, non vuol ch'a noi si sveli.
>
> (The power that fits bodies like ours
> to suffer torments, heat, and cold
> does not reveal the secret of its working.)
> (*Purgatorio* III, 31–33)

'[T]ormenti, caldi e geli' here echo the line 'ne le tenebre etterne, in caldo e 'n gelo' that defines Hell in the parallel canto (*Inferno* III, 85; quoted in the previous section). The new context is notable for the absence of the adjective 'etterno'. The verb 'sofferir' (31) works like the enantiosemic 'weathering', its opposite connotations 'to bear' and 'to feel' expressing comparable dynamics. By speaking of the experience of torment in atmospheric terms, then, the tercet above articulates a theme of the wider *Purgatorio* where the torments have a weathering effect on the souls even though weather phenomena are deliberately toned down in the canticle and never directly harnessed as instruments of torment as they are in *Inferno*.

The harmful potential of the weather is thematized more directly in the tales of Manfred of Hohenstaufen (*Purgatorio* III) and Jacopo del Cassero, Buonconte da Montefeltro, and Pia dei Tolomei (*Purgatorio*

---

25 Perhaps because as a virtuous pagan of Limbo he is unacquainted with Purgatory, Virgil does not say more here. Later in the canticle the poet Statius will give the technical, precise explanation that when the soul separates from its earthly body and gets to the afterlife, it can indeed create a body of air that has not only an appearance but also all the senses and can therefore be affected by physical pain (*Purgatorio* XXV, 19–108).

v), which foreground the extreme vulnerability of the mortal body to weather phenomena. These shades portray their earthly body as fluid, fragile, easily dispossessed — a body susceptible to being weathered and wounded irrecoverably.[26] The controlled environment in the terraces of Purgatory proper will eventually allow the dead to reclaim the experience of physical torment into a means for spiritual healing; however, at this early stage of Antepurgatory, the souls appear to be haunted still by fear of the potential dangers of physical exposure and vulnerability on Earth.[27] Such is the emblematic case of the nobleman Buonconte da Montefeltro, whom Dante meets among those who repented at the last minute before dying a violent death. Buonconte relates the dissolution of his own corpse on Earth as it fell prey to the force of the elements, embodied by a torrential flood. His speech contains the most extended description of the causes and effects of precipitation and the formation of rivers in the *Commedia*, which accurately follows Aristotle's *Meteorology*.[28] The rains and ensuing flood freeze, sweep, undo, spin, overcome, cover, and enclose Buonconte's corpse:

> Ben sai come ne l'aere si raccoglie
> quell'umido vapor che in acqua riede,
> tosto che sale dove 'l freddo il coglie.
>   [...] mosse il fummo e 'l vento
> per la virtù che sua natura diede.
>   Indi la valle, come 'l dì fu spento,

---

26   See Gary Cestaro, *Dante and the Grammar of the Nursing Body* (Notre Dame, IN: University of Notre Dame Press, 2003), pp. 109–34. As Cestaro argues: 'the souls of antepurgatory had come to depend upon the apparent solidity of their temporal bodies as emblematic of a stable individual identity. They had not paid sufficient attention to the inherent fluidity of bodies so evident — as canto 5 dramatically attests — in the text of the created universe. *Purgatorio* v shows us that temporal identity mistakenly depends upon bodily integrity, for just as the elemental body (of a person, of the earth, of the universe) is fragile and fluid, so is earthly personhood in time' (p. 110)

27   Antepurgatory is the first of the three parts of *Purgatorio*, which constitutes a transitional, dilatory space before the proper purgation can begin (*Purgatorio* i–ix).

28   Buonconte's tale is demonic in origin (*Purgatorio* xxv, 111–112) yet the description of its formation through the condensation ('si converse', 117) of vapour ('umido vapor', 110) into water ('acqua', 110, 117) at higher altitudes and lower temperatures ('tosto che sale dove 'l freddo il coglie', 111), which results in it falling down as rain ('la pioggia cadde', 118) is verisimilar and scientifically accurate according to Aristotle's *Meteorologica*, pp. 68–121 (i. ix–xiv. 346b16–353a28), and indeed, with some terminological tweaks, to modern meteorology.

> [...] coperse
> di nebbia; e 'l ciel di sopra fece intento,
>   sì che 'l pregno aere in acqua si converse;
> la pioggia cadde, e a' fossati venne
> di lei ciò che la terra non sofferse;
>   e come ai rivi grandi si convenne,
> ver' lo fiume real tanto veloce
> si ruinò, che nulla lo ritenne.
>   Lo corpo mio gelato in su la foce
> trovò l'Archian rubesto; e quel sospinse
> ne l'Arno, e sciolse al mio petto la croce
>   ch'i' fe; di me quando 'l dolor mi vinse;
> voltòmmi per le ripe e per lo fondo,
> poi di sua preda mi coperse e cinse.
>
>   (Surely you know how a column of moist air,
> rising to colder heights, condenses
> and once again is changed to water.
>   [...] natural power
> [...] roused the fog and wind.
>   Then, when the day was spent, he shrouded
> the valley [...]
> in mist, and darkened the sky with clouds
>   so that the pregnant air was turned to water.
> The rain fell and the overflow that earth
> could not absorb rushed to the gullies
>   and, gathering in surging torrents, poured
> headlong down the seaward stream
> with so much rage nothing could hold it back.
>   At its mouth the blood-red Archiano found
> my frozen corpse and swept it down the Arno,
> undoing at my chest the cross
>   my arms had made when I was overcome by pain.
> It spun me past its banks and to the bottom,
> then covered and enclosed me with its spoils.)
> (*Purgatorio* v, 109–29)

As a soul who has suffered a violent death, Buonconte is doubly aware of the vulnerability of his body. His powerful description is a reminder that in contrast to what happens in the Afterlife, vulnerability on Earth has limits: the living do not possess the same capacity for limitless harm that is proper to the body-of-air of the dead, and exposure will eventually result in annihilation (Figure 5).[29]

---

29   On the limits and sustainability of intensity and receptivity, see Rosi Braidotti, 'Intensive Genre and the Demise of Gender', *Angelaki*, 13.2 (2008), pp. 45–57 (p. 52).

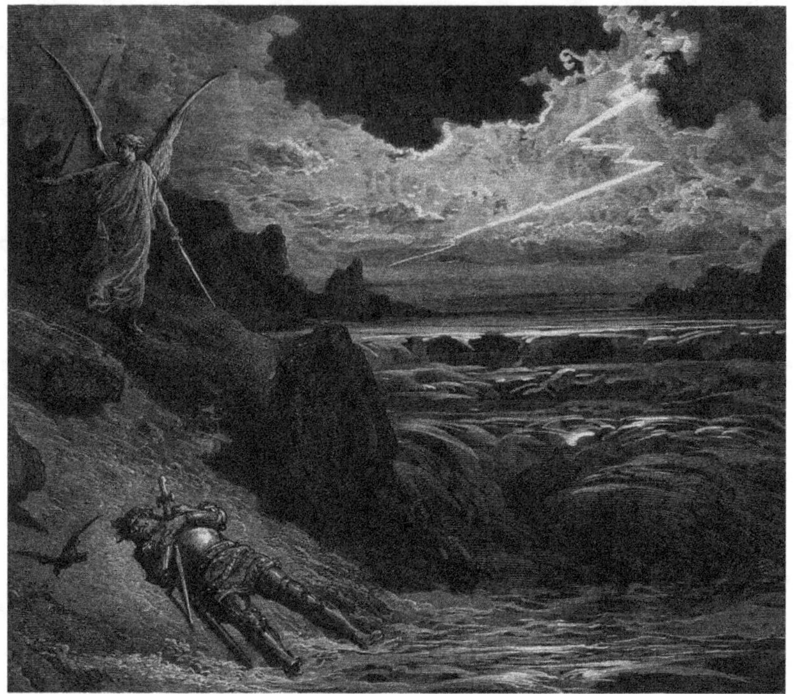

Figure 5. Buonconte's dispossessed body: 'the blood-red Archiano found
| my frozen corpse and swept it down the Arno' (*Purgatorio* v, 124–25).
Gustave Doré, *Purgatorio* v, 1868, wood engraving.
Credit: gallica.bnf.fr / BnF.

Antepurgatory plays this scene of unchecked vulnerability over
and over again, intertwining it, more often than not, with the violence
of the elements. This is seen in the first place with the tale of the
excommunicated king Manfred, whose body is wounded and broken
('rotta la persona', *Purgatorio* iii, 118) and whose bones ('l'ossa del
corpo mio', 127) are left at the mercy of the elements ('Or le bagna
la pioggia e move il vento | di fuor dal regno, quasi lungo 'l Verde,
| dov' e' le trasmutò a lume spento' [Now the rain washes and the
wind stirs them | beyond the Kingdom, near the Verde's banks, there
| where he brought them with his torches quenched], 130–32). The
scene is then repeated in the tale of the murdered Jacopo del Cassero,
who graphically describes his death by blood loss ('lì vid'io | de le mie
vene farsi in terra laco', *Purgatorio* v, 83–84) 'as bodily blood flows

back to join marsh, lake, and sea.'[30] Lastly, after Buonconte's tale, the dissolution of the earthly body also closes the canto in the pithy line by Pia dei Tolomei, who was apparently murdered by her husband: 'Siena made me, in Maremma I was undone' (Siena mi fé, disfecemi Maremma; *Purgatorio* v, 134). As these episodes show, there is only so much an earthly body can weather. Having established this, the rest of *Purgatorio* will shelter the purging shades from the inclement weather and sharpen the focus of their punishments in a regulated atmosphere where vulnerability can be reclaimed and turned into a means for positive transformation. It is on this regulated atmosphere that we reflect in the second part of this section.

The most distinctive feature of the purgatorial environment is a negative one: the absence of any adverse weather. The mountain of Purgatory is still part of Earth but, beginning with the seven terraces of Purgatory proper where the souls purge the residue of their earthly sins and recuperate their original perfection, its atmosphere is subject to a special dispensation. The microclimate of Purgatory proper is explained to Dante and Virgil by the Latin poet Statius, whom they encounter at the completion of his purgatorial process when he is ready to ascend to Heaven. Statius describes Purgatory as a regulated environment, free from weather changes:

> Cosa non è che sanza
> ordine senta la religïone
> de la montagna, o che sia fuor d'usanza.
>   Libero è qui da ogne alterazione:
> di quel che 'l ciel da sé in sé riceve
> esser ci puote, e non d'altro, cagione.
>   Per che non pioggia, non grando, non neve,
> non rugiada, non brina più su cade
> che la scaletta di tre gradi breve;
>   nuvole spesse non paion né rade,
> né coruscar, né figlia di Taumante,
> che di là cangia sovente contrade;
>   secco vapo non surge più avante
> ch'al sommo d'i' tre gradi ch'io parlai.
>
> (The mountain's holy law does not allow
> anything disordered or that violates its rule.

---

30   Cestaro, *Dante and the Grammar*, p. 124.

> Here nothing ever changes.
> Only by that which Heaven gathers from Itself,
> and from nothing else, can any change be wrought
> so that not rain nor hail nor snow
> nor dew nor hoarfrost falls above
> the gentle rise of those three steps below.
> Clouds, dense or broken, do not appear,
> nor lightning-flash, nor Thaumas' daughter,
> who appears in many places in the sky down there,
> nor does dry vapor rise beyond the highest
> of those three steps of which I spoke.)
> (*Purgatorio* XXI, 40–53)

The prevalent rhetorical mode in these lines is one of negation, which appear eleven times over fourteen lines, concentrating in the negative list of weather phenomena that are *not* in *Purgatorio*: rain, hail, snow, dew, hoarfrost (46–47); clouds, lightning-flash, rainbows, dry vapour (which caused winds) (49–50, 52). The phenomena excluded are not only those that were harnessed in Hell as punishments (wind in the circle of the lustful; rain, hail, and snow in the circle of the gluttons; lightning evoked by Capaneus in the circle of the violent; hoarfrost in the circle of the traitors) but also those that are represented in a more positive light in the liminal spaces of the shores of Antepurgatory and Eden (dew) and in Heaven (rainbows). This atmospheric regulation by exclusion is conceived in terms of order, rule, and norm: with two double negations we are told that the sacred rule *cannot* be affected by anything '*without* order' or '*outside* the norm' (41–42).[31] The rest of the quote gives this atmospheric control a positive spin, as the exclusion of bad weather in this regulated environment is described in the language of freedom: 'Libero è qui da ogne alterazione' (The mountain is free from all change; 43).

---

31 Manfredi Porena has understood the phrase 'sacra religïone | de la montagna' (*Purgatorio* XXI, 40–41) to refer not to the constitution of the mountain but more specifically to the 'community of the purging souls'. If this interpretation is correct, then the verb 'senta' ('to feel', 'to be affected', 41) would support the idea that the purging souls cannot feel or be affected by any distracting weather forces. See Manfredi Porena on *Purgatorio* XXI, 40–42; references to commentaries of the *Commedia* are taken from the Dartmouth Dante Project available online at <https://dante.dartmouth.edu/> [accessed 8 April 2020].

Freedom is a keyword of *Purgatorio*, strategically placed through the beginning, middle and end of the cantica.[32] The freedom to be attained in Purgatory is not conceived in terms of a positive liberty to do whatever one pleases but as a negative liberty from unorderly disposition and affect; in other words, as control of one's desires through reason. There thus seems to be a relation between this specific form of free subjectivity in the making and the atmosphere that enables it in *Purgatorio*. Purgatory, the realm predicated on the possibility of controlling passion and effecting (spiritual) change, is itself tightly controlled and free from all (atmospheric) change. To some of the readers of this paper in the early twenty-first century, the status of Dante's Purgatory as a fantasy of controlling and even harnessing the weather in a protected, productive, and well-structured environment may evoke problematic fantasies of geoengineering as a strategy to alter the effects or pace of climate change.[33] There is certainly a sense in which the atmospheric regulation is conceived, anthropocentrically, as a space for the souls to undertake their normative spiritual path. However, from the perspective of the souls of Purgatory, the mountain is not an opportunity for asserting their mastery over their environment, but a place where they can experience, exercise, and achieve, in all safety, a protected form of vulnerability. In this way, and in contrast with the extreme exposure which the damned attempt to weather, or that have the potential to annihilate the living, the vulnerability to pain depicted in *Purgatorio* is channelled into a productive experience of understanding and growth, a veritable transformation that gradually

---

32   Key passages are the opening canto, where Virgil famously refers to Dante as one who goes searching for freedom ('libertà va cercando', *Purgatorio* I, 71); the discourse of freedom is then theorised more at length in the central canti of the *Commedia*, *Purgatorio* XVI–XVIII, which discuss the theological doctrine of free will ('libero arbitrio', *Purgatorio* XVI, 71); and the word returns as the poet reaches the top of the mountain and Virgil proclaims that Dante's will is finally free ('libero, dritto e sano è tuo arbitrio', *Paradiso* XXVII, 143):

33   For a feminist critique of geoengineering in the face of climate change, see Holly Jean Buck, Andrea R. Gammon, and Christopher J. Preston, 'Gender and Geoengineering', *Hypatia*, 29.3 (2014), pp. 651–69. For a critique of architecture that adopts instead strategies of resilience: Orit Halpern, 'Hopeful Resilience', *e-flux*, 19 April 2017 <https://www.e-flux.com/architecture/accumulation/96421/hopeful-resilience/> [accessed 8 April 2020]. We are grateful to Alison Sperling for these insightful suggestions.

wears down the wrong dispositions of the past and re-opens the self to a correct form of love and desire.

This is the action of weathering in the Purgatory imagined by Dante. Earthly or infernal weathering involves the violent action of concrete weather phenomena; in Purgatory, these are suspended so that a more meaningful and productive form of weathering can take place, independent of the weather phenomena themselves but capturing their transformational powers. It is a beneficial connotation of 'weathering', like the action of airing one's linen or 'lifting [a hawk's] confinement and putting them back in their element'.[34] What is weathered away, in this weathering without weather, are the incrustations, accretions, and bad habits accumulated over the course of a lifetime, which targeted torments safely exfoliate, erode, and consume. As the gatekeeper of Purgatory Cato of Utica puts it on the shores of Antepurgatory, the mountain's purpose is precisely to help these souls shed their past accretions: 'spogliar[si] lo scoglio | ch'esser non lascia a voi Dio manifesto' (shed the slough | that lets not God be known to you; *Purgatorio* II, 122–23).[35] The punishments of *Purgatorio*, thus, do not coincide with a senseless exposure but operate weathering with focus, direction, and an end as a way to target, in progressive steps, the seven deadly dispositions of Pride, Envy, Wrath, Sloth, Greed, Gluttony, and Lust. In particular, the process of Dante's Purgatory is centred around the figure of the suffering Christ and imagined as the experience of suffering that teaches the soul how to gradually erode these dispositions and conform to Christ's gratuitous and selfless love.[36] As an example of this targeted weathering, we will turn to the sixth terrace, where the gluttons are punished not by the force of the elements but by their own longing for sweet-smelling fruits and a murmuring spring of fresh water, tantalizingly out of reach. Their

---

34 See Holzhey, 'Weathering Ambivalences: Between Language and Physics', in this volume, p. 29.

35 This process can be conceived in terms of the 'logic of supplementarity' inherent in the action of weathering, whereby something is gained through a process of weathering away; thus in *Purgatorio* the process of purgation transforms the souls spiritually as it erodes their disordered accretions. On the logic of supplementarity, see Damiano Sacco's chapter in this volume.

36 Manuele Gragnolati has written about the Christological paradigm of Dante's Purgatory and the concept of 'productive pain', *Experiencing the Afterlife*, pp. 89–137.

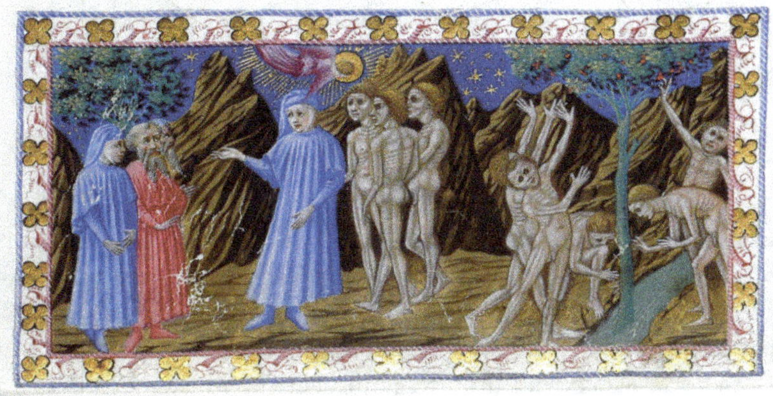

Figure 6. 'The sockets of their eyes resembled rings | without their
gems': the emaciated gluttons (*Purgatorio* XXIII, 31–32). Detail of a
miniature by Priamo della Quercia, *Purgatorio* XXIII, 1440s, MS Yates
Thompson 36, f. 107, The British Library, London.
Credit: The British Library/europeana.

environment is idyllic in all other respects. Yet, in their purgation, these
souls are worn to their bare bones: emaciated, their eyes hollow, their
face pale, their skinned stretch out over their bones (Figure 6):

> Ne li occhi era ciascuna oscura e cava,
> palida ne la faccia, e tanto scema
> che da l'ossa la pelle s'informava.
> Non credo che così a buccia strema
> Erisittone fosse fatto secco,
> per digiunar, quando più n'ebbe tema.
> Io dicea fra me stesso pensando: 'Ecco
> la gente che perdé Ierusalemme,
> quando Maria nel figlio diè di becco!'.
> Parean l'occhiaie anella sanza gemme:
> chi nel viso de li uomini legge 'omo'
> ben avria quivi conosciuta l'emme.

> (Their eyes were dark and sunken,
> their faces pales, their flesh so wasted
> that the skin took all its shape from bones.
> I do not believe that Erysichthon had become
> so consumed, to the very skin, by hunger
> when he was most in terror of it.
> I said to myself in thought:

> 'Behold the people who lost Jerusalem
> When Mary set her beak into her son!'
>   The sockets of their eyes resembled rings
> without their gems. He who reads 'omo''
> in men's faces would have easily made out the 'm'.)
> (*Purgatorio* XXIII, 22–33)

In addition to comparing the gluttons' emaciation to two horrible cases of starvation, the poem also associates it with Christ: the word 'omo' that the pilgrim reads on the face of the shades (32–33) recalls the passage in John's Gospel, where, during his Passion, the flagellated Christ is crowned with thorns and presented by Pilate to the crowd with the expression 'Ecce homo': 'Ecce homo' sounds very similar to the Dantesque 'legge omo', and 'Ecco' (28) and 'omo' (32) are rhyme words within four lines of each other.

In contrast with the damned from Hell, the distortion of the shades' features is a manifestation, not of sin, but of conforming to the crucified Christ, his selfless love, and productive pain. In a paradoxical way that does not mask the intensity of the suffering, the souls in Purgatory embrace pain, through identification with Christ, as a form of pleasure:

> E non pur una volta, questo spazzo
> girando, si rinfresca nostra pena:
> io dico pena, e dovria dir sollazzo,
>   ché quella voglia a li alberi ci mena
> che menò Cristo lieto a dire 'Elì',
> quando ne liberò con la sua vena.
>
> (And not once only, circling in this space,
> is our pain renewed.
> I speak of pain but should say solace,
>   for the same desire leads us to the trees
> that led Christ to utter *Elì* with such bliss
> when with the blood from His own veins He made us free.)
> (*Purgatorio* XXIII, 70–75)

The gluttons become increasingly raw and exposed but in a protected, controlled, and well-structured environment that does not destroy them but exfoliates their rigidity and allows them to recuperate the original likeness with God that sin had hidden. In the process of purgation, disorderly dispositions are softened, and the souls learn such virtues as humility, meekness, temperance, and generosity. They can experience a form of vulnerability that overcomes self-righteous and self-referential fixation and makes them 'inclined' and open to others.[37] Significantly, as Joan Ferrante has argued, the experience of Purgatory also teaches the souls to reconstruct societal bonds, rebuild a sense of community, and 'become citizens of the ideal society'.[38]

Dante's Purgatory is attractive in imagining the possibility for a productive experience of pain, a viable vulnerability, and an inclined subjectivity. At the same time, the importance of a highly regulated environment would seem to correspond to the widespread view that Butler, Gambetti, and Sabsay take as the starting point of their feminist critique, namely 'that vulnerability requires and implies the need for protection and the strengthening of paternalistic forms of power'.[39] However, Purgatory is meant as a transient rather than ideal state, and it prepares the souls for Heaven, where, as we will see in the next section, the weather conditions are far less restrained but the blessed no longer need protection.

HEAVENLY HEAT

At the top of the mountain of Purgatory, what awaits the newly weathered soul is the idyllic garden of Eden, a *locus amoenus* where spring is eternal ('qui primavera sempre e ogne frutto' [here it is always spring, with every fruit in season], *Purgatorio* xxviii, 143) and the atmosphere is characterised by 'un'aura dolce, senza mutamento' (A sweet breeze, without any change; *Purgatorio* xxviii, 7). This also is a controlled environment, one last stop for the souls to experiment

---

37   On the ethical posture of inclination, see Cavarero, *Inclinations*. Both in Antepurgatory and especially in the seven terraces of Purgatory proper, souls gather in groups and assume postures defying straightness and autonomy. For instance, the indolent Belacqua is found leaning over his knees among a group of late-repentants who are resting in the shade (*Purgatorio* iv, 103–109), the proud are bent under the weight of rocks (*Purgatorio* x, 130–39), the envious lean against the wall of the terrace and against each other (*Purgatorio* xiii, 59–60), and the avaricious lie flat on the ground (*Purgatorio* xix, 70–75).

38   Joan Ferrante, *The Political Vision of Dante's 'Comedy'* (Princeton, NJ: Princeton University Press, 1984), pp. 198–252 (p. 198).

39   Butler, Gambetti, and Sabsay, 'Introduction', p. 1.

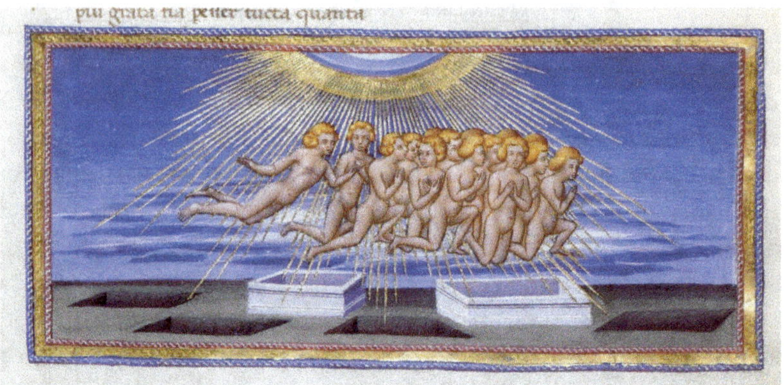

Figure 7. 'Nor will such shining have the power to harm us' (*Paradiso*
XIV, 58). Detail of a miniature by Giovanni di Paolo, *Paradiso* XIV,
1440s, MS Yates Thompson 36, f. 154, The British Library, London.
Credit: The British Library/europeana.

with exploration and wandering a while longer, before their leap to
Heaven. Given this portrayal of Eden, one might expect the garden to
be an anticipation of what Heaven might look like — a place of im-
perturbable bliss and enjoyment, free from the distraction and pain of
the elements' most adverse effects. However, Dante's representation of
Heaven overturns this comforting expectation. In *Paradiso* the weather
is not controlled or sublimated but, on the contrary, its intensity is
dialled up. The weather of the canticle does not feature precipitations,
supernatural phenomena, freezing temperatures, or earthquakes but is
dominated instead by a relentless atmospheric condition of extreme
light and heat — we call this the heavenly '*canicule*' after the heatwave
that hit the planet in the Summer of 2019, as we were beginning to
write this paper in France.

As Lino Pertile and Heather Webb pointed out, there is more fire
in *Paradiso* than in *Inferno*, and references to fire, heat, and burning
are accordingly much more numerous in the third canticle than in the
previous ones.[40] The condition of being in Dante's Heaven resembles
that of being exposed to a heatwave, which the blessed experience as a

---

40   Lino Pertile, 'L'antica fiamma: La metamorfosi del fuoco nella *Commedia* di Dante',
    The Italianist, 11.1 (1991), pp. 29–60; Heather Webb, *Dante's Persons: An Ethics of the
    Transhuman* (Oxford: Oxford University Press, 2016), pp. 123–62, esp. p. 125.

sensation of intense burning: they are 'infiammati' (inflamed; *Paradiso* III, 52) and 'ard[ono]' (burn; XXXI, 100). While light is the external and visible indication of the divine love informing Heaven, fire also manifests the intensity of the vision attained by the blessed souls and that of the joy resulting from it:

> La sua chiarezza séguita l'ardore;
> l'ardor la vision, e quella è tanta,
> quant'ha di grazia sovra sua valore.
>
> (Its brightness answers to our ardor,
> the ardor to our vision, and that is given
> in greater measure of grace that we deserve.)
> (*Paradiso* XIV, 40–42)

Having themselves become 'sempiterne fiamme' (eternal flames; XIV, 66) and 'lucenti incendi' (fiery lights; XIX, 100), the blessed souls are not only affected by the weather but also contribute to it insofar as they radiate the heat they feel back to one another. In this way, far from being simply immersed in the heatwave, the blessed are sources of extreme heat in turn.[41] As Heather Webb has shown, *ardore* qualifies 'the intensity of attention that one person can offer to another',[42] and the blessed souls' ardent burning is a sign that they have overcome any self-enclosure or rigidity and are now enjoying a form of radical dispossession that merges them with God and opens them to others. Yet, while the souls open up to the divine environment and melt with it, they are not completely annihilated and, paradoxically, their fusion occurs without fully dissolving them, their memories, desires, or consciousness.[43]

The heat and burning running throughout the *Paradiso* culminate in the final cantos of the poem. Dante the character's final leap into

---

41   See Pertile, 'L'antica fiamma', pp. 31–32. The heavenly condition of exposure to the heatwave and embodiment of it can be read as suggesting the collapse of distinctions between human beings and their environment. For this idea in contemporary new materialism and in particular in the work of Stacy Alaimo, and Astrida Neimanis and Rachel Loewen Walker, see Christoph F. E. Holzhey's chapter in the present volume.

42   Webb, *Dante's Persons*, p. 125.

43   On the paradox of Heaven as at once losing and finding oneself, see Manuele Gragnolati, 'Diffracting Dante's *Paradiso*: Transformation, Identity, and the Form of Desire', in *Reception, Translation, and Transformation of Italian Literature*, ed. by Brian Richardson, Guido Bonsaver, and Giuseppe Stellardi (Oxford: Legenda, 2017), pp. 352–66.

Transcendence can take place only when his *ardour* reaches its peak of intensity:[44]

> E io ch'al fine di tutt' i disii
> appropinquava, sì com'io dovea,
> l'ardor del desiderio in me finii.

> (And, as I neared the end of all desire,
> I extended to its limit, as was right,
> the ardor of the longing in my soul.)
> (*Paradiso* xxxiii, 46–48)

However, if the heatwave is the hallmark of Dante's Heaven, its status should not be taken for granted. Spiritualizing interpretations maintain that, unlike the weather phenomena of Hell, it is entirely and exclusively metaphorical, to be understood as a fire of love and desire.[45] In Lino Pertile's view, emblematic of this position, the fire of love is reified as a form of *contrapasso* in *Inferno* and has a therapeutic purpose at the end of the terrace of the lustful in *Purgatorio* xxvii, 10–57 (anticipated in xxv, 138–39), as a 'real' fire, with a flame that burns literally; but in Heaven, it is reduced to a metaphor whose meaning takes on positive connotations.[46] Instead, in stressing the concreteness of the extreme atmospheric conditions of Heaven and the intense burning of the blessed, we insist on the literal character of the heavenly *canicule* even as it acquires a spiritual dimension as a manifestation of the love and vision of Transcendence that are disclosed in Heaven.

Paradiso reiterates that the light and heat of heaven are intense enough to be destructive on any mortal body that were to be exposed to them. For instance, they are so violent that they must be temporarily tempered for the benefit of Dante, who is travelling through the afterlife with his earthly body and would otherwise burn alive. This restraint, which is reminiscent of the suspension of weather in *Purgatorio*,

---

44   See Webb, *Dante's Persons*, pp. 160–63. On this understanding of the term *finii*, see Lombardi, *The Wings of the Doves*, p. 125.

45   'il fuoco del *Paradiso*, contrariamente a quello infernale, non fa fumo ne brucia nessuno, perché è tutto e soltanto metaforico, e fuoco d'amore e di desiderio, ove non sia ardore di luce' (Pertile, 'L'antica fiamma', p. 30). Curiously, Pertile concedes that the spiritualising interpretations comes 'at the risk of contradicting Dante himself' (ibid.).

46   Pertile, 'L'antica fiamma', p. 30.

only lasts as long as Dante's journey, thus indicating the physical violence of the heavenly *canicule* by human standards. Beatrice illustrates its force by comparing it to the myth of Semele, who burned to ashes the moment she chose to see the pagan god Zeus face-to-face in all his splendour. For the protagonist Dante, who, exceptionally, is voyaging through Heaven, the myth of Semele still functions as a cautionary tale:

> E quella non ridea; ma 'S'io ridessi',
> mi cominciò, 'tu ti faresti quale
> fu Semelè quando di cener fessi;
>   ché la bellezza mia, che per le scale
> de l'etterno palazzo più s'accende,
> com'hai veduto, quanto più si sale,
>   se non si temperasse, tanto splende,
> che 'l tuo mortal podere, al suo fulgore,
> sarebbe fronda che trono scoscende.'
>
>   (She was not smiling. 'If I smiled,'
> she said, 'you would become what Semele became
> when she was turned to ashes,
>   for my beauty, which you have seen
> flame up more brilliantly the higher we ascend
> the stairs of this eternal palace,
>   is so resplendent that, were it not tempered
> in its blazing, your mortal powers would be
> like tree limbs rent and scorched by lightning.)
> (*Paradiso* XXI, 1–12)

Beatrice explains that if she were to smile fully, she would risk annihilating Dante's mortal body with her radiance like a lightning strikes a tree (11–12). Temporarily tempering her splendour (10), she makes heaven safe for Dante, and lets herself be seen.

Such self-restraint and protectiveness, as Beatrice displays in this passage, does not concern the fleshless souls of the blessed in their constant exposure to their environment. Far from sheltered and insulated, they are able to feel heavenly weather and burn with its ardour without being harmed. Similar to Hell, there is no change here but the blessed souls have a different way of 'weathering the storm' to the impermeable rigidity of a Capaneus: they are able to sustain the full intensity of the environment, yet they simultaneously demonstrate a radical receptivity to it, which is in turn an integral part of their bliss. While this ability, at once to receive and endure paradisiac warmth, is essential to the experience of the blessed souls, in the heaven of the Sun Solomon explains that earthly bodies will also be unharmed once they resurrect and reunite with their souls at the end of time:

> né potrà tanta luce affaticarne:
> ché li organi del corpo saran forti
> a tutto ciò che potrà dilettarne.

> (Nor will such shining have the power to harm us,
> For our body organs shall be strengthened
> to deal with all that can delight us.)
> (*Paradiso* XIV, 58–60)

The organs of the resurrected body are exposed but 'strengthened' (59), the 'shining' (58) of the flesh is intense but does not 'have the power to harm' them (58). The weather can be dialled up in Heaven precisely because the blessed are ready to enjoy intensity without annihilation (Figure 7).

Radically open even to the extreme conditions of its environment, the ideal subjectivity represented in *Paradiso* is not self-involved or defiant (as in Hell) or sheltered (as in Purgatory) but discovers that it does not have to fear being radically receptive even as it is radically exposed. The weathering of *Paradiso* constitutes an answer to the mitigated, 'safe' weathering of *Purgatorio* just as much as to the antagonistic weathering of *Inferno*. *Paradiso* dramatically removes the protected setting of *Purgatorio* and reveals a form of subjectivity that is finally capable of abandoning all rigidity and closure even in the most extreme of circumstances. Having relinquished aggressiveness, self-enclosure, and pretence of autonomy, heavenly subjectivity neither needs protection nor fears unmediated exposure, but is capable of enjoying the blinding light without having to close itself off from its burning intensity.

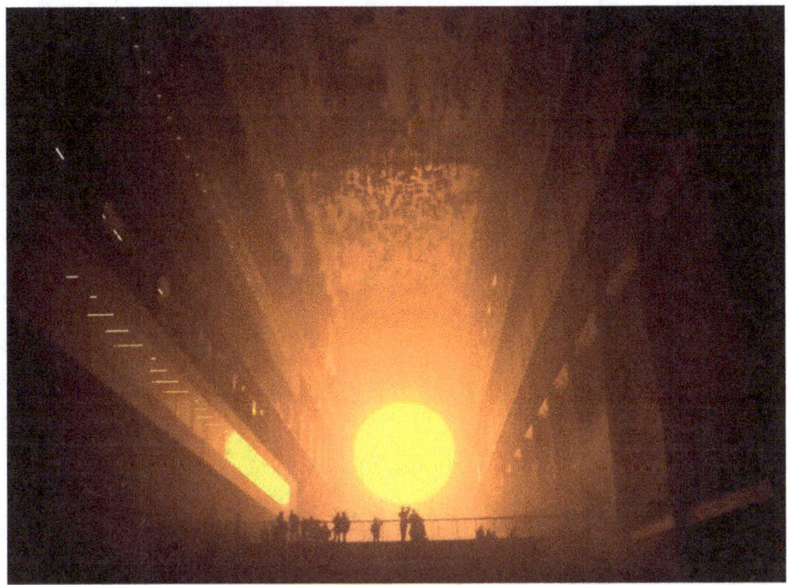

Figure 8. '[S]o much of the sky seemed set on fire | by the flaming sun' (*Paradiso* I, 79–80). Olafur Eliasson, *The Weather Project*, 16 October 2003 – 21 March 2004, Turbine Hall, Tate Modern, London. Credit: Bradley Clark/Wikimedia Commons.

Scaling from Weather to Climate

DANIEL LIU

> The interaction of all meteorological elements at a particular time in a particular place provides what we call the 'weather' [Wetter]. The weather is not an average atmospheric state, but rather the total impression or total effect of actually occurring atmospheric phenomena all at once within a particular, short period of time, at a certain hour, or even more strictly in a given moment. We speak of the weather of a certain day, but only of the 'climate' [Witterung] and hardly of the 'weather' of a whole year, because the longer the period, the more manifold and heterogenous are the weather phenomena that have occurred, which can be summarized only through the term 'climate.' Climate already indicates an abstraction, while weather is a real condition, an individual event singled out of the changing sequence of climate phenomena. A weather map shows the atmospheric phenomena taking place over a part of the earth's surface at a particular moment. There is no such thing as a weather map for months or a whole year, because the interplay of average temperature, average cloud cover, average wind, average rainfall, or monthly rainfall is not the weather.

> Julius Hann, *Lehrbuch der Meteorologie* (1901), p. 483

The theme 'weathering' in this volume assumes a set of climatic forces — both material and metaphorical — that act with some constancy or predictability on an object, as well as specifying the kind or kinds of temporalities with regard to the thing being weathered. One of our motivations for choosing 'weathering' as our theme is the clear and distinct ambiguity of the concept. In English, at least, the concepts 'weather' and 'weathered/weathering' are at once global and local, e.g., the way a thunderstorm is a locally contained event caused by larger-scale climatological patterns; they invoke recent events, historical disruptions across a handful of centuries, and even processes that stretch well into Earth's deep history. The weathering or weathering away of an object is temporally relative to both the object and the forces acting upon it. Weather is also an omnipresent condition — there's good weather and bad weather, but there's never *no* weather — and yet, from within the ivory tower, it's both containable and temporarily escapable thanks to durable construction methods and modern climate control technologies like fibreglass insulation, air conditioning, a steady supply of electricity, central heating, and cognitive dissonance.[1] As a friendly concept, weathering manages to tick all of the boxes of being everywhere and not everywhere at the same time, working as a capacious-enough concept that's both helpfully meaningful and vague, impossible to ignore and (as aforementioned) conveniently ignorable if need be.

Are all of these possible meanings of the weather actually commensurable with one another? Or is part of the appeal their incommensurability? One of the more powerful intellectual currents within Anthropocene discourse and the environmental humanities is a stress on incommensurability of individual thinkers or political actors when compared to the geographical, geological, and historical scales of anthropogenic climate change. The problem of scaling individual experience — be it through pragmatic experience, social contract theory, the Kantian a priori, the Cartesian criterion of clarity and distinctness, etc. — up to encompass the scale and nature of climate change has been a manifest political problem around global climate science since the mid-1980s, and has dramatically intensified since the early 2000s.[2]

---

1   Christina Sharpe, *In the Wake: On Blackness and Being* (Durham, NC: Duke University Press, 2016), chapter 4; on air conditioning see Bruno Latour, *Facing Gaia: Eight Lectures on the New Climatic Regime*, trans. by Catherine Porter (Cambridge: Polity, 2017), pp. 123–24.

2   Naomi Oreskes and Erik M. Conway, *Merchants of Doubt: How a Handful of Scientists Obscured the Truth on Issues from Tobacco Smoke to Global Warming* (New York: Bloomsbury, 2010).

A running exchange with Dipesh Chakrabarty, Julia Adeney Thomas, Robert Stockhammer is a good case in point. In 2009, Chakrabarty reflected that his own scholarship left him ill-equipped to conceptually tackle the political crises of global climate change:

> I realized that all my readings in theories of globalization, Marxist analysis of capital, subaltern studies, and postcolonial criticism over the last twenty-five years, while enormously useful in studying globalization, had not really prepared me for making sense of this planetary conjuncture within which humanity finds itself today.[3]

In 2012, Chakrabarty sensed that the problem of scale was becoming more acute within postcolonial historiography and theory, which has emphasized differences of cultural experience juxtaposed against processes of globalization. The sheer scale of climate change left 'experience' behind, in that, 'We cannot ever experience ourselves as a geophysical force — though we now *know* that this is one of the modes of our collective existence. We cannot send somebody out to experience in an unmediated manner this "force" on our behalf.'[4] More troublingly for Chakrabarty,

> We now also have a mode of existence in which we [...] are 'indifferent' or 'neutral' to questions of intrahuman justice [...]. This is why the need arises to view the human simultaneously on *contradictory* registers: as a geophysical force and as a political agent, as a bearer of rights and as author of actions; subject to both the stochastic forces of nature (being itself one such force collectively) and open to the contingency of individual human experience; belonging at once to differently scaled histories of the planet, of life and species, and of human societies.[5]

Even though the individual versus the general will has long been a stock problem in social contract theory, Stockhammer, following Chakrabarty's lead, has noted that global climate change in the last century

---

3 Dipesh Chakrabarty, 'The Climate of History: Four Theses', *Critical Inquiry*, 35.2 (Winter 2009), pp. 197–222 (p. 199) <https://doi.org/10.1086/596640>.

4 Dipesh Chakrabarty, 'Postcolonial Studies and the Challenge of Climate Change', *New Literary History*, 43.1 (2012), pp. 1–18 (p. 12) <https://doi.org/10.1353/nlh.2012.0007>.

5 Ibid., p. 15, emphasis added.

has created or intensified a fissure in the history of Western philosophy that had remained hidden: the two separate concepts of humanity, the rational *homo* of the philosophers and the species *Anthropos* of natural history. Whereas *homo* gestures to the universality of human reason and experience, the *Anthropos* signifies what is collectively common *despite* human diversity and inequality. This distinction leads Stockhammer to write, 'I am skeptical whether this model of individual enlightenment [*Homo*] can directly carry over to seven billion specimens of the species [*Anthropos*]', and, 'The commonality of *homo* is not comparable to the inequality within the *Anthropoi*.'[6] Picking up on Stockhammer's terminology and highlighting the contradictory or even 'incommensurable' concepts of the human, Chakrabarty responds,

> By introducing new questions of scale — astronomical scales for space, geological scales for time, and scales of evolutionary time for the history of life — all in search of understanding the relationship between the history of the planet's atmosphere and its life-carrying capacity, and thus promoting what may be called a life, or zoecentric, view of the history of the planet, the literature on global warming works at a tangent to the completely homocentric narrative of globalization.[7]

Not that either Chakrabarty or Thomas believe this incommensurability is *only* a hindrance. Thomas argues that just as paleobiology, microbiology, and biochemistry 'produce visions of "the human" that are incommensurable with one another, as well as with the historian's usual conception of personhood and society', for historians such in-

---

6   Robert Stockhammer, 'Philology in the Anthropocene', in *Meteorologies of Modernity: Weather and Climate Discourses in the Anthropocene*, ed. by Sarah Fekadu, Hanna Straß-Senol, and Tobias Döring (= *REAL: Yearbook of Research in English and American Literature*, 33 (Tübingen: Narr Francke Attempto, 2017)), pp. 43–64 (pp. 49–50).

7   Dipesh Chakrabarty, 'The Human Condition in the Anthropocene', in *The Tanner Lectures on Human Values*, 35, ed. by Mark Matheson (Salt Lake City: University of Utah Press, 2016), pp. 139–88 (p. 159), available online: <https://tannerlectures. utah.edu/Chakrabarty%20manuscript.pdf> [accessed 1 August 2020]. Chakrabarty replaces Stockhammer's term *Anthropos* with his quasi-Aristotelian *zoe* to come up with 'zoecentric' history.' On 'human agency over multiple and incommensurable scales' see Chakrabarty, 'Postcolonial Studies and the Challenge of Climate Change', p. 1.

commensurability and diversity are usually strengths, or at least are tolerated well enough.[8]

The historian of science Deborah Coen offers a different take on such 'incommensurability', that scaling, as well as awareness of scale effects, are themselves human concepts, and that the point at which different scales become 'incommensurable' is not fixed:

> The spatial and temporal dimensions of human life are historically and culturally contingent: they vary with differences in life span, degree of mobility, communications technologies, and cultures of remembering the dead. There is therefore no fixed meaning to the 'human scale' that could be set in opposition to 'the planetary'.[9]

In other words: How did we get to the point where individual experience, never mind community or even species experience, is assumed to be so small, while conceptions of either regional environments or planetary climates are assumed to be so large?[10] The problem is perhaps analogous, in early twenty-first-century political discourse, to the way the individual's experience has become politically and epistemologically unassailable against prevailing or 'dominant' narratives, especially when dealing with the experiences of those who are marginalized, forgotten, or historically oppressed. In both, the relationship between the general and the particular becomes undone, either by accident or through acts of deliberate resistance.[11] The question is not so much one of whether *all* grand narratives and generalities need to be done away with, but which generalities are now most useful, and how the contours of general theories are negotiated. As Coen writes, paraphrasing the nineteenth-century Austrian writer, Adalbert Stifter (1805–1868): 'In nature, as in human life [...] often the little things

---

8   Julia Adeney Thomas, 'History and Biology in the Anthropocene: Problems of Scale, Problems of Value', *American Historical Review*, 119.5 (December 2014), pp. 1587–1607 <https://doi.org/10.1093/ahr/119.5.1587>.

9   Deborah R. Coen, 'Big Is a Thing of the Past: Climate Change and Methodology in the History of Ideas', *Journal of the History of Ideas*, 77.2 (April 2016), pp. 305–21 (p. 308) <https://doi.org/10.1353/jhi.2016.0019>.

10 On the concept of regional, as opposed to local and national scales, see Jeremy Vetter, *Field Life: Science in the American West During the Railroad Era* (Pittsburgh, PA: University of Pittsburgh Press, 2016).

11 Ibid., pp. 62–63.

are most significant, once they are recognized as instances of a more general pattern, perceptible to observers everywhere.'[12]

The concepts *Homo, Anthropos*, the human, and the Anthropocene are not only abstractions, but extrapolations from a highly specific set of scientific and social scientific practices, and we need to pay attention to how these extrapolations are made. Likewise, rigorous conceptions of the weather and weathering demand more than just conceptual gesturing or figuration: it requires paying attention to the methods by which particular phenomena, experienced at the individual or immediately local scales, are stitched together to create accurate pictures of regional and ultimately global conditions. If we take 'weather' in its *most* everyday sense, then we ordinarily say it is the job of the weather reporter or *meteorologist* to take into account a wide range of regional patterns and information coming from a variety of well-placed sensors in order to generate a weather report, an anticipation of how much rain, wind, dryness, or thunderstorms I can expect in a given place. In this volume, by focusing on weather and weathering, we are re-examining how we transform a single weather event or the weathering of a single object into broader notions respectively of climate or maintenance. In contrast to the way Stockhammer's figurative *Homo* and *Anthropos* are simply *assumed* to be universal, the basic constructivist approach to the history and sociology of science demands that we explain empirically *how* scientific concepts become universal. There are, of course, a great many ways of doing so within science studies, but in this essay, I will assume that this 'how' demands examination of practices and methodologies. As the editors of a recent special journal issue on 'Experiencing the Global Environment' have written, 'Ways of experiencing the global[...]are by necessity always produced locally.'[13]

The remainder of this essay will examine two areas of scholarship in the history of sciences of scaling: Martin Rudwick's foundational work on the history of geology and Deborah Coen's recent study of

---

12   Deborah R. Coen, *Climate in Motion: Science, Empire, and the Problem of Scale* (Chicago: University of Chicago Press, 2018), p. 154.

13   Lino Camprubí and Philipp Lehmann, 'The Scales of Experience: Introduction to the Special Issue *Experiencing the Global Environment*', *Studies in History and Philosophy of Science Part A*, 70 (August 2018), pp. 1–5 <https://doi.org/10.1016/j.shpsa.2018.05.003>.

the origins of physical geography and climatology. These two cases provide important contrasts, illuminating the differences between natural philosophy and natural history, theory versus empirical research. Rudwick has argued that the major theoretical innovation that established modern geology was the shift from a relatively rigid style of ahistorical and deterministic geotheory to a geoscience that is highly attentive to historical contingencies of time and place. In other words, geologists had to learn how to scale up from local particularities and contingencies to reconstruct the history of the earth. Coen, by contrast, argues that modern climate science developed in the reverse fashion, from the active attempt to collect and synthesize local differences into physical theories of climatic change, effective at regional and global scales. How does this relate to the volume's overall theme of weather/weathering? Obviously, in the case of climatography, observation and recording of the weather at special observatories and stations was the new science's empirical foundation. In the case of early geology, scientists (Rudwick prefers the period-appropriate *savants*) travelled looking for places where the weather had worn away the Earth in a way that allowed one to see layers of different rocks or strata. Both sciences deal with the earth as a physical system, both sciences are clearly borne out by quite particular local human efforts, and both sciences were fundamental in the late twentieth-century formulation of the concept of the Anthropocene.

GEOLOGY: ENLIGHTENMENT IN ACTION

The evolutionary theorist and historian of science Stephen Jay Gould (1941–2002) wrote in 1988 that Sigmund Freud had forgotten the fourth great intellectual revolution of European scientific modernity. Freud had enumerated three: Copernicus' de-centring of the Earth into one of a multitude of planets, Darwin's demotion of man's special creation into the spectrum of the descent of species, and of course Freud's own revolution of subordinating rational action to the impulses of the subconscious. The fourth revolution, which Freud missed and Gould insisted upon, was the early nineteenth-century discovery of geological and cosmological deep time, the extension of the history of nature to millions and billions of years, in both breadth and depth.[14] But it has been Martin Rudwick's contention since his 2005 book *Bursting the Limits of Time* and emphasized in the 2008 sequel *Worlds Before Adam* that geology's essential modernity is not in its mere *extension* of time, a concept other sciences have potentially entertained. Rather, Rudwick argues that modern geology embraced a very particular *kind* of historicity and temporality unique to the history of the geosciences. Modern geology for Rudwick — perhaps modernity generally — is characterized by emphasis on the *contingency* of geohistory, not just its depth. Contingency in the history of nature means, to Rudwick, that the history of nature is 'as unrepeated, and as unpredictable, as human history itself'.[15] Modern geological theory that embraces this sense of deep historical contingency can help take local and regional rock formations and reconstruct the past in stepwise fashion. By analogy, this is akin to comparing the reconstruction of the evolutionary history of *Homo sapiens* to theories of the state of nature in moral philosophy: these clearly related endeavours to understand the human and the subsequent history of humanity nevertheless have totally different relationships to the distant and proximate past. This sense of historical contingency is, Rudwick argues, the product of the late eighteenth-century habit by natural philosophers to import methodological concepts from the history of Christian theology, specifically Biblical *chronology*, into the theories of the Earth. Without denying the importance of deep time, Rudwick's contention is particularly useful in our general consideration of weather/weathering, in that it insists on the duality of the contingency of particular events alongside the universality of the laws that govern them.

It is perhaps easier to understand what this contingent historicity is by contrasting it with the alternative temporalities that have been extant in European intellectual history. It is also a helpful way of qualifying what Rudwick means by history being unrepeatable and unpredictable: to be more exact, this means that a genuinely contingent human history or history of nature must be directionally cumulative

---

14   Stephen Jay Gould, *Time's Arrow, Time's Cycle: Myth and Metaphor in the Discovery of Geological Time* (Cambridge, MA: Harvard University Press, 1988), pp. 1–2.

15   Martin J. S. Rudwick, *Bursting the Limits of Time: The Reconstruction of Geohistory in the Age of Revolution* (Chicago: University of Chicago Press, 2005), p. 6. See also Rudwick, *Worlds Before Adam: The Reconstruction of Geohistory in the Age of Reform* (Chicago: University of Chicago Press, 2008).

(and therefore unrepeatable), and it also must not be preordained. For the most part, ancient Greek and Roman natural philosophy only provided its Latinate and Arabic descendants with a conception of nature as eternal, cyclical, and governed by forces that acted out of necessity. This was particularly true in Platonic cosmology, Aristotelian cosmology, and Ptolemaic astronomy, which took the eternal rotation of the stars around the earth, and the evident perfection of circles and spheres as the archetypes for both nature and causality generally. This kind of natural philosophy stood in stark contrast with the emphasis on free will in Christian theology and the Biblical drama of salvation. One of the great tasks of European and Arab scholarship through the Middle Ages was precisely to find ways to reconcile Greek philosophy's emphasis on the eternal on the one hand, and, on the other hand, Mosaic theology's emphasis on both the provisional nature of God's will and the voluntary nature of human faith. The histrionics surrounding the papal Condemnations of 1277 was but one famous episode, with church authorities alarmed by the radical Aristotelians' claims that an eternal universe was more logically consistent than the account of creation in Genesis.[16]

Additionally, the Aristotelian foundations of medieval Latin and Arabic natural philosophy provided only very crude ideas for understanding different scales of natural phenomena. Privileging the eternal, circular motion of the celestial sphere relegated the terrestrial as the realm of linear, or 'accidental' as opposed to perfectly circular and eternal 'natural' motion. The physics of the terrestrial sphere were effectively governed by the natural motions of the four elements in Aristotelian matter theory — i.e., that earth, water, air, and fire tended to sort themselves in layers, with earth 'falling' to the centre of the cosmos and fire rising to the interface of air and the celestial aether (*e.g.* in pre-Newtonian definitions of gravity). In this cosmology, the elements' terrestrial disorder meant this overarching, law-like tendency towards order would be interrupted by the proliferation of local events and causes. The terrestrial as the realm of the accidental proved to be a source of inspiration for natural philosophers seeking to reconcile

---

16   David C. Lindberg, *The Beginnings of Western Science*, 2nd edn (Chicago: University of Chicago Press, 2007), chapter 10.

the overarching eternalist framework of Greek metaphysics with the demand for theological contingency: for example, for the Lutheran reformer and pedagogue Phillip Melanchthon (1497–1560), elucidating the providential meaning of accidents (generally, in the metaphysical sense) was an essential way of fitting the Aristotelian natural philosophical corpus into reformed Christianity based on justification by faith alone.[17]

The terrestrial was therefore not *historical* so much as merely *accidental*, and terrestrial natural history was thus merely the corrupted subset of a naturally eternal cosmos. At least when it came to nature, Greek natural philosophy and its descendants up to the Scientific Revolution could explain specific natural phenomena with reference to extremely local causes and agents (e.g., in theories of vision),[18] but they were not capable of wholesale discovery, ordering, and reconstruction of events in time, deep or otherwise, according to Rudwick. In contrast, Biblical chronology, dynastic chronicles, epics, and narratives generally place events in a temporal sequence and seek to explain their sequence with any number of causes. Nor did this lack of interest in specific historical sequence substantially change during the Scientific Revolution. The introduction of the new mechanical philosophy by Descartes and the neo-Epicurean atomists in the sixteenth and seventeenth centuries managed to replace the eternalism of Aristotelian cosmology with a linear history of the universe, albeit one strongly shot through with determinism. The mechanical philosophy's determinism was directional — linear motion was now 'natural', while active intervention was required for circular motion — but although it could in principle be used to reconstruct the history of the universe, in practice the mechanical philosophy's explicitly abbreviated causality limited scientists to ad hoc guesses about particular types of geological events. These ad hoc 'theories of the earth' traced their lineage to Descartes own theory of the creation of mountains in his 1644 *Principia Philosophiæ* (part 4, sections 41–44), in which Descartes suggested mountains were caused by differential heating and cooling of

17   Sachiko Kusukawa, *The Transformation of Natural Philosophy: The Case of Philip Melanchthon* (Cambridge: Cambridge University Press, 1995).

18   David C. Lindberg, *Theories of Vision from Al-Kindi to Kepler*, rev. edn (Chicago: University of Chicago Press 1996).

the Earth by the Sun (Fig. 1). This kind of directional, if broadly deterministic theory culminated in Buffon's theory of the cooling earth: in his *Histoire Naturelle* (1749–89), he argued that all of the planets formed when comets struck the Sun, tearing off lumps of superheated material that cooled as over time. Inspired by the evident fact that mines become hotter the deeper they are excavated, Buffon went as far as commissioning a blacksmith to heat iron balls of different sizes, and studied the way heat loss varied by the size of the sphere: based on these studies, Buffon argued in print that the Earth was approximately 75,000 years old, though in private he speculated that it was as high as 10 million.[19] Whatever the particular age of the Earth might be in these theories, however, they were largely based on a premise that a small set of initial conditions and mechanisms could account for the entire course of geohistorical events in a deterministic, predictable fashion, 'from Fireball to Snowball, under the constant laws of nature.'[20] They were, by definition, global in scope, albeit 'global' relative to cosmology, rather than relative to anything approaching human history of human experience. This indoor theorizing was often dismissed as indulgent speculation. Nevertheless, these kinds of 'Fireball to Snowball' theories by Buffon and others provided for a deeper history of the Earth, now conceivably millions of years old.

They also created the first tentative link between theories of the Earth's development with a different domain of investigation: geognosy, what today we might call stratigraphy, the description of the ordering of *layers* of different kinds of rocks into strata (Figure 2). In the eighteenth century and earlier, geognosy was a descriptive part of the sciences of mining and quarrying: layers of rock were studied in order to anticipate where in the Earth valuable ores or minerals could be found. In most areas, the layers of rock formed regular *sequences* from topsoil down to bedrock granite: mine engineers knew that these sequences of strata were fairly regular across local and even regional distances, since they had already dug into the earth or examined exposed outcrops.[21] The clearly layered and seemingly orderly sequence

---

19   Martin J. S. Rudwick, *Earth's Deep History: How It Was Discovered and Why It Matters* (Chicago: University of Chicago Press, 2014), pp. 65–66.

20   Ibid.

21   Rudwick, *Bursting the Limits of Time*, chapters 2 and 4.

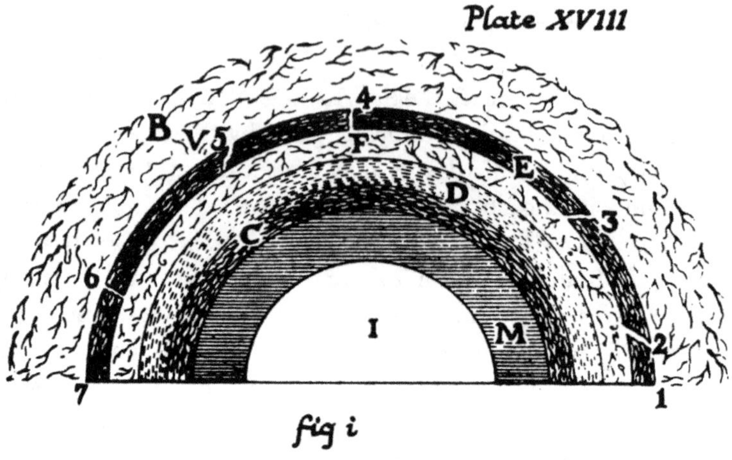

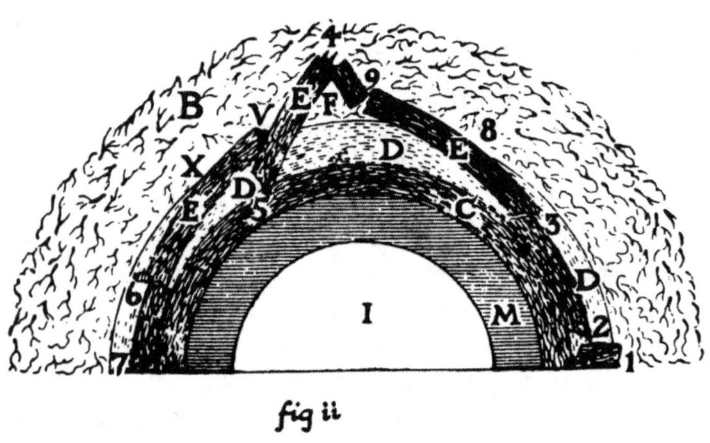

Figure 1. Descartes' 'buckling crust' theory of the Earth, from *Principia Philosophiæ* (1644). The surface crust of the Earth (*E*) has pores or cracks (1–7) that connect the atmosphere (*B*) and *F*, a layer of rarefied matter beneath the Earth's crust; when the sun heats the Earth, heated fragments of *F* push themselves up through the crust *E*, but then cooled air *B* sinks through the pores of the Earth's crust, expanding this body and causing the crust to buckle upward. These buckles cause both the formation of mountains and press the lower masses *D* and *C* upward, causing the creation of oceans at fragments 2–3 and 6–7.

of strata had made early geotheory plausible, and early geotheory like-wise tried to mobilize the regularity of rock strata to create theories of the Earth. In what Rudwick calls the 'standard model' of pre-modern geology, as the Earth cools, its surface becomes a giant ocean, and further cooling causes minerals to precipitate and sediment into layers, with each layer differing due to its relative age and by its chemical composition.[22] These theories could thus explain why 'basement' or 'Primary' rocks like granite, schist, gneiss, and marble were usually found below the lighter, 'Secondary' rocks like sandstone, shale, and limestone. Buffon's and other theories following the standard model could potentially take geognosy — ordinarily a descriptive, classifica-tory, and structural science — and transform it into evidence of the Earth's deep history.

But the Earth is not so regular, and planetary-scale causal theor-ies like the late eighteenth/early nineteenth-century standard model struggled to account for the increasing amounts of local variation being studied and recorded by miners, physical geographers, and mineralo-gists. Critics of 'Enlightenment rationality' tend to miss the way that amateur and expert savants in the eighteenth century also obsessively collected examples of nature's diversity, often desiring particularly strange specimens that explicitly defied extant theories or rationaliza-tions of nature. Strange or beautiful rocks and fossils would be removed from their original context precisely for their peculiar or exemplary character and be placed in mineralogical collections; these collected specimens could be compared by simple visual examination, through more advanced optical analysis, or even through more destructive chemical analysis. Chemical analysis could raise some uncomfortable questions about the standard model. Why, for instance, was heavy basalt so often found in strata *on top of*, for example, lighter sediment-ary strata like sandstone or limestone? Did this mean basalt was a compressed sandstone? Or, as some geotheorists in the eighteenth century suggested, was basalt *volcanic* in origin — thus adding unex-pected complexity to the standard model of geological history?[23]

---

22   Ibid., pp. 172–74.
23   Ibid., pp. 62–63.

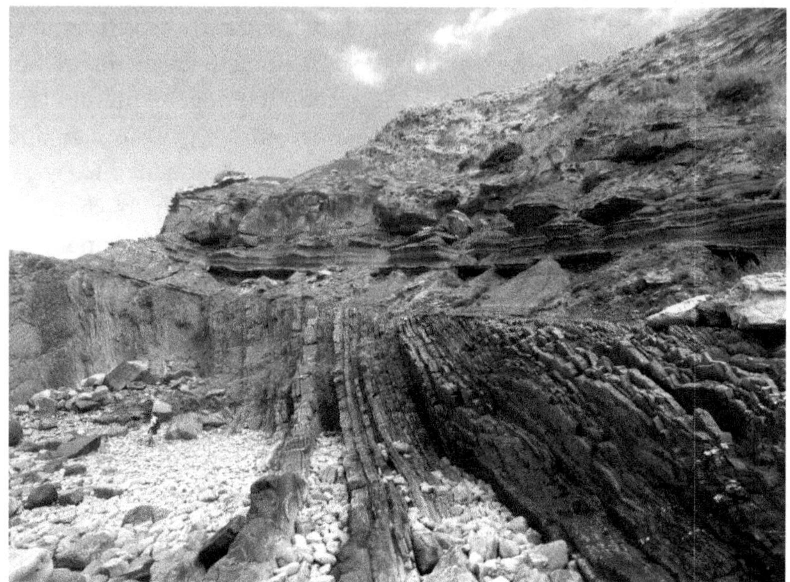

Figure 2. Angular unconformity at Praia do Telheiro, near Sagres in
Algarve Portugal. It shows Late Triassic red and yellow planar
sandstones resting on top of tilted black shales and greywackes of
Carboniferous age, deformed during the Variscan orogeny. Photograph
by André Cortesão, Creative Commons Attribution 3.0 Unported license
<https://commons.wikimedia.org/wiki/File:Angular_Unconformity_
at_Praia_do_Telheiro_in_Algarve_in_Portugal.png>.

The most broadly synthetic method of addressing these questions
about the Earth's geological diversity would, by the middle of the nineteenth century, be found in physical geography and geognosy, which,
above all else, privileged outdoor fieldwork over the collection and
comparison of objects. The turn of the century in Europe witnessed a
unique boom in geological fieldwork, though the reasons for the boom
varied in different places: in Britain it became inexplicably fashionable
for leisured gentleman to explore their physical environments, while
in Central Europe minor and major states alike established mining
schools as a cameralistic response to the economic devastation of the
Seven Years' War.[24] Initially, both these amateur and professional en-

---

24   Ursula Klein, *Humboldts Preussen: Wissenschaft und Technik im Aufbruch* (Darmstadt:
     Wissenschaftliche Buchgesellschaft, 2015).

deavours were much alike in scale but unlike in dimension. As already mentioned, mining scientists in places like the Ore Mountains on the border of Saxony and Bohemia sought to understand the local sequence of the Earth's strata in order to anticipate where veins of ore (and later coal) might be found before undertaking the costly work of digging mine shafts. Mining savants above all, like Abraham Gottlob Werner (1749–1817), thus sought to understand the sequence of strata on the *vertical* axis in particular mining districts. Strata are not simply layered in parallel sequences as the standard model — or, for that matter, the Aristotelian model — would suggest, like a cake, but rather many sit at different angles. Certain well-established strata could be found in vastly different thicknesses in different places. Most critical were *unconformities*, places where some strata might be layered at sharp angles to others, or a stratum is highly uneven, or perhaps missing entirely, or even found unexpectedly intruding on a predicted sequence. Some unconformities are visibly evident, others quite subtle and visible only to someone looking for it; some strata simply do not show clear orientation at all, looking more like a mass of rubble. These difficulties made expertise valuable particular in the professional setting of mining and geognosy, but amateurs could nevertheless do the basic work, since the basic instruments were quite minimal: all one needed was a hammer, shovel, a hand lens, free time, and transportation to seek out weathered cliff faces or hills with exposed layers of rock. At the same time, long personal experience with the rocks of a local region was necessary to understand all of the variation that was possible, and to discriminate between similar-looking strata, in order to correlate the sequence of formations from one place to another.[25]

The mining professionals had the advantage of being able to enlist labour to dig, but they also considered their knowledge to be both relatively localized and purely descriptive: initially, geognosy was not tied to particular theories of the Earth or ideas about Earth's history. But over the course of the first half of the nineteenth century, as more and more local areas had their strata mapped, the early geologists grew increasingly confident that they could understand the stratigraphy of

---

25   Martin J. S. Rudwick, *The Great Devonian Controversy: The Shaping of Scientific Knowledge Among Gentlemanly Specialists* (Chicago: University of Chicago Press, 1985), pp. 37–54.

whole regions by induction, without needing to direct empirical evidence from each individual locale. Moreover, the growing network of amateurs in Britain meant that studies of local formations could be compared: by 1822 the Geological Society of London counted 313 members living in or near London, and an additional 328 'non-resident' members living overseas, all of whom received published *Proceedings* that summarized members' reports.[26] The amateurs in Britain had the advantage of sheer numbers and a growing system of scientific sociability that could coordinate the efforts of a larger number of less-expert local explorers. These collective efforts would culminate in some of the most impressive examples of the synthesis of experiential knowledge in natural history: George Bellas Greenough (1778–1885) and William Smith's (1769–1839) grand geological maps of regions as large as the entirety of England (Fig. 3), with Smith making his map entirely through his own surveying work. By mid-century, British geologists were crisscrossing the globe, taking advantage of global travel secured by Britain's naval supremacy, in order to conduct intensive geological surveys in the field. The Scottish geologist Roderick Murchison (1792–1871) made expeditions to nearly every corner of the globe, from Australia to British-controlled India to the Russian Baltic: his work in stitching together the stratigraphy of so many areas of the Earth was not only in service of geological theory, e.g. determining the global distribution of the sequence of strata, but equally importantly his work aided imperial and colonial authorities in planning gold, coal, and other mining projects that ultimately sustained the imperial endeavour. At every point in Murchison's journey, the basic tools of investigation were the same: travel to many locations, examine extant outcroppings, map and chart formations along horizontal and vertical axes.[27]

Identifying and associating the order of strata across such large distances ultimately required more than just the examination of the rocks themselves, the differences among which could be exceedingly subtle, or, in the case of some unconformities, absent entirely. The great success of unlocking the sequence of strata across the globe owed

---

26   Ibid., pp. 18–27.

27   Robert A. Stafford, *Scientist of Empire: Sir Roderick Murchison, Scientific Exploration, and Victorian Imperialism* (Cambridge: Cambridge University Press, 1989).

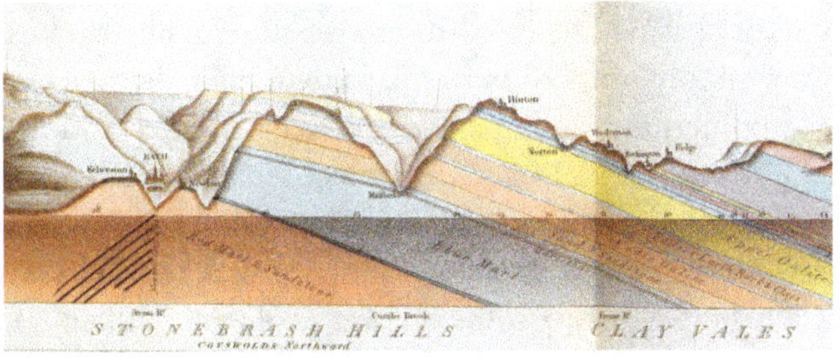

Figure 3. Part of William Smith's map of geological sections in Somerset, England, 1819, showing the sedimentary strata of sandstone, marl, and limestone. William Smith, *Section of the Strata through Hampshire and Wiltshire to Bath, on the Road from Bath to Salisbury* (London: John Cary, 1819).

much to the growing recognition in the nineteenth century that the order of rock strata were correlated to the kinds of *fossils* that geologists and geognosists found in each of the strata. The distinctiveness of the fossil bones, shells, and occasionally plants in each stratum became aids for identifying the order of strata across regions where the rocks themselves were not the same, or just hard to identify: Smith's grand maps of the strata of England owed much to his ability to use 'characteristic fossils' to identify strata. But these observable consistencies across strata and fossil beds eventually became a way to understand both fossils and strata as clues for the reconstruction of a linear, progressive, and contingent history of the Earth. As early as 1801, the naturalist Georges Cuvier (1769–1832) remarked, 'the older the beds in which these bones are found, the more they differ from those of animals we know today.'[28] As geologists and collectors alike started to plot out where certain kinds of fossils were found — a task that required experience both out in the field and inside the museum — it became apparent that the top-most, 'youngest' strata bore fossils that were similar to many known living species, while fossils in deeper, 'older' strata were often much stranger. Whereas in the late eighteenth century early geologists had suggested that the presumably law-like character of geological change might make the history of the Earth cyclical or eternal, the fossil evidence accumulating in the early nine-

---

28   Georges Cuvier, 'Espèces de quadrupèdes' (1801), p. 260, quoted in Rudwick, *Bursting the Limits of Time*, p. 424.

teenth century seemed to show otherwise. The fossils that were being found were simply not like bones of known animals, suggesting that large scale extinctions accompanied the successive deposition of rocks into strata. Moreover, as the correlations of fossil types and strata became stronger, it became possible to imagine a reconstruction of the actual past world that these fossils came from. A most dramatic case in 1822 by the English theologian and geologist William Buckland (1784–1856) demonstrated that it was even possible to reimagine not only ecosystems, but even the daily lives of animals that lived in a very distant time. The cave, discovered by miners in 1821 working in a limestone quarry in Kirkdale, in Yorkshire, was filled with fossil bones of elephants, hyenas, rats, horses, bears, oxen, and rhinoceroses. Yet both the entrance of the cave and the cave itself was too small for any of these larger animals to go in. Buckland realized that the cave must have been home to a hyena den, and that the largest bones must have been dragged into the cave by the hyenas, as shown by the toothmarks on the large bones and abundant 'calcareous excrement' found within the gravel and silt. The petrified dung would be the key to the reconstruction: by comparing the fossil excrement with specimens from English zoos, Buckland demonstrated that the fossils were most likely dragged in as scavenged food by the hyenas, and not washed into the cave — either by periodic flooding or by Biblical deluge.[29]

Buckland's reconstruction of the Kirkdale cave made it possible to, as Rudwick puts it, 'construct a conceptual time machine' moving backward from recent cases into the deep past.[30] This kind of stitching together of the past from localized elements into maps and narratives stood in stark contrast to earlier attempts to create theories starting from cosmological scales. As Rudwick argues in *Earth's Deep History*, by the middle of the nineteenth century geology had adopted many of its conceptual frameworks not from geophysics but rather from secular and sacred history: the coins, artefacts, and documents of history and historiography were made analogous to the rocks, fossils, and formations of geology. Although elements of this analogy can be debated, it nevertheless suggests how modern geology can be considered as a

---

29   Ibid., chapter 8.
30   Rudwick, *Earth's Deep History*, p. 125.

science of *scaling up* localized, individualized experience into grand narratives of the history of the Earth.

CLIMATOLOGY: FROM EXPERIENCE TO THEORY

The epigraph at the top of this chapter, taken from the meteorology textbook by the Austrian climatologist Julius Hann (1839–1921), highlights the fundamental epistemological difference marked by the concepts 'weather' and 'climate': we can go outside and experience the weather through our senses and instruments, but if we are to collect our experience into knowledge about the climate, then we have to resort to something other than experience. It does not follow that weather is real and climate a fiction: it simply means that the two are grasped by different means. The history of climatology and meteorology in some sense runs in the opposite direction from the history of geology and theories of the Earth. Whereas the latter began at cosmological scales and gained local-historical granularity, the sciences of weather and climate began with the assumption that local weather events were both highly variable and highly place-specific. Climate science only later acquired a theoretical generality that could tie large-scale movements of air, water, and heat together with the particularities of a local landscape.

Meteorology and weather forecasting have probably been practiced by every human society through some means, though the modern combination of ship-borne observation of navigable winds and long-term records from weather stations to analyse large-scale climatic phenomena began in the late-1700s, with the mobilization of the thermometer, barometer, and hygrometer.[31] Well into the nineteenth century, alerts for potentially catastrophic weather events required someone to directly observe an incoming storm — by ship in many colonial coastal ports, by observation stations everywhere else.[32] The historian Richard Grove has argued that the first global climatic

---

31   H. Howard Frisinger, *The History of Meteorology: To 1800* (New York: Science History Publications, 1977).

32   See Robert M. Rouphail, 'Cyclonic Ecology: Sugar, Cyclone Science, and the Limits of Empire in Mauritius and the Indian Ocean World, 1870s–1930s', *Isis*, 110.1 (March 2019), pp. 48–67 <https://doi.org/10.1086/702729>.

event to be accurately recorded was probably the Great El Niño of 1790–1794, when the British imperial officials simultaneously recorded barometric readings, droughts, and reports of crop failures in the Caribbean, northern China, Australia, Mauritius, and most critically Madras and Bengal.[33] But noticing the simultaneity of far-flung events does not amount to noticing and naming one climatic event: in the case of the El Niño Southern Oscillation, a complete theory only emerged in the 1960s, with major revisions made through the 1980s. Until the 1870s, the gathering of data and creation of meteorological maps and tables had only a very limited theoretical payoff.[34] As Deborah Coen argues in *Climate in Motion*, taking climatology from rules of thumb to scientific theories of global climate required new physical theories of heat as well as literary techniques for describing movement across scales.

For Coen, the Austro-Hungarian Empire was a political entity that was particularly suited for the creation of an integrated science of climatology: a contiguous land empire that encompassed many peoples, languages, and terrains. Coen argues that finding political unity in the Empire meant searching for the forces and tensions that tied together the parts into the whole through *dynamics*, rather than simply assuming parts are instantiations of an *a priori* whole or natural category.[35] Mapping and collecting, which were so crucial to British, Dutch, and Spanish imperial projects, were augmented by projects to determine why diversity persisted across an integrated space: it was important to fully catalogue local contrasts, but an additional step was needed to turn this collection of facts into scientific knowledge.[36]

In Austrian climatology, the additional force came through different applications of thermodynamics in order to explain the accumulation, movement, and dispersal of atmospheric energy. For example,

---

33   Mike Davis, *Late Victorian Holocausts: El Niño Famines and the Making of the Third World* (London: Verso, 2002), pp. 216–18; Richard Grove and George Adamson, *El Niño in World History*, Palgrave Studies in World Environmental History (London: Palgrave Macmillan, 2018), chapter 4.

34   Azadeh Achbari and Frans van Lunteren, 'Dutch Skies, Global Laws: The British Creation of "Buys Ballot's Law"', *Historical Studies in the Natural Sciences*, 46.1 (February 2016), pp. 1–43 <https://doi.org/10.1525/hsns.2016.46.1.1>.

35   Coen, *Climate in Motion*, p. 32.

36   Ibid., pp. 139–42, 153.

the Austrian geographer Alexander Supan (1847–1920) pioneered the discovery and use of pressure and temperature gradients, mapped to particular geographical regions, where atmospheric energy accumulated and dispersed along predictable lines.[37] Doing so revealed that the distribution of climatic patterns was not itself driven by measured wind speed, but rather by the movement the pressure systems that drove the wind. But by far the most important climatological theory to come out of imperial Austrian climate science was Max Margules' (1856-1920) theory of the 'available potential energy' (APE) of the atmosphere.[38] Margules, a physicist at the Austrian Imperial *Zentralanstalt für Meteorologie und Geomagnetismus* (ZAMG), argued that the stability of pressure gradients themselves had to be accounted for by measuring the energy capacity and (thermodynamic) work done by moving masses of air and moisture. By considering the dynamics of weather as 'pendulous oscillations' of unequal masses of air as a first principle (Fig. 4), Margules' APE model implies that winds, storms, and pressure gradients were caused by the movement of warm and cold bodies of air — a concept that is fundamentally a mathematical abstraction of direct experience — and that movement of warmer or colder air horizontally across the landscape has significant effects on the vertical distribution of atmospheric heat, pressure, and moisture.[39] Here was the grand unifying theory: all weather phenomena must be understood as the energetic effect of bodies of air moving across the land and up and down the atmosphere, and the terrain itself thus has a powerful effect on the movement of these masses of air. In the 1950s, the American meteorologist Edward Lorenz (1917–2008) would broaden Margules' theory of storm generation into a general theory of atmospheric circulation, a theory that makes the movement of heat into the root cause of all weather phenomena.[40]

---

37   Ibid., pp. 172–74.

38   Ibid., pp. 199–202.

39   Max Margules, 'On the Energy of Storms', in *The Mechanics of the Earth's Atmosphere*, trans. by Cleveland Abbe (Washington, DC: Smithsonian, 1910), pp. 533–95.

40   Edward N. Lorenz, 'Available Potential Energy and the Maintenance of the General Circulation', *Tellus* 7.2 (January 1955), pp. 157–67 <https://doi.org/10.3402/tellusa. v7i2.8796>; Edward N. Lorenz, *The Nature and Theory of the General Circulation of the Atmosphere* (Geneva: World Meteorological Organization, 1967).

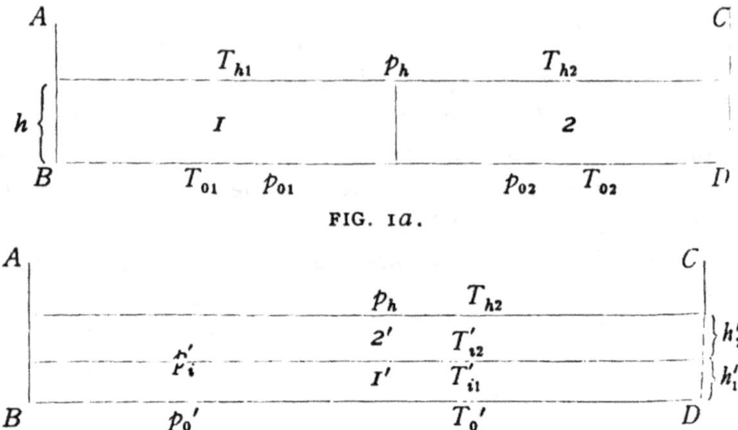

Figure 4. Max Margules' 1904 schematic showing an initial state (above) of vertically differentiated temperature (T_n) and pressure (P_n) differences (spatially divided by P_h), which results in the subsequent state (below) of horizontally differentiated layers of air at different temperatures and pressures. Max Margules, 'On the Energy of Storms', p. 536.

CONCLUSION

Experience, Lino Camprubí and Phillip Lehmann argue, scales.[41] Models and theories of the climate are not generated solely by abstraction, but historically come from people observing rolling clouds near and far, measuring the fall of atmospheric pressure, feeling their skin becoming clammier as the humidity rises: the dynamic experience of the weather is not only felt by one individual, but by many, and these experiences and measurements are recorded, sorted, and eventually calculated to become the science of the climate. This is in large part because there is not one monolithic 'experience'. Experience has different modes of feeling and seeing that are augmented by time, technologies, and, once accumulated, in expertise. The instruments and techniques of experience in early geology were collections, reports, and eventually maps and guides to landscapes. The scale of geographical and geological maps provides a good case in point: they are clearly generated by experience, but a map in the hands of its user becomes a tool to

---

41   Camprubí and Lehmann, 'The Scales of Experience'.

augment experience as well. The study of the cumulative and recursive effect of experiences turned into tools and representations has become one of the core tenets of empirical science studies in the twenty-first century,[42] despite the fact that such recursiveness can lead to a sense of vertigo and disorientation.[43]

In this essay I have tried to juxtapose two different ways experience and science scaled. In Rudwick's studies of the history of geology, theories of the Earth originate from the Aristotelian and Cartesian theories operating at essentially cosmological scales, and much of what makes geology 'modern' is its contrasting ability to account for very small-scale, local variations of phenomena within the context of planetary laws. Coen's account of the history of climatography and climatology, in contrast, begins with the historically widespread assumption of the local, small-scale specificity and variability of the weather, and only through the use of high-quality record keeping and modelling using thermodynamic laws does a picture of climatological dynamics arise. In both, the interplay of natural history and natural philosophy is centre stage, and one does not operate well without the other.

But what are we to make of the kinds of distant theorizing and exploration of nature, which in both of the cases presented here is conceptualized largely as a world prior to or absent the human species — the *Anthropos* and the *Homo* mentioned at the start of the essay? As Julia Adeney Thomas observes of Chakrabarty's original analysis of the concept of the Anthropocene, the challenge is not *only* in scaling as such, which would be a problem of method and methodology in the historical sciences, but in what is being scaled. For Thomas, the distinction between *Homo* and Anthropos, or 'the Human' and 'the human species'

> is not something humanist historians can *understand* through self-reflection in Wilhelm Dilthey's sense, where historical consciousness is 'a mode of self-knowledge', or in R. G. Collingwood's sense, where historical comprehension rests fundamentally not on reconstructing the past but on reen-

---

42   Bruno Latour, *Pandora's Hope: Essays on the Reality of Science Studies* (Cambridge, MA: Harvard University Press, 1999).

43   Coen, 'Big Is a Thing of the Past', p. 309.

> acting 'in our own minds the experience of the past.' While
> 'species' may work for paleobiologists comparing, say, the
> fossil records of Eemian biota from 130,000 years ago with
> modern organisms, theirs is a labor of reconstruction as op-
> posed to one of self-reflection or mental reenactment.[44]

I would like to close this meditation on weathering by suggesting that this disjuncture Chakrabarty highlights between the human as a political actor and humanity as a planetary force is loosely analogous to the distinction between the self-reflective subject and the self-negating analyst. During the early-1990s debates on historical and scientific objectivity, the historian Thomas Haskell argued that attempts to cast the concept of objectivity itself as both fictional and disingenuous ran the risk of turning any historical scholarship into propaganda, and any possible utterance into an expression of will:

> But to shrug off the capacity for detachment as entirely il-
> lusory — to claim that since none of the standpoints the
> self is capable of imagining are *really* that of 'the other', but
> are self-produced (as is certainly the case), and to argue that
> all viewpoints therefore are *indistinguishably* contaminated
> by selfishness or group interest or the omnipresent Nietz-
> schean will — is to turn a blind eye to distinctions that all
> of us routinely make and confidently act upon, and thereby
> to blur all that distinguishes villainy from decency, veracity
> from mendacity, in everyday affairs. Not to mince words, it is
> to defame the species. Fairness and honesty are qualities we
> can rightfully demand of human beings, and those qualities
> require a very substantial measure of self-overcoming.[45]

Since these debates, historians of science have argued that objectivity is itself a historically specific kind of subjectivity and set of values that scientists work to cultivate, so much so that objectivity has it-self become essentially synonymous with scientific knowledge and practice.[46] Haskell argues that the species — Stockhammer's *Homo*

---

44   Thomas, 'History and Biology in the Anthropocene', p. 1592.

45   Thomas L. Haskell, 'Objectivity Is Not Neutrality: Rhetoric Vs. Practice in Peter
     Novick's *That Noble Dream*', *History and Theory*, 29.2 (May 1990), pp. 129–57 <https:
     //doi.org/10.2307/2505222>.

46   Lorraine Daston and Peter Galison, 'The Image of Objectivity', *Representations*, 40
     (1992), pp. 81–128; Theodore M. Porter, 'The Objective Self', *Victorian Studies* 50.4

— must be capable of some kind or kinds of detachment, alienation, impartial judgement, and empathy towards the other, and this itself requires a degree of personal cultivation. It is precisely this recasting and scaling-up of the personal experience of the weather to a global understanding of climate, and the scaling-down of geological theory to understand one's local landscape or patch of the Earth, that demands personal experience as well as alienation from it.

(2008), pp. 641–47; Jimena Canales, *A Tenth of a Second: A History* (Chicago: University of Chicago Press, 2009).

TRACES

Enduring Ornament

AMELIA GROOM AND M. TY

> Truly great actor more seriously in character he carries — slips
>   into: than you — W.C. — are in what you try to show off
>   in: force.
> Force ripples — vibrates life — muscle in action one visible form.
> You: brittle — breaking — decaying iron — eaten by rustworm.
>
> Elsa von Freytag-Loringhoven, 'Mineself — Minesoul — And
>   — Mine — Cast-Iron Lover' (1919)

> There have been occasional accidental spills onto the works,
> including two separate vomiting incidents. Despite immediate
> attention from on-site conservation staff, the acidity of the vomit
> caused spots of clean etched metal to appear on the surface, which
> were impossible to blend in with the rest of the work without
> polishing the entire surface. A few brightly etched areas therefore
> remain.
>
> Sculpture conservators at the Tate reporting on the condition of
>   Carl Andre's Minimalist metal floor sculptures (2013)

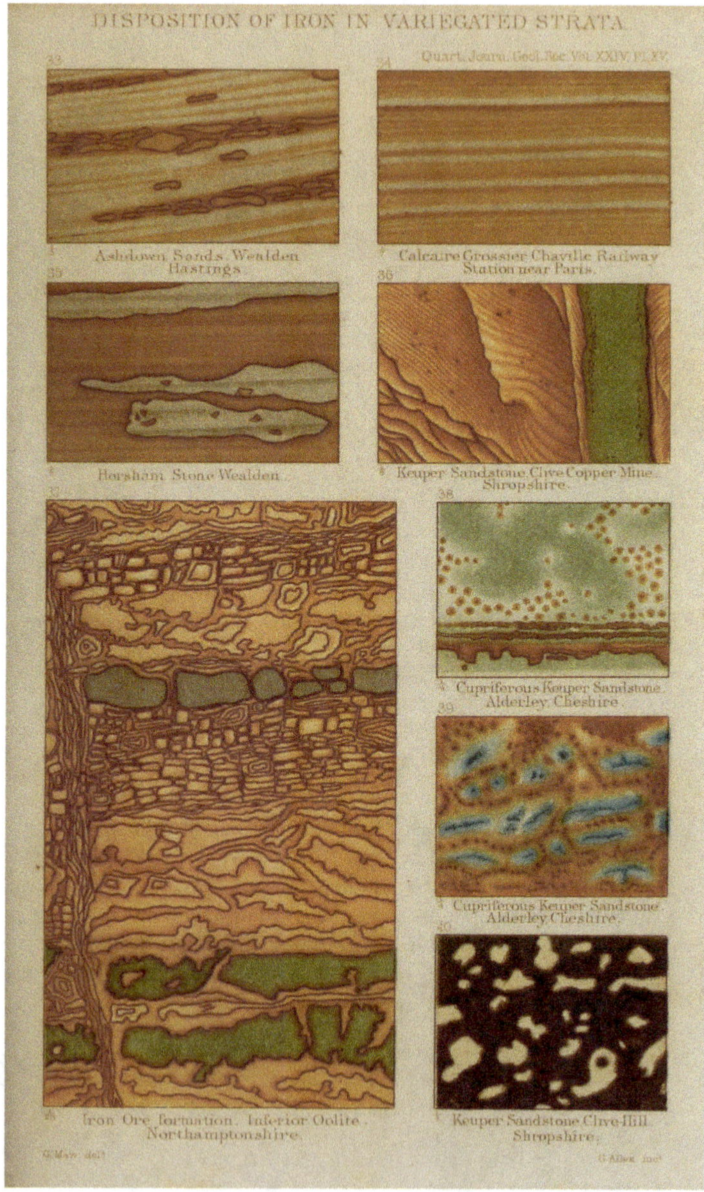

Figures 1 and 2. *Ferruginous Variation*, colour plates included in the publication of George Maw's paper 'On the Disposition of Iron in Variegated Strata', *The Quarterly Journal of the Geological Society of London*, 24 (1868), pp. 351–400.

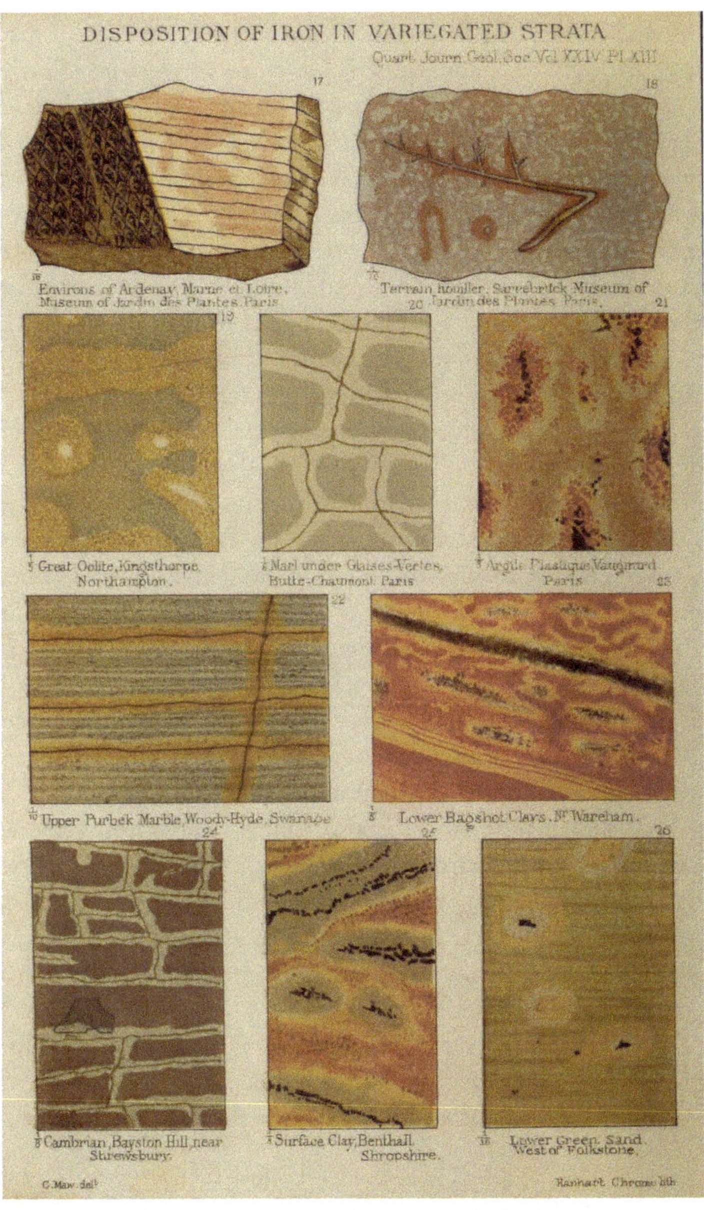

Maw's paper begins: 'Of those secondary changes which have modified the original chemical and physical constitution of rocks none seem to have more largely affected their aspect than the recombinations and rearrangements of iron.'

In his *Arcades Project*, Walter Benjamin remarks on the enthusiasm with which capitalist modernity would come to greet iron construction.[1] Celebrated for its strength, versatility, and durability, iron served as the innumerable vertebrate of the railway system and as the ballast of transitory spaces of exchange: bridges, shopping arcades, exhibition halls, train stations, luxury restaurants, and the reading rooms of eminent libraries. When checkered by glass, iron allowed interior spaces to be both sheltered and cascaded in light; trees could be housed indoors, and greenhouses could grow gardens even in the freeze of winter. Architecture also found a gateway to unprecedented verticality; by force of iron, colonial modernity extended its horizontal and upward reach, with train tracks going distant and buildings breaching the sky.

In the nineteenth century, iron also comes to exceed its functional role and to assume an ascendant place in the capitalist imaginary. Cultural investment in its magical properties amplifies to the extent that the rings of Saturn were imagined as a cast-iron balcony, on which the inhabitants of that faraway planet would step out for an evening stroll.[2] Meanwhile, in symbolist literature, hairstyles were said to take inspiration from the wrought-iron designs found in the built environment.[3]

When entering into metaphor, iron usually plays the part of strength, stubbornness, impenetrability, tyranny — think of 'iron man', an 'iron will', the 'iron curtain', 'ruling with an iron fist', or 'the iron control of the slavedriver', as Frederick Douglass would name it.[4] Lying in wait within iron, though, is the potential for its decomposition into rust. As a gradual transition into soft powdery flakes, rust registers the dimension of time in the material, reminding us that even iron is susceptible to its own undoing.

Iron, thus, presents particular problems for the long term. For archivists, paperclips and staples are prime enemies because, when they start to rust, they discolour and erode the pages they fasten. For

---

1   See convolute F of Walter Benjamin, *The Arcades Project*, trans. by Howard Eiland and Kevin McLaughlin (Cambridge, MA: Harvard University Press, 1999).

2   Ibid., p. 8. Benjamin refers here to an illustration from Jean Ignace Isidore Gérard Grandville's 1844 *Un autre monde* (1844).

3   André Thérive, 'Les Livres', *Le Temps*, 25 June 1936, cited in ibid., p. 553 [S5a,1].

4   Frederick Douglass, *The Life and Times of Frederick Douglass* (Boston: De Wolfe, Fiske & Co., 1892), p. 47.

someone restoring an old house, small metal hinges, screws and latches are an issue because, once rust comes onto the scene, it augments and accelerates ruination. Similarly, a cotton jacket with plenty of life left in it can be worsted by its metal buttons, fusing with rust and then bleeding out, staining and eating away at the rest of the garment.[5] While iron is thought of as a stronger material than the likes of paper, wood, and cloth, its sensitivity to the elements can mark it out as the centre of fragility. '[I]f there be one crevice through which a single drop can fall,' Douglass writes, 'it will certainly rust off the slave's chain.'[6]

Along with its etymological affiliation with red, the word 'rust' is coloured by a history of uses, which include the sense of 'degenerating in idleness' or becoming 'impaired by inaction'.[7] In old slang, to be 'in rust', meant to be out of work or resting; today we talk about an acquired language or skill becoming 'a little rusty' when it seizes up through disuse. Sometimes actual rust and its metaphoric senses of dereliction and decay collapse into one another, as in the Rust Belt — a derogatory epithet for the deindustrialized cityscapes of the United States, stretching from the Great Lakes to New York, where economic and population decline are signalled through enormous abandoned mills and weapons plants that are literally rusting away.

At the same time, rust has also been an emblem of relentlessness: it is a renowned insomniac. The title of Neil Young's live album *Rust Never Sleeps* (1979) came from the band Devo, whose members had previously done graphic design work for Rust-Oleum, a company that manufactures rust-preventative coatings.[8]

Like dust, rust puts everyone who has to deal with it into a Sisyphean situation. 'Stainless steel' is a misleading name; it's an iron-derived metal that stains *less*, but it isn't stain proof. 'Rustproofing' is also an impossibility — it's an optimistic term in the auto industry for

---

5   Recommended remedy, successfully tested by the authors on a sunny day on Tempel-hofer Feld: saturate the rust stains with lemon juice and leave the garment in direct sunlight. The stains will vanish, but the metal buttons will need to be removed and replaced, or the rust will make a comeback.

6   Douglass, p. 130.

7   Cf. 'Rust, n.1 and adj.' and 'Rust, v.1', in *OED Online* (Oxford: Oxford University Press, 2020) <https://www.oed.com/view/Entry/169112> and <https://www.oed.com/view/Entry/169115> [accessed 2 July 2020].

8   Jimmy McDonough, *Shakey: Neil Young's Biography* (New York: Random House, 2010), p. 531.

techniques of delay that always require periodic re-enactment. While the oxides of other metals can form 'passivating' layers (which make the metal *less active* by forming a stable sealant, cutting off further oxidation), the default behaviour of rust is to expand on the surface and then flake away, exposing new layers for further corrosion. Rust keeps iron active, by always reaching out into the world and then breaking off and inviting the world in, to keep gnawing away at the material's insides.

In modern economic and militaristic terms, this spells disaster. The US government spends tens of billions of dollars every year in direct costs in the fight against rust. In 2004, the Department of Defense declared *war on rust* with their new 'corrosion prevention and control program', CorrDefense.[9] As Jonathan Waldman chronicles in his book *Rust: The Longest War*, rust has been called 'the pervasive menace', 'the great destroyer', 'the ruthless enemy', and 'the evil'.[10]

Rusts are also pathogenic fungi, named so because of their powdery, storm of Jupiter colour. Plants who have contracted rust really do appear as though their stems and leaves are corroding away, and when these fungi show up on crops they can wreak havoc. In the nineteenth century, the arrival of a rust fungus on the island of Sri Lanka led to the rapid and total collapse of its coffee industry, which the British had coercively cultivated into one of the largest and most lucrative in the world.[11] After examining spores that had been collected from plantations abroad, a chief botanist at Kew Gardens named the fungus *Hemileia vastatrix*, the 'half-smooth devastator'.

Enabled by colonial networks of transit, and by the imperial imperative to consign land to monoculture, coffee rust threatened to become a global epidemic. Spores of rust could ride on railways, steamships, and airplanes trafficking the spoils of the plantation — could hang on the clothes and bodies of labourers who travelled routes of trade.

---

9   See the hilariously bad video 'Pentagon declares War on Rust', uploaded to YouTube by user noahmax6000 <https://youtu.be/qoME4gFEWFQ> [accessed 1 July 2020].

10   Jonathan Waldman, *Rust: The Longest War* (New York: Simon and Schuster, 2015), pp. 6–7.

11   British forces prepared the island for large-scale coffee production by destroying native rice fields, carrying out massacres to deter rebellion, and placing the land at the disposal of British planters, who recruited labour from a population that, until that point, had largely practiced diversified subsistence farming within local communities.

By 1920, the rust had reached many of the coffee-producing countries in Asia and Africa; by the 1970s it was starting to show up in South America.[12] Since then, fungicides and new strains of crop have been engineered to resist rust's proliferation. But *la roya*, as it's called in Central America,[13] has continued to return with greater intensity and at higher altitudes, as climate irregularities encourage its propagation.[14] As lands across the Americas succumb to rust and fall fallow, farmers and wage labourers are pressed to migrate toward northern borders that largely refuse them.

In the past, agricultural combat against rust remained a relatively local affair. In ancient Rome, when large spreads of wheat had reddened with rust, they used to say that foxes with torches tied to their tails — running — had set the fields on fire.[15] Robigalia was a festival held by the Romans every spring, when they would ask the goddess of rust, Robigo, to please stay away from the crops — offering her red wine and the entrails of red puppies instead. In his account of the sacrificial festival, Ovid records a prayer to Robigo that solicits her to redirect her destructive powers towards weapons of destruction. 'Forbear, I pray you, and take your rough hands from the harvest [...]. Attack first not the tender crops, but harsh iron.' '[M]ay the weapons of war be stained with rust, and when anyone tries to draw a sword from its sheath, may he feel it stick through long disuse', bids the priest.[16] Rust, if you must ruin things, at least ruin that which ruins; make yourself useful by introducing uselessness into the instruments of violence.

'Destroy first what can destroy others' — this springtime petition sees an ethics of anti-violence in rust's capacity to de-functionalize:

---

12   See Stuart McCook, *Coffee Is Not Forever: A Global History of the Coffee Leaf Rust* (Athens: Ohio University Press, 2019).

13   The word also carries the sense of 'blight'.

14   In Guatemala, The Federación de Cooperativas Agricolas has formed 'Anti-Rust Brigades', which spray farms with fungicide. Jacques Avelino, Marco Cristancho, Selena Georgiou, and others, 'The Coffee Rust Crises in Colombia and Central America (2008–2013): Impacts, Plausible Causes and Proposed Solutions', *Food Security*, 7.2 (2015), pp. 303–21.

15   J.C. Zadoks, *On the Political Economy of Plant Disease Epidemics* (Wageningen: Wageningen Academic Publishers, 2008), p. 25.

16   Ovid, 'A Prayer to Robigo', *Fasti*, iv.905–32, quoted in Mary Beard, John North, and Simon Price, *Religions of Rome*, 2 vols (Cambridge: Cambridge University Press, 1998), ii: A Sourcebook, p. 32.

rust could accomplish disarmament even if the will to power remained unchecked. The naval and army commander Pliny the Elder likewise sensed the promise of rust's inhuman power, which, without directly partaking in military contest, could render it inoperative. Writing in his *Naturalis Historia* about the uses of iron in weaponry and war, he reflects with particular despair on the missile, which he considers 'the most criminal artifice that has been devised by the human mind, for, as if to bring death [...] with still greater rapidity, we have given wings to iron and taught it to fly.' He then considers rust, and concludes that the 'benevolence of nature' has limited the power of iron by inflicting rust on it as a penalty, 'making nothing in the world more mortal than that which is most hostile to mortality'.[17]

*

Rust can signal a once-functional object's disuse, while also ensuring its future uselessness. Think of a rusted bicycle or padlock; the less you have used it, the less you can use it. It is perhaps appropriate, then, that one of the only ways that the substance of rust is usefully put to work is in that pursuit most commonly opposed to utility: the ornamental. Through a reframing of *stain* as *dye*, rust lends itself to the production of pigments for paints, inks, and cosmetics. It is only when the metals are oxidized — when they have 'breath put into them', in John Ruskin's words — that they begin to function as colouring agents.[18]

When the artist Baroness Elsa von Freytag-Loringhoven, walking to New York's city hall to get married for the third time in 1913, picked up an abandoned rusty iron ring off the street and renamed it *Enduring Ornament*, she was compelled perhaps by the object's show of time in colour — its mottled persistence through its fall from utility. Met by her eye, rust is renewed as ready-made adornment.[19]

---

17   Pliny, *Natural History*, 10 vols (Cambridge, MA: Harvard University Press, 1938–62), ix: *Books 33–35*, trans. by H. Rackham, Loeb Classical Library, 394 (1952), p. 231.

18   John Ruskin, 'The Work of Iron in Nature, Art, and Policy', in *The Two Paths: Being Lectures on Art and its Application to Decoration and Manufacture Delivered in 1858–9* (West Lafayette, IN: Parlor Press, 2004), pp. 93.

19   Freytag-Loringhoven's friend Marcel Duchamp would exhibit the 'first' readymade the following year. Irene Gammel, *Baroness Elsa: Gender, Dada* (Cambridge, MA: MIT Press, 2003), p. 161.

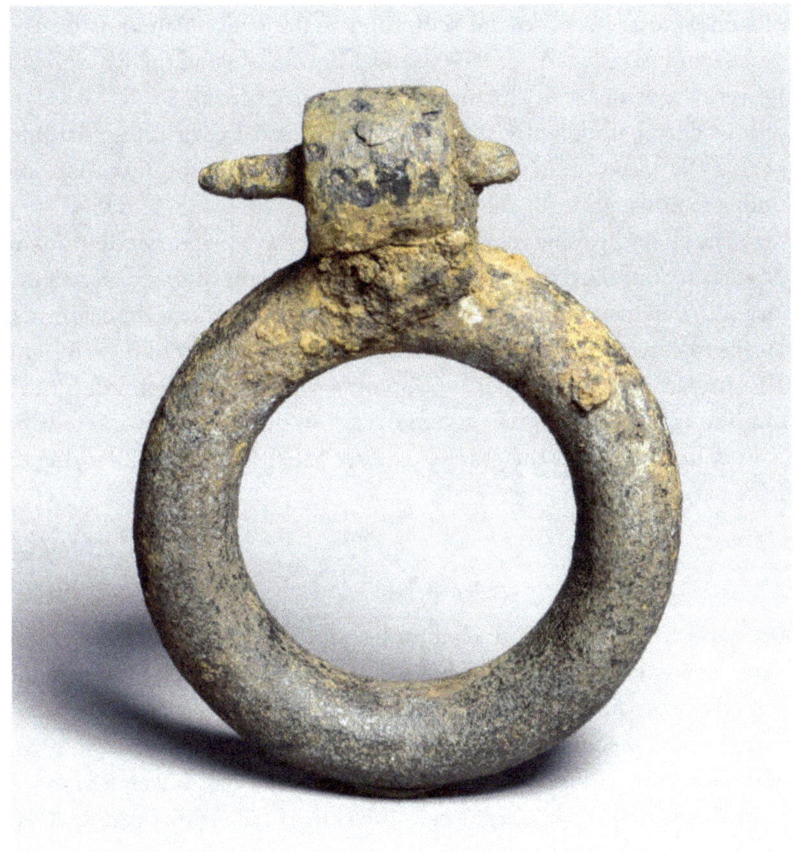

Figure 3. Baroness Elsa von Freytag-Loringhoven, *Enduring Ornament*
(1913), found rusted metal ring, approximately 3 1/2 inches in
diameter. Mark Kelman Collection, New York.

The artist most readily associated with rust today is probably the
American sculptor Richard Serra, whose uncompromising prowess of
production had earned him the title, 'man of steel'.[20] Serra's work has
long pressed against the limits of infrastructural support, requiring ship
yards, big cranes, steel mills, outsourced labour, and lots of money.

---

20   The nickname also makes reference to Serra's time working in a steel mill in Cali-
      fornia during his student years. Calvin Tomkins, 'Man of Steel', *The New Yorker*,
      5 August 2002 <http://www.newyorker.com/magazine/2002/08/05/man-of-steel>
      [accessed 2 July 2020].

His enormous rusted metal sculptures make major demands on the spaces they occupy. In her 1990 essay 'Minimalism and the Rhetoric of Power', the feminist art historian Anna Chave recounts that Leo Castelli Gallery had recently shored up the floors of their industrial loft, so that the space could exhibit Serra's works without totally collapsing under their weight.[21]

The sheer heaviness of Serra's sculptures is a primary component of what is supposed to be impressive about them; their exact weights and dimensions are routinely advertised in their official descriptions. While making a clear bid to permanence, the extremity of their weight also invests the objects with a potential violence, as testified by the numerous injuries — and on one occasion, death — of workers who have collapsed under the gravity of Serra's abstractions while trying to install them.[22]

*

In 1981, the artist David Hammons took a piss on *T.W.U.*, one of Serra's massive assemblies of pre-weathered steel, which had been installed the previous year in the gentrifying downtown neighbourhood of Tribeca. The sculpture was sponsored by a wealthy German gallerist, and New York's Public Art Fund website vaunts that it weighed more than 72 tons (65,000 kilograms). The title of Hammons's short-lived intervention is *Pissed Off*.

---

21   Anna C. Chave, 'Minimalism and the Rhetoric of Power', *Arts Magazine*, 64.5 (January 1990), pp. 44–63 (p. 44).

22   In 1971, Raymond Johnson was killed by one of the 5212-pound steel plates comprising Serra's 'Sculpture No. 3', which Johnson was helping to install at the Walker Art Center in Minneapolis. His wife filed a lawsuit against Serra, whom the courts acquitted from guilt. The fatality and trial did not seem to alter Serra's practice of producing sculptures so grandiose in their dimensions that anyone handling them would be placed at risk of injury. In 1988, another of Serra's enormous free-standing works fell on top of installers Daniel Hafner and Joseph Gallo at Leo Castelli Gallery. Gallo's right leg was crushed, and later amputated. Of the incident, Serra has said the following: 'Some reporter asked me about my relationship to the accident. I don't think that my relationship is open to interpretation or speculation. I think it's *my* relationship to it. Rigging is a dangerous business. Danger is something that surrounds that activity. The sculpture when it's erected is not dangerous.' Richard Serra, 'Interview by Robert Morgan', in Richard Serra, *Writings/Interviews* (Chicago: University of Chicago Press, 1994), p. 191. See United States Court of Appeals, Eighth Circuit, Janet Johnson v. Richard Serra, et al., March 10, 1975. Don Terry, 'A 16-Ton Sculpture Falls, Injuring 2', *The New York Times*, 27 October 1988, Section B, p. 6.

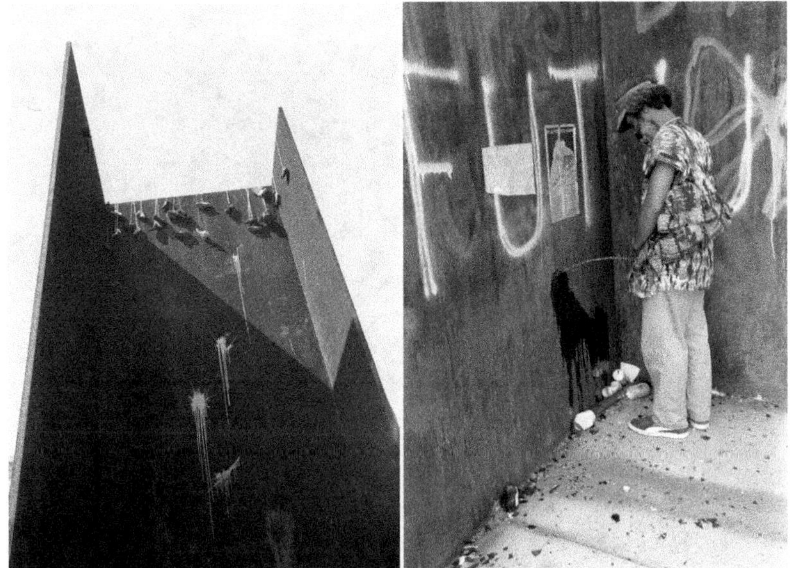

Figures 4–5. David Hammons, *Shoe Tree* (1981) and *Pissed Off* (1981).
Photographs by Dawoud Bey. Copyright Dawoud Bey; courtesy of
Stephen Daiter Gallery.

As is often the case with Hammons, the facts about this piece are fuzzy.[23] The artist had his friend Dawoud Bey document the act — along with another work that is now known as *Shoe Tree* (1981), where twenty-five pairs of kicks were draped by their straps and laces over the top of Serra's three-story tall sculpture, turning his monument of high art into just another prop for the transient idiom of the street. But Hammons didn't show the black-and-white photographs publicly until nine years later, and they still leave us guessing about what happened outside their frames, and what happened before and after the moments they capture.

Do the pictures refer to a one-off event, or a sustained habit, or a re-enactment for the purpose of documentation? Were the shoes thrown up all at once, all by Hammons? Or did he gradually add to shoes already flung, maybe over several days, maybe taking a piss each

---

23   See Elena Filipovic, *David Hammons: Bliz-aard Ball Sale* (London: Afterall Books, 2017) and Abbe Schriber, '"Those Who Know Don't Tell": David Hammons c. 1981', *Women & Performance: A Journal of Feminist Theory*, 29.1 (2019), pp. 41–61.

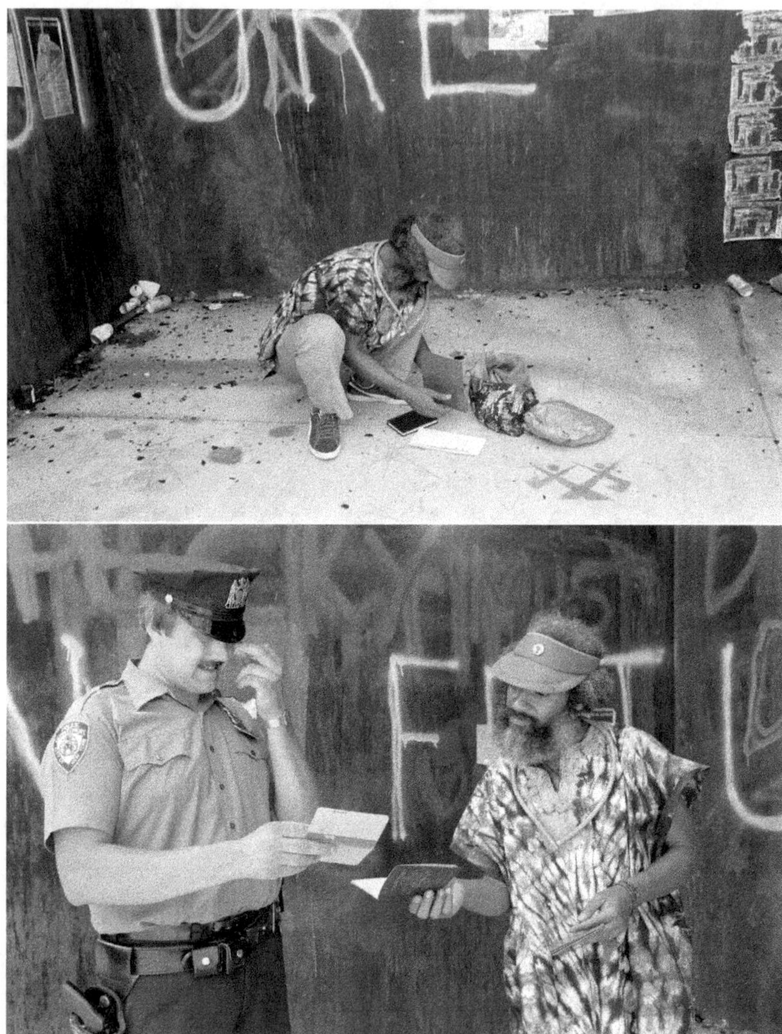

Figures 6–7. David Hammons, *Pissed Off* (1981). Photographs by Dawoud Bey. Copyright Dawoud Bey; courtesy of Stephen Daiter Gallery.

time? Was there an audience, besides Bey? And what happened with the white cop who is shown talking to Hammons in a number of the photographs? Is Hammons being arrested, or receiving a warning? Is he talking his way out of a fine?

In 1981 in New York City, anti-loitering campaigns and the criminalization of 'vagrancy' were feeding into the city's pro-development agenda, as unemployment and homelessness were skyrocketing following large-scale withdrawals of social services. The industrial neighbourhood of Tribeca had been recently re-zoned so that investors could convert it into a new housing market; this was the first time ever in New York's history when loft housing was made legal for those who weren't artists.[24] There was also a dearth of public lavatories in the city, which meant that the only way one could avoid pissing in public was to become a paying customer in a restaurant or bar, or else risk being charged with indecent exposure.[25] And, as the pictures of Hammons and the officer remind us, gentrification was secured by anti-black policing.

Hammons exhibited the images for the first time in 1990, as part of the group show *Illegal America* at Exit Art.[26] A short statement he wrote for the exhibition reads:

> *Pissed Off* is about the fact that in New York City a man doesn't have any public access to relieve himself in a decent manner. There is no way for a gentleman to relieve himself in a gentlemanly way without having to buy a drink. Keeps the rage going.[27]

*

Serra has been infamously iron-willed about the site-specificity of his public pieces. In 1981 (the same year as *Pissed Off*), his *Tilted Arc* was installed in a plaza outside a government building a few blocks away from *T.W.U.* At 120 feet long and 12 feet high, the solid wall of steel formed a domineering and blank-faced block to the area's daily commuters, who couldn't see past it and had to take detours around

---

24   See chapter nine of Aaron Shkuda, *The Lofts of SoHo: Gentrification, Art, and Industry in New York, 1950–1980* (Chicago: University of Chicago Press, 2016).

25   See Abbe Schriber, "'Those Who Know Don't Tell'".

26   Ibid. In addition to the *Illegal America* exhibition at Exit Art in 1990, the images were also included in the exhibition catalogue *David Hammons: Rousing the Rubble* (New York: P.S. 1 Contemporary Art Center, 1990).

27   The statement is reproduced in Abbe Schriber, "'Those Who Know Don't Tell'", p. 48.

it.[28] When hundreds of government workers petitioned for it to be repositioned or relocated, the artist sued the public agency that had commissioned the project, insisting that 'to remove the work is to destroy the work'.[29]

While Serra's sculptures are specifically situated in public places (and with public funding, in the case of *Tilted Arc*), they're also meant to be impervious to the lived realities of their surroundings.[30] Despite this, and despite the artist's defensive resistance to the time of contingency that comes after the execution of his authorial intention, many of Serra's site-specific works around the world have become impromptu but well-established urinals. Something about their placement in busy thoroughfares, combined with the degree of shelter and privacy offered by their big rusty facades, makes them perfect spaces for responding to nature's calls. It's safe to say that as long as cities fail to provide adequate public facilities, Serra's weatherproof monuments will continue to have a stench of piss about them.

Quite against themselves, Serra's outdoor sculptures also tend to become broad canvases for public commentary — with messages inscribed in the rust, writing his facades out of their timelessness. As soon as it was installed, the *T.W.U.* piece was customized by its neighbourhood. The immensity of its scale and the starkness of its surfaces made it well suited as a blank slate for graffiti and posters — so the dubious claim to autonomous purity is actually what ensured that the Minimalist sculpture became contaminated by the reality onto which

---

28   Chave cites Danny Katz, who worked as a clerk in the building at the plaza where *Tilted Arc* was installed, who said: 'It's not a great plaza by international standards, but it is a small refuge and place of revival for people who ride to work in steel containers, work in sealed rooms, and breathe recirculated air all day. Is the purpose of art in public places to seal off a route of escape, to stress the absence of joy and hope? I can't believe this was the artistic intention, yet to my sadness, this for me has been the dominant effect of the work, and it's all the fault of the location and position. I can accept anything in art, but I can't accept physical assault and physical destruction of pathetic human activity. No work of art created with a contempt for ordinary humanity and without respect for the common element of human experience can be great' (Chave, 'Minimalism', p. 60).

29   Richard Serra, *Writings/Interviews*, p. 194. For more on the *Tilted Arc* debacle, see *The Destruction of Tilted Arc: Documents*, ed. by Clara Weyergraf-Serra and Martha Buskirk (Cambridge, MA: MIT Press, 1991).

30   Chave cites Serra's own account of what it means for him to conceive of a work for a public place: 'one has to consider the traffic flow, but not necessarily worry about the indigenous community, and get caught up in the politics of the site' (Chave, 'Minimalism', p. 58).

it imposed itself. Paint was splattered on its surfaces, garbage tumble-weeded around it, and there was, almost certainly, piss. Then David Hammons comes along and participates in this existing repertoire of furtive and improvisational urban practices, where authorship is blurry or irrelevant, and where forms are necessarily transient.

*

Another work that has Serra's big weathered walls in the background is Andrea Fraser's 2001 video *Little Frank and His Carp*.[31] With just over six minutes of shaky footage that was shot with hidden cameras,[32] the video shows Fraser taking herself on a tour of the Guggenheim Museum in Bilbao, which was designed by Frank Gehry, the titan of contemporary architecture, whom Fraser's title addresses in the diminutive. Walking through the museum's atrium with the official audio guide pressed to her ear, its strap around her wrist, Fraser performs a radical susceptibility to the disembodied voice, which instructs visitors exactly where to go, how to feel, and how to appreciate what they are looking at:

> If you haven't already done so, walk away from the desk where you picked up this guide and out into the great high space of the atrium. Isn't this a wonderful place? It's uplifting. It's like a gothic cathedral, you can feel your soul rise up in the building around you.

Rather than resist the bathos of her automated tutor — by, say, turning the device off — Fraser abandons herself to its powers of suggestion. When the voice tells her to look up at the archways, her head follows.

---

31   This video can be viewed at *UbuWeb* <http://ubu.com/film/fraser_frank.html> [accessed 2 July 2020].

32   In an essay that accompanies this work, Fraser mentions how aggressively the Guggenheim Bilbao controls the circulation of images of the museum's architecture; while visitors are encouraged to touch the walls, they are strictly prohibited from taking any photographs. Fraser also relays an anecdote of a local artist who, after making macaroni shaped like Gehry's building, was threatened with a lawsuit. The museum's vigilance about its own image makes the artist's intervention in this site all the more provocative. Andrea Fraser, 'Isn't This a Wonderful Place? (A Tour of a Tour of the Guggenheim Bilbao)', in *Museum Highlights: The Writings of Andrea Fraser*, ed. by Alexander Alberro (Cambridge, MA: MIT Press, 2005), pp. 233–59 (p. 245).

When he directs her to turn around and admire the glass tower, she swivels on cue. When he speaks of the 'heart of the museum', she touches her breast. When he explains pedantically that modern art is 'demanding, complicated, bewildering', her brows contract in consternation.

The artist never speaks, and while the video begins with the ambient sounds of the museum, the audio track is soon replaced with the generic museal voiceover that arrives through the wand of information. The camerawork also participates in the play of acquiescence, as it cuts to show whatever she is told to look at. But this perfect compliance — if not obedience — to the dictation of experience by the voice of institutional authority gradually takes a turn, as a transgressive mode of sensuality starts to emerge from the practice of listening all too well.

> Every surface of this space curves, only the floor is straight. These curves are gentle but in their huge scale powerfully sensual. You'll see people going up to the walls and stroking them. You might feel a desire to do so yourself. These curving surfaces have a direct appeal that has nothing to do with age or class or education [...]. This pillar is clad in panels of limestone. Run your hand over them. Feel how smooth it is....

When the video is two and a half minutes in, Fraser bites her own fist. By the fourth minute, she is hiking up her bright green dress to reveal a white thong, and caressing her own ass as she presses herself against Gehry's curved pillar. She consummates the enjoyment of the universal through its de-sublimation, and her impersonally prompted exhibitionism recodes the solemnity of aesthetic education into the comedy of the improperly erotic.[33]

When the narrator prompts her to pause the audio guide, she does so, ambling to the next room to await further instruction. The

---

33   'These curving surfaces have a direct appeal that has nothing to do with age or class or education', the Guggenheim Bilbao's voiceover insists, before explaining how the building was made by computers and robots — as the product, in Fraser's words, 'of a world in which the human labour of production does not exist'. While museumgoers are instructed to touch the walls of the building and 'feel how smooth it is', Fraser's essay reflects on the social realities that are being smoothed-over here — from local unemployment and poverty to the precarization of labour in and through art institutions and the franchised spectacularization of museums made into 'corporate entertainment complexes' (ibid.).

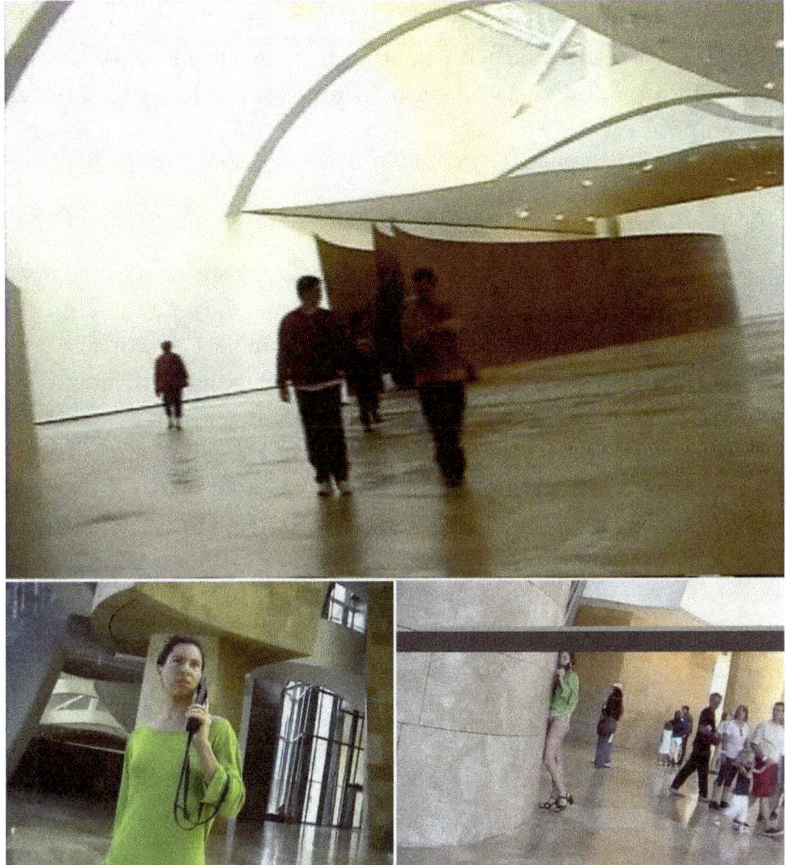

Figures 8–10. Andrea Fraser, *Little Frank and His Carp* (2001), standard
definition video. Video stills. Courtesy the artist.

video cuts to a museum-goer touching his hand to the wall where
Fraser has just had her encounter, before ending on a shot of Serra's
180-ton, 15.85-meter-long *Snake* (1994-97) — a 'big slab of rusty
steel' (Fraser's description) that critics have variously described as
'undulating' and 'flirty' in its 'wanton curviness'.[34] By the time she
arrives in the space, Fraser has libidinally charged the embodiment

---

34   Ibid., p. 243. Richard Cork, *Breaking Down the Barriers: Art in the 1990s* (New Haven,
      CT: Yale University Press, 2003), p. 515. Deborah Solomon, 'Richard Serra Is Carrying
      the Weight of the World', *The New York Times*, 28 August 2019.

of the abstract 'phenomenological subject'[35] that Minimalist artworks like Serra's are credited with inviting into engagement — and she has roused platitudes about participatory art to the point of their discomposure.

*

Fraser's illicit encounter with the defiantly blank surfaces of the institution recalls an anecdote at the start of Anna Chave's essay on the relations of power that play out through Minimalist artworks. At the Museum of Modern Art in New York, two teenage girls are interacting with a polished brass box on the floor, which is an untitled Donald Judd sculpture. Their first response is to kick it and laugh, then they use it as a mirror to fix their hair, and finally they bend down and kiss their reflections on its surface. Witnessing all this from a distance, Chave recounts that she was struck by the fact that the museum guard who stood nearby made no attempt to intervene. She goes on to argue that 'the object's look of absolute, or "plain power"', as Judd described it, 'helps explain the perception that it did not need or merit protecting'.[36]

The tendencies that came to define American Minimalism as it emerged in the 1960s included the explicit use of industrial materials and procedures, and the absence of any frame or plinth for the art object. Positioned on the same ground as the viewer, the Minimalist sculpture might have appeared more 'exposed', more vulnerable to being touched or attacked — except that the self-consciously hardy and non-precious materiality, and the techniques of outsourced mass production, served at the same time to negate any dimension of fragility.

Serra's contribution to Minimalism was to render its objects on an ever more monumental scale, and the installation at the Guggenheim Bilbao is one of his biggest-ever works. It occupies the museum's largest gallery, which was specifically built to house the installation as a permanent centrepiece. 'Contemporary art is *big*', the official voiceover in Fraser's video explains, as she reaches the Serra room. 'In fact, some of it is enormous!'

---

35   See Hal Foster, 'The Crux of Minimalism', in Hal Foster, *The Return of the Real: The Avant-Garde at the End of the Century* (Cambridge, MA: MIT Press, 1996), pp. 35–71.
36   Chave, p. 44.

The curvaceous surfaces that we see Fraser enjoy in her video seem to be left unaffected by her excessively compliant (and wonderfully inappropriate) masturbatory caress. Similarly, Hammons's piss and shoes have got nothing on the immense solidity and claims to posterity that are embodied in Serra's work. They might cause some olfactory disruption, and prove difficult to take down, but the stench would pass within a matter of days, the shoes in some weeks, while the towering steel walls would remain indefinitely and indifferently upright.[37]

By messing with registers of macho monumentalism, though, these transitory interventions bring its humorlessness and impervious self-importance into sharp relief. The steely indifference of Serra's surfaces, along with the logic of final conquest that they embody, may seem to impress a sense of futility on such leaky and libidinal gestures as those enacted by Hammons and Fraser. But it is precisely by making minimal claim to staying power that such acts of fleeting disturbance underscore the ultimate futility of trying to close off the relationship between an object and its world.

For decades, Serra has steeled his works against the weather by using pre-treated COR-TEN, which is the generic trademark name for US Steel's weathering steel, whose alloy is designed to stave off the weathering effects of the weather, by accelerating and then harnessing the rusting process. Rust is welcomed onto the surface, but only as a technique of controlled passivation: once the coating of oxidation has formed over the exposed metal, it is supposed to stabilize and shut out the environment, thereby eliminating the need for ongoing re-painting or other costly anti-rust maintenance measures. This is the idea with weathering steel; the steel is weathered so as to refuse the weather, with a paradoxically protective layer of corrosion.[38]

When US Steel opened the US Steel Tower as their headquarters in Pittsburgh in 1970, the building was supposed to be a showpiece for their COR-TEN product, with columns of the weathering steel running right up the sixty-four story skyscraper. Within months, though,

---

37   Serra, apparently, was not pleased. Filipovic, *David Hammons*, p. 70.

38   In this sense, COR-TEN's design is in keeping with the original architectural sense of 'weathering', which refers to the parts of the building that were meant to 'throw off the rain' or otherwise stave the weather off. Mohsen Mostafavi and David Leatherbarrow, *On Weathering: The Life of Buildings in Time* (Cambridge, MA: MIT Press, 1993).

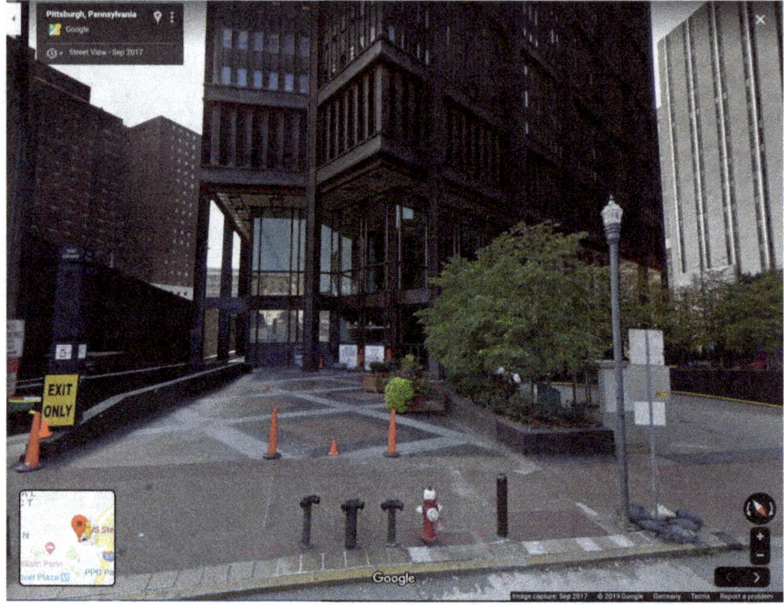

Figure 11. US Steel Tower in Pittsburgh, as it appears in Google Maps
Street View.

as the COR-TEN underwent its initial phase of anti-corrosive corrosion, the building started to bleed, with iron oxides seeping out
and staining the sidewalks and nearby buildings. Literally red-faced,
the corporation orchestrated an extensive clean-up effort. But Google
Maps Street View confirms that parts of the pavement around the
tower still have a rusty tinge to them.

We recently went to have an irl look at Serra's big COR-TEN sculpture that stands outside the Berliner Philharmonie, at the southern
edge of Tiergarten. Besides the presence of graffiti, garbage, weeds,
and an abandoned long-stemmed rose — which were not altogether
unexpected — we noticed that the solid metal panels are failing in
their weather resistance, and literally leaking out into their surrounds.
They're standing strong, very strong and very still, but the ground
around them shows ornamental stripes of fluid red, where the rust is
carrying the resistant sculpture away from itself. This is rust: a gathering of red that is followed by its own scattering; a material archive of
exposure that does not keep itself but flakes apart and seeps away.

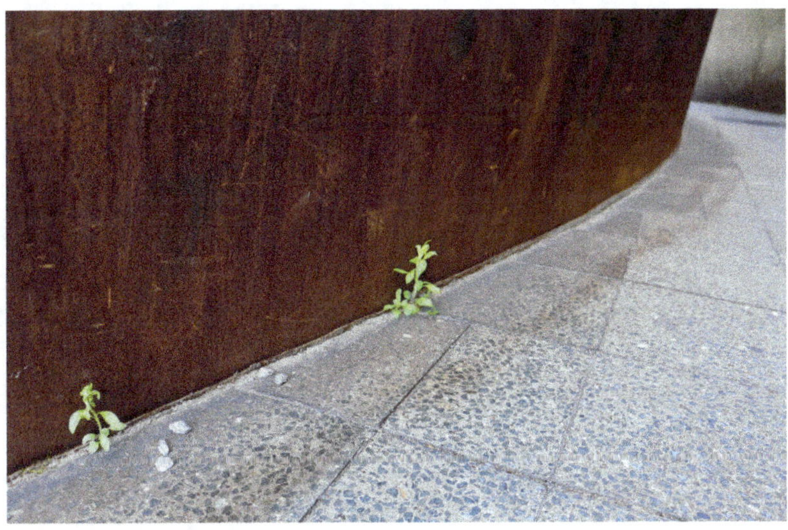

Figure 12. Richard Serra's *Berlin Junction* (1987), giving off its red.
Photograph taken by the authors on 21 May, the Ascension Day of 2020.

The Weathering of the Trace
Agamben's Presupposition of Derrida

DAMIANO SACCO

The urgency of the question of the status of the trace can perhaps in no way be justified, it can only be asserted. The trace 'itself', Derrida argues, cannot be done justice to — the trace, another name for justice, cannot be justified. The urgency of the question of the trace is unfolded in this essay alongside a principal axis instituted by the following question: is it possible that the trace might be weathering away? Is it altogether possible for the trace to weather away like a *material* trace would, a trace imprinted in the mud or in the snow, a trace exposed to the elements? It is not immediately clear how one should think the weathering of the trace — to which elements would the trace be exposed? To Heidegger's earth? To his forgetting of air? To Nietzsche's fear of water? To everyone's obsession with fire? Or is it the case, instead, that the trace has in fact already withered away — that there are no more traces to be found? Notwithstanding, one should at least justify the possibility of addressing the question of the trace under the heading of weathering, at least justify the possibility of articulating the question alongside a guideline that does not immediately appear to move in the vicinities of the trace. The principal standpoint from which this reflection moves is then the one which enables the thinking of the movement of the trace together with a certain notion of weathering. When a building, a stone, or a monument are exposed to the elements, it can be argued that a certain logic of 'supplementarity' is at work, a familiar kind of addition by subtraction or subtraction by addition: the monument *gains* something by being weathered — it gains a new status by something perhaps being removed or weathered off its surface, it gains something through a subtraction — and, at the same time, the monument *loses* something, its original status, through the additional supplement or sedimentation of the elements — it loses something through an addition. There is then an extent to which weathering, according to this logic of supplementarity, as the deferral of an origin that has always already been weathered, as an exposure to the elements, as an exposure to the Other, as an exposure that precedes all fantasies of self-presence, as the opening of temporality itself, but also, as will be made clear in the other contributions to this volume, as the logic of the archive — the logic of what remains alive of the dead and what is already dead of the living — as the haunting of memory, as the work of mourning, as the creation *and* erasure of physical traces — there is an extent to which the movement of the trace and this notion of weathering can be thought together.

The question at stake in this essay, however, is not that of weathering, but rather that of the weathering of the trace (objective genitive).[1] This question turns out to be problematic if approached from the current standpoint, for the weathering of the trace would stand for a weathering of weathering itself, for the trace of the trace 'itself'. This is a well-known problem, or feature, of deconstruction: namely, the aporia that arises when one attempts to think the possibility of a transformation or weathering *of* the very opening of temporality, *of* spacing, *of* the very exposure that first makes any weathering possible. To posit that the trace is liable to any notion of transformation, modification, or weathering would be to resort, precisely, to a possibility for change for which the trace will have always been the very opening. This is a feature that is known, in Aristotle (but not in Plato), as anhypotheticity (or, before Meillassoux's intervention, more commonly as

---

1   The expression 'weathering of the trace' has two meanings: when the genitive is taken as subjective, it attributes the performance of weathering to the trace, signalling that the trace is the source or principle of weathering; when the genitive is taken as objective, it is the trace to be subjected or exposed to weathering. This latter case will be explored as the subject matter of the essay.

elenchus): that is, the impossibility to attempt to refute (*elenchein*) a certain principle, of non-contradiction in Aristotle's case, without having of necessity to resort to it. The question of the weathering of the trace is then equivalent to that of anhypotheticity, a question of self-referentiality with which continental thought seems to keep confronting itself — by asking whether being is, whether the trace is, whether *die Sprache spricht*, whether contingency is contingent, whether plasticity is plastic, whether weathering weathers, and so forth. According to different topologies, the boundary of language — its limit — is either simple or, rather, consists of a certain fold that turns in upon itself. Deconstruction takes the following stance: there can be no trace of the trace, no deconstruction of deconstruction, no autoimmunity of autoimmunity, no hymen of the hymen, no *glas* of *glas*, no weathering of weathering. Justice, another name for deconstruction, Derrida states, is undeconstructible; the trace, as autoimmunity, is not liable to any autoimmunitary reaction, be that a permanent autoimmunitary disease or a seasonal allergy.[2] The aim of this essay is to confront the question of the anhypotheticity of the trace — the question of the weathering of the trace — with the claim that the trace itself would be inscribed in a certain history, not quite a temporal one, through an inscription that it has not itself written — the trace would be inscribed in a history that has come to an end. This is Agamben's claim.

I

For over forty years, from his first *Stanzas* through to *What Is Philosophy?*, Agamben has time and again engaged with the standpoint of deconstruction: an engagement that has at times been overt, at times covert, at times self-effacing, and at times, of necessity, unaware of itself. In the impossibility to render justice to this pluri-decennial confrontation, the hope is that this inevitably partial re-enactment might shed light on the question of rendering justice itself — to a text, to a reading, to justice itself. If the principle of reason is one of *reddendae*

---

2   For a different approach to the question of anhypotheticity, which points to the undecidability of the status of contingency, deconstruction, etc., see Damiano Sacco, 'Of *Apousia* and *Parousia*: The Correlation between Heidegger and Meillassoux', *Pli*, 30 (2019), pp. 141–63.

rationis, the anhypotheticity of justice deals precisely with the impossibility of rendering justice to justice itself. The plan is to present Agamben's claim on the status of the trace and to then outline his own proposal.

The principal claim made by Agamben is that, since Aristotle, our experience of language has been shaped by one particular *modus operandi*, to wit, the presuppositional one. Agamben argues that with Aristotle we observe the inception of a structuring guideline throughout which language will operate as a determinate apparatus (*dispositivo*): namely, one that is responsible for the 'the scission of being into a *hypokeimenon*, something lying-at-the-base (the being named or indicated of a singular existent, insofar as it is not said of a subject but is a presupposition for every discourse) and that which is said on the presupposition of it'.[3] To predicate in language always means having *pre*-supposed, *a posteriori*, the existence of a substratum or hypostasis that precedes all predicates. Agamben writes:

> As soon as there is language, the named thing is presupposed as the nonlinguistic or the unrelated with which language has established its relation. This presupposing power is so strong that we imagine the non-linguistic as something unsayable and unrelated, which we somehow try to grasp as such, without realizing that in this way we are simply trying to grasp the shadow of language. In this sense, the unsayable is a genuinely linguistic category, which can be conceived only by a speaking being.[4]

The trajectory of the history of Western metaphysics, a trajectory that Heidegger and Derrida read as being indexed by certain order of presence, a metaphysics of presence — this trajectory is re-interpreted by Agamben as that of the history of a certain experience of language, precisely a language that is inherently presuppositional, that cannot help but *pre*-suppose, after taking place, a prior, non-linguistic substratum that it itself constitutes retroactively. The self-presence of the signified, namely the target of Heideggerian destruction and Derridean

---

3   Giorgio Agamben, *The Use of Bodies*, trans. by Adam Kotsko (Stanford, CA: Stanford University Press, 2016), pp. 131–32.

4   Giorgio Agamben, *What Is Philosophy?*, trans. by Lorenzo Chiesa (Stanford, CA: Stanford University Press, 2018), p. 35.

deconstruction, should be traced, according to Agamben, to the self-presence of the retroactive positing of the linguistic presupposition, the self-presence of the non-linguistic presupposition. The history of metaphysics coincides then with the history of the presuppositional experience of language: 'It is in the structure of presupposition that the interweaving of being and language, ontology and logic that constitutes Western metaphysics is articulated.'[5] The history of metaphysics, rather than being constituted by a number of inscrutable sendings destined by a giving that will forever elude being given itself — a giving nevertheless constrained by the double binds of unconcealment and concealment (*Un-verborgenheit*), disclosure and withdrawal (*Enthüllung, Entzug*), appropriation and expropriation (*Ereignis, Enteignis*) — this history is rather to find its material inscription in the development of a science of language as well as in the uncovering of the presupposing structure that underlies the Western experience of language. An uncovering that follows the material conditions of 'centuries of humble analysis and grammatical education, through which language [*lingua, (langue)*] has been extracted from speech [*parola, (parole)*] and interiorized as knowledge.'[6]

This reading enables Agamben to ground the trajectory of the history of metaphysics — a trajectory that according to Heidegger moves along an axis indexed by the objectification (*Vergegenständlichung, Objektivierung*) and constant presence (*beständige Anwesenheit*) of the existent — on the development of a science of language that progressively uncovers the logic of presupposition, of the self-presence of the presupposed, of the institution of a subject of language, and so forth. Moreover, both the inception and the conclusion of the history of metaphysics find their own rationales: Aristotle's inception marks the beginning of the presuppositional experience of language, and, at the

---

5   Agamben, *The Use of Bodies*, p. 119.

6   Giorgio Agamben, 'La parola e il sapere', *aut aut*, 179–80 (September–December 1980), pp. 155–66 (p. 157; my translation): 'It is sufficient to reflect, even for just a moment, to realize that, while speech [*parola*], the concrete instance of discourse, is something that can be experienced immediately and concretely, language [*lingua*] is nothing but a construction of science that originates in speech. In order for something like language to even just be conceived of, in order for it to become something firmer and more real than speech, centuries, even millennia, of grammatical and logical reflection on language have been necessary.'

other end, the development of the modern science of linguistics that takes place from Bopp through to Saussure and Benveniste marks the accomplishment of this experience. Agamben writes:

> This is the Copernican revolution that the thought of our time inherits from nihilism: we are the first human beings who have become completely conscious of language. For the first time, what preceding generations called God, Being, spirit, unconscious appear to us as what they are: names for language.[7]

And he continues:

> The primordial character of the word is now completely revealed, and no new figure of the divine, no new historical destiny can lift itself out of language. [...] If God was the name of language, 'God is dead' can only mean that there is no longer a name for language.[8]

Crucially, this reading provides Agamben with a foothold that enables him to extend the history of metaphysics just enough to also include Derrida and the trace. Derrida's thought comes to represent, in Agamben's reading, the end of the trajectory beginning with Aristotle: the end of the presupposing experience of language. Agamben's gesture consists in claiming that the trace, in not being able to escape the presuppositional experience of language, rather brings it to its conclusion: the trace is, Agamben argues, presupposition of nothing *but* of itself — the trace is inscribed in the history of metaphysics *as self-presupposition*. The self-presence of the presupposed is forever deferred by the trace precisely because the action of presupposition comes to be shifted, at each turn, to act upon itself: the trace does not presuppose a self-present signified, but rather keeps presupposing a presupposition to each presupposition. The immediacy of the internal voice has always already presupposed the mediation of an external writing, which in turn can exist as a mediation or an externality only if it has presupposed ... and so forth, with the movement of arche-writing or trace standing

---

7   Giorgio Agamben, 'The Idea of Language', in Agamben, *Potentialities*, ed. and trans. by Daniel Heller-Roazen (Stanford, CA: Stanford University Press, 1999), pp. 39–47 (p. 45).

8   Ibid.

precisely for the differing and deferral operated by the process of self-presupposition. Agamben writes:

> For there to be the signification of an intentionality and not of an object, it is necessary that the term signify itself, but *signify itself only insofar as it signifies*. It is thus necessary that the *intentio* neither be a referent nor, for that matter, simply refer to an object. In the semiotic scheme by which *aliquid stat pro aliquo*, A stands for B, the *intentio* cannot indicate the first *aliquid* or the second; it must, rather, above all refer to the 'standing for' itself. The aporia of Derrida's terminology is that in it, one *standing for* stands for another *standing for*, without anything like an objective referent constituting itself in its presence. But, accordingly, the very notion of sense (of 'standing for') then enters into a state of crisis. This is the particular rigour of Derrida's terminology.[9]

The trace, as self-presupposition, is then inscribed in the history of the presuppositional experience of language as its necessary completion. According to a recurrent strategy, Agamben performs a gesture that enables him to include a certain element in a system through its very exclusion, namely to include the graphic element of the trace as the negative, i.e. the inverse/reverse, of the history of onto-theology.[10] Through a logic of the exception, a logic of *ex-capio*, the trace is included in the history of metaphysics precisely by its conformity, albeit by means of its negation, to the presuppositional structure of language, i.e. by excluding or disenabling the retroactive presupposition of a referent. The weathering of the trace (subjective genitive) — the trace as weathering — stands according to Agamben as the completion of the history of metaphysics.[11]

---

9   Ibid., p. 212, translation modified.

10   See, e.g., Agamben, *What Is Philosophy?*, pp. 19–20 or Giorgio Agamben, *Language and Death: The Place of Negativity*, trans. by Karen E. Pinkus with Michael Hardt (Minneapolis: University of Minnesota Press, 1991), pp. 38–40.

11   Agamben repeatedly grounds his assessment of the trace on Aristotle's *De Interpretatione* and on its ancient commentators. Agamben argues that the articulation between *phōnē* and *logos*, between bare voice and signifying language, can take place only thanks to the function of the letter, *gramma*, both element and sign of the voice: 'Insofar as it is the *element of that of which it is a sign*, it has the privileged status of being an *index sui*, self-demonstration; like *protē ousia*, of which it constitutes the linguistic cipher, it shows itself, but only insofar as it *was* in the voice, that is, insofar as it always already belongs to the past. The *gramma* is thus the form of presupposition itself and nothing

II

Before attempting to render justice to this reading, before asking whether the trace can effectively be included through an exclusion or whether it has the potential of deactivating the logic of the exception, it will be necessary to provide a brief outline of Agamben's own proposal. Having delimited the domain of metaphysics by means of a certain experience of language that runs from Aristotle to Derrida, Agamben resorts to the Heideggerian need for a step-back-beyond in order to move beyond the presuppositional history of language. This step back, which according to Heidegger should prepare the springing board or the run-up space for the leap (*Satz*) beyond metaphysics, is then quite literally a step back from Aristotle, namely a certain return to Plato's theory of ideas and quest for a principle freed from all presuppositions, an *archē anypothetos*. It is then exactly in the space articulated by the two different notions of anhypotheticity that a confrontation between Derrida and Agamben is to be staged. On the one hand, anhypotheticity as the impossibility to contest a principle without having necessarily to resort to it (to argue that the trace would presuppose a more original opening would precisely mean to resort to a notion of presupposition that is a prerogative of the trace); on the other hand, anhypotheticity as the attempt to do away with the logic of presupposition *altogether*, namely to turn to an experience of language that knows nothing of presuppositions, be they simple or self-referential.

The entry point to this different notion of anhypotheticity is then the following: if the unsayable, the non-linguistic, is nothing but the

---

else' (Agamben, 'The Thing Itself', in Agamben, *Potentialities*, pp. 27–38 (p. 37); see also Agamben, 'Tradition of the Immemorial', in Agamben, *Potentialities*, pp. 104–15 (pp. 111, 113)). Signifying language, Agamben argues, is always articulated (*enarthros*) and *phōnē enarthros* means *phōnē engrammatos, vox quae scribi potest* (Agamben, 'Philosophy and Linguistics', in Agamben, *Potentialities*, pp. 62–76 (p. 75)): 'The letter, as the interpreter of the voice, does not itself need any other interpreter. It is the final interpreter, beyond which no *hermēneia* is possible: the limit of all interpretation' (ibid., p. 37). He can therefore conclude: 'What has reached completion is in fact not the natural history of humanity, but that most special epochal history in which the *hermēneia* of speech as a language [*lingua*] — that is, as an intentional intertwining of terms, concepts, things, and letters that takes place in the voice through the *grammata* — had destined the West' (*What is Philosophy?*, p. 23). In the following it will be shown that the trace, neither *gramma* nor *phōnē*, neither positing nor presupposing, can neither be said to be within nor to be without the history of metaphysics.

presupposition of language, the shadow that language necessarily casts in its taking place, it is on the contrary the sayable (*il dicibile*), the sayability of the sayable, that with which philosophy should concern itself:

> It is not the unsayable but the sayable that constitutes the problem philosophy must at each turn confront again. The unsayable is in fact nothing else than a presupposition of language. [...] The unsayable is a genuinely linguistic category, which can be conceived only by a speaking being. [...] On the other hand, the sayable is a non-linguistic but genuinely ontological category. The elimination of the unsayable in language coincides with the exhibition of the sayable as a philosophical task.[12]

Precisely the task of exhibiting, or even exposing, the pure sayability of the sayable can, according to Agamben, be attended to by turning to Plato's theory of ideas. Neither does the idea, the 'thing itself', have a proper name nor is it homonymous with the thing: 'the "circle itself" (*autos ho kyklos*) seizes the circle not at the level of signification but in its pure having a name, in that pure sayability that alone makes discourse and knowledge possible.'[13] The specific performance of the pronoun *autos* is that of signalling a notion of sameness that, in contrast to the notion of mere identity (*ipse* and *das Selbe* rather than *idem* or *das Gleiche*), articulates the matter of thinking since the Heideggerian intervention. A certain notion of sameness of being and thought comes then to be articulated anew in Plato's theory of ideas: the idea belongs neither to thought nor to being, neither to *langue* nor to *parole*, it does not substantialize or abstract an ideal world, but rather, *as* event of language, deactivates and neutralizes these oppositions by joining together the thing with its being named:

> In this way, Plato problematizes the pure and irreducible givenness of language. At this point — where the name is resumed from and in its naming the thing, and the thing is resumed from and in its being named by the name — the

---

12   Agamben, *What Is philosophy?*, p. 35.
13   Ibid., p. 58.

world and language are in contact, that is, they are united only by an absence of representation.[14]

The promise of a different experience of language is to be waged on the contemplation of the event of language, on a suspension of what (*quid*) is being said to attend to the fact that (*quod*) it is being said. According to Agamben, in this shift, 'the whole modern theory of signification is called into question.'[15] This is the step back from the presuppositional experience of language that prepares for the leap beyond metaphysics:

> Language, which for human beings mediates all things and all knowledge, is itself immediate. Nothing immediate can be reached by speaking beings — nothing, that is, except language itself, mediation itself. For human beings, such an *immediate mediation* constitutes the sole possibility of reaching a principle freed of every presupposition, including self-presupposition. Such an *immediate mediation* alone, in other words, allows human beings to reach that *arkhē anypotethos*, that 'unpresupposed principle' that Plato, in the *Republic*, presents as the *telos*, fulfilment and end of *autos ho logos*, language itself [...]. There can be no true human community on the basis of a presupposition — be it a nation, a language, or even the a priori of communication of which hermeneutics speaks. What unites human beings among themselves is not a nature, a voice, or a common imprisonment in signifying language; it is the vision of language itself and, therefore, the experience of language's limits, its *end*. A true community can only be a community that is not presupposed.[16]

If the weathering of the trace, the trace as weathering, constitutes the consummation of the history of metaphysics, it is then a notion of the weather, a notion of the event of language freed of all presuppositions, that which sets forth the promise of a different experience of language.

III

The principle of justice — the anhypotheticity of justice — precludes the rendering of justice to the trace, the rendering of justice to justice.

---

14   Ibid., p. 65.

15   Ibid., p. 60.

16   Agamben, 'The Idea of Language', p. 47.

There is nevertheless a minimal gap that separates the movement of the trace from what Agamben refers to — a minimal gap that affords a rendering of justice. Every positing (*Setzung*), in taking place, points to a prior positing as to a presupposition (*Voraussetzung*) of its very taking place: namely, in the very act of positing, *it* — the positing itself — is presupposed to its own performance. The logic of positing and presupposing, the logic of reflection, finds perhaps its most natural fulfilment in being posited *itself* as one moment of the unfolding of an ideal Substance/Subject, to wit, Hegel's Spirit. Spirit, in positing its object, finds itself as the very presupposition of this positing; that is to say, Spirit finds itself — its own interiority — *in* the exteriority of the object it has itself posited. Positing, by being posited itself, presupposes itself; presupposition, in being itself posited becomes self-presupposition. Given this logic of self-presupposition — namely, given the dialectics between *Setzung* and *Voraussetzung* that locates in each positing a presupposition which comes itself to be posited — then, the movement or inscription of the trace can be said to be neither equal nor different, neither internal nor external, to this economy of self-presupposition. Between the restricted economy of self-presupposition and the generalized one of the trace, there is not a fully constituted difference, but precisely the trace of a difference, the difference of a trace.[17] The stakes and the promise of the whole Derridean project lie precisely in exhibiting and demonstrating, by means of an ex-hibiting that is a de-monstration, that the very condition of possibility of the restricted economy of *Setzung* and *Voraussetzung*, of positing and presupposing, is a moment that *of necessity* exceeds this economy. The economy of reflection is set into play neither by a positing nor by a presupposing, but rather by the excess of an ex-positing or of an ex-posure: the excess of an *Aussetzung*. The exposure that first makes possible this economy and that, at the same time, exceeds the aegis of its logic — the abstract negativity that cannot be drained by any determinate one, the gift that precedes all notions of accountability, the unconditional hospitality

---

17   One should confront here with the claim found in Derrida's 1964–65 seminar that the 'difference' between Hegel and Heidegger, between *Erinnerung* and *Destruktion*, 'is thus as close as possible to *nothing*'. Jacques Derrida, *Heidegger: The Question of Being and History*, trans. by Geoffrey Bennington (Chicago: University of Chicago Press, 2016), p. 9.

for the unposited Other, and so forth — this excess is found again, at each step, *within* the economy itself in a certain distancing of positing from itself: a distancing that does not quite amount to a full difference precisely because it does not distance two positings, but a positing and the other positing that will have been presupposed *only* by virtue of this very distancing. The trace is therefore not simply presupposition of itself, the trace does not *institute* a restricted economy of *Setzung-Voraussetzung*, but rather renders the latter *destitute* — i.e. it renders it justice — through the inscription of the generalized economy of *Setzung*-Aussetzung-*Voraussetzung*. Accordingly, every positing takes place by means of an exposure that is neither posited nor presupposed, every presupposing takes place by virtue of a non-posited exposure of positing, every exposure inscribes an economy of positing and presupposing.

Beyond Derrida — one could quote here a whole series of texts *in toto* — it is perhaps Hamacher the one to have most insisted in letting this structure emerge across the tradition. In Kant, where the very fact that the order of the posited is taken as the order of being ('The concept of position or positing (*Position oder Setzung*) is completely simple and is the same as the concept of Being'[18]) entails that positing itself cannot quite be said 'to be': 'it means that positing, affected by something other than Being understood as position, never *is* — never "is" according to its own sense of "is," according to the sense of thetic Being.'[19] In Fichte:

> Fichte's proposition can be characterized in this way: in order for the proposition to be able to realize its constative character through which the identity of the I with itself is designated as Being, it needs an absolutely nonrelational, performative positing, a sheer act that can be neither the action of an I nor an action in relation to an I, hence no action of consciousness and no intentional correlate of consciousness.[20]

---

18   Werner Hamacher, 'Premises', in Hamacher, *Premises: Essays on Philosophy and Literature from Kant to Celan*, trans. by Peter Fenves (Cambridge, MA: Harvard University Press, 1996), pp. 1–43 (p. 11; quoting from Kant's *Critique of Pure Reason*).

19   Ibid., p. 14.

20   Werner Hamacher, 'Position Exposed: Friedrich Schlegel's Poetological Transposition of Fichte's Absolute Proposition', in Hamacher, *Premises*, pp. 222–60 (p. 234).

In Hegel:

> Hegel does not dissolve the aporia of understanding. On the
> contrary, for him, the aporia constitutes the resistance from
> which experience must rebound and turn back on itself. By
> supposing that the incomprehensible has a meaning, spirit
> understands it as its object and understands itself as its posit-
> ing. […] [Spirit] takes the only path that the blockage of the
> aporia leaves open: a path back to itself.[21]

And, of course, in Heidegger:

> In the essay 'On the Essence of Truth,' he [Heidegger] does
> not use the terminology of understanding and anticipation
> but that of letting, leaving, and ex-posing: 'As this letting-be,
> it exposes itself to beings as such and transposes all comport-
> ment into the open. Letting-be, that is, freedom, is in itself
> ex-posing [*aus-setzend*], ek-sistent. Seen from the perspective
> of the essence of truth, the essence of freedom shows itself as
> exposure [*Aussetzung*] to the unconcealment of beings.' […]
> As the ex-posure of positing — the *Aussetzung der Setzung*, the
> interruption of every positional act, the exposition of every
> possible position — it draws on an opening, an unposited
> space, and a place impossible to posit.[22]

It is from this standpoint that weathering, or the trace, appears not
simply as an infinite regression of an always-already weathered existent, but rather as the emergence of this economy by means of an
exposure to its unweatherable condition of possibility — an exposure
to the event of the weather. The weather, the *factum* of language, constitutes the *archē anypothetos*, the giving of the economy of weathering
— an economy that will always contain the inscription of a trace that
cannot be weathered by anhypotheticity. In order to distance himself
from Derrida, Agamben misses the opportunity to see that this distancing arises only by his mis-positing of the trace — a mis-positing that
reveals the two projects to be perhaps as close as they could be. For,
on the one hand, the event of language as *archē anypothetos* gives rise

---

21   Hamacher, 'Premises', pp. 7–9.

22   Hamacher, 'Premises', p. 38; quoting from Heidegger's 'On the Essence of Truth'.

to an economy of positing and presupposing in which one can always find the inscription of a trace, a trace that cannot be weathered by anhypotheticity. Conversely, by virtue of its own anhypotheticity, the trace precludes positing from positing itself by inscribing a distancing within positing itself: the event of positing, the weather, constitutes an *archē anypothetos*. To think the weathering or the anhypotheticity of the trace amounts then to thinking the event of language, the event of the weather, as *archē anypothetos*. Weather and weathering, event of language and trace, abandoned being and exposed positing, *archē anypothetos* and anhypotheticity of the lack of *archē* — but also, *bando* and *bande*, *potenza* and *puissance/potence*, *soglia* and *hymen*, and so forth — Agamben and Derrida's projects are tangent to each other without any possibility of being disjoined. One should mark each of the following words by Hamacher: 'Positing is exposed positing; abandoned by itself, it is thus ex-position.'[23] This essay is perhaps only a long exegesis of this one sentence, of the relation between the exposure of positing and the exceptional *bando* of abandoned being.[24] Hamacher articulates this relation as follows:

> It thus becomes clear that there can be a position — and thus Being, subject, language, and understanding — only from the ex-position of this position: only, therefore, from what is precisely not an understanding of Being as position, not a subject, not a language, and not an understanding — and is, moreover, not a negation of any of these but the opening of every one. Only as an ex-posed, abandoned subject is there

---

23   Hamacher, 'Premises', p. 15. One should confront once again with the 'difference' between Hegel and Heidegger as found in Derrida's 1964–65 seminar, see previous note.

24   See also Jean-Luc Nancy, 'Abandoned Being', in *The Birth to Presence*, trans. by Brian Holmes (Stanford, CA: Stanford University Press, 1993), pp. 36–47. Equivalent readings could have been performed by substituting exposure (*Aussetzung*) with either the de-posing (*Ent-setzung*) of positing (*Setzung*) or with its trans-posing (*Über-setzung*). Hamacher writes: 'Translation [*Übersetzung*] is the exposition of languages in language [...]. In it, language exposes positing itself and being as the position of another being — or of another as being — which for its part presents itself not positively, [...] but rather only as the movement of this ex-posure [*Aus-setzung*] and de-posing [*Ent-setzung*] of positing [*Setzung*].' Werner Hamacher, 'Intensive Languages', trans. by Ira Allen and Steven Tester, *MLN*, 127.3 (April 2012), pp. 485–541 (p. 536). In this regard, see also Heidegger's discussion of the *Grundstimmung* of *Entsetzung*, Benjamin's work on translation, on the *Entsetzung* of the law, Paul's *katargēsis*, Agamben's destituent potential, and so forth.

a subject in the first place, and only as ex-posed, disrupted
language and understanding is there anything like language or
understanding at all.[25]

The guiding question of this essay, the question of the weathering of
the trace, is then inseparable from that of the event of the weather, of
the *factum* of language. The two questions point, albeit in opposite directions, to one and the same matter, to the constitutive impossibility to
think within language either an *archē anypothetos* or the anhypotheticity of a lack of *archē*. This rift within language, this internal fissure,
is not to be taken as an infinitely distant boundary that establishes a
limit with the real, but as the remnant of an encounter, the mark of the
loss that language has had to sustain in order to constitute itself, the
sacrifice through which language has had to make itself *sacer*, through
which language has had to abandon itself. The impossibility to think
the weathering of the trace and the failure to think the event of language *are* — finally without any metaphoricity — the real, the Other
exposed to the Other, language exposed to itself:

> The auto-parekbasis of language as such. It is the movement
> that leaps out of the uncontainable excess of speaking over
> the spoken, of positing over every positivity, of the act of
> positing over its fixation in the position of subjectivity. [...]
> Language speaks as absolute ex-position: as *ekbasis*, as excess,
> interruption, and opening up.[26]

There can be no trace 'itself' and there can be no *autos* 'itself'.

IV

The urgency of the question at stake is seen to both propel the analysis
forward and to put a halt to it — precisely for a lack of time. Had the
question not been so urgent, one could have articulated the same logic,
one could have attempted to apply the same change of coordinates

---

25   Hamacher, 'Premises', p. 16.

26   Hamacher, 'Position Exposed', p. 254. Parekbasis marks the speech that the chorus
      would give to the people in the middle of the play by stepping out (*ekbasis*) of the
      piece and of the limits of the proscenium, 'a complete interruption and *Aufhebung* of
      the play'. See ibid., p. 248.

between the trace and the event of language, along other axes: following the guideline of language, concerning the performativity of the performative and the sacrament of language; following the guideline of the law, through the two readings of 'Before the Law'; following the guideline of the name, concerning the inscription of the trace in every proper name and the lack of a name for the name; following the question of matter, the question of the *khōra*; following the guideline of the promise, the question of messianism, both between Derrida and Agamben and between Derrida and Benjamin; following many other guidelines.[27] But had the questions not been so urgent, one would have had no reason to follow these guidelines to begin with. My own promise then, urgently.

We have already heard Agamben claiming that the experience of language that has structured our tradition, an experience that when made non-thetically thematic constitutes the sought after *archē anypothetos* — this experience of language is that of an immediate mediation. Said otherwise, language *as* the medium that gives access must itself be immediate, it can posit something only insofar as it is itself not posited. Were that not the case, rather than letting the existent come forth, it would hinder this process by its own obtrusiveness, it would itself appear and conceal the existent. With the assistance of a number of eminent predecessors, let us designate this conception of language by the epithet 'weak', or, equivalently, by the epithet 'little' — not comparatively, as opposed to a strong one, but absolutely so:

---

27   For what concerns the question of the performative see, e.g., Jacques Derrida, *Specters of Marx: The State of the Debt, the Work of Mourning, and the New International*, trans. by Peggy Kamuf (London: Routledge, 1994) and Giorgio Agamben, *The Sacrament of Language: An Archaeology of the Oath*, trans. by Adam Kotsko (Stanford, CA: Stanford University Press, 2011). For the reading of Kafka see Jacques Derrida, 'Before the Law', trans. by Avital Ronell and Christine Roulston, in his *Acts of Literature*, ed. by Derek Attridge (London: Routledge, 1992), pp. 181–220, and Giorgio Agamben, *Homo Sacer: Sovereign Power and Bare Life*, trans. by Daniel Heller-Roazen (Stanford, CA: Stanford University Press, 1998). For the question of the name and of the *khōra*, see Jacques Derrida, *On the Name*, trans. by David Wood, John P. Leavey, Jr., and Ian McLeod (Stanford, CA: Stanford University Press, 1995) and Giorgio Agamben, '*Pardes*: The Writing of Potentiality', in *Potentialities*, pp. 205–19. For an attempt at the question of the promise, see Damiano Sacco, 'Highest Openness: On Agamben's Promise', in *Openness and Medieval Culture*, ed. by Manuele Gragnolati and Almut Suerbaum (Berlin: ICI Berlin Press, forthcoming), and references therein.

This movement of language from the withdrawal, this non-positional and presuppositionless language of freedom, is, according to one possible reading of Schlegel's note, 'little'. It does not show an object that would be little but shows 'how little' its showing is and thus shows that there is language.[28]

And again:

The 'weakness' of *logos* [*to tōn logōn asthenes*, Plato's Seventh Letter 343a1] therefore consists precisely in the fact that it is not capable of bringing this very knowability and sameness to expression; it must transform the knowability of beings that is at issue in it in a presupposition.[29]

And again:

To this presupposing structure of language corresponds the specificity of its way of being, which amounts to the fact that it must remove itself in order to make the named thing be. This is the nature of language Duns Scotus has in mind when he defines the relation as *ens debilissimum* and adds that it is for this reason so difficult to know. Language is ontologically very weak, in the sense that it cannot but disappear in the thing it names, otherwise, rather than designating or unveiling the thing, it would hinder its comprehension.[30]

And again:

As Meister Eckhart writes, if the form through which we know a thing were itself something, it would lead us to its knowledge and turn away from the knowledge of the thing. The risk of being itself perceived as a thing, and of separating us from what it should reveal to us, is until the end consubstantial with language. Not being able to say itself while it says other things, that is, its being always ecstatically in the place of the other, is the unmistakable signature and, at the same time, the original taint of human language.[31]

---

28   Hamacher, 'Position Exposed', p. 259.
29   Agamben, 'The Thing Itself', p. 33.
30   Agamben, *What Is Philosophy?*, pp. 9–10.
31   Ibid., p. 10.

The event of language constitutes an *archē anypothetos* by virtue of the weakness of language, that is, by virtue of the impossibility of making thetic by means of language while, at the same time, making language itself thetic. The aim of this essay has been to argue that the weakness of language, its presuppositional economy and the ex-position or trace that inscribes this economy are coextensive and indissociable from one another.

Firstly, the weakness of language entails a presuppositional economy. Every positing, by virtue of its very being a *weak* positing, cannot be posited insofar as it is positing — it therefore *points to* a presupposed that must have posited it: a presupposed that can be itself weakly posited, thus pointing to a new presupposition.

Secondly, the presuppositional economy has always been exposed to the inscription of the trace. The dialectics of positing and presupposing takes place only by virtue of the *écart* that separates the posited from the presupposed before the latter has been posited and a full difference has been constituted between the two — an *écart* that is in fact a self-spacing of positing itself.

Thirdly, the trace or ex-position of positing entails that positing is always weak positing. Positing, as ex-posed positing, is always inhabited by a self-spacing that distances positing and the presupposed that must have posited it. This self-spacing of positing precludes positing from positing itself — it makes positing weak.

There is therefore no presupposition or condition of possibility to the economy of presupposition (by anhypotheticity), but rather only a quasi-presupposition, a condition of possibility that, according to the logic of the quasi-transcendental, is, at the same time, a moment of impossibility in the economy that it itself makes possible. Positing is weak positing and positing is ex-posed positing. Or, to repeat Hamacher's words: 'Positing is exposed positing; abandoned by itself, it is thus ex-position.' It is then quite clear that the task can be neither that of finding a prior presupposed to either version of anhypotheticity nor that of uncovering the hidden ground of the trace. The very quest for what the trace has secretly presupposed or pre-excluded is then irrevocably bound to fail from the start: the logic of presupposition itself is inscribed by the ex-position of the trace and there can be no presupposed to an *archē anypothetos*.

V

Is this then the whole story? Once again, as for Hegel, Heidegger, Derrida, and Agamben, the limits of a certain history and of a certain experience of language have been traced, a new end has been marked: the end of the history of philosophy, of the history of being, of the history of presence, of the history of a certain experience of language. And yet, every time a closure is declared, the very performance of this gesture seems to backreact on the closure itself, and to propel its movement one step forward: to a certain extent, the history of philosophy has not ended with Hegel only because Hegel has marked its end. Is it then possible that the destruction and deconstruction of presence might have not left presence unaffected — that the exposition of positing might have not left positing itself present in the same way? Said otherwise, is there a potential for the system of *Setzung-Aussetzung-Voraussetzung* to affect itself, or to be affected — but, of necessity, neither in the simple mode of an auto-affection nor in that of a hetero-affection?

The positing of all intentionality, be that linguistic, technical, or phenomenological, operates according to a certain notion of accountability of the medium or contribution that gives rise to the order of presence of positing. As soon as intentionality posits a certain order of presence, the accountability of the contribution that gives rise to this positing *points* to the presupposed of this order of presence: a presupposed that corresponds to the subtraction of the contribution of the linguistic, technological, or phenomenological mediation, and thus reaches a non-linguistic, external, in-itself presence. The first two paragraphs of the Introduction to the *Phenomenology of Spirit* present this notion of accountability for what concerns the mediation that we are to have with the Absolute, taking as model either the active reshaping operated by an instrument on a thing ('it is obvious that the use of an instrument [*Werkzeug*] on a thing [*Sache*] certainly does not let it be what it is for itself, but rather sets out to reshape and alter it')[32] or the passive transmission operated by light ('a more or less passive medium through which the light of truth reaches us, then

---

32   G. W. F. Hegel, *Hegel's Phenomenology of Spirit*, trans. by A. V. Miller (Oxford: Oxford University Press, 1977), §73, p. 46. See also Levinas's discussion of these two technolo-

again we do not receive the truth as it is in itself, but only as it exists through and in this medium').[33] This conception of the medium that affords intentionality or positing — once again language, the hand, light — is the target of the destruction and deconstruction of presence, of the constant presence (*beständige Anwesenheit*) that underlies even the restlessness of Spirit. Most certainly, one should hasten to point out that Hegel proceeds to argue that this conception of the instrumentality of cognition is completely inadequate to think the Absolute, that we cannot learn how to swim before venturing into the water, and so forth: we must rather *presuppose* the Absolute and cognition *not* to be separated and in need of *external* mediation to begin with. It is nevertheless the case that Hegel, in order to set off the logic of presupposition, considers only the accountable mediation between two present 'things' — even in the case of the Absolute itself: 'If we subtract from a reshaped thing what the instrument has done to it, then the thing [*Ding*] — here the Absolute — becomes for us exactly what it was before this consequently superfluous effort.'[34]

This notion of mediation comes to lose its status of accountability once philosophy — or perhaps, as Agamben would have it, 'centuries of humble analysis and grammatical education' —firmly establishes the lack of any hierarchically prior element that would be able to structure and complete the differential chain of mediations: there is neither a 'transcendental (or, rather, transcendent) signified' that would afford a linguistic value to every signifier nor a first being that would afford an 'ontological' value to all beings. The mediation or contribution that brings about presence is then revealed as being neither accountable nor, let alone, transparent or diaphanous. The import of the medium that brings about presence cannot be determined by any meta-element, it can be neither accounted for nor be disregarded: the contribution of the medium that pro-duces presence is, crucially, *a priori unaccountable*. Unaccountable means that presence is brought about or pro-duced through a contribution that is neither null nor accountable, but rather one that is to remain structurally undetermined

---

gical/optic metaphors in Emmanuel Levinas, *Otherwise than Being, or, Beyond Essence,* trans. by Alphonso Lingis (Dordrecht: Nijhoff, 1981), p. 17.

33 Hegel, *Phenomenology of Spirit,* §73, p. 46.

34 Ibid., §73, pp. 46–47; translation modified.

— for to account for it one would need to resort to an additional unaccountable mediation. The contributions of language, of the hand, of light, in bringing about presence cannot be determined: there is no distillation procedure through which the contribution could be isolated and subtracted from presence in order to restore, or at least infer, a self-presence anterior to the contribution of the medium. In the order of unaccountable presence, it becomes impossible to separate what is medium, and what is substance; what is for-us, and what is in-itself; what is described, and what is constituted. Crucially, the unaccountability of the medium precludes the subtraction of the contribution that has brought about the order of presence — a subtraction that would otherwise point towards the presupposed as to a non-linguistic and self-present hypostasis. There is no substratum that is changed by a relation, but only a relation that bars the substratum.

If on the one hand the contribution of the medium cannot be subtracted to infer a prior order of self-presence that would precede the mediated presence, it is nevertheless the case that positing, in taking place, still points to the site of its emergence, to the site of a presupposition. But since it is not an order of presence that can be presupposed, since a presupposed presence is actually barred by positing itself, the minimal determination that can be taken to precede the order of unaccountable presence is then one of potentiality: a tendency or liability for events of presence to arise through unaccountable contributions. This potentiality is in no way a determination of a substratum or an attribute of a self-present substance, but rather a possibility *for* determinations and attributes to come to presence. This order of potentiality, then, quite clearly neither 'is' nor 'is not': it is presupposed by the order of unaccountable presence only to the extent that the 'sub' of this pre-*sub*-position cannot be said to participate in the self-presence of a substratum, hypostasis or *hypokeimenon*. On the other hand, the order of unaccountable presence can be said 'to be' only to the extent that the mark 'is' now comes to signal a presence that cannot be disjoined from the medium that has produced it. The shift at stake is not simply one between two modes of saying or gathering the existent: from a saying according to a notion of substance and attributes (*kata ta skēmata tēs katēgorias*) to a saying according to potentiality and actuality (*kata dynamin / kata energeian*), as dictated by Aristotle.

It is rather a shift in the horizon of presence that underlies as much *dynamis* as *energeia*, as *ousia*, as *metabolē*, as *kinēsis*, and so forth — a shift that displaces each and every of these concepts. Metaphysical presence, constant presence, is in turn promised by the order of potentiality and barred by the order of a shifted actuality, but, as such, it is never attained.

Crucially, the shift from constant to unaccountable presence breaks neither with the weakness of language nor with the economy of presupposition and ex-position of the trace: the order of presence of the posited and of the presupposed is changed by the inscription of the trace *while* respecting the generalized economy of positing, presupposing, and ex-posure. Positing takes place in a different order of presence, but as weak and self-spaced positing, it still points to a 'presupposed' — a presupposed that is not reached by the subtraction of an accountable contribution, but one that, by virtue of the very impossibility of this subtraction, cannot be said to enjoy an autonomous self-presence: as such, the order of the presupposed is not that of a self-present substratum, but that of a potentiality for unaccountable presence to take place. In turn, then, the economy affords the positing of this presupposed: a positing that itself can only take place through a new unaccountable contribution and by pointing to a new prior potential presupposed. At each step, the trace of a difference distances the unaccountable positing from its unaccountably potential presupposed. The trace that distances unaccountable presence from its potential presupposed is neither the same nor different from the trace that distances constant presence from itself. It can only be said that the trace respects the presuppositional economy and the principles of anhypotheticity. Weak and unaccountable language — language that in positing cannot be posited and language that entails no transcendent signified or metalanguage — still respects the economy of presupposition, anhypotheticity, and trace. There can be no more originary principle that would account for a change or a weathering of presence and of the trace: the economy of presence and trace has the potential of affecting itself by means of a hetero-affection.

*

After having gone through all the figures of presence, it is presence itself, the order of the posited and of the presupposed — the order of metaphysics — that comes to be shifted. The image in the mirror, the reflected image, is still the same — present. As a present image, it still points to a presupposed of which it is but a reflection. And yet, the destruction and deconstruction of this order of presence have exposed the un-reflectable condition of possibility of reflection itself: the tain of the mirror, the opaque foil that covers the back of the mirror, which, according to Derrida and Gasché, in making reflection possible, cannot itself be reflected. The opaqueness of the tain precludes the closure of all chains of reflection: there can be no close system of self-present substances and reflected images — the tain cannot be reflected. If the system of values of presence and light cannot be determined, then the import, the contribution of light cannot be determined — as Levinas writes: 'A light is needed to see the light.'[35] It is then impossible to separate, in the presence of the image, what is the reflected and what is the reflector, what is the result and what is the medium. The contribution of light does not precipitate at the bottom of the image, it cannot be removed to infer the presence of that which is reflected. 'Before' the reflection there is not something waiting to be altered by light: this retroactive positing is replaced by that of a potentiality that can be actualized through different unaccountable contributions. And yet, the contribution of light is neither null nor infinite, light is neither transparent nor opaque. In turning to see where the light comes from, in positing the presupposition through another light, a new unaccountable presence appears, and with it a new presupposition is assumed. The economy of reflection, the economy of positing and presupposing, is at the same time preserved and transformed. Constant presence and unaccountable presence cannot be distinguished: the image in the mirror is still the same, but one can no longer think of it *as an image of* any substance. The non-linguistic, the non-technological, the non-phenomenological are still shadows and presuppositions of language, of the hand, of experience — but there is no non-linguistic, non-technological or non-phenomenological substance, only possi-

---

35   Emmanuel Levinas, *Totality and Infinity: An Essay on Exteriority*, trans. by Alphonso
     Lingis (The Hague: Nijhoff, 1979), p. 192.

bilities for different languages, different hands, different experiences. The order of presence of the signifier, of the concept, of consciousness are transformed and yet they preserve the economy of positing and presupposing. Presentation and representation can be claimed to persist only if presence itself cannot be accounted for: Hamacher himself puts forward 'the possibility of thinking about understanding no longer as an archi-eschatological self-appropriation, no longer as a making-present, as a presentation or appresentation, but as an always singular alteration and thus an alteration of the very concept of understanding.'[36] In the unaccountability of the present, truth as unconcealment (*alētheia*) and truth as correspondence (*adaequatio*) correspond to one another: *adaequatio* of *alētheia* and *adaequatio*. Equivalently, *adaequatio* is unconcealed: *alētheia* of *adaequatio*.[37]

Whether presence has the potential to change again, whether its unaccountability can change and persist at the same time, how the trace is to weather through it all — the contribution of the question to thinking is neither that of an instrument on a thing nor that of the light for the eye; the contribution of the question to thinking is rather the incitement or soliciting of the potential of thinking to produce further unaccountable questions.

Exposed and abandoned language, lacking a final word, only comes forth in unaccountable presence.

Exposed and abandoned philosophy, lacking an abiding standpoint, only takes place through unaccountable contributions.

Exposed and abandoned weather, lacking an unweathered origin, only takes place through unaccountable weatherings.

---

36   Hamacher, 'Premises', p. 35.

37   Contrast the *alētheia* of *adaequatio* and the *adaequatio* of *alētheia* and *adaequatio* of the order of unaccountable presence with the trace between *alētheia* and *adaequatio/homoiōsis* in the order of constant presence. See e.g. Jacques Derrida, *Dissemination*, trans. by Barbara Johnson (Chicago: University of Chicago Press, 1981), p. 192. It is perhaps to be remarked that Derrida will have remained silent throughout this essay. But then again, the question at stake has been that of the impossibility for the trace to render justice to itself, a question addressed most evidently not in order to find the what or the who that could render justice to the trace, but with the aim of halting that very search.

Glaze
Or Formulas to Get through Bad Weather
UMUT YILDIRIM

On the condition that my words will fully be considered, I can announce the evidence that I rely on.

The fact that a shadow — too engulfed in an apprehension as dark as rotten flesh to tend to my shortness of breath, kindly caressing my hair while I followed him up the two-foot stairs of the dark corridor — recommends that I not be afraid, certainly counts as evidence! Buried shadow. Huh. shad. ow. Huh huh shadow. Huh.

Hahahahah hah ha huh. Some shadow! I know from his rapid heartbeat, his dilated pupils and his tobacco breath, that there is no shadow. He is my corpulent, yet quite young father and, according to him, a burglar has broken into our modest rental house. I no longer remember which, since we moved so many times.

It happens. They always break in. Each time, the light oozing down the corridor (from where the apartment door, which is meant to be closed, has been broken) becomes sensory evidence and makes my father say, 'A burglar has broken in.' My father turns into a shadow, and then something happens to his pupils. Because every time he becomes a shadow, I turn into a Cyclops who can predict the future with an adventure-craving weariness, I drop my backpack from my shoulder with a huff. This is what will happen next: my father will pick up my bag, hold my hand, and with a nervous smile he will say, 'Come on, darling!'. In quick little steps, he will take me outside, somewhere he deems safe, and, without actually commanding me, in a curt hiss between a plea and a recommendation, he will ask me to wait. I will frown because I do not like to wait, or at least I do not like to be made to wait. My father will go into the building and then into our apartment. If there is no burglar, he will come back to where he left me. If there is indeed a burglar, my father will have to heroically eject him from our house.

Throughout the years, I have become convinced that he *can* expel burglars from our house because, now that I think about it, my dearest father Cem would cry while watching Akira Kurosawa films in his early thirties. He gathered bay leaves from inside sea bass, fertilized jasmine, is an admirer of magnolias, and was an Akiraphile Samurai. A samurai! If a burglar, may he die of thirst on the steep stairs of the corridor, knew that he would face a samurai, would he dare break into our home? Not at all. Even if that's true, what if Samur Cem needs help?

On one occasion, when I got tired of waiting, I tried to follow him inside. He picked me up and galloped us away the moment he saw his Cyclops daughter, standing in the beam of light from the open door at the end of the stairs, hoping to help him expel burglars. I must have perceived that he had not appreciated my action, for although he had not yelled at me, never again did I refuse his request to wait outside. He needs to be able to take care of himself. As you can understand, I cannot always save him.

While waiting and thinking about these things, omitting the fact that he would later become intimately attached to Kurosawa in the period of early maturity, which neither he nor I have yet reached, I wake up to his nervous and deep voice, rousing me from my reverie. I find him with a smile freed of anxiety, his hand freed of anxiety extending in a soft gesture to my bored of being bored hair. 'The burglar's gone, sweetheart', he says. High five! I pick up my bag from the floor, he lifts me to his lap, I throw my arms around his neck, and we enter our home.

The burglars do not take anything from the house. We are transient, a Cyclops family of three, and we own nothing of value. Before we came out as Cyclops, we used to receive many visitors: pipes were smoked, books were discussed, guitars were played to loud cheering, and raucous laughter would break out — not that they visit anymore, whatever. It is true that we have our own features and belongings, and it is also true that we have nothing worth stealing. These burglars have been unable to achieve anything other than sticking their bear's feet into our home and breaking our things.

Who are these burglars, and what do they want from us?

[*An underfired piece requires a lot of glazing.*]

~

[*First: it is important to know for which body, temperature, and atmosphere you are mixing the glazing. Weathered glaze bubbles, cracks, and crazes over time.*]

[*Basic glazes: RO, RO_2 {PbO, Na_2O, K_2O, Li_2O, BaO, CaO, MgO, ZnO, SrO}*] We are playing remote tickle. No touching is allowed. Only talking. So we are tickling without touching. While kicking around on the floor, I am yelling, 'Father, stop!' and laughing. He makes up nicknames for me, too. Ö ZÜ is my favourite. It is uttered in this fashion, 'Öööööööööö Zü!'. In the years that followed, many tried to repeat this one and failed, because they were unaware of the original intonation, God bless them. Then, on account of the bread slices I burnt at breakfast one morning, he called me 'Coal-master Mustafa'. But that one did not stick. He called me 'Ruskating', after I referred to Russian figure skating as such. Next, he changed to calling me 'Özika-Honorika-Valentinika-Tatata!'.

He had a moderate sympathy for all things Soviet, the kind that does not recklessly produce hammers and sickles wherever it goes. At first, I thought it was merely a literary and philosophical interest (he loves to read) until he bought me Ilin and Segal's *How Man Became a Giant*, as every socialist does for their offspring. It may have been my first year of primary school. A person is, of course, old enough to grasp materialist philosophy at seven years old. And I had been through a pre-curriculum, which was gently anthropological in its nature. I knew about things like 'worker uncles' and 'worker aunts', 'class', *bourjoya, revolutionanny, communix, anarchix, imperialix,* and fair distribution, not merely from the place they occupied in the lexicon of the militant, but also from personal experience. I have long been aware that bourgeois women who get their hair blow-dried and wear red nail

polish have betrayed our cause, to such an extent that right around that
age, my militant's destiny made me attack my beautiful mother with a
slobbery growl of 'bourjoya' as she sat in the hairdresser's chair.

Later, as I collected Debussy and Schnittke records from the fra-
grant second-hand booksellers in Beyoğlu; as I admired the powerful
fragility of Mümtaz and Nuran's love in Ahmet Hamdi's *Huzur*; as I
looked for C's footprints on Kumbaracı Yokuşu after reading Yusuf
Atılgan's *Aylak Adam*, though I cared little for C's fallen virility; as I was
reading, alternatively, Begoña Aretxaga, Jacques Prévert, J. H. Prynne,
and Audre Lorde in hazy London cafés; as I was cooking mussels with
white wine and sea bass with plums that I collected from Antigoni
Island; as I fell in love with both Sicilian lace and Concrete music; as I
was cloudgazing, doing all these herebys, I would have that militancy
removed. What I mean is, if it is not in the essence of the object, flat-
tening sharpness looks unpleasant on a human being. Therefore, since
most socialists never get the opportunity to have children because
they are murdered, imprisoned, crippled by torture, busy with militant
activities or undergoing a nervous breakdown, as the child of the few
socialists blessed with kids, I quickly neutralize *How Man Became a
Giant* instead of reading it cover to cover as I ought to because my
mind is perpetually in the sea, in hopscotch, in Chinese jump rope,
in dodgeball and in skittle hide-and-seek — I am completely obsessed
with scheming ways to pluck the cherry tree before it is too late in the
year, obsessed with geometry and the logic puzzles of the magazine *Science and Technology* and what not, these type of things. I'm an incurable
romantic. I write poetry.

> Wherefore these falling leaves?
> And, why these endless pains?
> Why is it that I miss you,
> Every day, once anew?

[*Amphoteric glazes:* R_2O_3 $\{Al_2O_3, B_2O_3\}$] With my hair in a twist
from distance-flirting, and my collar unstarched on my throwaway
school uniform, as a seven year-old *je t'aime*, I sense it! Samur would
get me started on Ilin and Segal, then he would destroy me with
brick-sized ova-evski books, and, good God, he would prepare me for
Poulantzas or something! Since my vigilant, golden-hearted mother

Roza swore to protect her offspring from anything unexpected, she has herself became a panther, subject to the unexpected. She would protect me from reading banned books. However, concerning these matters, there's no trusting Samur — he will just throw a book in front of you, you may read it with interest just because it came from Samur. So, what do we learn? Since he knew so much about these things, Samur would keep these bricks away from me. I am a militant girl-child. If a sister is the kind of comrade with whom one cannot voluntarily and openly make love, a child is the kind of comrade who thankfully goes unnoticed as such. I must take measures, as you will appreciate.

[*Acidic glazes: RO_2 {SiO_2, SnO_2, TiO_2, ZrO_2}*] Özika-Honorika-Valentinika-Tatata! He really likes this nickname. Although it is really long, he can repeat it without getting bored. He bursts into a crescendo of laughter at the Tatata. He is wildly happy! I laugh it off. As you know, there's no use in being a child around a child. I let him act like a rascal because he has suffered a lot, though I am not entirely sure why and how. I may have developed this opinion because his heart went boom boom BOOM BOOMM while moving up the steep stairs of the dark corridor. And when the burglars came, something would happen to his pupils. My eyes are on Samur. Though he does not realize it, I know that I need to protect him. That's why my eyes are on myself.

~

[*In addition to the raw materials used in glazes, there are also metal oxides that will render them impervious to crackling effects of weathering. During the development of the glaze at high temperatures, these oxides fulfil various functions.*]

[*Glassifiers: SiO_2, B_2O_3*] Hrrr hrrrrr harh h h h h haaaarrhhhh rah rah rah hhh h. The shadow is running quickly. The orange street light blends into the sooty black walls — topped with shards of glass — of a sugar factory on a narrow street. Samur is running hhhhrrr haaarh hhhr. He is panting. I'm unable to touch his dark shadow. I can't tell if it's him who is running, or if his shadow has taken over him. The silhouette looks like Samur: his athletic body, his longish hair, his turtleneck sweater and bellbottom pants, his long-fingered hands extruding from his jacket. That is Samur! I am not sure. That is Samur! He is running.

Others are running after him. Samuhhhr hhhhhh haaarhg is running.
The others are right behind him: tap TAP clump CLUMP! Samur runs.
They can't catch him.

[*Fusers and stabilizers, respectively: Na_2O, K_2O, Li_2O, PbO, B_2O_3;*
CaO, MgO, BaO, Al_2O_3, PbO, ZnO] On that day, when they arrived
in one of the working-class neighbourhoods where I grew up, in a
manner unbefitting a samurai, the policemen put Samur into their van,
pressing his head down and twisting his long swan's neck. Unlike what
happens in the recurring running dream that has been haunting me for
years, Samur failed to turn into a shadow. He was caught. While huge-
legged and larger-bellied old women stood behind the van, saying:
this happened and that happened, so it happened, ah is that what
happened, did this happen, it did so happen, with my football in hand,
dressed in my shorts and standing on tiptoe, I tried to create a view
through the what-a-shame, what-a-pity hips that blocked me. Finally,
I saw my father. Waving at me from the window, he looked more
perplexed than I had ever seen him. He was gesticulating. I'll be back
tonight, he said. We will cook before my mom comes home. My father
cooks and does the dishes. I wipe them dry. I'm not tall enough yet to
reach the kitchen cupboards and put them away.

[*Matte glazes and opacifiers, respectively: ZnO, TiO_2, CaO, BaO;*
SnO_2, $ZrSiO_4$, ZrO_2, TiO_2] Oh Samur from the window, from the
police van, from the world that twisted your swan's neck, why do you
wave? Why can't I come with you? Alright. I'll wait if I must. But Samur,
under these conditions, as we both know you may never come home.

[*Crystallisers: ZnO, TiO_2, CaO, Cr_2O_3*] Her face whitewashed and
grey, my mother comes. She is about to break, and yet she listens to the
women talking, as though the events they speak of have no connection
to us. I hide under her coat. Samur does not come home that night.
With hope, I wait for him. He does not come home for another week.
I could not protect him. My tears flow dry, and my neck twists, like an
intensely green leaf that gently lands on the ground as it gets too heavy
for her huge palm tree.

~

Then his long fingers were all warped
crooked, gnarled smitten smitten
the devil got into his hangnails
the nail enveloped his soul
his teeth retreated into their gums and fell off.
In the end, his nose got hairy
his hands were all tied
Then he got a hump
his feet shuffle and stumbled as he walked
his breath faded
his fingers turned yellow
ether, he became ether
Samur went from bad to worse.

The revolution collapsed, and melancholy ate my father up. Samur settled into a regime of glorious, self-involved pain. Sadness penetrated Samur, the radiant child, the dissenting genie, the rebel boy fallen in love with black bile. The bile scorched him and burned him. The bay leafs wilted, the jasmines faded, the magnolias fainted, the lemons sagged. And Samur unleashed his anger on everyone.

~

While Samur fell in love with black bile, and burglars kept pillaging our home, I started my second year at a new primary school. Pretty Erol, who died from heroin when he was seventeen, and his mother, Nigâr Hanım Teyze, who forced the neighbourhood indoors on Friday nights when she cooked tripe, and her daughter, Melek Abla, whose scarred face was said to be warped from walking on hot embers during the evening call to prayer; the alcoholic former-policeman, Mr. Dipstick whose name I cannot recall, and his wife the porcelain fiend, Çiçek Hanım Teyze, who he regularly beat; the cheerful mother of three daughters and one son, Mavi Hanım Teyze, who slept with neighbour-hood men for pocket change while her husband laboured in Libya, and their daughters, the malicious Hülya, the evil-eyed Oya, and the supple Nida, who was so educated and graceful that she did not appear to belong to her family; the donkey-eyed and very smart daughter of Muzaffer Hanım Teyze from apartment 10, Selma Abla, who always had a book; and the oldest of the seven children in apartment 9, Pınar Abla, who Selma eternally loved, the only girl in the neighbourhood

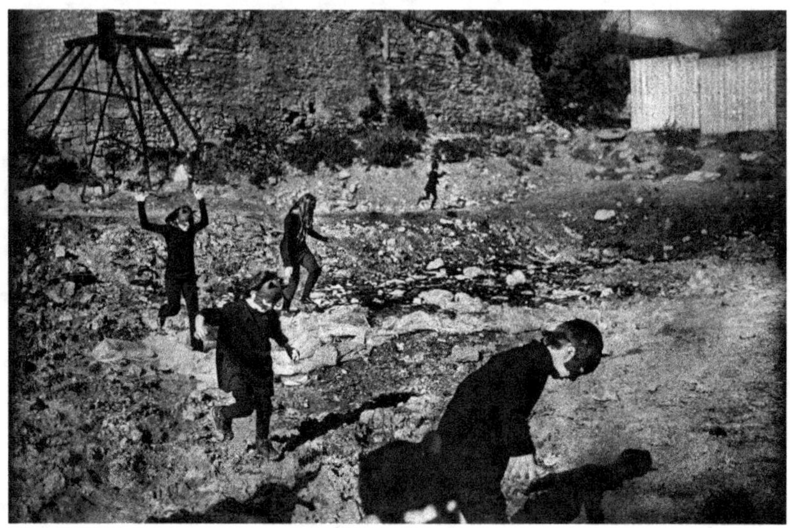

Yusuf Sevinçli, *Post 023-Istanbul*, 2012, courtesy of the artist.

to attend university — I was transferred to a primary school in the council estates of an ancient Istanbul slum that embraced these people and many other similar ones.

Occasionally, the adolescent boys, who communicated by transmitters, played us songs from Orhan, Müslüm, Fikret, the Eagles, and Chicago. The tunes would get under my skin while we ran around in the sun with my friends among the oleaster, plum, mulberry, and cherry trees, and later, in the poppy fields, we heard arabesque melodies when we took off on flying horses. We escaped the tables of evening drinkers who lived in derelict houses, a bit further away, with curiosity, we poked our noses into the gypsy neighbourhood. Is there anything more pleasant than being surprised? Every child should run free in the streets. Here we are with our heads miles above the clouds, our gravity-hating knees covered in wounds. In those years, when everything was a wonder, I forgot about Samur. And the burglars. For ten years or so.

~

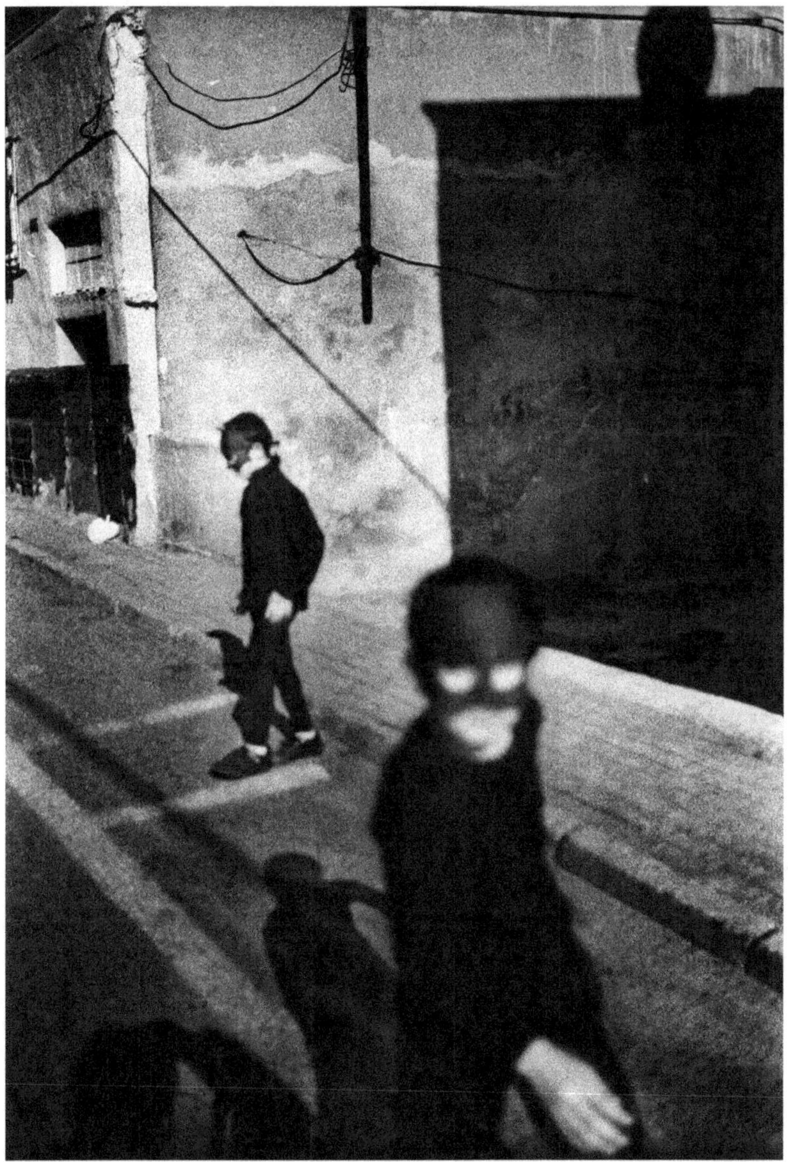

Yusuf Sevinçli, *Post 024-Istanbul*, 2012, courtesy of the artist.

[*Weathered glaze can collapse.*]

I am scraping slightly burnt bread slices with a knife, and Samur is setting the table. My mother is frowning calmly at the newspaper. We have never been a family that constantly hangs out together, in close quarters, in each other's hair, on top of each other, in a tangle. We each live in our own space, so when we are together, especially if it happens to be during breakfast at the start of the day, it can be precious and intense — we turn into a political organization. This is a breakfast table organization where the recent political conjuncture is evaluated, literature is discussed, a bit of gossip is exchanged to spice things up, mind you, Samur only learnt how to gossip with a laugh after turning sixty-five, which made us very happy, decisions concerning the household are made, propositions concerning cats, dogs, plants, trees, and human health and development are discussed, criticisms are expressed, voices are raised, tears are shed, laughs are full, and kisses are sweet, and everything is prepared with love. A lot of love.

According to an article in the paper, which my mother left on the table as she went to the door, a person named Abdullah Öcalan, the leader of an organization called the PKK, is a supporter of the Galatasaray football club. So? I think. Two-thirds of the people of Turkey commit this error. Why is this newsworthy? While I am scraping a piece of bread, I ask Samur: 'What's the PKK, Father?'. He gives me a look of disappointment that cannot hide his aspirational agenda. 'What a shame', he says, to no one in particular; yes, he says that, and leaves the table.

He did not have to leave in this manner. Samur had previously taught me the meanings of Kurdistan and Kurdish. On a weekend when I was confused, attempting to understand the concept of absolute borders separating regions and countries that I was fed at primary school, I had asked for his help. He did not make my task any easier. 'This here', he had said, indicating a place called South Eastern Anatolia, 'is an area in our country. But this place, according to some, is the northern part of a place called Kurdistan.'

    — Why has it been drawn like this, as though it has always
        been this way?
    — To make it easier.

> — It's not easy. If it is both this way and that way, why is it only
> drawn like this? Who is drawing these borders? Who
> is filling in their insides?
> — Well, borders are not absolute; they can change.
> — (Though I felt that the *imperialix* and the bosses were
> involved in this mess, I did not stray off topic.) How
> can they change?
> — Referendum.
> — (Yay! An unfamiliar word!) How does that work?
> — The people who live there can change the boundaries
> through democratic means if they so desire.

At first it seemed plausible. Democracy. I knew about that. It meant that workers would be happy. Other than kids, but not counting my classmate, Serkan Dal, who worked as a shoeshine boy, everyone I knew worked: my mother, my granny, Samur. All the adults I knew worked, or were looking for work, so all adults should be happy. But what would happen to Serkan Dal? Someone is always left out. Alright, let's focus: all creatures on earth live inside these borders, cats and dogs, granny's geraniums, even the imagination-deficient people who drew the borders and filled in their insides. Serkan Dal as well. (Although Serkan Dal did not want to work, and in that case, he may not have had any connection with a democracy that made people happy, and he may not have had any connection with the referendum, therefore what was supposed to happen to the happiness of those who did not work and who did not want to work?) Argh, I could not wrap my head around it. If we leave Serkan Dal to the side, (but how could we leave him out? We shared a desk. And I know he wants to smash his shoe-shine brush into five pieces on the floor. CRACK!) While thinking through this puzzle of democracy, my teacher's voice startled me, asking what we learned over the weekend. I blurted out, 'Referendum!' and was sent home for the day. So, what? I threw my schoolbag to the ground and climbed the cherry tree, getting in my practice before summertime.

As Samur returned to the table with tea, and my mother returned with toast, I do not know what it is that touched me, but I could not contain myself:

> — You should not have left me with Mama Rezzan.
> — Why do you mention Mama Rezzan now?

— You can't be cross with me, Dad. I can be cross with you.

— You don't say! And why is that?, said Samur.

— There's something. If I feel so…

— What does Mama Rezzan have anything to do with this?

— Oh dear!, said my mother. She was a very important, very lovely person. A bit on the opportunistic side, a bit of a revisionist, but that's fine.

— You should not have left me with Mama Rezzan.

— Özgür, what are you saying?

— They shot up the place.

— What are you saying?

— You weren't there when the fascists fired, only Mama Rezzan and I were home. She shoved me under the table. That's why we made it out alive.

— Darling, what are you saying?

— Özgür, for god's sake. Is such a thing possible?

— Of course, it's possible! Plus, that day, as the military police came in to apprehend you, weren't you the one who handed me over to Süheyla Abla who was sleeping inside, oblivious to the event? Süheyla Abla and I made it out alive because we were hiding behind the sofa!

The choir continues rehashing the same motifs: My child, what are you saying? My child, is it possible? My child, where does this come from now? While they keep trying to prove that these two tales are not real as I would come to understand and accept in the upcoming years, I am turning inside out with a gurgling sound, to-the-point-of-no-return. I explode like a fire:

— And who were those burglars!? What did they want from us!?

[*Glazing gives the body to which it is applied a shiny and smooth surface. Since it forms a non-conductive barrier, it protects the body from weathering, insulating it. The glazing also provides mechanical resistance and electrical isolation. It protects the body from acids, bases, scratches, and impacts. It ensures hygiene, prevents the proliferation of microorganisms and limits their actions. It prevents dirt build-up and ensures easy cleaning. It brings colour and textural features to the surface and increases the aesthetic value of the object.*]

TRANSLATED FROM TURKISH BY UMUR ÇELIKYAY

LAYERS

Weathering Weather
Atmospheric Geographies of the Guiana Shield
YOLANDA ARIADNE COLLINS

INTRODUCTION

As the climate changes, so too must our ways of grappling with the interconnectivities that it lays bare. Increasingly, artistic and academic renderings of climate change are demonstrating the need for human beings to rethink, restate, and reshape their connections to their environments.[1] A subset of these renderings has turned towards the weather to identify the shared atmospheric and lived experiences it orients and engenders.[2] Weather, along with its associated processes of weathering

---

1   Yolanda Ariadne Collins, 'How REDD+ Governs: Multiple Forest Environmentalities in Guyana and Suriname', *Environment and Planning E: Nature and Space*, 3.2 (2020), pp. 323–45 <https://doi.org/10.1177/2514848619860748>; Robert Fletcher, 'Environmentality Unbound: Multiple Governmentalities in Environmental Politics', *Geoforum*, 85, Supplement C (2017), pp. 311–15 <https://doi.org/10.1016/j.geoforum.2017.06.009>; Malcolm Miles, 'Representing Nature: Art and Climate Change', *Cultural Geographies*, 17.1 (2010), pp. 19–35 <https://doi.org/10.1177/1474474009349997>.

2   Tim Ingold, *The Life of Lines* (Abingdon: Routledge, 2015); Astrida Neimanis and Jennifer Mae Hamilton, 'Open Space Weathering', *Feminist Review*, 118.1 (2018), pp. 80–84; Astrida Neimanis and Rachel Loewen Walker, 'Weathering: Climate Change and the "Thick Time" of Transcorporeality', *Hypatia*, 29.3 (2014), pp. 558–75; Christina Sharpe, *In the Wake: On Blackness and Being* (Durham, NC: Duke University Press, 2016); Eliza de Vet and Lesley Head, 'Everyday Weather-Ways: Negotiating the Temporalities of Home and Work in Melbourne, Australia', *Geoforum*, 108 (2020), pp. 267–74 <https://doi.org/10.1016/j.geoforum.2019.08.022>.

and being weathered, which I will explore in its various aspects, is largely taken for granted within scholarship that is most concerned with analysing the spatially differentiated social, cultural, and historical relationship of human beings with their natural environments. The air and the ever-changing atmospheric constellations referred to as weather exist as spaces between physical objects and the human and non-human beings that form the focus of academic analyses within the social sciences.[3] A focus on weather, however, may provide a useful window into how these spaces, along with relationships between human and non-human beings and their natural environments, can be examined.

In line with scholarship that connected the adoption of fossil fuels in the United Kingdom centuries ago to current rising temperatures and melting ice at the earth's South Pole, I suggest that efforts to re-think human-environment relationships must recognize that 'climate change is a messy mix-up of time scales'.[4] The human-environment relationship is simultaneously immediate and futural, grounded and atmospheric, fluid and embedded. This instability acts as an oppositional counterpart to the dominant depiction of climate change and climate policy as a singular, coherent force being rolled out and differentially manifested in spaces and places around the world, managed through coherent logics and top-down governing approaches.[5] Attention to weather, air, and atmosphere in analyses of climate change can challenge these entrenched ways of seeing the world, such as those that bifurcate human beings and nature, while troubling assumptions that enable the dominance of one over the other. This destabilization resonates, for example, with the challenge presented to any 'culture' that is resistant to the incorporation of technological objects by its recognition of some more useful and welcome aspects of said objects.[6]

---

3   Stephen Graham, 'Life Support: The Political Ecology of Urban Air', *City*, 19.2–3 (2015), pp. 192–215; see also Ingold, *The Life of Lines*.

4   Andreas Malm, *Fossil Capital: The Rise of Steam Power and the Roots of Global Warming* (London: Verso, 2016).

5   Karin Bäckstrand and Eva Lövbrand, 'Planting Trees to Mitigate Climate Change: Contested Discourses of Ecological Modernization, Green Governmentality and Civic Environmentalism', *Global Environmental Politics*, 6.1 (2006), pp. 50–75.

6   Gilbert Simondon, *On the Mode of Existence of Technological Objects*, trans. by Cécile Malaspina and John Rogove (Minneapolis: Univocal, 2017).

In what follows, I take natural geographic formations for granted instead of human-imposed borders. I recognize the messy time scales of climate change while challenging the 'false opposition between the local as immobile or grounded and the global as mobile and ubiquitous'.[7] I focus on the term weather(ing), which I define later, in both its geophysical and linguistic registers in the English language. I suggest that one of the possible relationships between weather(ing) and climate change is its operation in, above, through, and on the geological formation called the Guiana Shield, located in the north of the South American continent. In so doing, I tease out its peculiar atmospheric and place-specific qualities. I recognize the interconnectivity of temporalities pointed to by Andreas Malm in *Fossil Capital* but refrain from advocating for a 'collapse (of) any notion of distinct space and time'[8] as do Astrida Neimanis and Rachel Loewen Walker in their programmatic essay on 'Weathering'. My arguments do not represent an attempt to retell the stories told about the earth through the natural sciences. On the contrary, I pursue an answer to the question of how paying attention to the English word 'weather', in both its noun and verb forms, can make the relationship between geological, biological, and social activities perceptible outside of ongoing global efforts by the social to exploit the resources of the biological and geological. I construct an image of a circular atmosphere, which is locally accessible yet locally unbounded, while pushing back on atmosphere's traditional limitation of referring to above-ground relations.[9] Like Neel Ahuja in her essay on 'Intimate Atmospheres', I recognize the atmosphere's 'contradictory figuration as a space of geology and life, and a background that forges exchange between social and physical processes'.[10] Finally, I limit my reflections on the socio-political aspects of weathering to the two independent countries situated within the Guiana Shield, those of Guyana and Suriname.

---

7   Ash Amin, 'Placing Globalization', *Theory, Culture & Society*, 14.2 (1997), pp. 123–37 (p. 131).

8   Neimanis and Loewen Walker, 'Weathering', p. 569.

9   Neel Ahuja, 'Intimate Atmospheres: Queer Theory in a Time of Extinctions', *GLQ: A Journal of Lesbian and Gay Studies*, 21.2–3 (2015), pp. 365–85.

10   Ibid., p. 370.

A POLITICAL ECOLOGY OF ATMOSPHERES

Investigations into the relationship between the international political economy and the environment take place within the tradition of political ecology, which explores the detrimental environmental and social effects of the dominant economic system. It does so by integrating methods from ecological anthropology to examine the role culture plays in these dynamics and interactions.[11] The discipline of political ecology pays significant attention to the relationship between both current and historical international political economy on one hand, and the environment on the other. It focuses especially on the relationship between capitalist and neoliberal endeavours and the societies supporting them.

Political ecology has been strongly critiqued for focusing too much on 'politics' to the detriment of the 'ecology'.[12] In developing this critique, Andrew P. Vayda and Bradley B. Walters argued in *Against Political Ecology* that the tendency of self-styled political ecologists to focus on politics in distant view of the environment assumes a direct connection between politics and environmental change that is not always there. Instead, they suggest that connections between politics and environmental change be sought out and proven rather than determined from the outset as a determining factor in that change.[13] While the now well-established connection between politics and climate change, as an example of environmental change, already challenges the openness to non-political factors advocated for by Vayda and Walters, I suggest that attention to weather(ing) may form a useful addition to the political ecology framework due to the weather(ing)'s simultaneous reference to the earth's natural and physical processes of resilience and change, and to atmospheric constellations of nature and climate change. After all, as noted by political ecologist Raymond Bryant (1998), 'unequal power relations are as likely to be "inscribed" in the air or the water as they are to be "embedded" in the land.'[14]

---

11   Raymond L. Bryant, 'Power, Knowledge and Political Ecology in the Third World: A Review', *Progress in Physical Geography*, 22.1 (1998), pp. 79–94.

12   Andrew P. Vayda and Bradley B. Walters, 'Against Political Ecology', *Human Ecology*, 27.1 (1999), pp. 167–79.

13   Ibid.

14   Bryant, 'Power, Knowledge and Political Ecology in the Third World', p. 89.

'Weather' in its noun form is defined by the Merriam-Webster dictionary as 'the state of the atmosphere with respect to heat or cold, wetness or dryness, calm or storm, clearness or cloudiness; state or vicissitude of life or fortune; and/or disagreeable atmospheric conditions'.[15] The verb 'weather', on the other hand, is defined as 'expos[ing] to the open air: subject to the action of the elements; to bear up against and come safely through; weather a storm or crisis; to undergo or endure the action of the elements; and of or relating to the side facing the wind'.[16] Naturally, these definitions of the weather and the process of weathering have been operationalized in the academic literature in a variety of ways.

Christina Sharpe, writing from the perspective of critical race theory, has conceived of the weather in terms of social climates. For her, the weather is 'the totality of our environments; the weather is the total climate; and that climate is antiblack'.[17] Anthropologist Tim Ingold, in arguing for greater recognition of how the world is shaped by weather, challenged the overreliance of some disciplines, among them anthropology, on 'the hard physicality of the world' as it is described by archaeologist Bjørnar Olsen quoted by Ingold, for understanding environments.[18] He calls into question the manner in which the environment is interpreted and envisaged as a 'clutter of solid objects' ignoring the 'aerial dimension of bodily movement and experience'.[19] He asserts that within the efforts to understand how people engage with the things of the world through analyses — by taking into account the agency of people, the agency of objects, or even hybrid people–object agencies — little attention has been paid to air. In a critique fully extendable to the interdisciplinary framework of political ecology,[20] Ingold states that this is simply because 'within the terms of accepted discourse, air is unthinkable'.[21]

---

15   'Weather', in *Merriam-Webster Dictionary.com* (Springfield, MA: Merriam-Webster, 2020) <https://www.merriam-webster.com/dictionary/weather> [accessed 20 February 2020].

16   Ibid.

17   Sharpe, *In the Wake*, p. 96.

18   Ingold, *The Life of Lines*, p. 69.

19   Ibid.

20   See Graham's 'Life Support' for an exception.

21   Ingold, *The Life of Lines*, p. 69.

Gender and cultural studies theorists Astrida Neimanis and her co-authors, Jennifer Hamilton and Rachel Loewen Walker, see weathering as useful for conveying how climate change is being felt by people within 'the fleshy, damp immediacy of our own embodied existences'.[22] For them, weathering is 'a particular way of understanding how bodies, places, and the weather are all inter-implicated in our climate-changing world'.[23] The authors argue that weathering 'describes socially, culturally, politically and materially differentiated bodies in relation to the materiality of place, across a thickness of historical, geological and climatological time'.[24] Particularly useful here for political ecology is their recognition that 'not all bodies weather the same; weathering is a situated phenomenon embedded in social and political worlds'.[25]

In a radically different use of the term, architectural theorists Mohsen Mostafavi and David Leatherbarrow focus on the weathering of architecture to explain that weathering is not only a subtraction, insofar it destroys that which was constructed, but that it also has to be recognized as adding certain qualities to the weathered artefact. Weathering, in this productive sense, is a process of 'unending deterioration', 'the continuous metamorphosis of the building itself'.[26]

Hence, while furthering engagement with how bodies, places, and the weather are implicated in the climate changing world described by Neimanis and Hamilton and racialized by Sharpe, I join Ingold by looking past the 'hard physicality' of world to follow Mostafavi and Leatherbarrow's recognition of weathering as that which produces and transforms. I interrogate weathering in the Guiana Shield by seeing weathering as:

- Exposing to the open air and subjecting to the action of the elements.

- Becoming deteriorated by excessive exposure to bad weather.

---

22   Neimanis and Loewen Walker, 'Weathering', p. 559.

23   Neimanis and Hamilton, 'Open Space Weathering', p. 80.

24   Ibid., pp. 80–81.

25   Ibid., p. 81.

26   Mohsen Mostafavi and David Leatherbarrow, *On Weathering: The Life of Buildings in Time* (Cambridge, MA: MIT Press, 1993), p. 16.

- To become prominent or isolated by the decay or disintegration of the surrounding rock.

- The breaking down of rocks, soil, and minerals as well as wood and artificial materials through contact with the Earth's atmosphere, water, and biological organisms. Weathering occurs in situ, that is, in the same place, with little or no movement, and thus should not be confused with erosion, which involves the movement of rocks and minerals by agents such as water, ice, snow, wind, waves, and gravity and then being transported and deposited in other locations. [27]

And, as I propose in the sections that follow: 'to influence and generate weather patterns'.

ATMOSPHERE

The weather is an insufficient signifier of the climate. It is overly mutable and short-lived. The significance of the weather in relation to the climate at any given time needs to be determined by situating its occurrence into averages qualified according to a linear timeline. Neimanis and Loewen Walker look to overcome the different temporalities of longer-term climate and shorter-term weather by collapsing them into a conception of 'thick time', seen as 'a transcorporeal stretching between present, future, and past, that foregrounds a non-chronological durationality'.[28] In my analysis of how the Guiana Shield weathers, however, I will retain temporal distinctions and adhere to what might appear to them a rather conventional linear conception of time. I do this because my effort to facilitate dialogue between the social scientific discipline of political ecology and the interdisciplinary concept of weathering requires that the potential for the attribution of responsibility be maintained. Hence, in order for connections to be made cross-temporally and for the responsibility of these actions to be attributed to specific actors operating in particular times and places, the maintenance of the distinctions embedded in linear time

---

27   Vladimir A. Obruchev, *Fundamentals of Geology: Popular Outline* (Moscow: Foreign Languages Publishing House, 1959), p. 75.

28   Neimanis and Loewen Walker, 'Weathering', p. 561.

is paramount. Overall then, I suggest that focusing on the weather and processes of weathering has the potential to bring particular places like the Guiana Shield into view, situating them in the geographic coordinate system of linear latitudinal and longitudinal spatial geographies, much like observations of the weather within climate models, through the ordinary linearity of time that retains its capacity for representing connections between the past and the present. It is through these interactions that atmospheres emerge.

HOW THE GUIANA SHIELD WAS WEATHERED

> From sufficient altitude, the Shield resembles an old weathered island surrounded by flat Tertiary and Quaternary sediments.[29]

Politically, the region known as the Guiana Shield is governed by six states including Colombia, Venezuela, Guyana, Suriname, French Guiana, and Brazil.[30] Geologically, however, the Guiana Shield is known to be a formation that has been stable in geological terms, unaffected by mountain building activity for a thousand million years. A massif of hard Proterozoic rocks, the Shield can mostly be found between the Orinoco and Amazon river basins. Its parental rocks are low in mineral content but are susceptible to high rates of weathering, resulting in poor to very poor nutrient content.[31] This, in turn, results in low nutrient soil since '[s]oil is the layer of weathered material overlying bedrock' that then goes on to support plant life.[32]

The gradual weathering undergone by the Guiana Shield is captured in contemporary art theorist Amelia Groom's evocative description of the process of fragmentation:

---

29   Allan K. Gibbs and Christopher Norman Barron, *The Geology of the Guiana Shield*, Oxford Monographs on Geology and Geophysics, 22 (Oxford: Oxford University Press Oxford, 1993), p. 3.

30   Philippa Haden, 'Forestry Issues in the Guiana Shield Region: A Perspective on Guyana and Suriname', 1999 <https://www.odi.org/sites/odi.org.uk/files/odi-assets/publications-opinion-files/5700.pdf> [accessed 1 July 2020].

31   Ibid.

32   Graham R. Thompson and Jonathan Turk, *Introduction to Physical Geology* (Fort Worth, TX: Saunders College Publishing, 1998).

> Pieces of rock keep multiplying through further breakage, with their insides becoming new outsides. They gradually leave more of themselves behind, acquiring the edges that suggest autonomy and self-containment while moving always into pluralized partiality, via loss, until the undecidable moment where they become sand, the granular representation of time itself.[33]

Through the slow process of loss, multiplication, and transformation, the Guiana Shield has been weathered over millions of years, as it continuously has been shaped by interactions with the elements. Yet the Guiana Shield is representative of weathering not only in terms of the destruction of rock. It also weathers in ways not captured in the literary meaning of the term. The Shield influences weather, as I will show later.

The hard rocks of the Guiana Shield weather as they are subjected to the natural forces they encounter daily, such as heat, rain, water, and wind. The rocks are weathered by weather in combination with plants and minute organisms. On a daily basis, rocks are exposed to sunlight, which heats them intensely. They then cool down over the course of the night. These daily fluctuations in temperature ensure that, during the day, rocks expand and, during the night, they contract. Despite the fact that these expansions and contractions are hardly noticeable to human observers, their repeated occurrence over hundreds and thousands of years take their toll, as rock particles weaken over time.[34]

Water also helps in the work of weathering since porous, multi-cracked rock absorbs more moisture, while solid rocks absorb less. The repeated action of wetting and drying rock also wears down the internal adhesion of the rocks. Water, in particular, contributes to the weathering of rocks because it carries with itself gases from the atmosphere, such as carbon dioxide, which may have been produced by the burning of fuel or the oxidation of various substances. Through water, these gases are put into direct contact with the rocks. The water carrying these gases has a more significant impact on the weathering of rocks than in the case of water in which these gases are not present.

---

33 Amelia Groom, *Beverly Buchanan: Marsh Ruins* (London: Afterall Books, forthcoming in 2021).

34 Obruchev, *Fundamentals of Geology*.

Plant and fungi species also weather rocks as lichens colonize even the smoothest of rocks. Wind carries spores of lichens into microscopic cracks, and/or the rain carries them as they stick together on the surface of rocks. As they germinate, they become firmly lodged in the rocks. Drawing on the moisture they are able to absorb from the rocks, they eventually corrode the rock's surface and widen the cracks that develop there. Grains of sand and dust brought by the wind or water more easily adhere to rock that had been corroded, filling the cracks. Tree roots also cause rock particles to break down, and eventually dust accumulates to such an extent that soil appears, necessary for the growth of further vegetation. The seeds of these plants also fall, through wind and rain, into the cracks and dust in spaces between lichen colonies that are situated on the rocks, eventually germinating.[35]

Vegetation eventually smothers the lichens working their way down into the cracks of the rock, corroding the surface of the rock further. As cracks widen and more dust gathers, along with the remains of dead grass and their roots, a place emerges where shrubs and trees and larger types of vegetation can take root. As they grow, their roots act as wedges, further widening the cracks in the rock. The natural forces of heat, frost, dew, and water affect the internal cohesion of the rock. But further, they help other forces of nature to interact with the rock.[36] As Vladimir A. Obruchev notes, 'from a rock subjected to weathering, the rain washes away liberated grains.'[37] He continues, 'The rain, as it collects in grooves, slowly wears away nicks in the rock. The wind, on the other hand, acts to disperse liberated sand and dust particles and carries them away.'[38] Yet, it is as a result of this process through which the Shield is physically weathered that the Shield is, in turn, able to generate weather itself, as I describe in what follows.

HOW THE GUIANA SHIELD WEATHERS

The Guiana Shield generates and influences the formation of weather patterns through its hydrological function, a role that impacts the well-

---

35   Ibid.
36   Ibid.
37   Ibid., p. 80.
38   Ibid., p. 79.

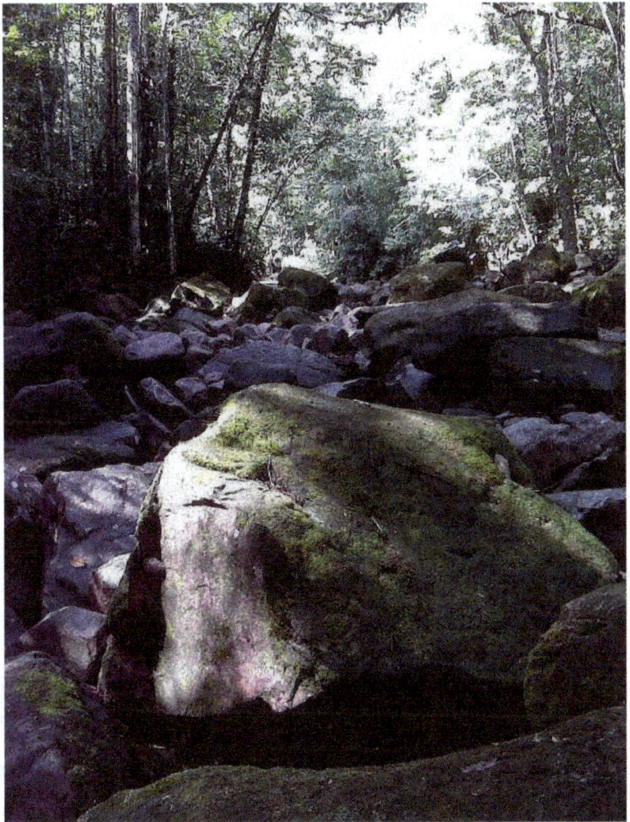

Figure 1. Weathered Rock and Emerging Vegetation in Kaieteur National
Park, Guyana, 2010. Photo credit: Oronde Drakes.

being of the wider Amazon basin, one of the few relatively intact
forest ecosystems on Earth.[39] The weathering of rock over millennia
generated the soil of the Guiana Shield as 'granular representations
of time'[40] within which tropical rainforest was able to take root. The
rainforest that emerged is remarkable in abundance, diversity, and rate
of botanical endemism.[41]

---

39   Haden, 'Forestry Issues in the Guiana Shield Region'.
40   Groom, *Beverly Buchanan*.
41   Haden, 'Forestry Issues in the Guiana Shield Region'.

Focusing on the weather understood as exposure to air and the elements calls to mind a hierarchy between the weather and that being weathered, between that which is above ground and that which is grounded. This hierarchical, layered approach to weathering is downward facing yet expansive. Hence, although the Shield was formed, in part, through this downward facing weathering relationship, its vegetation also produces weather in a manner that signals a reverse upward approach to influencing weather. Their combination is, hence, a circular relationship of different manifestations of weather(ing).

Allan K. Gibbs and Christopher Norman Barron, authors of one of the few academic texts on the geology of the Guiana Shield, refer unwittingly to the unidirectional nature of the forests as they quote an anonymous geologist:

> The close-pressing trees, large and small, instinctively draw one's gaze upward, looking for light. But the crown of the forest, 30–40m above, forms a dense canopy. Only where a forest giant has finally given up the struggle and fallen, dragging down its neighbours in a long roar of sound, only then is there a chance of seeing clear sky, and a place for the geologist to read his [sic] instruments without much difficulty, or to eat his sandwiches beside one of the clear streams that he may be fortunate enough to find.[42]

Forests, by and large, stand upright. As the above-quoted geologist looking for a place to read his instrument finds in the forests of the Guiana Shield, trees grow upward, standing so densely together that the search for cracks of light coming through their overlapping canopies may prove futile. For the single human standing in these forests, the forests are giants, forcing her to gaze upward to see the sky beyond their canopies. While rooted in the soil, forests continually mediate with air, negotiating between the creation and absorption of oxygen and carbon dioxide. Forests are fuelled and nurtured within the vertical space between air and land, remaining horizontally stationary but vertically unconstrained, except perhaps by other trees competing with each other and with the human within them for access to the sun's light.

---

42   Gibbs and Barron, *Geology of the Guiana Shield*.

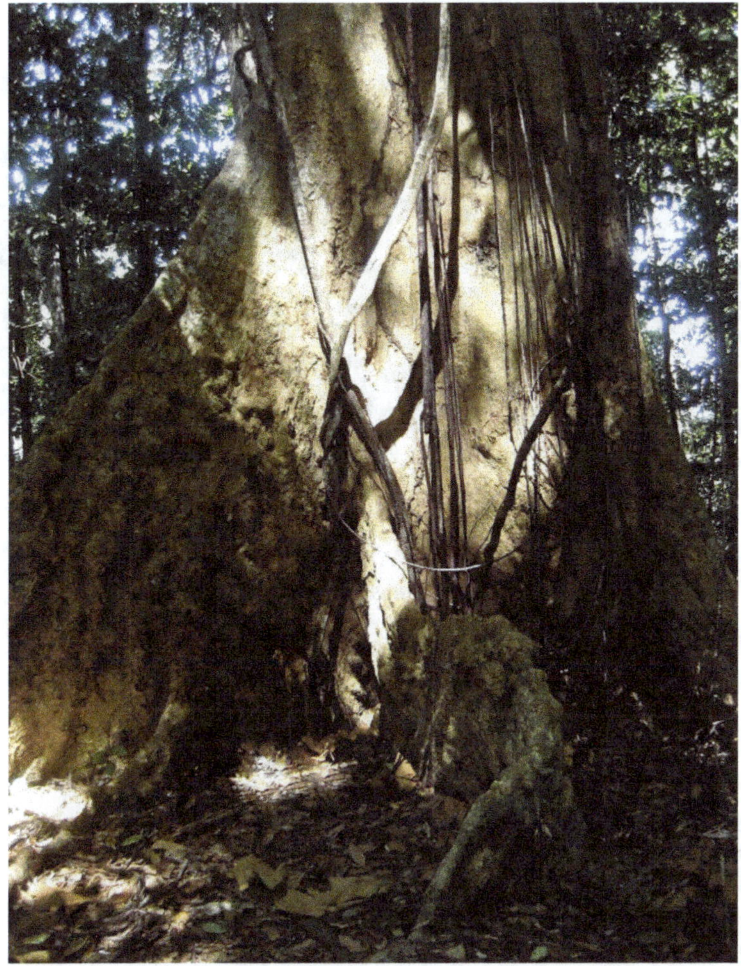

Figure 2. Cracks of Light in the Forests of Brownsberg Nature Park, Suriname, 2014. Photo by author.

The verticality of the forests as they move from soil to atmosphere is more than just visible. Emerging vertically from weathered rock, the forests of the Guiana Shield also *influences* weather. The forests of the Guiana Shield are guardians of the water cycle of the South American continent.[43] As hydrologist Isabella Bovolo described:

---

43   C. Isabella Bovolo, Thomas Wagner, Geoff Parkin, David Hein-Griggs, Ryan Pereira, and Richard Jones, 'The Guiana Shield Rainforests — Overlooked Guardians of South

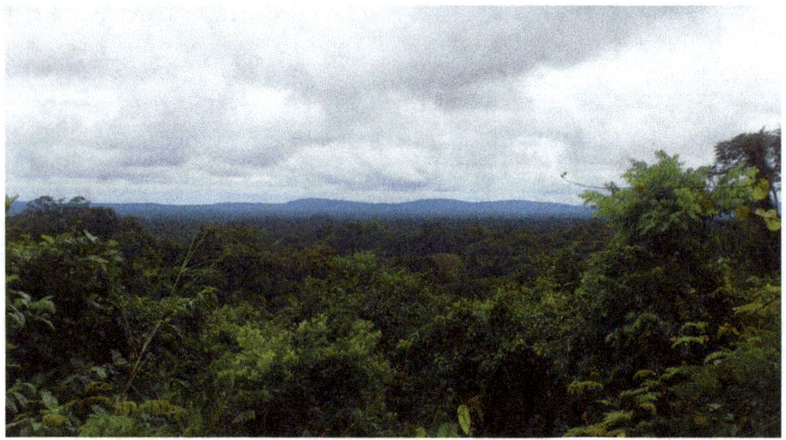

Figure 3. A View of Dense Canopy from a Mountain, Mahdia, Guyana, 2014. Photo by author.

> [D]eforesting less than a third of the Guiana Shield, in areas currently under threat from mining, logging, and agricultural activities, could result in significant changes in the water cycle across the continent. This includes large variations in temperature and precipitation affecting areas 4000 km away, impacting ecosystems and economies, with consequences for society.[44]

Land-use change in the Guiana Shield, 'even if small in spatial scale, but occurring in particularly sensitive hot-spots, can alter the flow of atmospheric rivers, with large consequences'.[45] A focus on the cycles of weather shows that because the Guiana Shield is vulnerable to immense pressure from extractive activity on and within it, its ability to prevent and magnify further climatic changes is reduced.

With the unidirectional connections of geology and atmospheres now outlined, I now turn towards situating these interactions in relation to the actions of the states, people, and colonial histories that magnify and are magnified by these dynamics.

American Climate', *Environmental Research Letters*, 13.7 (2018) <https://doi.org/10.1088/1748-9326/aacf60>.

44   Ibid., p. 1.

45   Ibid.

ABOVE AND BELOW GROUND

Political geographers Adam Bobbette and Amy Donovan point out
that the classical conception of geopolitics saw the concept of the state
as a spatial configuration on the surface of the earth, with the political dramas of sovereign territories playing out across these territorial
surfaces. Bobbette and Donovan highlight that critical geopolitics have
since challenged this framework. Political geographers, they explain,
such as Bruce Braun, Stuart Elden, and Gavin Bridge, have since
thickened the horizontal and classical spatial understanding of the
state by demonstrating how territory claimed by the state is constituted
vertically, showing how 'the depth of political processes extend into
and through the geos'.[46] I take this further, however, by considering
also how the state and its territorialization also has effects that go from
the surface to the atmosphere.

Claims made by states on subsoil and biological life point to
the need for a vertical, perhaps layered, approach to understanding
territory. Similarly, I argue, these claims should be recognized as
continuing upward past the canopies of trees to include the unrelent-
ingly spatially unbounded atmosphere, especially within the effort to
rethink the human-environment relation in view of climate change.
States and their claims on land, life, and atmospheres also have a key
role in discussions of the geological and linguistic registers of weathering. This is because the process of creating the states that now support
the authority with which the governments of Guyana and Suriname
are able to manage sections of the Guiana Shield (including those
'particularly sensitive hotspots' outlined by Bovolo)[47] was made possible through approximately five hundred years of colonialism.[48] This
colonial experience went hand in hand with the development and
expansion of geology as a science. I describe this experience in the
following section.

---

46   Adam Bobbette and Amy Donovan, 'Political Geology: An Introduction', in *Political
      Geology: Active Stratigraphies and the Making of Life*, ed. by Adam Bobbette and Amy
      Donovan (Berlin: Springer, 2019), pp. 1–34 (p. 1).
47   Bovolo and others, 'The Guiana Shield Rainforests'.
48   Sidney Wilfred Mintz, *Sweetness and Power* (New York: Viking New York, 1985).

COLONIAL GEOLOGY

Since the discovery of the land that became Guyana and Suriname, in the late fifteenth century to the early sixteenth century, the people residing on the Guiana Shield have weathered colonial histories and continue, despite the granting of independence in 1966 and 1975, respectively, to endure postcolonial injustices. It is through this colonial experience that the population of Guyana and Suriname came to include non-indigenous groups. The people now residing on the Guiana Shield and within its forests interact with, magnify, and live with the natural and social weathering processes of the Shield.

As '(in)human geographer' Kathryn Yusoff explains, geology is part and parcel of processes of racialization, by no means innocent with respect to the histories of colonialism, slavery, and environmental devastation that rely upon it.[49] This was also partly demonstrated in Gibbs and Barron's *The Geology of the Guiana Shield* cited earlier.[50] Now, almost three decades past its publication date, a re-reading of this book brings into view the way geology, lauded as a noble but unrewarding calling, sweeps aside or even propagates the colonial encounter.

Gibbs and Barron traced geology, recognized as a science in the beginning of the nineteenth century, back to the demand for finding mineral deposits in pre-historic times. Gibbs and Barron note that Alexander von Humboldt ascended the Orinoco in 1800 and discovered the Cassiquiare Canal, 'linking it with the Negro and hence with the Amazon'.[51] The authors describe him as 'truly an example for his present-day successors, and also an example of the many European and North American geologists who gave up the comforts of homes and universities to demonstrate by example the internationality of geology'.[52] In recognizing the geological contributions of Venezuelan nationals in mapping the Venezuelan Amazon, they further describe early gold exploration in Guyana by Dutch mining engineers and John

---

49   Kathryn Yusoff, *A Billion Black Anthropocenes or None* (Minneapolis: University of Minnesota Press, 2018).
50   Gibbs and Barron, *Geology of the Guiana Shield*.
51   Ibid., p. 99.
52   Ibid., p. 10.

Harrison, who discovered Guyana's bauxite deposits. They continued by describing how geological mapping of the then 'colony' of Guyana was tied to the search for base metals. According to Gibbs and Barron, Harrison published 'many papers on the geology of the country, the weathering of its rocks, and finally the miner's bible, "The Geology of the Goldfields of British Guyana", in 1908'.[53]

Notably, Gibbs and Barron draw attention to the fact that, as they put it, the 'Guyanaization of the survey of Guyana's mineral deposits started in 1959, and the first Guyanese director, Dr. S. Singh, was appointed in 1966', the year of Guyana's independence. They continue by explicitly tying geological knowledge to mining, stating that 'Guyana's principal gold deposits was published as "Bulletin 38" by Ronald McDonald', who they describe as an experienced Canadian economic geologist. This Bulletin was instrumental for summarizing the significant data on dozens of old gold mines and workings. It still represents, according to Gibbs and Barron, the '"sourcebook" of prospective mining companies'. On the Surinamese side, which receives substantially less attention in this part of their elaboration, the authors write that 'the "grand old man" of Surinamese geology was undoubtedly IJzerman'. In addition, they recognize that aid in mapping Suriname was provided by Dr. Prem and his team in the Netherlands, Suriname's colonial masters. Gibbs and Barron then tie the development of geological maps and surveys to the large bauxite industry that subsequently developed in Suriname, along with its hydroelectric scheme and 'helpful' petroleum industry.[54]

These developments of geology as a science operationalized, in part, within colonial Guyana and Suriname went hand in hand with the exploitative practices that defined slavery, indentureship, and colonialism in these two countries. These exploitative practices were enacted upon populations who simultaneously weathered them and came to influence the weather in turn, as I will detail next.

---

53   Ibid.
54   Ibid.

THE PEOPLE WHO WEATHER(ED)

The circumstances of forest-dwelling communities in Guyana and Suriname are particularly reflective of the circular nature of weathering, as in withstanding oppressive conditions, and in influencing and generating weather patterns. The indigenous inhabitants of the forests of the Guiana Shield were diverse, spread over at least nine different tribes in Guyana alone. They lived in ways that were considerate of the natural environment but that did not conform to utopian ideas of a harmonious and conflict-free life. Over time, however, as these communities were confronted by European colonizers, they were forced to move away from the Shield's coastal areas. They took up residence deeper in the forests as conflicts with the newcomers arose and escalated. Over the following centuries, the colonizers relocated comparatively vast numbers of people from Africa, Asia, and Europe to work on the plantations they had developed on the coasts.

Those brought to these lands to work forcibly or under exploitative conditions also found ways of rebelling. The maroon communities of Suriname exemplify this rebellion.[55] Maroon communities were established within the rainforests of the Guiana Shield. They are the descendants of formerly enslaved Africans who were brought to labour on the coastal plantations and managed to escape. They fled to the forests and learned how to survive in them partly from the indigenous communities already living there. This escape was by no means peaceful. Wars were frequently waged against the emerging maroon communities whose members made it their mission to attack plantations and to liberate other enslaved people. In the 1760s, peace treaties were signed between the colonizers and the maroon communities, allowing the latter to live autonomously in the forests, prohibiting future

---

55   I opted not to capitalize the words 'indigenous' or 'maroon' because I use these words primarily as adjectives. Maroon and indigenous groups in Guyana and Suriname have their own names and titles that they have used for centuries, for example, the Saramaka in Suriname, now classed as maroon, and the Wapishana in Guyana, now classed as indigenous. In this paper, I pay careful attention to how people brought to and found in the Guiana Shield were labelled by external powers according to the demands of capital accumulation and in the interest of racial hierarchies. I therefore resist the urge to act in a manner similar to that which I critique by cementing the identities of these groups of communities through capitalization according to externally imposed groupings and identities.

settlers from molesting them, and compelling them to respect the customary laws they had established.[56] Maroon communities in Suriname can be said to have weathered forced relocation to unfamiliar lands, attempts to subjugate them to horrific slave systems, and the challenges that came with establishing new, cohesive communities within the forests.

However, Suriname's independence in 1975 did not see maroon and indigenous rights included in the constitution of the new Surinamese state. Indigenous communities had also gained autonomy through peace treaties with the Dutch colonizers. As a result of Suriname's independence, the new Surinamese state claimed and continues to claim the land on which maroon and indigenous communities reside, along with the resources above and beneath that land. Some of the maroon communities were further disadvantaged when a few years prior to the state's independence, a hydropower dam was built by the colonial government. The dam, intended to provide cheap electricity for the industry that intentionally weathered rock by 'multiplying its insides'[57] in the successful search for bauxite, forced the relocation of some maroon communities to land near a modern-day nature conservation park. Again, in unfamiliar environments, those maroon community members turned towards the industry that had magnified their disadvantage, joining the effort to 'multiply the insides of rock'[58] but this time in search of gold. Now, gold mining, known to be the largest driver of deforestation in both Guyana and Suriname, and the related issue of land rights, demonstrate the manner in which these communities both weather (rock) and are weathered (by political climates) cumulatively throughout their lives in the forests of the Guiana Shield. Even Suriname's independent government has recognized the legacy of previous injustices carried out against these maroon communities in granting miners from the communities the right to continue mining for gold within the nearby conservation park. The state government, too, recognizes that these communities also face the challenge of finding

---

56   Marieke Heemskerk, *Rights to Land and Resources for Indigenous Peoples and Maroons in Suriname* (Paramaribo: Amazon Conservation Team, 2005) <http://www.act-suriname.org/wp-content/uploads/2015/02/ACT_land-rights-report-2005.pdf> [accessed 2 August 2017].

57   Groom, *Beverly Buchanan.*

58   Ibid.

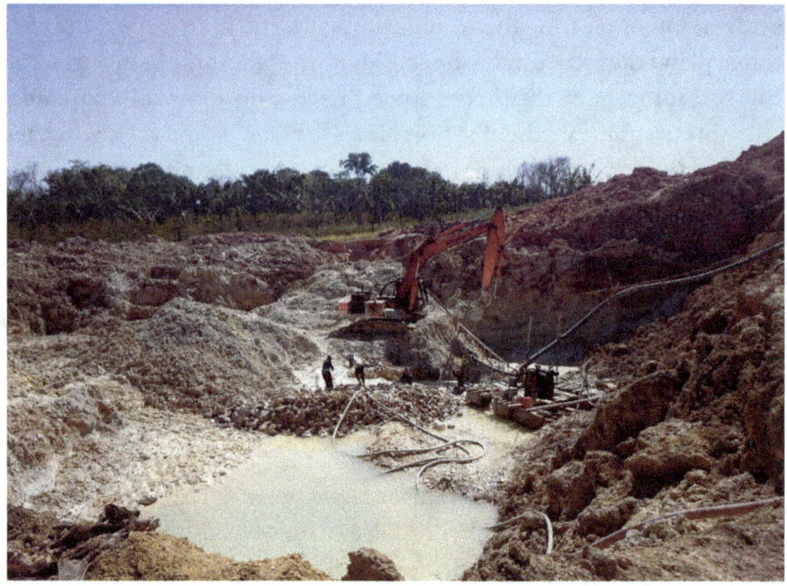

Figure 4. Gold Mining Operations taking place near Brownsweg,
Suriname, 2014. Photo by author.

land for gold mining due to the fact that they are often expelled from
lands when large-scale mining concessions are granted by the state
government.[59]

In Guyana, the development of maroon communities was limited
because some indigenous communities worked with the colonizers to
stop enslaved Africans from seeking refuge in the forests. Nonetheless, complications around access to the land remain. While indigenous communities in Guyana benefit from the Amerindian Act, which
serves as the legal basis on which the right to the land of Amerindian
communities is established, the efficacy of the act is challenged by an
organization that represents indigenous people in Guyana. An analysis carried out by this organization, called the Amerindian Peoples
Association, stated that the discriminatory norms rooted in Guyana's
colonial period continue to be manifested in the Guyana's national
legal framework. These norms support the idea that all the land not

---

59   Interviewee, 2014.

privately titled land in the country, and hence the sub- and above- soil, is solely the domain of the state.[60]

In reference to circumstances similar to those earlier described for the case of Suriname, the report described that once the British colonial power seized control of the country from the Dutch in the nineteenth century, the rights to the lands of indigenous people were annulled. The power to determine the use of the land, and to pass the previously mentioned Amerindian Act, passed to the state government, which now grants forestry and mining concessions in the areas considered customary lands by the Amerindians. In their efforts to weather the vicissitudes of their lives in the forests, communities based there use the materials in the forests around them in ways that contribute to the problem of climate change.

In 2014, I conducted fieldwork in Guyana and Suriname on forest conservation initiatives taking place there. Eddy, a community member of a relocated maroon community in Suriname, explained how the communities use the above- and below-ground resources to which they have access to survive.[61] In these and other ways, people residing on the Guiana Shield engage in racialized economic relations that cause the Shield to be weathered and to influence weather. They are important elements in any effort to rethink the situated and layered human-environment relationship within the larger framework of global climate change. The circumstances of forest communities demonstrate how actions that took place in the colonial past continue to impact the climate-changing present and future, multiplying vulnerabilities they faced for centuries through the atmosphere to the rest of the earth. The communities exemplify particularly well the recognition

---

60   *Indigenous Peoples' Rights, Forests and Climate Policies in Guyana: A Special Report*, ed. by Kate Dooley and Tom Griffiths (Georgetown, Guyana: Amerindian Peoples Association, 2014).

61   Eddy explained that 'We are not waiting for money from the government. We want to decide for ourselves on what we are going to do and make our own decisions. We were moved fifty-five years ago. You have to see what kind of house they gave us. We had to live in it with a husband, wife, three to four children. It is too small. We want to have our own rights, make our own decisions, build our own houses, and do everything by ourselves without the government telling us what to do. How is it even possible to live in this house for a whole family? We try to make our own houses so we use the rainforests. We use wood, gravel, we use everything that we can find in the rainforests, we use to build our own house' (Interviewee, 2014).

by Neimanis and Hamilton that not all bodies weather the same.[62]
Moreover, the differentiated weathering of bodies in the Guiana Shield
go on to influence social weather patterns in other parts of the globe,
as I detail next.

SOCIALLY DIFFERENTIATED WEATHERING

Just as continental weather patterns are influenced by the forests of the
Guiana Shield, so are social weather patterns influenced by the events
taking place there. This is demonstrated in how the system of socially
differentiated and racialized weathering of the bodies populating the
Shield went on to influence social climates around the world. This
influence becomes visible once it is situated within the spatial and
social geographies of the dominant capitalist system.

The coloniality of power, as defined by sociologist Anibal Quijano
in *Coloniality of Power and Eurocentrism in Latin America*, connects
these colonial histories with the creation and institutionalization of
race and global capitalism. Quijano traces how capital became the organizing principle or axis around which all other social relations took
shape in the Americas, of which the Guiana Shield is a part.[63] Hence,
as capitalism expanded and deepened, so did constructions of race as
fundamental to the structuring of social and economic relations. The
exclusive control of the circulation of resources produced in the Americas by people categorized as 'Whites', went hand in hand with the
concentration of the commodification of the labour force for 'White'
workers. This constellation meant that capital:

> [A]s a specific social relation, could be concentrated in the
> geographic region that then received the name of Europe.
> So Europe or, more specifically, Western Europe emerged as
> a new historical entity and identity and as the central place
> of the new pattern of world-Eurocentered colonial/modern
> capitalist power.[64]

---

62   Neimanis and Hamilton, 'Weathering'.
63   Anibal Quijano, 'Coloniality of Power and Eurocentrism in Latin America', *Interna-
      tional Sociology*, 15.2 (2000), pp. 215–32.
64   Quijano, 'Coloniality of Power', pp. 217–18.

These racialized dynamics played an instrumental role in the emergence of modern Guyana and Suriname. As I previously wrote of the racialized distribution of labour in Guyana, colonial racial structuring meant that white planters headed the social order with the support of the colonial authorities, controlling most of the land and capital. Chinese and Portuguese groups in Guyana, after being freed from laws that prevented them from acquiring land, became smallholders who practiced market gardening that led to their eminence in trade and commerce. Villages established by formerly enslaved people worked as seasonal labour on the plantations while living on lands considered marginal to the colonial authorities. East Indian descendants laboured on the plantations year-round, while Amerindians continued to live in and to depend on the forests in the interior locations of the country. In the nineteenth century, a black, middle class developed and came to dominate the urban areas while East Indians populated some rural areas, farming rice on land that the colonial masters granted them. Some of the descendants of the formerly enslaved, as previously described, turned to gold mining in the forest areas.[65]

In the productive and generative sense in which I conceptualize weathering, the Guiana Shield can be seen to have had a similar atmospheric effect of structuring racialized capital relations within the emergent system of world capitalism. These racialized relations are situated in but not limited to the spatial geographies of the Guiana Shield.

As I also wrote of Suriname's racialized division of labour, Creoles, as the descendants of formerly enslaved people are called in Suriname, began to dominate Suriname's political scene. Maroon communities remained suspicious of Creole dominance, having been sceptical of the granting of Suriname's independence since they had by then developed an amicable relationship with the colonizers with whom their ancestors had signed peace agreements. While racialized economic separations in Suriname diminished somewhat on the coast where most of the population lives, they remain strong in the forests where some maroon communities have established dominance in gold mining and

---

65 Yolanda Ariadne Collins, 'Colonial Residue: REDD+, Territorialisation and the Racialized Subject in Guyana and Suriname', *Geoforum*, 106 (2019), pp. 38–47 <https://doi.org/10.1016/j.geoforum.2019.07.019>.

indigenous communities opt largely to work towards maintaining their subsistence practices.[66]

This racialized system of categorizing labour that became fundamental to the development of capitalism originated in the Americas, eventually becoming institutionalized in the dominant global capitalist system.[67] In his particular representation of a temporal schism, Quijano explained that '[t]he relations between European and non-Europeans suffered a temporal alteration: all non-Europe belonged to the past, and so it was possible to think about relations between them in an evolutionary perspective'.[68] This resulted in an evolutionary perspective according to which all-non Europeans could be situated along a historical chain in comparison to Europeans, ranging from, 'primitive' to 'civilized', from 'irrational' to 'rational', from 'traditional' to 'modern', from 'magic-mythic' to 'scientific', *en route* to eventual Europeanization and modernization.[69] Hence, these temporal alterations, cemented in part in Guyana and Suriname, continue to linger in the modes of production and exploitation characteristic of current capitalist orders.

ATMOSPHERIC GEOGRAPHIES

Man-made or not, weathering plays a fundamental role in the potential of the Guiana Shield to affect both physical and social weather patterns. The weathering and fragmentation of the Guiana Shield unearths gold, diamonds, and oil beneath the soil; and has the now familiar, double-edged effect of increasing carbon in the atmosphere through the burning of fossil fuels to sustain the mechanized aspects of these activities. The production of certain commodities, like gold and bauxite, is made possible through the intentional, human-induced weathering of rock and soil. Forests and other vegetation become the victims of economic activity that cause weathering as they are cleared to access these timeworn minerals beneath the soil. This weathering then goes on to affect the weather by reducing the capacity of forests

---

66　Ibid.
67　Quijano, 'Coloniality of Power'.
68　Ibid., p. 221.
69　Ibid.

in the area to maintain the Amazon's hydrological function. Oil, also produced in Guyana and Suriname, is especially notable in how it goes on to magnify these weathering dynamics, leading directly to increased carbon in the atmosphere that, completing the loop, increases the potential to rainfall infused with atmospheric gases to speed up the weathering of rock, as previously described, and to speed up the slow process of weathering rock.

Racialized social climates[70] are also bound up in biophysical process of weathering, as racialized, colonial, and capitalist relations established and schematized in the Guiana Shield went on to inform and support the dominance of capitalist relations on a global scale. I hope to have demonstrated that reimagining human-environment relations by focusing on weather and the process of weather(ing) can bring into view the circular manner through which activities and relations taking place across linear time and space affect each other and shape particular places. This attention to weather and weathering has shown that it is possible to bring different geological, biological, and social activities, as well as different disciplinary insights into sustained and critical dialogue with each other outside of attempts of one to exploit the other. This endeavour, undertaken by exploring how weather and processes of weathering culminate in the climate changing social and ecological atmosphere, arrives at the somewhat unsurprising conclusion: What goes up must come down.

Nevertheless, with 'weathering' representing form, function, and activity, I posit that attention to the weather might be a useful complementary addition to political ecology frameworks. Weathering represents a useful prompt for urging political ecologists to refocus on the iterative and ongoing interaction between the natural environment and the social, potentially balancing the framework's current social leaning to the detriment of the physical, a critique to which the discipline has found itself susceptible. Weathering can remind political ecologists that it is possible to interrogate human-environment relationships without overlooking or over-relying on the social or upon the capitalist, economic factors that are often the source of their ire.

---

70   Sharpe, *In the Wake.*

'Locked out in nature'
Films on the European Asylum System, Latent Violence, and Ghosts

ANJA SUNHYUN MICHAELSEN

> It is not a case of dead or missing persons sui
> generis, but of the ghost as a social figure.
>
> Avery Gordon, *Ghostly Matters*

While watching documentaries about asylum facilities in Europe, I notice that they are often filmed in the most scenic surroundings. For example, in Fernand Melgar's *La Forteresse*, the 'Reception and Processing Centre' (*Empfangs- und Verfahrenszentrum*) for asylum seekers is located in Vallorbe, Switzerland, at the North-Eastern tip of the Jura National Park, close to the French border, within a landscape of mountains and forests.[1] *Zentralflughafen THF* documents the temporary accommodations set up for asylum seekers in the former Tempelhof Airport in Berlin from 2015 to 2018.[2] The building faces Tempelhofer Feld, a former airfield, which now serves Berliners and tourists as a unique space for leisure activities, including beekeeping and every type

---

1   *La Forteresse*, dir. by Fernand Melgar (2008).
2   *Zentralflughafen THF*, dir. by Karim Aïnouz (2018) <https://www.zentralflughafen-thf.de/> [accessed 7 June 2020].

of recreational sport. The Tempelhofer Feld includes partly wild, growing nature in the middle of the city, and it offers a rare open sky. In
Forst, the accommodation for asylum seekers is cut off from public
transportation and surrounded by a thick forest near the East German
city of Jena.[3] In these documentaries, asylum facilities are located in
or close to landscapes that are often associated with tourism, leisure,
and retreat.[4] This proximity to nature could be understood as exterior
or removed from ordinary life — spatially and, as in the case of *Zentralflughafen THF*, conceptually — as far away from 'civilization'. The
scenic location of the asylum facilities troubles the notion of nature as
an escape resort — to go 'off the grid', free for at least a limited amount
of time from state surveillance.[5]

The concept of 'weathering' implies a relation between interior
and exterior, and a state of exposure to the forces of nature. In
In the Wake, Christina Sharpe conceptualizes 'the weather' as all-
encompassing antiblackness, as 'the totality of our environments', 'the
total climate'. This understanding of weathering highlights how systemic racism permeates all boundaries. In Sharpe's case (she reads Toni
Morrison's *Beloved*), it collapses the borders between 'free' and 'unfree'
states.[6] Clear distinctions between inside and outside, exposure and
protection are deeply unsettled in Sharpe's account. In the following,
I ask to what extent systemic racism collapses the relation between
inside and outside of the European asylum system. In the films that
I will discuss, images of nature exemplify different kinds of exposure,
literal and conceptual. Nature, in various ways, becomes apparent as an
instrument of violence, even if one is provided with food and shelter.
We can assume that the locations of the asylum facilities have been
chosen because of state efforts to separate and isolate the world of

---

3   *Forst*, dir. by Ascan Breuer, Ursula Hansbauer, Wolfgang Konrad, in cooperation
     with The Voice Refugee Forum and others (2005) <http://www.forstfilm.com/> [ac-
     cessed 7 June 2020].

4   Another recent example outside of Europe shows a refugee camp in the jungle on
     beautiful Easter Island in Australia. See *Island of Hungry Ghosts*, dir. by Gabrielle Brady
     (2018) <http://www.christmasislandfilm.com/> [accessed 7 June 2020].

5   I want to thank Alison Sperling, Amelia Groom, and M. Ty for drawing my attention
     to this aspect and for generally and substantially furthering the text with their careful
     commenting.

6   Christina Sharpe, *In the Wake: On Blackness and Being* (Durham, NC: Duke University
     Press, 2016), p. 200.

asylum. Nature hides the facilities from plain sight and conceals the violence within them from view; it functions as a means of physical separation in *La Forteresse* and *Forst*. It also is used to dominate and control the person in the process of seeking asylum, as exemplified in the aerial images in *View from Above*.[7] And, nature is used directly as murder weapon at the European borders, as can be seen in the underwater shots in *Purple Sea*.[8]

A NON-SPACE FOR THE STATELESS

The asylum facilities are not just geographically cut off and remote from urban life but constitute, rather, a 'non-space' in the way Hannah Arendt describes refugee internment camps. For Arendt, the problem of the refugee is the problem of statelessness, politically or *de facto*:

> Every attempt by international conferences to establish some legal status for stateless people failed because no agreement could possibly replace the territory to which an alien, within the framework of existing law, must be deportable. All discussions about the refugee problems revolved around this one question: How can the refugee be made deportable again? The second World War and the DP camps were not necessary to show that the only practical substitute for a nonexistent homeland was an internment camp. Indeed, as early as the thirties this was the only 'country' the world had to offer the stateless.[9]

Handling 'non-deportable' subjects required the creation of special places, a foreign 'country' of its own kind on the territory of a host nation, a space outside of the trinity of territory — people — state. The treatment of Jews and Armenians exemplify, for Arendt, how falling outside of one distinct state's responsibility implies the loss of the 'right to have (civil) rights'. Such a loss of the very pre-condition of claiming rights makes the respective subjects vulnerable to both arbitrary violence and systematic annihilation, in the home country, and on foreign

---

7   *View from Above*, dir. by Hiwa K (2017).

8   *Purple Sea*, dir. by Amel Alzakout and Khaled Abdulwahed (2020) <https:// purplesea.pong-berlin.de/>.

9   Hannah Arendt, *The Origins of Totalitarianism* (London: Harcourt Brace Jovanovich, 1973), p. 284.

territory. Without a state authority capable and willing to enforce legal protection, refugees are *de facto* 'outlawed' — regardless of their actions, simply because of what they 'are' — and exposed to arbitrary rule.[10] The fact that Greece recently declared a 'state of emergency' that suspends the Geneva Convention of 1949, as well as additional international asylum laws, confirms the continuing relevance of Arendt's analysis for the contemporary moment.[11] The absence of the right to have rights enables the intentional killing, systematic neglect, and letting die of refugees within and at the European borders. The extreme violence must not be understood as exceptional or excessive, but as a direct consequence of the asylum seekers' status, fundamentally unprotected by the law.[12] In the German version of *The Origins of Totalitarianism* Arendt writes:

> The existence of such a category of people poses a twofold danger to the civilized world. Their unrelatedness to the world, their worldlessness, is like an invitation to murder, inasmuch as the death of people who stand outside all worldly references of a legal, social and political nature remains without any consequences for the survivors. When they are murdered, it is as if no one has been wronged or even harmed.[13]

I understand Arendt's notion of 'worldlessness' not in a metaphysical sense but as the name for a situation in which '*all worldly references of a legal, social and political nature*' do not apply to oneself in the same way

---

10   Ibid., p. 282.

11   'Greece suspends asylum applications as migrants seek to leave Turkey', *BBC News* (1 March 2020) <https://www.bbc.com/news/world-europe-51695468> [accessed 7 June 2020]. Whether the numerous attempts to prove the illegality of the 'suspension' of international asylum law have consequences remains to be seen.

12   Elliot Douglas, 'Germany: New Accusations of Police Violence in Death of Asylum-Seeker', *Deutsche Welle* (2 November 2019) <https://www.dw.com/en/germany-new-accusations-of-police-violence-in-death-of-asylum-seeker/a-51067499> [accessed 7 June 2020].

13   'Die Existenz solch einer Kategorie von Menschen birgt für die zivilisierte Welt eine zweifache Gefahr. Ihre Unbezogenheit zur Welt, ihre Weltlosigkeit ist wie eine Aufforderung zum Mord, insofern der Tod von Menschen, die außerhalb aller weltlichen Bezüge rechtlicher, sozialer und politischer Art stehen, ohne jede Konsequenzen für die Überlebenden bleibt. Wenn man sie mordet, ist es, als sei niemandem ein Unrecht oder auch nur ein Leid geschehen.' Hannah Arendt, *Elemente und Ursprünge totaler Herrschaft* (Frankfurt a.M.: Europäische Verlagsanstalt, 1955), p. 766. This passage is not present in the English version.

as they do to non-refugees, a situation in which these references and the world to which they belong — a world that one is at the mercy of — somehow seem to not concern oneself. To 'stand outside all worldly references' in this sense has far-reaching consequences. For Arendt, it makes murder permissible, 'invites' murder.

To what extent do contemporary asylum facilities constitute a 'country' for those 'without a country', and hence a space of comparable existential threat to its inhabitants? How does the lethal undercurrent of statelessness impact the situation in the facilities? And how does the violent structure of the European asylum system 'make itself known' in the documentaries? In the films mentioned above, images of 'nature', in different ways, indicate a space of being 'outlawed', not as freedom from the law (in the sense of escape) but as existing outside of the 'pale of the law' (which permits indeterminate confinement and murder). To a certain extent, state territoriality, and thereby protection (at least in theory) from arbitrary violence, are suspended. This does not mean that in asylum facilities unrestricted violence is necessarily enacted but that violence is always latent.

What interests me in these documentaries are the ghostly traces of the latent possibility of violence. The ghosts here are not Freud's suppressed unfamiliar familiar, a metaphor for psychic processes. Instead, my understanding of the ghostly draws closer to Raymond Williams's 'structure of feeling' — something that is present and potent but not fully ascertainable in conceptual terms.[14] In the documentaries, murderous, systemic violence is present without showing itself openly, in the way Avery Gordon considers haunting as a dimension of violence whose force exerts itself apart from explicit exploitation and oppression:

> [H]aunting is one way in which abusive systems of power make themselves known and their impacts felt in everyday life, especially when they are supposedly over and done with (slavery, for instance) or when their oppressive nature is denied (as in free labor or national security). [...] Haunting is not the same as being exploited, traumatized, or oppressed, although it usually involves these experiences or is produced

---

14   Raymond Williams, 'Structure of Feeling', in *Marxism and Literature* (Oxford: Oxford University Press, 1977), pp. 128–35.

> by them. What's distinctive about haunting is that it is an ani-
> mated state in which a repressed or unresolved social violence
> is making itself known, sometimes very directly, sometimes
> more obliquely.[15]

In the films, systemic violence makes itself known in images of nature. In *La Forteresse* and *Forst*, mountains and forests separate the world of the asylum seekers from Europe, on European territory. In *Zentralflug-hafen THF*, nature is the space of leisure and recreation from which the asylum seekers are separated. Repeatedly, across several films (*Forst, View from Above, Purple Sea*), aerial images point to the sky as sphere of surveillance and control in the asylum context. Here, nature, i.e. the sky, is turned into a tool of domination. In *Purple Sea*, the Aegean sea functions directly as murder weapon used by the European asylum system. Nature is not a metaphor in these films. Silently, in the form of trees and air, rocks and water, it is the instrument with which systemic violence is enacted. Without showing violence explicitly, nature in these films, in different ways, indicates its pervasive, latent presence.

SEPARATED BY NATURE

In *La Forteresse* — 'Fortress Europe' resonates in the title — the asylum facility includes the accommodation as well as the offices where the interviews are conducted, on the basis of which the asylum seekers are transferred to other places or are deported. In the housing units, each room contains four bunk beds. They are cramped, but people help and support each other. There is a large dining room and a program to keep the children occupied. The residents learn German, play football in the courtyard, and pray together. Once, a couple of inhabitants are sent to do some forest work for a change of scenery. They drink tea from thermos flasks and eat a kind of picnic of cheese and kiwis, which the camera captures with a close-up shot (it is puzzling what the camera/I pay attention to). Back at the shelter there is a lot of hoopla as one of the asylum seekers is stuck in his rubber boot. The head of the facility lends a hand to help free him. The staff are obviously trying to

---

15   Avery Gordon, *Ghostly Matters: Haunting and the Sociological Imagination* (Min-
      neapolis: University of Minnesota Press, 2008), p. xvi.

create a humane atmosphere. In a team meeting, the traumatization of asylum seekers is acknowledged and everyone is asked to 'show some humanity' (there seem to be no social workers or psychologists on site). The fact that the security guards take away the asylum seekers' musical instruments, to prevent them being used as weapons, causes laughter all around. The asylum seekers, it seems, are not subject to abusive treatment. In the interviews they are assisted by translators, they are listened to.

The facility appears as a mix of a youth hostel, welfare institution, and prison. The employees serve as social workers, administrators, judges, police and prison guards at the same time. The facility follows the rule of 'carceral humanitarianism':

> Under carceral humanitarianism, detention *is* shelter and materializes the double meaning of security, as securing against a threat through violence and offering security from the threat of violence. Humanitarian governmentality produces irregularized bodies as simultaneously a threat to security and a life to be secured: a life to be saved *and* made secure, seized, possessed, fastened to an apparatus of care that is also an apparatus of capture, control, and ruination.[16]

In the uncomfortable laughter at the idea of music instruments being used as weapons, the double meaning of security Debarati Sanyal points to resonates. The security measure prevents obvious abuse of the refugees but renders them as a potential threat, suspicious, nonetheless.

In this observant, rather quiet representation of the Swiss asylum system, which includes no spoken commentary, it is above all nature that suggests that something is wrong. The facility is surrounded by snow-covered mountains; it is cold, and it rains. Instead of prison walls, there is thick forest. Nature blocks the view. It separates this world from the world outside which is Europe. The images of isolating and confining nature frame the social interactions within the facility. They remind the viewer of the precarious grounds on which daily life in

---

16   Debarati Sanyal, 'Humanitarian Detention and Figures of Persistence at the Border', *Critical Times*, 2.3 (December 2019), pp. 435–65 (pp. 438–39) (emphases in original).

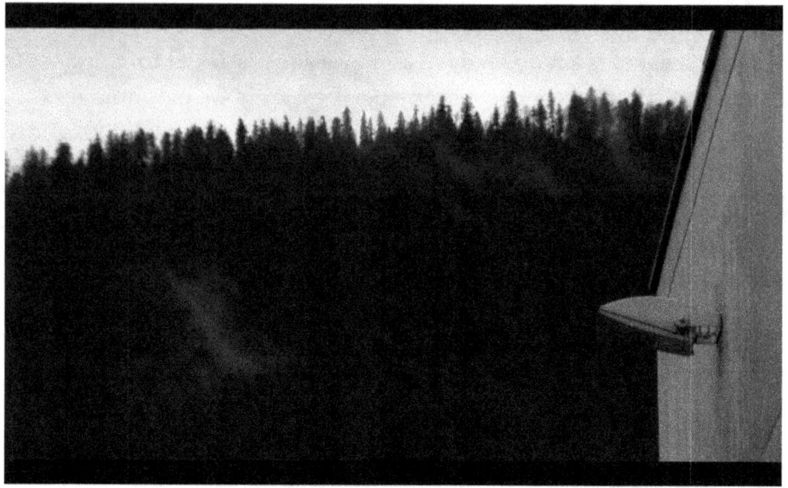

Figure 1. *La Forteresse*, film still. Image © 2008 Fernand Melgar.

detention takes place.[17] Those asked to behave humanely hold, in their hands, the power over the asylum seekers' lives.

THE INTERVIEW

Indirect reminders of these precarious grounds permeate the film. Repeatedly, *La Forteresse* shows excerpts of asylum interviews, during which officers ask refugees to describe their journey to Switzerland. They inquire about entry routes and state persecution. They compare earlier versions to the accounts of family members, they point to gaps and contradictions and register the emotional state of the applicant. In her book on the European asylum practices, the author Dina Nayeri develops a polemical narrative theory in which she compares the storytelling of asylum seekers to literary writing:

> [T]o pass an asylum interview, you don't just need a true story. [...] To satisfy an asylum officer takes the same narrative sophistication it takes to please book critics. At once

---

17   There is a spatial inversion happening, built into the hillside, the accommodation appears as a fortress within the 'Fortress Europe'. Geography and nature separate the accommodation — i.e. the socio-political Outside of Europe — and the outside, i.e. the Inside of Europe.

logical and judgmental of demeanor, both are on guard for manipulation and emotional trickery. Stick to the concrete, the five senses, they say. Sound natural, human, but also dazzle with your prose. Make me cry, but a whiff of sentimentality and you're done.[18]

At one point in *La Forteresse*, the decision-maker decides that the story did not convince her, that it seemed 'too stereotypical'. It seems implausible to her that the asylum seeker made the journey he recounts. He talked about it, she explains to her colleague, as if he was telling another person's story. She rejects his application on the grounds of incredibility.[19] The problem, however, might not be the story's validity but that 'credibility' is structurally impossible:

> [T]he asylum officer, who appropriates the rules of good storytelling, fails to realise, when sitting across a petitioning refugee, that you are speaking to a *character* in the story, not the *author*. [...] In practice, much still depends on what each asylum officer finds credible. For that, the refugee must take control of the story and behave as the storyteller, not just a character.[20]

In the end, the asylum seeker must embody both the position of the storyteller *and* of the story's subject. They must give an objective account without appearing detached, 'as if telling someone else's story'. Based on Nayeri's book, we can assume that asylum seekers are well aware of this impossible narrative requirement. In *La Forteresse*, suspicion takes hold of the entire film. The employees are alert to lies, contradictions, missing memories, too much emotion, or too little.

The camera participates in the credibility test, as it focuses on the asylum seekers' faces and bodies and records their movements, ges-

---

18   Dina Nayeri, *The Ungrateful Refugee* (Edinburgh: Canongate, 2019), pp. 242–43.

19   The process might be this trivial and arbitrary. In *Die Entscheider* (dir. by Susanne Ofteringer, 1992) the filmmaker asks her interview partners, two 'decision-makers' at the Central Admission Point for asylum seekers in Cologne, what enables them to assess the credibility of asylum seekers. Expert knowledge, professional experience and knowledge of human nature, they answer. Other disclosures from the film: the interviews take place in a friendly atmosphere. They are not interrogations. The decisions are mostly correct. The decision makers do not consider themselves as in a specifically powerful position. *Die Entscheider* exposes their alarming lack of awareness for their role within the asylum system.

20   Ibid., p. 263.

tures, and voices as they tell their story. The film's audience is put into
the position of the judge as well. Is the story true? Are the tears real?
What is revealed by the posture, the facial expressions, the look into
the camera? The asylum seekers tell their story to a triple audience: the
interviewer, the camera, and the film's audience. But in this paranoid
situation, everyone is tested — the asylum seekers, the staff members
as well as the film *and* its audience. Everyone turns into subject and
object of suspicion. Is the interviewer 'humane enough', 'unbiased',
racist? Do I agree with her decision? Is the film 'biased', manipulative,
is it critical enough? Am I 'biased', manipulated, critical enough? The
testing continues outside of the interview scenes, it makes no difference which situation is shown. The asylum seekers' interactions with
one another and with the staff are equally subject to it. Suspicion is
the undercurrent of the entire film despite its humane impression. The
film does not produce a voyeuristic gaze in the proper sense, the fact of
observation is in no way hidden. The story is told *for* the interviewer,
the camera, and the audience. And still the film creates the most paranoid viewing situation in which everyone is suspected to deceive and
misjudge.

LOCKED OUT IN NATURE

In *La Forteresse*, the asylum facility is hidden by Swiss mountains. The
asylum seekers are under constant surveillance and the film uninten-
tionally participates in it. Despite the overtly sympathetic depiction,
the film creates the feeling of being locked in, in this remote space, in
the logic of impossible authentication. The more experimental film,
Forst, helps to understand how nature in the asylum context *is* the
space of claustrophobia, a space in which one is locked in and out at
the same time. The film, which was made in cooperation with refugee
organizations in Germany such as The Voice Refugee Forum, Women
in Exile, and Caravan for the Rights of Migrants and Refugees, depicts
an accommodation for asylum seekers in the city of Forst. Forst is
the small town's name, but it is also a German term for 'forest'. The
accommodation is located in an actual forest. The film gives only a
blurred impression of the building and its surroundings, the images

of the accommodation and the forest merge into an undistinguishable entity. The latter extends the former, just like the mountains in *La Forteresse* constitute an external part of the facility. In *Forst*, the forest is the prison.

Forst is not a typical documentary film. The filmmakers call it an 'un-documentary', which could refer to its experimental aesthetics, as well as to the status of those who are invisible in ordinary life:

> *Forst* is a portrayal. The documentary tells about a forest in the middle of Europe far from the urban world and from civilisation which is home to a peculiar community of the banished — it is a world for the stranded. A diffuse system that still has total control makes sure that this world doesn't show itself, that it doesn't pop up in our reality and become a disturbance.[21]

The film conveys the reality of this 'community of the banished', but its aesthetics — abstract black and white images, with asynchronic sound and voice-overs — maintains opacity of the scene and its subjects and prevents objectification by the viewer and exposure to state control. Unlike *La Forteresse* the human faces and figures are kept out of the frame, shown only as silhouettes. By not assigning bodies to stories the film resists to individualize and authenticate the question of asylum. In this sense, it documents and 'un-documents' at the same time.

The building and its surroundings are abstract to a degree in which they are still recognizable, but perspective and framing emphasize geometric structures and light patterns, atmospheres. A fragmented narrative plot remains unresolved. *Forst* begins with an unlocated voice-over and a black screen that tells of the narrator's arrival at a place beyond the reach of public transportation. Other voices follow. They tell of personal experiences within the asylum system, but they do not give exactly biographical accounts.

In a central scene, white-clad appearances with unidentifiable faces slowly emerge from the forest. *Forst* explicitly stages the refugee as the social figure of the ghost. The film avoids the credibility logic

---

21   ForstFilm.com, 2005 <http://www.forstfilm.com/> [accessed 7 June 2020].

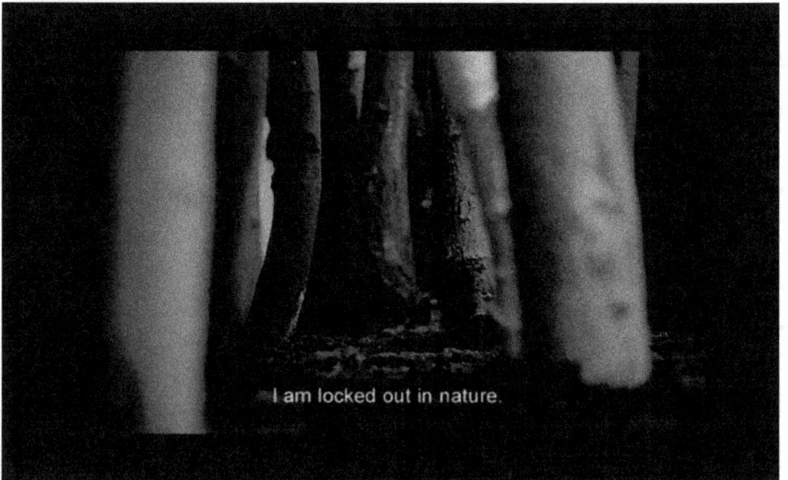

Figures 2 and 3. *Forst*, film still. Image credit: Ascan Breuer, Ursula Hansbauer, Wolfgang Konrad, Ben Pointeker, Julia Lazarus, wr.

that was exhibited in *La Forteresse*. Instead, it tells of the current situation in Europe and of the state practices aimed at isolating the asylum seekers to prevent solidarity and political organization. 'I am locked out in nature', the first narrator says — not allowed in despite already having arrived in Europe but instead confined in nature, the space of the Outside within.

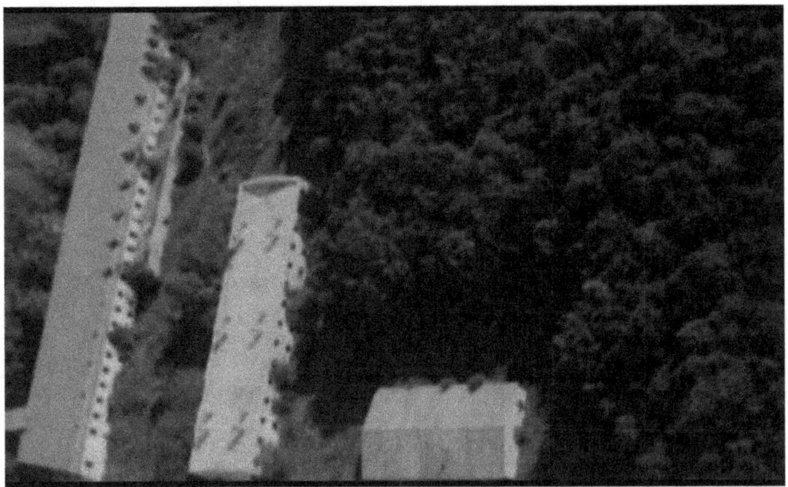

Figure 4. *Forst*, film still. Image credit: Ascan Breuer, Ursula Hansbauer, Wolfgang Konrad, Ben Pointeker, Julia Lazarus, wr.

VIEW FROM ABOVE

In *La Forteresse* and *Forst* nature appears as that which blocks the view, isolates, and confines. As viewers, our view is equally confined in the paranoid space. In a disorienting way and with very different aesthetics, both films do not provide access to the world beyond the mountains and forests, paralleling the asylum seekers' and the audience's perspective. In both films, the camera operates on ground level but *Forst* also includes some helicopter shots of the thick forest from above.

In the films, nature mostly organizes the separation between Europe's interior and exterior horizontally. The helicopter shots indicate a vertical dimension of separation which conceptually resonates with the interview scenes in *La Forteresse*. To assume the perspective of the author can also be understood as a change from a (character's) view from below to a view, as it were, from above.

View from Above is the title of an experimental video piece by Hiwa K, which allows one to understand how the aerial view of surveillance and the authorial narrator's bird's eye view in the asylum interview are folded into one another. Produced for documenta 14 in Kassel in 2017, the video tells the story of M who flees from the northern, Kurdish part of Iraq and applies for asylum 'in one of the Schengen countries'. His application is rejected because Kurdistan is considered a 'safe zone' by the UN, which denies the latter's inhabitants any claim to asylum. M applies in a different country. This time he makes the statement that he comes from the 'unsafe zone', which he proves in the interview by showing detailed cartographic knowledge of the city K in the non-Kurdish part of Iraq. The decision-maker is impressed and grants him asylum. *View from Above* transgresses the border into the fictional. Its mode remains ambiguous. Perhaps the story is autobiographical, perhaps it contains a collective experience, or still something other than that. It remains as fictional and as real as the arbitrary cuts in the political map of 'safe' and 'unsafe' zones, of economic and political refugees, of subjects worthy or unworthy of living, and living well.

The story, co-written by Hiwa K and Lawrence Abu Hamdan, is told off screen by K as narrator with calm and gentle intonation. In the beginning, we hear a disembodied, disorienting voice over a black screen. It tells the story of M, not chronologically (as I recounted it above), instead it starts in the middle, jumping back and forth through-out. Visually, the video consists of slow tracking shots over a curious miniature model of the war-torn German city of Kassel in 1945. The model was built in the 1950s, is made out of sand, cardboard, and plaster, and was commissioned by the city of Kassel. It shows the city centre in May 1945, when eighty percent of the city was destroyed by air raids. The model is based on aerial photographs taken by the same allied forces. Meant to commemorate the defeat of the National Socialist regime, it was stowed away after its construction in a storage room in the Kassel City Hall for years, only to be exhibited in 1983.[22] During documenta 14, the model and Hiwa K's video were presented in adjacent rooms. Both are now part of the museum's permanent exhibition.[23]

---

22   Jörg Steinbach, 'Kassel in Schutt und Asche: Trümmermodell wieder zu sehen', *Hessische Niedersächsische Allgemeine* (2 March 2016) <https://www.hna.de/kassel/kassel-schutt-asche-6171148.html> [accessed 7 June 2020].

23   'Documenta 14-Arbeit "View from Above" von Hiwa K ist in das Stadtmuseum zurück-gekehrt (27 May 2019) <https://www.kassel.de/pressemitteilungen/2019/mai/view-from-above-von-hiwa-k-ist-in-das-stadtmuseum-kassel-zurueckgekehrt.php> [accessed 7 June 2020].

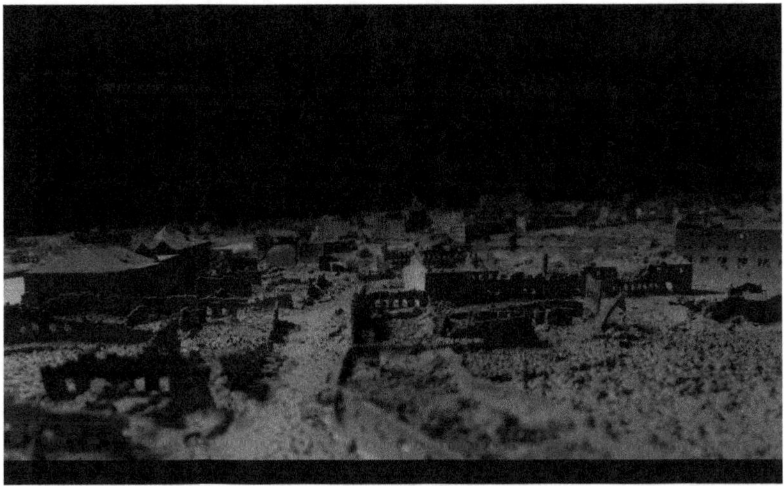

Figure 5. *View from Above*, film still. Image credit: Hiwa K.

View from Above uses explicit aesthetic means to create a ghostly atmosphere. Hiwa K's voice stands out from the acoustic environment, in which otherwise only the technical hum of the camera/drone can be heard. Visually, this eerie atmosphere is intensified by the slow camera movements, as well as by the contrasting pitch black background and the illuminated model, creating sharp, accentuated shadows. Sound and image technology isolate the voice and the model from their surroundings. The camera travels through the model of the destroyed city, in which, next to the ruins, a few miniature trees are still standing, but no human figures are included. The model not only preserves a war-destroyed city, but a city without survivors — a ghost town. The relationship between image and narrative is not easily determined. What does the story of an Iraqi asylum seeker have to do with the German defeat in 1945? The narrative seems to suggest a fatalist understanding. 'All cities have destruction in common', the narrator says at one point.

Narrative and image share a common perspective — the view from above. M memorizes the city of K by looking at its map from a bird's eye view, which, as we learn from the Kassel model, is the perspective of war. Some of the visuals in *View from Above* are reminiscent of the infrared images familiar from various military operations, as part of the

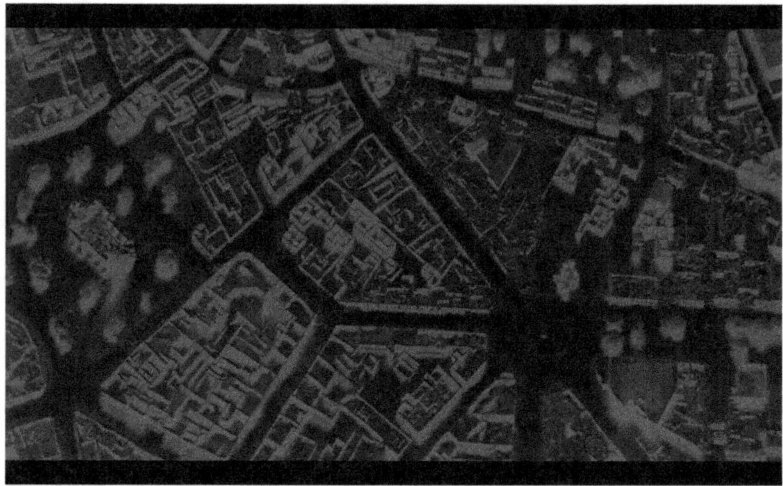

Figure 6. *View from Above*, video still. Image credit: Hiwa K.

'occupation of the skies', as Achille Mbembe refers to it.[24] It is also the perspective of the authorial narrator as it is required in the asylum interview. Just as the camera swiftly pans from the ground level of the city model to a bird's eye view, M needs to lift himself up into the air, to leave his position of the powerless to be able to look down on the map drawn by those in power.

It is a violent change of perspective. Telling one's own story is often considered a form of empowerment, possibly even more so if one masters the ability to obscure the distinction between fiction and truth. In the asylum interview, telling one's story requires a form of narrative mastery unavailable for most. Another version, which can be found in written form on Hiwa K's website, reads:

> The people from J taught him everything and helped him draw the map of their town, all the while asking him questions to confirm that he had mastered everything about J.
>
> When M finally had his refugee interview, the official was quite surprised, even impressed. He asked M questions about the geography of the town, and compared M's answers to a map. M's answers demonstrated knowledge of J as it was seen from above.

---

24   Achille Mbembe, 'Necropolitics', *Public Culture*, 15.1 (2003), pp. 11-40 (p. 29).

> It took only twenty minutes for the official to grant M refugee status. Meanwhile, thousands of people who were actually from J and other cities in the unsafe zone waited as long as ten to fifteen years for the same thing, because their answers only demonstrated knowledge of their towns from the ground.[25]

The story can very well be understood as an example of the 'autonomy of migration',[26] which will continue despite all efforts to close Europe off. But it also points to something beyond solidarity and resistance, raising the question of the costs of the bird's eye view. By juxtaposing the Kassel model and today's asylum system, *View from Above* points to the use of the bird's eye view as equally instrument of domination and of survival. 'To lift oneself up' here requires to adopt a militarized perspective on life lived on the ground. M must bear to leave behind all those who have helped him, and with them the life he lived. Ultimately, in *View from Above* the bird's eye view leads to M's amnesia. While the narrator repeatedly reminds M how he succeeded in the asylum process, M seems to have forgotten all about it. The right of residence, the story suggests, comes at the price of losing all connection with the asylum seeker's former life.

POSTSCRIPT

Premiered at the Berlinale film festival 2020, *Purple Sea* re-examines, in a shocking manner, the question of violence in the European asylum system. The film consists of images recorded by the camera which the artist Amel Alzakout tied around her wrist while crossing the Aegean Sea, from Istanbul to Lesbos. Alzakout had first fled Syria to Istanbul where she lived for a couple of years. When she decided to make the crossing to Europe, the boat fell apart shortly after departure, leaving a couple of hundred refugees to drown. Visually, the hour-long film

---

25 Hiwa K, 'A View from Above' <http://www.hiwak.net/anecdotes/a-view-from-above/> [accessed 7 June 2020].

26 Yann Moulier Boutang, 'No Longer Reserve Army: Theses on the Autonomy of Migration and the Necessary End of the Regime of Labour Migration', *Jungle World* (3 April 2002) <https://jungle.world/artikel/2002/14/nicht-laenger-reservearmee> [accessed 7 June 2020].

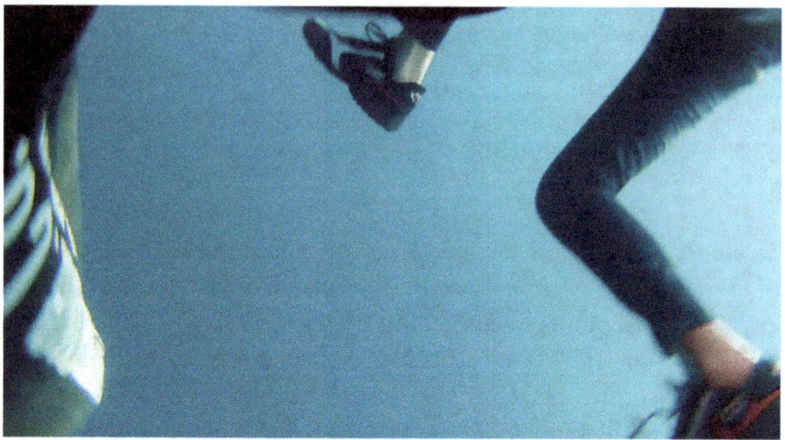

Figure 7. *Purple Sea*, film still. Image credit: PURPLE SEA © pong
film/Alzakout 2020.

is comprised almost entirely of the under-water shots taken by the
camera on Alzakout's wrist.[27]

In the voice-over, Alzakout narrates a conversational text that she
co-wrote years after she arrived in Berlin with others who were involved in the filmmaking process. She describes personal perceptions
and feelings during the time before the trip, as well as thoughts and
events leading up to the moment at sea, whose images feature in the
film. The shots, which, as Alzakout says, are not hers but those of the
camera, show clothed bodies up to the neck, moving, or not, objects
floating in the water, cigarettes, shoes. I understand these images as
neither from below nor from above. They embody neither the asylum
seekers' nor the decision makers' perspective but are technical images
of their own kind. The camera registers, records what floats in front of
it. It films the death zone with maximal absence of intention, without
authenticating, or even witnessing anything, leaving the viewer alone
with the images. Disconcertingly, their immersive quality allows us to
easily forget that what we see are actual human beings left to die. It
requires the audience's conscious effort to not be carried away by the
beauty of the underwater shots. Abruptly, the viewer is reminded of
their meaning in a couple of moments when Alzakout's arm with the

---

27   'Synopsis', Purple Sea, 2019 <https://purplesea.pong-berlin.de/en/16/synopsis>
     [accessed 7 June 2020]. The original footage is much longer.

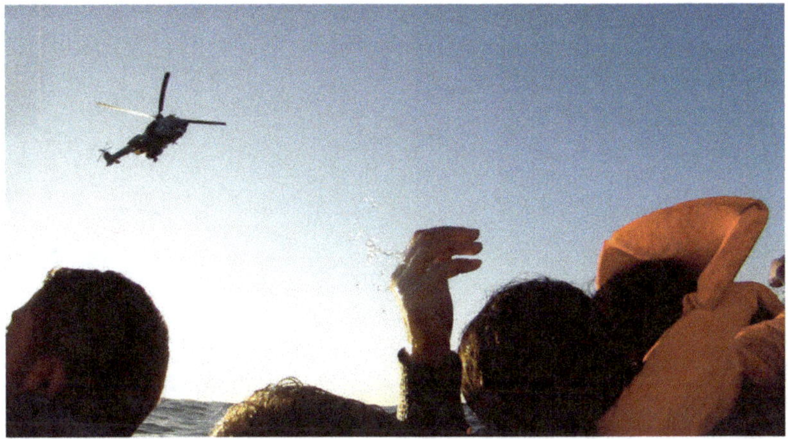

Figure 8. *Purple Sea*, film still. Image credit: PURPLE SEA © pong film/Alzakout 2020.

camera shoots out of the water, as she protests against a helicopter that circles above.

In the underwater shots, the view is limited to a few metres. The intense colour and texture of the water and the muffled sounds allows for the viewer to become lost in the images. Now, the blinding sunlight, shrill whistling sounds, people in the water shouting, and the noise of the rotating propeller blades overwhelm the perception. The helicopter is not there to rescue. Instead, it creates waves that endanger those in the water even more. A tiny red dot indicates that someone in the helicopter is filming, from above.[28]

In the previous films, nature served as a means of separation between Europe's interior and exterior, within Europe, which included hiding systemic violence from view. Indirectly or directly, *La Forteresse*, *Forst*, and *View from Above* convey an inherent violence in the European asylum system, in the housing, the processing, the interviews, as a haunting quality especially of nature images. Systemic violence strongly makes itself felt in the claustrophobic and eerie atmospheres of the films and in the images of the refugees as ghostly figures. In contrast, the images in *Purple Sea* seem haunted by nothing. Nothing is hidden or latent. The film lays bare the absolute violence that is the European asylum system, for everyone to see openly.

---

28   There is much more to be said about *Purple Sea*.

On Bad Weather
Heidegger, Arendt, and Political Beginnings
FACUNDO VEGA

> The great trouble is that human nature, which
> might otherwise develop smoothly, is as depend-
> ent upon luck as seed is upon good weather.
>
> Hannah Arendt

If 'datability' made any sense, 2020 will hand down a particular term: virus. In the domain of thinking, the magnitude of this new crisis in life-in-common made visible an invariant: the shortcomings in philosophy to deal with *the unexpected*.[1] The point is, of course, not to suggest that philosophy should have predicted and offered keys to theoretically apprehend what could not be fully perceived in advance. Rather, what is happening — the current events that we are experiencing — invites theorists to be attentive to the ordinary world they are confronted by. But this invitation is pending.

Though the extent of the crisis we are traversing is not known, the contours of the problem I try to illustrate are not brand new. In

---

1   See, among others, Giorgio Agamben, *A che punto siamo? L'epidemia come politica* (Macerata: Quodlibet, 2020) and Alain Badiou, 'Sur la situation épidémique', *Quartier général. Le Média libre*<https://qg.media/2020/03/26/sur-la-situation-epidemique-par-alain-badiou/> [accessed 30 March 2020].

fact, the consequences of the love of philosophy for 'the extraordinary' are as old as the laughter of the Thracian girl.[2] Enamoured by their own 'radicality', philosophers have purportedly abandoned the world even for the sake of discovering and scrutinizing it. In dealing with this issue in an *Auseinandersetzung* with Martin Heidegger, Hannah Arendt returned to the promise of politics. For Arendt, the validity of this question about politics, of great importance in today's milieu, is inextricably related to the matter of the 'beginning': a beginning, Arendt notes, which is animated 'not by the strength of one architect but by the combined power of the many'.[3] By dealing with Arendt's 'beginning' and avoiding exceptionalist stridencies, I hope to open up a space to re-ask: How to begin anew? What can and should be learned during this *intermezzo*? What can and should be the promise of politics today?

In the current situation, when the very act of 'beginning' is confined, the temptation is to deal with the questions I posed by postulating the need of a magnificent event, breaking into and interrupting the normal course of history. Positing a hiatus in time to found a *new time* has, according to Arendt, political implications. In her rendition, in fact, 'revolutions are the only political events which confront us directly and inevitably with the problem of beginning.'[4] But revolutions are not only foundationalist events that break history in two. When Arendt thematizes the revolutionary power to constitute life-in-common and refers to the Mayflower Compact, she strikingly wonders whether its signatories 'had been prompted to "covenant" because of the *bad weather*'.[5] Vis-à-vis the splendour and grandeur of a new beginning, the 'bad weather' appears as a vivid reminder that the 'earliest

---

2   On the anecdote about the Thracian servant-girl ridiculing Thales for falling into a well while observing the motion of celestial bodies see, among others: Plato, *Theaetetus*, ed. by Bernard Williams, M. J. Levett, and Myles Burnyeat (Indianapolis, IN: Hackett, 1992), p. 44; Martin Heidegger, *Die Frage nach dem Ding. Zu Kants Lehre von den transzendentalen Grundsätzen* (Tübingen: Niemeyer, 1962), p. 2; Hannah Arendt, *The Life of the Mind*, ed. by Mary McCarthy, 2 vols (New York: Harcourt Brace Jovanovich, 1977–78), I: *Thinking* (1977), pp. 82–83; Hans Blumenberg, *Das Lachen der Thrakerin. Eine Urgeschichte der Theorie* (Frankfurt a.M.: Suhrkamp, 1987); Jacques Taminiaux, *La Fille de Thrace et le penseur professionnel. Arendt et Heidegger* (Paris: Payot, 1992).

3   Hannah Arendt, *On Revolution* (London: Penguin, 1990), p. 214.

4   Ibid., p. 21.

5   Ibid., p. 167; my emphasis. Arendt adds that 'the bad-weather theory, which I find rather suggestive, is contained in the "Massachusetts" article in the *Encyclopaedia Britannica*, 11th edition, vol. XVII' (Arendt, *On Revolution*, p. 306).

written constitution in history' and its creative power also originated out of contingency and the ordinary variation of fortune.[6]

In order to erode foundationalist narratives about political institution, I will re-stage Arendt's confrontation with Heidegger regarding 'political beginnings'. Keeping the reference to 'bad weather' in mind, this essay will proceed in three parts. Firstly, I will sketch Heidegger's exceptionalist account of 'new beginnings'. By fusing origin and rule in the will of a single person, I will claim that Heidegger conceives of beginnings as extraordinary, exceptional, and singular moments. Secondly, I will briefly examine Arendt's dispute with Heidegger's work from 1946 to 1958, from manifest enmity due to the latter's commitment to German totalitarianism, to recognition of intellectual gratitude. My aim in this case will be to foreground how, according to Arendt, 'the Heidegger case' (*der Fall Heidegger*) conveys the 'philosophico-political problem', that is to say, the ineradicable tension between the domains of 'philosophy' and 'politics'. Arendt's critical examination of the 'philosophico-political problem', in turn, offers new insights that reveal two distinctive ways of conceiving 'beginnings'. For Heidegger, the 'beginning' expresses — either politically or philosophically — a radical event imbued with an ontological dignity that surpasses any plurality. For Arendt, on the contrary, the 'beginning' seems to stage an an-archic display that is political insofar as it happens 'between' human beings. Finally, this theoretical trajectory will allow me to show how, after her confrontation with Heidegger's work — which, paradoxically, is both the epitome of the philosophical tradition *and* the way to overcome its deadlocks — Arendt provides an original answer to the question of the status of 'political beginnings'. Aware of the particular conditions of political modernity — which, for her, is

---

6   The article of the *Encyclopaedia Britannica* quoted by Arendt emphasizes that 'in the early winter of 1620 [the passengers of the Mayflower] made the coast of Cape Cod; they had intended to make their landfall farther south, within the jurisdiction of the Virginia Company, which had granted them a patent; but *stress of weather* prevented their doing so. Finding themselves without warrant in a region beyond their patent, and threatened with the desertion of disaffected members of their company (probably all servants or men of the 'lesser' sort) unless concessions were made to these, they drew up and signed before landing a democratic compact of government which is accounted the earliest written constitution in history' (*The Encyclopaedia Britannica: A Dictionary of Arts, Sciences, Literature and General Information*, 11th edn, 29 vols (London: The Encyclopaedia Britannica Company, 1911), XVII, p. 858; my emphasis).

rooted in an 'abyssal ground' — Arendt seeks, time and again, coordinates with which to elucidate the act of political institution. In the face of current theoretical perspectives that advocate a return to ontology in order to account for the 'exceptional' origin of life-in-common,[7] I propose that Arendt invites us to recognize the 'principle of anarchy' innate to 'political beginnings'. And I claim that this an-archic matter that animates political foundations, always already exposed to 'bad weather', cannot be absorbed by exceptionalist invocations of the 'history of Being'.

THE TALE OF THE FOX AND THE FASCINATION WITH THE NEW BEGINNING

After not speaking to each other for seventeen years following a grievous falling out, Arendt and Heidegger reconnect in 1950. Three years later, Arendt writes a bittersweet parable about Heidegger in her *Denktagebuch*, a story that hints at the fragility of their 'friendship'. Seeking to capture 'the true story of Heidegger the fox' (*die wahre Geschichte von dem Fuchs Heidegger*), she claims:

[T]he fox who lived in the trap said proudly: 'So many are visiting me in my trap that I have become the best of all foxes.' And there is some truth in that, too: Nobody knows the nature of traps [*Fallenwesen*] better than one who sits in a trap his whole life long.[8]

Arendt's tale of the fox conjures the endless construction of a burrow — one that, because of the fox's determination to perfect it, ends up becoming a dead-end. But the story gets even more dramatic if this particular fox can, thanks to his cleverness, entrap future generations of thinkers. In the most lugubrious reading of the saga, everything the fox touches gives into his charms. The corollary of this terrifying version of the tale is troubling: even surpassing interpretations guided by

---

7   See, among others, Oliver Marchart, *Post-Foundational Political Thought: Political Difference in Nancy, Lefort, Badiou and Laclau* (Edinburgh: Edinburgh University Press, 2007); Marchart, *Die politische Differenz. Zum Denken des Politischen bei Nancy, Lefort, Badiou, Laclau und Agamben* (Berlin: Suhrkamp, 2010).

8   Hannah Arendt, *Denktagebuch: 1950 bis 1973*, ed. by Ursula Ludz and Ingeborg Nordmann, 2 vols (Munich: Piper, 2002), I, p. 404; English trans. as 'Heidegger the Fox', in *Essays in Understanding: 1930–1974. Formation, Exile, and Totalitarianism*, ed. by Jerome Kohn (New York: Schocken, 2005), p. 362.

scandal and the 'anxiety of influence', Arendt is, shockingly, assimilated into the 'destruction of thought' (*destruction de la pensée*) supposedly fostered by her former professor, the fox Heidegger.[9]

Looking to Arendt's parable without falling into a conventional narrative of personal intrigue between the two protagonists, however, will help us to observe that, by being both 'faithful and not faithful' to Heidegger,[10] she offers important insights to delineate the contours of the Heideggerian trap as well as its implications within the domain of political foundation. Heidegger's thought is certainly one of the main bases from which Arendt challenges the failures of the philosophical tradition. But she also sees her former professor's work as the prime example of intellectual hubris that utterly failed to heed life-in-common. Put differently, for Arendt the post-totalitarian political crisis could not be understood if the crisis of philosophy was not tackled, and Heidegger blatantly manifested that theoretical and political quandary.

Several recently-published seminars delivered by Heidegger in the 1930s as well as the *Schwarzen Hefte*,[11] to be sure, complicate Arendt's ambivalent stance toward him. Heidegger, *malgré* Arendt,

---

9   See Elzbieta Ettinger, *Hannah Arendt/Martin Heidegger* (New Haven, CT: Yale University Press, 1995); Richard Wolin, *Heidegger's Children. Hannah Arendt, Karl Löwith, Hans Jonas, and Herbert Marcuse* (Princeton, NJ: Princeton University Press, 2015); Emmanuel Faye, *Arendt et Heidegger. Extermination nazie et destruction de la pensée* (Paris: Albin Michel, 2016).

10   By sending a copy of *Vita activa oder Vom tätigen Leben* to Heidegger via her publisher, Arendt made a confession to him: 'Re Vita activa: The dedication of this book has been omitted. | How could I dedicate it to you | trusted one | *to whom I was faithful* | *and not faithful* [dem ich die Treue gehalten | und nicht gehalten habe] | And in both cases with love'. See Hannah Arendt and Martin Heidegger, *Hannah Arendt/Martin Heidegger. Briefe 1925 bis 1975 und andere Zeugnisse* (Frankfurt a.M.: Klostermann, 1998), p. 319; English trans. as *Letters: 1925–1975*, ed. by Ursula Ludz (New York: Harcourt, 2004), p. 261; my emphasis, translation modified.

11   Martin Heidegger, *Gesamtausgabe*, 102 vols (Frankfurt a.M.: Klostermann, 1975–), XXXVIII: *Logik als die Frage nach dem Wesen der Sprache*, ed. by Günter Seubold (1998); XXXVI/XXXVII: *Sein und Wahrheit*, ed. by Hartmut Tietjen (2001); 'Hegel, "Rechtsphilosophie"', 'Hegel, Rechtsphilosophie. WS 34/35. Mitschrift Wilhelm Hallwachs', 'Hegel, Rechtsphilosophie. WS 34/35. Protokolle', LXXXVI: *Seminare. Hegel-Schelling*, ed. by Peter Trawny (2011), pp. 55–184, pp. 549–611, pp. 613–55; XCIV: *Überlegungen II-IV (Schwarze Hefte 1931–1938)*, ed. by Peter Trawny (2014); XCV: *Überlegungen VII-XI (Schwarze Hefte 1938/1939)*, ed. by Peter Trawny (2014); XCVI: *Überlegungen XII-XV (Schwarze Hefte 1939-1941)*, ed. by Peter Trawny (2014); XCVII: *Anmerkungen I-V (Schwarze Hefte 1942-1948)*, ed. by Peter Trawny (2015); 'Über Wesen und Begriff von Natur, Geschichte und Staat. Übung aus dem Wintersemester 1933/34', in *Heidegger und der Nationalsozialismus. Dokumente*, ed. by Alfred Denker and Holger Zaborowski (Freiburg: Alber, 2009), pp. 53–88.

can no longer be envisioned as the 'hidden king' (*heimlicher König*) of thought, who took a brief detour around Syracuse due to a *déformation professionnelle*.[12] After all, he explicitly links 'ontology' and 'politics' through the notion of 'beginning'. By conflating both realms, Heidegger's position on the 'history of Being' takes a narrative bent: it is encompassed by a 'beginning' (*Anfang*) and an 'end' (*Ende*) or, more accurately, by two 'beginnings' — *erster* and *anderer* — and an 'end' embodied by what he terms machination (*Machenschaft*). This narrative, which of course has protagonists — namely, 'the Greeks' and 'the Germans' — is animated on a metapolitical level.[13] What Heidegger's metapolitics (*Metapolitik*) — understood as both rejection and constitution of the world — names is his own 'onto-historical' (*seinsgeschichtliche*) reflection on the *Anfang*. For Heidegger, then, 'the history of Being' invigorates political life; tuned into the implications of the Greek 'first beginning', Germany, understood as an ontological force, should effect a 'second beginning'.

The essence of the German people, epitomized by the leader, is the groundwork for Heidegger's preaching on the 'foundation' and the 'new beginning'. This exceptionalist rendition of *Anfänge* cannot be weathered; it cannot be subjected to the action of the elements: it seems to be incorruptible. The absolute power of the *Führer* and the fusion of governmental command in one person were salient features of the new German reality. At the time, in *Über Wesen und Begriff von Natur, Geschichte und Staat* (*Wintersemester* 1933/34), Heidegger upheld the idea that the leader's will knew no bounds since he was the ontological interpreter of the people and the state.[14] The *Führerprinzip* praised by Heidegger, in turn, instantiates the 'onto-historical' and extra-political foundation of 'the political', as well as the political institution of the will of *a single* man. One man, or better, *this* man, is not the shepherd of Being; Being, rather, seems to be shepherd of the leader. The leader is the 'preparer of the danger, the decider

---

12   Hannah Arendt, 'Martin Heidegger ist achtzig Jahre alt', in *Antwort. Martin Heidegger im Gespräch*, ed. by Günther Neske and Emil Kettering (Tübingen: Neske, 1988), pp. 232–46 (pp. 233 and 243–45).

13   See Heidegger, *Überlegungen II-IV*, pp. 115, 116, and 124.

14   Heidegger, 'Über Wesen und Begriff von Natur, Geschichte und Staat', p. 77.

of the struggle (*Kampfes*), and the guardian of its new truths'.[15] In 'Hegel, "Rechtsphilosophie"' (*Wintersemester* 1934/35), in particular, Heidegger will assert:

The unification of powers in the Dasein of the leader is not a mere coupling and heaping up (quantitative), but rather in itself already the starting point [*Beginn*] of the development of an originally new [*ursprünglich neuen*] — but still undeveloped — beginning [*Anfangs*].[16]

The German 'revolution', as Heidegger conceived it, laid the foundation for more than the mere seizure of power.

Crucial, in this sense, is the distinction that Heidegger draws between the notions of 'starting point' (*Beginn*), 'beginning' (*Anfang*), and 'origin' (*Ur-sprung*) of the state.[17] For Heidegger, the 'starting point' is left behind as the 'occurrence' (*Geschehen*) unfolds. The 'beginning', meanwhile, irradiates unparalleled energy in its own 'occurrence'. The radicalism of the Heideggerian 'beginning' is evidenced in a foundational act that rests on the figure of the leader. According to Heidegger, the leader does not contemplate the political reality but shapes it. His intervention is historical and reveals a truth embodied in danger and *pólemos*.[18] If Heidegger once spoke of an event that 'can only be compared to the change at the beginning [*Anfang*] of the intellectual history of the Western human being in general',[19] he now uses the notion of 'another beginning' (*anderer Anfang*) to refer to that same phenomenon. Heidegger's thinking takes this new turn in the context of a discussion of what he envisions as 'our people' (*unser Volk*), which is at once the 'most endangered people' (*gefährdetstes Volk*) and the 'metaphysical people' (*metaphysisches Volk*).[20] Later, for Heidegger, not only the statesman, but also the poet and the thinker will be the

---

15   Heidegger, 'Hegel, "Rechtsphilosophie"', p. 170.

16   Ibid., p. 73.

17   Ibid., pp. 74–75. Richard Polt states that 'the main point here is that the chronological beginning of a process, its "starting point", is not necessarily an "inception" in the Heideggerian sense'. See Richard Polt, 'Self-Assertion as Founding', in Martin Heidegger, *On Hegel's Philosophy of Right: The 1934–35 Seminar and Interpretative Essays*, ed. by Peter Trawny, Marcia Sá Cavalcante Schuback, and Michael Marder (London: Bloomsbury, 2014), pp. 67–81 (p. 74).

18   Heidegger, 'Hegel, "Rechtsphilosophie"', p. 177.

19   Heidegger, *Logik als die Frage nach dem Wesen der Sprache*, p. 132.

20   Martin Heidegger, *Gesamtausgabe*, 102 vols (Frankfurt a.M.: Klostermann, 1975–), XL: *Einführung in die Metaphysik*, ed. by Petra Jaeger (1983), p. 41.

ones who express the radical self-affirmation and self-foundation of the people: all of them must grapple with the question of who can initiate the 'beginning'. But, beyond any good or bad weather, in the previous and foundationalist instance that we examined, Heidegger assumes that philosophy — or rather, *his philosophy* — in conjunction with the creation of the new leader is what drives the 'new beginning'.[21]

LOOKING INTO THE EXCEPTIONALIST TRAP: THE PHILOSOPHICO-POLITICAL AS PROBLEM

Centred on the 'anxiety of influence' and personal intrigue, the most catastrophic interpretation of the tale of the fox lets out a deafening cry in response to Heidegger's exceptionalist description of the 'beginning' of a 'we' evident in *Über Wesen und Begriff von Natur, Geschichte und Staat*, and 'Hegel, "Rechtsphilosophie"'. The cleverness of this animal, combined with its evil nature, is adduced to entrap everyone wandering around under its spell. Heidegger's trap, the philosophical positing of a political beginning as ontologically exceptional, appears in this rendition as a totalitarian realization imbued with unavoidable magnetism. Arendt, considered merely under Heidegger's shadow, cannot but accentuate the predicament. Subjugated to her former professor's enchantment, she, according to this version, 'advocate[s] a form of salvation, based on a superficially seductive — though equally Heideggerian — vision of being-with (*Mitsein*). This vision leads her to conceive a paradigm of the *polis* that excludes most of humanity: long ago, the slave, the foreigner, the barbarian; today, the worker, the employee — in short, the multitude of those not immortalized by the heroic grandeur of political action [*la grandeur héroïque de l'agir politique*].'[22] Conflating Heidegger's and Arendt's theoretical impulses, this interpretation disregards her *Auseinandersetzung* with *der Fall Heidegger* — which is symptomatic since, even today, in the wake of a new episode of it due to the recent publication of the *Schwarzen Hefte*, interpretations tend either to denounce or to exculpate.

---

21   This tendency culminates when he asserts that 'in sixty years, our state will certainly not be led by the *Führer* anymore; but what happens *then* is up to *us*. *This is why* we must philosophize [*Deshalb* müssen wir philosophieren]' (Heidegger, 'Hegel, Rechtsphilosophie. WS 34/35. Mitschrift Wilhelm Hallwachs', p. 560; emphasis in original).

22   Faye, *Arendt et Heidegger*, p. 512.

Even notions like 'metapolitics', which Heidegger ties to the 'end of "philosophy"' (*Ende der 'Philosophie'*), the 'metaphysics of Dasein' (*Metaphysik des Daseins*), the 'historical people' (*geschichtliches Volk*) and, of course, the 'new beginning' (*neuer Anfang*),[23] are envisioned as part of a dispute that can, under no circumstances, be allowed to sully philosophy. Heidegger's defenders assert time and again that the greatest philosopher of the twentieth century never scrutinized political issues explicitly — which is simply false. Heidegger's accusers contend that his work can in no way be conceived as philosophy, since the author was an enthusiastic supporter of German totalitarianism.[24] Although one of Heidegger's post-war aspirations was to protect his philosophical project from readings that emphasize its political implications, Arendt herself had, by 1946, started to examine this issue.

Far from the praise of Heidegger's philosophical endeavour voiced in, for instance, her 1930 essay 'Philosophie und Soziologie', Arendt challenges what she terms 'Heideggerian functionalism' in her 1946 text 'What Is Existenz Philosophy?'.[25] Central in her argument is the inability of Heidegger and, *mutatis mutandis*, of philosophy, to rigorously interrogate the status of plurality and life-in-common. Heidegger is, according to Arendt, the last German Romantic and, as such, he is completely irresponsible politically. The most patent expression of this 'oblivion of politics' is the fact that Heidegger's thinking focuses on the question of the 'Self'. 'This ideal of the Self follows as a consequence of Heidegger's making of man what God was in earlier ontology', Arendt argues. And she adds that 'a being of this highest order is conceivable only as single and unique and knowing no equals'. In sum, 'the essential character of the Self is its absolute Self-ness, its radical separation from

---

23   Heidegger, *Überlegungen II-IV*, pp. 115 and 124.

24   The paradigmatic cases of this dyad, which ultimately safeguards the immaculate site of philosophy are: Friedrich-Wilhelm von Herrmann and Francesco Alfieri, *Martin Heidegger. La verita' sui Quaderni Neri* (Brescia: Morcelliana Editrice, 2016) and Emmanuel Faye, *Heidegger, l'introduction du nazisme dans la philosophie. Autour des séminaires inédits de 1933–1935* (Paris: Albin Michel, 2005). Exceptions to the aforementioned impasse are, among others: Peter Trawny and Andrew Mitchell, eds, *Heidegger, die Juden, noch einmal* (Frankfurt a.M.: Klostermann, 2015); Andrew Mitchell and Peter Trawny, eds, *Heidegger's Black Notebooks. Responses to Anti-Semitism* (New York: Columbia University Press, 2017).

25   Hannah Arendt, 'Philosophie und Soziologie. Anläßlich Karl Mannheims *Ideologie und Utopie*', *Die Gesellschaft*, 7.1 (1930), pp. 163–76; 'What Is Existenz Philosophy?', in her *Essays in Understanding*, pp. 163–87 (p. 178).

all its fellows.'[26] The climax of this invective is the brief tale in Arendt's *Denktagebuch* where, as noted, she compares Heidegger to a fox.

The Arendtian tale of the fox, nonetheless, is not her last word about Heidegger nor is it a fate she was condemned to. For Arendt, the figure of Heidegger represents an enigma at the core of the irresolvable dispute between 'philosophy' and 'politics'. Arendt will never cease to theorize what is at stake in the 'philosophico-political problem' — a crucial aspect of her critical interpretation of Heidegger's project in later essays.[27] To fully understand this 'problem', we must bear in mind the series of works she wrote starting after the war and through the publication of *The Human Condition* in 1958.[28]

Of those writings, 'Concern with Politics in Recent European Philosophical Thought' deserves special attention.[29] In it, Arendt discusses Heidegger's emphasis on 'historicity' (*Geschichtlichkeit*) to show that, for him, human history coincides with the history of Being. Expressing a new critical approach — one at odds with her vision in 'What Is Existenz Philosophy?' — Arendt argues that neither a transcendent spirit nor an absolute are revealed in Heidegger's ontology. A philosopher informed by the Heideggerian lesson would not attempt to institute a vision of herself as a wise being who searches for eternal patterns to understand human affairs that are, by definition, perishable. For Arendt, this new understanding 'opens the way to a reexamination of the whole realm of politics in light of elementary human experiences [and the discarding of] traditional concepts and judgments'. Heidegger, then, is envisioned as an author who reads the old texts

---

26   Ibid., pp. 180 and 181.

27   See Arendt, *On Revolution; Between Past and Future: Eight Exercises in Political Thought* (New York: Penguin, 1993); *The Life of the Mind.*

28   In reference to that last work, Arendt lets Heidegger know that it 'came directly out of the first Freiburg days [*Freiburger Tagen*] and hence owes practically everything to you in every respect [*schuldet Dir in jeder Hinsicht so ziemlich alles*]' (Arendt in *Hannah Arendt / Martin Heidegger*, p. 149; *Letters*, p. 124). Remarkably, Arendt mistakenly writes 'Freiburger' instead of 'Marburger'.

29   See Arendt, 'Concern with Politics in Recent European Philosophical Thought', in *Essays in Understanding*, pp. 428–47. See also 'Concern with Politics in Recent European Philosophical Thought', in *Perspektiven politischen Denkens. Beiträge anläßlich des 100. Geburtstags von Hannah Arendt*, ed. by Antonia Grunenberg, Waltraud Meints, Oliver Bruns, and Christine Harckensee (Frankfurt a.M.: Peter Lang Verlag, 2008), pp. 11–31; 'Concern with Politics in Recent European Philosophical Thought', in *The Modern Challenge to Tradition: Fragmente eines Buchs*, ed. by Barbara Hahn and James McFarland (Göttingen: Wallstein Verlag, 2018), pp. 560–92.

with new eyes. In response to a patent expression of the 'philosophico-political problem' — mainly, the observation that philosophy mostly deals with human being in the singular, whereas politics deals with human beings in the plural — Heidegger's notion of 'world' (*Welt*) is, for Arendt, insightful. Insofar as Heidegger 'defines human existence as being-in-the-world', Arendt claims that 'he insists on giving philosophic significance to structures of everyday life that are completely incomprehensible if man is not primarily understood as being together with others'.[30]

With this extended prolegomenon, I attempt to explicitly release Arendt's argument from any possible subordination to the process of coming to terms with Heidegger's totalitarian commitment. Arendt's work should function neither as mere repercussion of Heidegger's nor as protection against its most inadmissible tendencies. Indeed, many theorists have considered how Arendt thinks both *with and against* Heidegger.[31] Stressing her critical stance, my examination of the Arendtian notion of 'political beginning' shows its intertwinement with the 'an-archic principle' of politics, a term to which I will return in the third part of this essay.

Beyond any personal impulse that might have animated Arendt's endeavour,[32] her discussion of the concept of 'beginning' can only be

---

30   Arendt, 'Concern with Politics in Recent European Philosophical Thought', in *Essays in Understanding*, pp. 432 and 443.

31   See, notably, Simona Forti, *Vita della mente e tempo della polis* (Milano: Franco Angeli, 1996), pp. 43–87; Peg Birmingham, 'Heidegger and Arendt: The Birth of Political Action and Speech', in *Heidegger and Practical Philosophy*, ed. by François Raffoul and David Pettigrew (Albany: State University of New York Press, 2002), pp. 191–202; Miguel Abensour, *Hannah Arendt contre la philosophie politique?* (Paris: Sens & Tonka, 2006); Miguel Abensour, 'Contre la souveraineté de la philosophie sur la politique. La Lecture arendtienne du mythe de la caverne', in *Hannah Arendt. Crises de l'état-nation. Pensées alternatives*, ed. by Anne Kupiec, Martine Leibovici, Géraldine Muhlmann, and Etienne Tassin (Paris: Sens & Tonka), pp. 341–68. See also Margaret Canovan, 'Socrates or Heidegger? Hannah Arendt's Reflections on Philosophy and Politics', *Social Research*, 57.1 (1990), pp. 135–65; Dana Villa, *Arendt and Heidegger: The Fate of the Political* (Princeton, NJ: Princeton University Press, 1996); Antonia Grunenberg, *Hannah Arendt und Martin Heidegger. Geschichte einer Liebe* (Munich: Piper, 2006); Taminiaux, *La Fille de Thrace et le penseur professionnel*; Jacques Taminiaux, 'La Déconstruction arendtienne des vues politiques de Heidegger', *Cahiers philosophiques*, 3.111 (2007), pp. 16–30; Dieter Thomä, 'Hannah Arendt. Liebe zur Welt', in *Heidegger Handbuch. Leben-Werk-Wirkung*, ed. by Dieter Thomä (Stuttgart: Metzler, 2013), pp. 397–402.

32   Strikingly, Arendt affirms that 'sometimes I ask myself what is more difficult — to teach the Germans a sense of politics [*einen Sinn für Politik*] or to impart to the Americans a

properly understood if her persistent confrontation with the philosophical tradition is taken into account. While Arendt's engagement
with the question of the 'beginning' is not systematic, it does run
through all of her work, as does her interest in the related 'principle' or
'principles' of action. From *Der Liebesbegriff bei Augustin* through *The
Life of the Mind*, along with mentions in her key texts,[33] the 'beginning'
is omnipresent in the Arendtian world. While many have examined this
notion in her political theory,[34] one aspect of it — Arendt's dispute
with Heidegger over the ways of narrating the 'beginning' — has been
largely overlooked.

Considering her former professor's radical stance on the *Anfang*,[35]
Arendt's dictum that 'against philosophy only philosophy helps' (*Ge-*

---

light dusting of philosophy [*einen leichten Dunst auch nur von Philosophie*]'. See *Hannah Arendt–Karl Jaspers Briefwechsel. 1926–1969*, ed. by Lotte Köhler and Hans Saner (Munich: Piper, 1985), p. 165.

33   See, among others, Hannah Arendt, *Der Liebesbegriff bei Augustin. Versuch einer philosophischen Interpretation* (Hildesheim: Olms, 2006); *Was ist Politik? Fragmente aus dem Nachlaß*, ed. by Ursula Ludz and Kurt Sontheimer (Munich: Piper, 1993); *The Origins of Totalitarianism* (New York: Meridian, 1958); 'On the Nature of Totalitarianism: An Essay in Understanding', in her *Essays in Understanding*, pp. 328–60; *The Human Condition* (Chicago: Chicago University Press, 1998); *On Revolution*; *Between Past and Future*, *The Life of the Mind*.

34   See, among others, Bonnie Honig, 'Declarations of Independence: Arendt and Derrida on the Problem of Founding a Republic', *The American Political Science Review*, 85.1 (1991), pp. 97–113; Margaret Canovan, *Hannah Arendt: A Reinterpretation of Her Political Thought* (Cambridge: Cambridge University Press, 1992), pp. 136–55; Linda Zerilli, 'Castoriadis, Arendt, and the Problem of the New', *Constellations*, 9.4 (2002), pp. 540–53; Allan Keenan, 'Promises, Promises: The Abyss of Freedom and the Loss of the Political in the Work of Hannah Arendt', in his *Democracy in Question. Democratic Openness in a Time of Political Closure* (Stanford, CA: Stanford University Press, 2003), pp. 76–101; Andreas Kalyvas, *Democracy and the Politics of the Extraordinary: Max Weber, Carl Schmitt, and Hannah Arendt* (Cambridge: Cambridge University Press, 2008), pp. 187–300; Patchen Markell, 'The Rule of the People: Arendt, Archê, and Democracy', *The American Political Science Review*, 100.1 (2006), pp. 1–14; Lucy Cane, 'Hannah Arendt on the Principles of Political Action', *European Journal of Political Theory*, 14.1 (2015), pp. 55–75; Claudia Hilb, 'El principio del *initium*', in *Revolución y violencia en la filosofía de Hannah Arendt*, ed. by Marco Estrada Saavedra and María Teresa Muñoz (México D.F.: El Colegio de México, 2015), pp. 67–102.

35   See, in particular, Heidegger, *Gesamtausgabe*, 102 vols (Frankfurt a.M.: Klostermann, 1975–), xxxv: *Der Anfang der abendländischen Philosophie. Auslegung des Anaximander und Parmenides*, ed. by Peter Trawny (2012); lxv: *Beiträge zur Philosophie (Vom Ereignis)*, ed. by Friedrich-Wilhelm von Herrmann (1994); lv: *Heraklit. Der Anfang des abendländischen Denkens. Logik. Heraklits Lehre vom Logos*, ed. by Manfred Frings (1987); lxx: *Über den Anfang*, ed. by Paola-Ludovika Coriando (2005); lxxi: *Das Ereignis*, ed. by Friedrich-Wilhelm von Herrmann (2009); lxxiii.1–2: *Zum Ereignis-Denken*, ed. by Peter Trawny (2013).

gen Philosophie hilft nur Philosophie) must not be disregarded:[36] to interrogate the question of the politicality of the 'beginning' in an Arendtian fashion requires scrutinizing its philosophical vein in order to deactivate the exceptionalist impulses inherent to the act of beginning. Arendt acknowledges this important facet of the 'philosophico-political problem' against the backdrop of modern revolutions and totalitarianism. She does not brush aside the pitfall of exceptionalism when she returns to Heidegger's thinking only to go beyond it since, for her, the politicality of the 'beginning' lies in its plural character: beginnings are, in Arendt's view, set off by the 'endless variety of a multitude whose majesty resided in its very plurality'.[37]

Bypassing the scandal sparked by a catastrophic interpretation of the tale of the fox, I have attempted to bring to light a theoretical impasse: either interpreters have disregarded how Arendt's notion of 'beginning' is rooted in her *Auseinandersetzung* with Heidegger or they have taken that dispute into account but overlooked the risks inherent to the Heideggerian understanding of the 'beginning' as an extraordinary event. In order to fully address the question of 'beginning', it is, I argue, vital to return to that impasse. Once it is disentangled, it becomes evident that both a 'principle of an-archy' and the basic experience of its *common* institution animate political foundation. It is at the core of 'bad weather', then, that a promise to withstand and multiply beginnings lies.

WEATHERING BEGINNINGS OR THE AN-ARCHIC PROMISE

The story of Heidegger and Arendt was re-written more than once. During her first semester at the Philipps-Universität Marburg, Arendt attended Heidegger's seminar on Plato's *Sophist*, which included a reading of Aristotle's *Nicomachean Ethics*. This first encounter had lasting theoretical consequences in Arendt's work and, particularly, in her contention with the philosophical tradition. Indeed, her interest in the

---

36   See Arendt's letter to Dolf Sternberger dated 26 August 1949 in Hannah Arendt, *Wahrheit gibt es nur zu zweien. Briefe an die Freunde*, ed. by Ingeborg Nordmann (Munich: Piper, 2013), p. 86.

37   Arendt, *On Revolution*, 93. See also Hannah Arendt, 'Philosophy and Politics', *Social Research*, 57.1 (1990), pp. 73–103.

notion of 'beginning' emerged precisely during the 'Marburg days'. As Arendt reminds us, though, intense engagement with this topic is not incidental: the question of 'political beginnings' is as old as philosophical concerns with politics in general.[38] Approaching the atavisms of tradition as a means to engage the abyssal character of political modernity, Arendt undertakes a far-reaching theoretical investigation that releases 'political beginnings' from the pure spontaneity of the great event and *the given*.

Despite not having access to the recently published seminars and notebooks in which Heidegger advocates a fusion of 'ontology' and 'politics' as a key to understanding the 'new beginning', Arendt refutes some of his basic assumptions on founding moments in politics. If, in the Heideggerian constellation, grasping an extraordinary beginning and the great mission of a 'we' is based on the repudiation of clumsy repetition and requires 'destroying destruction' (*détruire la destruction*),[39] if that *neuer Anfang* is inextricably related to a 'fundamental experience' (*Grunderfahrung*) expressed in the figures of 'danger' (*Gefahr*), 'self-affirmation' (*Selbstbehauptung*), and 'destiny' (*Schicksal*),[40] then, by contrast, the Arendtian endeavour focuses on what, in reference to the formulation of one of her most sophisticated collaborators, Reiner Schürmann, we might call the 'an-archic principle' inherent in every 'beginning'.[41] Arendt's 'political beginning' lies beyond an exceptionalist scene that seeks to bring to a halt the decline of the West and, to that end, exacerbates the intimate fusion of 'ontology' and 'politics', of the *Dasein* and the German people.

In releasing 'beginning' from its ontological substratum, Arendt, *thinking with and against* Heidegger, returns to the question of 'political inception'. She observes that the *Anfang* is *based on* the paradox of its self-institution. This realization, I argue, evidences that Arendt's rendition of 'political beginnings' constitutes one of the highest points

---

38 In her 1969 birthday tribute to Heidegger, Arendt states: 'Plato once remarked that "*the beginning* [Anfang] *is also a god*; so long as he dwells among human beings, he redeems all things" (*Laws* 775)' (Arendt, 'Martin Heidegger ist achtzig Jahre alt', p. 232; my emphasis).

39 See Jean-Luc Nancy, *Banalité de Heidegger* (Paris: Éditions Galilée, 2015), p. 42.

40 Heidegger, *Überlegungen II-IV*, pp. 160–62.

41 See Reiner Schürmann, *Le Principe d'anarchie. Heidegger et la question de l'agir* (Paris: Éditions du Seuil, 1982).

in her examination of the ineradicable tension between 'philosophy' and 'politics'. Without absolutes — which implies questioning philosophical intervention in the political domain — 'beginnings' cannot be grounded on the itineraries of an exceptionalist 'history of Being' or of 'history as drama of being' (*l'histoire comme drame de l'être*).[42] 'Beginnings' undergo, rather, the an-archic pluralization at stake in any extra-ordinary act of political foundation. 'An-archic' has a specific meaning: to 'begin' with, the *archē* of a principle inheres the fusion of 'its beginning (*commencement*) and its rule (*commandement*)'.[43] Conversely, the anarchic '*lacks simple ultimacy*' and counteracts any *principial* reference by being a 'force of dislocation, of plurification' regarding fully constituted *archē* as point of origin and governance.[44]

Through an understanding of 'beginning' as a conjunction of inaugural actions governed by an 'an-archic principle', Arendt can elaborate a response both to the widespread confusion regarding the domains of labour, work, and action, and to the traditional representation of the Platonic myth of the cave where the polis, grounded on the *agáthōn*, is, ultimately, assumed to be the founding myth of every political theory. Arendt's critical assessment of the philosophical tradition — from Plato and Aristotle to Hobbes, Marx, and Heidegger — shows that, in elaborating the notion of 'beginning', she is trying to find ways of thematizing political groundings without upholding a principle that lies beyond human affairs. The 'an-archic principle' innate to the 'beginning' can only exist in confrontation with the provenance of the One as fusion of origin and rule. Politically, it implies that 'power under the condition of human plurality can never amount to omnipotence, and laws residing on human power can never be absolute'.[45] Detecting the limits and promises of an an-archic 'beginning' — a 'beginning' *without banisters* — means, then, bringing to the fore the contours of the exceptionalist Heideggerian trap. And that is no mean feat. Arendt herself

---

42   For this formulation, see Alain Badiou, *Le Séminaire. Heidegger. L'Être 3 — Figure du retrait. 1986–1987* (Paris: Fayard, 2015), p. 122.

43   Schürmann, *Le Principe d'anarchie*, p. 42.

44   Schürmann, 'Technicity, Topology, Tragedy: Heidegger on "That Which Saves" in the Global Reach', in *Technology in the Western Political Tradition*, ed. by Arthur M. Melzer, Jerry Weinberger, and M. Richard Zimman (Ithaca, NY: Cornell University Press, 1993), pp. 190–213 (p. 199); *Le Principe d'anarchie*, p. 16.

45   Arendt, *On Revolution*, p. 39.

pointed out the risks of her former professor's siren song: 'Come here, everyone; this is a trap, the most beautiful trap in the world [*die schönste Falle der Welt*].'[46]

One way of circumventing the magnetism of a trap that offers the ecstasy of the extraordinary is to associate the 'an-archic principle' of 'beginning' with the basic experience of 'bad weather' — a weather that, expressing the force of contingency, ameliorates exceptionalist myths around the grandeur and singularity of political foundations. Arendt vehemently contests narratives that constrict the 'manyness of beginnings'. The figure of the great founder understood as an ontological supplement of 'the political' must give way to the idea of democratic 'ordinary glories'. Arendt's commitment to a 'politics of the ordinary', to be sure, does not mean suppressing that which erupts unpredictably or that which challenges the status quo.[47] At stake in the 'an-archic principle' of 'political beginnings' is not the contraposition of ordinary and extraordinary moments, but rather recognition of 'anonymous glory'. That is why Arendt appreciates the 'nameless heroes' (*namenlose Helden*), the 'common man' (*gewöhnlicher Mensch*), the 'anybody and everybody' (*irgendwer und jedermann*) who is 'ruled by his laws and not by mysterious forces [*geheimnisvolle Kräfte*] emanating from above or from below'.[48]

Ultimately, my returning to Arendt's *Auseinandersetzung* with Heidegger, to the *sotto voce* dispute between them over how to narrate the experience of the 'beginning', was not merely an exegetic matter. It was

---

46   Arendt, *Denktagebuch*, p. 403; 'Heidegger the Fox', p. 362.

47   Arendt makes this point crystal clear by affirming that 'the *common* and the *ordinary* must remain our primary concern, the daily food of our thought — if only because it is from them that the *uncommon* and the *extraordinary* emerge'. Hannah Arendt, 'Action and the Pursuit of Happiness', Paper delivered at the Meeting of the American Political Science Association, The Hannah Arendt Papers at the Library of Congress, MSS Box 61, 1960, pp. 1–21 (p. 2; my emphasis). See also Kalyvas, *Democracy and the Politics of the Extraordinary*, p. 224; Bonnie Honig, *Emergency Politics: Paradox, Law, Democracy* (Princeton, NJ: Princeton University Press, 2009), p. xviii.

48   Hannah Arendt, 'Franz Kafka, von neuem gewürdigt', *Die Wandlung*, 1.12 (1945/1946), pp. 1050–62 (pp. 1058 and 1062); 'Franz Kafka', in her *Die verborgene Tradition. Essays* (Frankfurt a.M.: Suhrkamp, 1976), pp. 95–116 (pp. 108 and 115); 'Franz Kafka: A Revaluation. On the Occasion of the Twentieth Anniversary of his Death', in her *Essays in Understanding*, pp. 69–80 (pp. 76 and 80). See also Étienne Tassin, 'Les Gloires ordinaires: Actualité du concept arendtien d'espace public', *Cahiers Sens Public*, 15–16 (2013), pp. 23–36; Patchen Markell, 'Anonymous Glory', *European Journal of Political Theory*, 16.1 (2017), pp. 77–99.

also an attempt to open up a space to re-ask what the promise of politics should be today. Current struggles against climate change, exploitation, neo-colonialism, extractivism, patriarchy, and racism, prove that a 'politics of the ordinary' cannot rely on redemptive figures that incarnate the myth of leadership. Beginning anew, thus, can only commence if we accept that, not anymore univocal, 'political beginnings' should stage and enact the plural 'power of the many'. The storms can only be weathered if beginnings appear as they are: common and mundane occurrences that hold in them the potential to interdigitate, proliferate, and to push towards a radicalization of the democratic adventure.

FLOODS

Representing the World, Weathering its End
Arthur Bispo do Rosário's Ecology of the Ship

MARLON MIGUEL

PRE SCRIPTUM

If one looks at the definition of the word 'weather', one will find an intrinsic relation to the sea and the ship.[1] 'Weather' is, on the one hand, a noun that refers to 'the state of the atmosphere at a particular place and time', and, on the other, a verb, meaning:

1. to expose to open air and, therefore, to begin a process of transformation or alteration due to 'long exposure to the atmosphere'

2. 'to bear up against and come safely through', commonly referred to a ship coming 'safely through a storm' ('the sturdy boat had

---

1   I would like to acknowledge the support of some people that made this text possible. First of all, the team of the Museu Bispo do Rosário Arte Contemporânea, in particular, the curator Ricardo Resende for authorizing the publication and sending the images of Bispo's works, as well as the coordinator for education and curatorship of the Museum, Diana Kolker. The latter kindly received me in the Museum in November 2019 and was a crucial interlocutor for writing this text. I thank also Tania Rivera for the essential exchanges around Bispo's work, as well as Eleonora Fabião and Márcio Seligmann-Silva for sending me their papers, which are quoted in this chapter. Finally, I thank Delfina Cabrera and Claudia Peppel for their crucial commentaries and for the discussions around this piece during the last year.

weathered the storm well'); 'to make good, bad, etc. weather of
a ship'; to behave well or ill in a storm. And then, by extension
and, more metaphorically, 'to live through a difficult situation or
a problem', 'to undergo or endure the action of the elements'.[2]

Etymologically, 'weather' comes from the old English *weder* (air,
sky, breeze, storm, tempest) and the Proto-Germanic *wedra* (wind,
weather). In the seventeenth century, it was associated with the idea
of 'coming through safely' and often with 'a ship riding out a storm'. In
nautical use, it appears also as an adjective, meaning 'toward the wind'
(opposed thus to 'lee'). An expression such as 'under the weather',
for example, also comes from nautical vocabulary and before evolving
to the connotation it carries today of feeling unwell, it originally expressed the action of going down, below, under the deck and away
from the elements. Later, in the course of the eighteenth century,
'weather' gets tied to exposure as a metaphor. In Latin, *tempestas*
means 'season', 'weather', 'bad weather', 'tempest/storm', but also time,
and we know how the French *temps*, Spanish *tiempo*, Portuguese and
Italian *tempo* mean both the time and the weather — the only exception in Latin languages is the Romanian, which has *timp* and
vremea, meaning 'time' and 'weather', although strangely *vremea* can
also be used as 'time'. Latin languages also have the derived terms of
*tempestade/tempest/tempête/tempesta/tormenta/temporal(e)/*etc. It is
thus remarkable that the terms in both Latin and Germanic languages
evolved in a nearly parallel fashion; and even though the Germanic
languages make the distinction between 'time' and 'weather', the latter
remains associated with the passing of time and the idea of 'going
through'. As verb, 'weather' condenses the two meanings and synthe-
tizes them into a certain contradiction: it relates to both the passing
and the effects of time and the resistance to time and its effects.

INTRODUCTION

In this chapter, I would like to explore a constellation of issues that
run through Arthur Bispo do Rosário's work and posit how these

---

2   See *Merriam-Webster.com Dictionary* (Springfield, MA: Merriam-Webster, 2020)
     <https://www.merriam-webster.com/>, *OED Online* (Oxford: Oxford University
     Press, 2020) <https://www.oed.com/>, and *Online Etymology Dictionary* <https:
     //www.etymonline.com/> [accessed 28 June 2020].

works — and the topics they engage — reveal an intriguing relationship between weather/weathering, sea, memory, and artistic production. These terms are to be read, on the one hand, in the context of Bispo's eschatological narrative: his 'mission' of representing the world through objects that can weather till the end of times. But, on the other hand and beyond the artist's assumed discourse, his constructions are also a way of weathering obliteration and oblivion — of weathering the 'natural' fate he was destined for because of his racial, social, and clinical status. His objects — and among them, several types of ships — contribute to an inventive strategy to deal with memory and the process of recollection.

In 2017 and 2018, I collaborated on the exhibition *Lugares do delírio* (Places of Delirium), curated by the researcher and psychoanalyst Tania Rivera. The exhibition combined works of well-known artists from the established art circuit (such as Cildo Meireles and Lygia Clark) and those of more or less well-known 'mad' artists. In fact, the curator's aim was not so much to talk about madness, but rather about delirium, or about how, in her words:

> [T]he field of the artistic production can be rigorously taken as cultural field of the construction of reality. In the art, one has deliriums [*delira-se*, a verb in Portuguese], the thought leaves its usual rails, the imaginary rails that fix the 'common' reality in which we alienate ourselves.[3]

By shifting, thus, the perspective from madness to delirium, Rivera reactivates the Freudian gesture, which looks at psychiatric 'disorders' as positive phenomena. In the case of the delirium, this means seeing it as a form of the production of subjectivity, an 'attempt at a cure or a reconstruction'.[4]

---

3   Fatima Pinheiro and Tania Rivera, 'In Situ | Lugares do Delírio — Entrevista com Tania Rivera', *Subversos* (2017); my translation <http://subversos.com.br/in-situ-lugares-do-delirio-entrevista-com-tania-rivera/> [accessed 28 June 2020]. See also Tania Rivera, 'Museu dos delírios — notas sobre a exposição *Lugares do delírio*', *Ao Largo*, 6 (2018) <https://www.maxwell.vrac.puc-rio.br/33478/33478.PDF> [accessed 28 June 2020].

4   Sigmund Freud, 'Neurosis and Psychosis', in *The Standard Edition of the Complete Psychological Works of Sigmund Freud*, ed. and trans. by James Strachey, 24 vols (London: Hogarth, 1953–74), xix: *The Ego and the Id and Other Works (1923–25)* (1961), pp. 147–54 (p. 151).

To my surprise, when I arrived at the Art Museum of Rio de Janeiro (MAR), in the beginning of the exhibition's installation, I found mainly boats. The patients of the public mental health system, many of whom were Afro-descendants — as is common in the Brazilian psychiatric system — had built most of these objects. There were boats by, among others, Maurício Flandeiro (from Cariri in northeastern Brazil and patient of the public mental health system), Arlindo Oliveira and Luiz Carlos Marques (both attending the therapeutic space Gaia Atelier, at the Colônia Juliano Moreira, in Rio de Janeiro). Alongside these works, one could see also those built by Bispo do Rosário. They were very prominent, and it was clear that he was a key figure in the exhibition — he gave coherence to that strange ocean of objects displayed in the museum space. That particular institution seemed also the perfect place to host the exhibition as it is called MAR — 'sea', in Portuguese — and was recently built in the renewed waterfront district of Rio de Janeiro.[5]

My first association when observing this emerging milieu was Michel Foucault's *History of Madness*, its discussion of the ship of fools, and the mysterious relationship between water, navigation, and madness stressed therein.[6] And indeed, in the exhibition, by collect-

---

5   The exhibition was originally proposed by curator and art critic Paulo Herkenhoff, curated by Tania Rivera. It was first shown at the Museum of Art of Rio (MAR), from 2 February to 17 September 2017 and subsequently, in an expanded version, at the SESC Pompeia, in São Paulo, from 12 April to 2 July 2018. About the MAR, see footnote 9.

6   'So the ship of fools was heavily loaded with meaning, and clearly carried a great social force. On the one hand, it had incontestably practical functions, as entrusting a madman to the care of boatmen meant that he would no longer roam around the city walls, and ensured that he would travel far and be a prisoner of his own departure. But there was more: water brought its own dark symbolic charge, carrying away, but purifying too. Navigation brought man face to face with the uncertainty of destiny, where each is left to himself and every departure might always be the last. The madman on his crazy boat sets sail for the other world, and it is from the other world that he comes when he disembarks. This enforced navigation is both rigorous division and absolute Passage, serving to underline in real and imaginary terms the *liminal* situation of the mad in medieval society. It was a highly symbolic role, made clear by the mental geography involved, where the madman was *confined at the gates of the cities*. His exclusion was his confinement, and if he had no *prison* other than the *threshold* itself he was still detained at this place of passage. In a highly symbolic position he is placed on the inside of the outside, or vice versa. A posture that is still his today, if we admit that what was once the visible fortress of social order is now the castle of our own consciousness. Water and navigation had that role to play. Locked in the ship from which he could not escape, the madman was handed over to the thousand-armed river, to the sea where all paths cross, and the great uncertainty that surrounds all things. A

ing ships, Rivera also tried to reframe the question of madness — as already noted — towards that of delirium, emphasizing the productive, creative force of the latter. In this way, she also echoed the proposal of the curator and art theoretician Frederico Morais, primarily responsible for the acknowledgement of the importance of Bispo's works, as well as for their reception in the art world. According to Morais, Bispo's deliriums should be seen as an attempt at 'ordering of ideas, [an] elaboration of concepts'.[7] As we will see, Bispo's production is a way of (re)building a world, a form of organizing what the medical order called his 'disorder' — 'paranoid schizophrenia', 'delusion of grandeur', etc. according to the several diagnoses he had received throughout his life.

However, I think there is more. Bispo's objects (and among them, ships) can be also the source of a series of radically different questions sending us to other seas. These questions relate, in particular, to a reflection on the ocean and the water beyond their only 'metaphysical' dimensions — or as a 'paradigmatic metaphor for existence'.[8] They relate also to memory in a world that is, we must more than ever acknowledge, necessarily marked by the transatlantic slave trade.[9]

---

prisoner in the midst of the ultimate freedom, on the most open road of all, chained solidly to the infinite crossroads. He is the Passenger *par excellence*, the prisoner of the passage. It is not known where he will land, and when he lands, he knows not whence he came' (Michel Foucault, *History of Madness*, ed. by Jean Khalfa, trans. by Jonathan Murphy (London: Routledge, 2006), pp. 10–11).

7   Frederico Morais, *Arthur Bispo do Rosario: arte além da loucura* (Rio de Janeiro: Livre Galeria e Nau Editora, 2013), p. 66; my translation.

8   Hans Blumenberg, *Shipwreck with Spectator: Paradigm of a Metaphor for Existence*, trans. by Steven Rendall (Cambridge, MA: MIT Press, 1996).

9   In this sense, the position of the MAR in Rio de Janeiro's social and political geography adds a layer of complexity to my analysis that I should at least acknowledge. The museum was opened in March 2013 as part of the renovation project of Rio's city centre for the 2014 World Cup and 2016 Olympic Games. This area of Rio is historically very important. During the eighteenth and nineteenth centuries, not far from the Museum, a large slave market used to take place. Close to it, there was a vast slave cemetery (*Cemitério dos Pretos Novos*), which was built over and for a very long time forgotten, to be found again only at the end of the 1990s. It became, in 2005, the institute for black (or 'negro', *preto*) memory *Instituto de Pesquisa e Memória Pretos Novos*. The city centre renovation project was very ambiguous and highly problematic, based on a neoliberal agenda preoccupied more with attracting investments and tourism to the city than with progressive social change. Many people in the region were expelled from their homes. The populations living in the *favelas* around the area — such as the Morro da Providencia, the first favela built in Rio de Janeiro at the end of nineteenth century — were targeted in particular. The Institute became undesirable because it stood in the

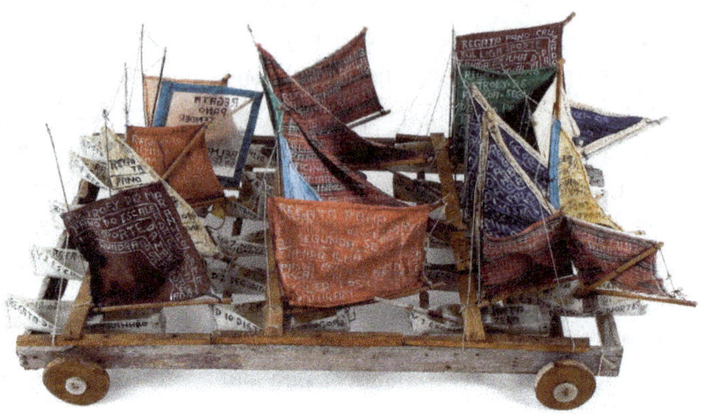

Figure 1. *Vinte e Um Veleiros* (Twenty-One Sailboats), Museu Bispo do Rosário Collection. Photography: Rodrigo Lopes.

In this sense, I would like to suggest, inspired by the reflections of other contemporary thinkers, to look at Bispo do Rosário's production through the prism of decolonial critique and blackness. I propose to emphasize an aspect that was for a long time avoided in the analyses of Bispo's works, namely, that they are produced by a black man, in a society profoundly marked by racist and colonial elements.[10] The many ships he produced throughout his life can be read as part of an 'ecology of the ship'. They constitute forms that deal with, that assemble, and reassemble mnemonic elements inscribed in his body.

---

way of a projected new line of the tramway system. Now, without public resources since 2017, the Institute is at risk again of being shuttered for good and hence exemplifies the national agenda of an erasure of memory and counter-memory. Despite having been born of this very city project, the MAR itself is now also at risk and has been targeted by the current municipal government.

10 I am of course not the only one emphasizing this dimension, neglected for too long. Ricardo Aquino, for example, also remarked upon the 'efforts in whitening Arthur Bispo do Rosário; of not evidencing his Negritude or his African background': Ricardo Aquino, 'From Picturesque to Points in Time: A Biographical Image', in *Arthur Bispo do Rosário*, ed. by Emanoel Araújo and others, curated by Wilson Lazaro; trans. by Regina Alfarano (Rio de Janeiro: Réptil, 2012), pp. 48–105 (p. 51).

BISPO DO ROSÁRIO, THE MAN AND HIS MISSION

Bispo spent most of his life inside psychiatric institutions, and there is an important nexus between elements of his life, his psychotic deliriums and his production of hundreds of objects, many of them ships or forms that relate to the sea. For a long time, little was known about the artist, but archival research, interviews with those who knew him, in addition to the few interviews Bispo gave himself, and a more thorough analysis of his oeuvre have made it possible to at least partially reconstruct his biography.

An important work regarding his trajectory is that of his biographer Luciana Hidalgo, who assembled key data and managed to shed light upon Bispo's mysterious past. Arthur Bispo do Rosário Paes was born around 1909–11, in Japaratuba, Sergipe, in northeastern Brazil.[11] The city of Japaratuba was originally a Tupi village, whose population was diminished by a smallpox outbreak in the eighteenth century. Following the outbreak, the city was occupied by a Carmelites mission for a period of time — the *Japaratuba Mission*, a name that appears in one of Bispo's embroideries — and it remained a very Catholic city. Bispo spent his first years immersed in a religious environment of processions, moral customs, stories of sins and blessed martyrs, mixed with elements of African and indigenous traditions. The small city also developed an important tradition of embroidery. Some years later, records say that his parents moved with him to Bahia to work at a cacao farm.[12] At the age of fifteen, he joined the Navy, and then moved to Rio.[13] He also became a pugilist and, after being expelled from the Navy for 'disciplinary reasons' — according to Navy records — he started to work at the Rio's electricity company and later as a

---

11   Three registers were found concerning Bispo's birth date: 14 May 1909 (Navy register), 16 March 1911 (electricity company register) and his baptism certificate found in the church of Japaratuba from which one can deduce that he was born most probably in the first week of July. Cf. Luciana Hidalgo, *Arthur Bispo do Rosário. O senhor do Labirinto* (Rio de Janeiro: Rocco, 2011), pp. 30–31.

12   For an analysis of the different documents and texts regarding these records, see also Viviane Trindade Borges, *Do esquecimento ao tombamento. A invenção de Arthur Bispo do Rosário* (doctoral dissertation, Universidade Federal do Rio Grande do Sul, 2010), pp. 36–59 <https://www.lume.ufrgs.br/handle/10183/22989> [accessed 28 June 2020].

13   He started to work at the Navy in 1925. Records say that he was sent by his father, although some speculate that he was sold to the Navy, a common practice at the time.

domestic worker for a bourgeois family (the Leone family) — where he would clean the house, go to the market, and serve as bodyguard of the patriarch (not for a salary, which he refused as a matter of principle, but for food and lodging). He finally worked for two years as a handyman at a clinic owned by the patriarch's brother-in-law, again refusing a salary, since he saw salaries as the origin of all sins. The attic of the clinic became his living place and studio.

One night, on 22 December 1938, he had what was probably his first 'episode': seven angels descended on the Earth, transported and left him at the Botafogo neighbourhood, from where he began a peregrination to a church in the city centre. This crucial event consists, for him, in a moment of revelation: he is Jesus Christ — or, in other variants he gave, his son or 'Arthur Jesus', as he would sign some of his works — and had come to Earth to judge the dead and the living, to govern a new world, which he would recreate after its destruction through fire. Like many other biographical details of his life, which appear in his works, this date and the tale narrating the event were embroidered in a big banner (Figure 2) and repeated by himself in interviews given at the Colônia towards the end of his life.[14]

From this moment on, Bispo claims that he started to hear voices obliging him to work and to produce his objects. In an interview, he claims that it was not an option not to work, even if he did not want to. He was given a divine task by these 'voices' and had no other choice but to comply — thus he would claim to be their 'slave' or also 'slave of the Lord'.[15]

After what could be considered his major episode, Bispo wandered for two days before being arrested by the police. The police record defines him as such: a 'wandering black beggar ["indigent"], bearing no documents'.[16] He was then sent to the Hospital Nacional dos Alienados in December 1938 and to the Colônia Juliano Moreira in January

---

14   See *O prisioneiro da passagem: Arthur Bispo do Rosário*, dir. by Hugo Denizart (Centro Nacional de Produção Independente, 1982) <https://www.youtube.com/watch?v=PjgP1LYLZOU> [accessed 28 June 2020], a title (The prisoner of the passage) that echoes Foucault's passage about the ship of fools quoted above; as well as *O Bispo*, dir. by Fernando Gabeira (Globo TV, 1985) <https://www.youtube.com/watch?v=x9wc-_XoCcw> [accessed 28 June 2020].

15   *O Bispo* (1985), at ca. 8:00.

16   Luciana Hidalgo, *Arthur Bispo do Rosário*, p. 18.

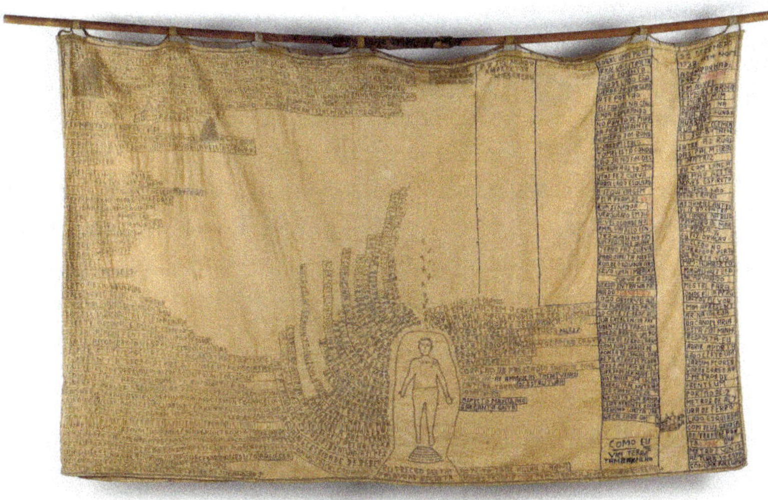

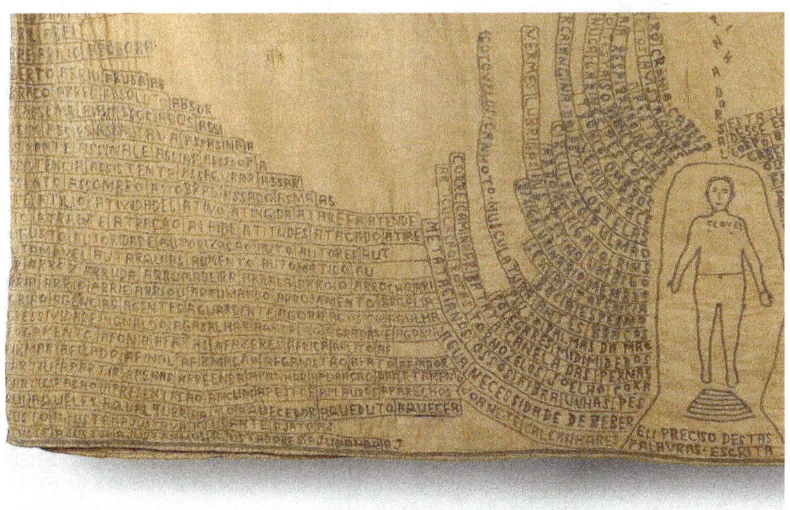

Figure 2. Above: *Eu Preciso Destas Palavras. Escrita* (*I Need This Words in Writing*), Museu Bispo do Rosário Collection. Photography: Rodrigo Lopes. Below: Detail.

1939, becoming patient number 01662. As a typical poor, black figure of Brazilian society, he was just another person without a name, history, or identity — a mere black 'indigent', according to the police record, to be locked away. When he died, fifty years later, his clinical record amounted to barely a few words.

Bispo would go back and forth between these two institutions (with some stays also at the Centro Psiquiátrico Nacional/Centro Psiquiátrico Pedro II) until 1948.[17] In 1964, he came back to the Colônia, where he then stayed until his death in 1988. In 1967, according to research conducted by Frederico Morais, he was put into a small cell of six square meters. In this period, he again started to hear voices obliging him to work, to produce his objects and reminding him about his salvation mission on Earth:[18]

> My mission is that, it is to achieve that, what I have to the following day [is] to represent the existence of Earth that is there, everything I did. [...] I will be preparing and packing [*encaixotando*, boxing] the things. Because the order is to pack.[19]

---

17   The psychiatrist Nise da Silveira ran a studio (which later, in 1952, would become the Museum of Images of the Unconscious) inside the Centro Psiquiátrico Nacional. Silveira emphasized the creation of a favourable working environment for artistic endeavours and considered the patient's production crucial instruments for the scientific study of psychosis. She organized permanent exhibitions and collaborated with figures such as the art critic Mário Pedrosa and the artist Almir Mavignier. Bispo was interned in other sections, and there is no evidence of an encounter with Silveira. The Colônia Juliano Moreira also contained an art section, with occupational activities and a painting workshop, being used in particular in the 1950s. See João Henrique Queiroz de Araújo and Ana Maria Jacó-Vilela, 'The Experience of Art at the Juliano Moreira Colony in the 1950s', trans. by Rebecca Atkinson, *História, Ciências, Saúde-Manguinhos*, 25.2 (2018) <https://doi.org/10.1590/s0104-59702018000200002>. However, Bispo was not there during this period. In fact, he went back to Colônia within a week of the 1964 military *coup* and remained institutionalized during the 'years of lead', coinciding with the worst period of the Brazilian psychiatric system.

18   For a certain time, researchers would consider this moment key to the beginning of his production. Photos taken by Jean Manzon in 1943, however, show Bispo already dressed in his 'presentation mantle' next to a big ship built by him, Bianca Bernardo, 'Quem você deixaria entrar em sua cela sem precisar acertar a cor da sua aura?', in *Das virgens em cardumes e da cor das auras*, ed. by Daniela Labra (São Paulo: WMF Martins Fontes, 2016), pp. 122–35 (p. 126). Ricardo Aquino also mentions a drawing of a boat dating from the 1930s, in his 'From Picturesque to Points in Time', p. 87.

19   Bispo do Rosário interviewed by Conceição Robaina, quoted in Flavia dos Santos Corpas, *Arthur Bispo do Rosario: Do claustro infinito à instalação de um nome* (doctoral thesis, Pontifícia Universidade Católica PUC-Rio, 2014), p. 90; my translation <https://www.maxwell.vrac.puc-rio.br/35039/35039.PDF> [accessed 28 June 2020]. According to Corpas, Bispo talks about a mission at least since 1938 and a medical record of the Centro Psiquiátrico Nacional (without date, but certainly between 1938 and 1948) states, in principle, his claim: 'it is a mission to reform the world we live' (ibid., p. 57).

After a certain period of time, he left this cell and started to progressively occupy other larger cells and spaces at the hospital — up to eleven cells at the end of his life — that constituted at the same time his living space and studio. He transformed this enclosed space into a living installation, a sort of labyrinth of hallways, galleries, and passages, which were constantly rearranged. In some cells, he stocked objects and raw materials (bricks, tiles, glass shards, wood sticks, syringes, etc.); others were rearranged and installed with the different pieces; in others, he lived, kept kitchen appliances, which allowed him to barter coffee, for example, for materials and tools from other patients. This generous allotment of asylum spaces only became possible thanks to the particular position he managed to occupy at the Colônia: he cleaned the space, took care of other patients, and also played the role of 'sheriff', beating, for example, patients in moments of crises, or administering medication prescribed by the doctors. Patients, doctors, and the personnel accepted and even respected Bispo's strange manners, giving him space to do things more or less as he wanted.

Bispo exercised a sort of ascetic practice, eating very little, and even entering long periods of fasting. He believed he needed to, in his words, 'dry' in order to achieve 'his transformation' and become a 'saint'. He avoided the same medications he gave to other patients, afraid of 'lulling his senses'. His cells constituted also a fortified territory and only those capable of 'naming the colour of his aura' — blue — were given access to it. Whenever he felt the voices were again too strongly present, he would lock himself in his cell and avoid contact with others, sometimes lasting several months. That is, as I am tempted to put it, whenever he felt he was excessively *under the weather*, that his *inner turmoil* had become unbearable, he would seek refuge in his cell.

The conditions of the psychiatric asylums in Brazil at the time were truly terrible and the way in which the Brazilian system was structured early on implemented principles of eugenics and ideas of a necessary 'cleansing of the race', which undoubtedly explains why Bispo remained confined over so many years, just as in general black subjects spend disproportionately more time in asylums than white subjects.[20]

---

20   For more precise data and a history of the Brazilian psychiatric system, I refer to another article recently written: Marlon Miguel, 'Psychiatric Power: Exclusion and

That said, in contrast, for example, to Antonin Artaud, Bispo himself did not view his confinement at the psychiatric hospital was as a torment but as a 'sign of recognition' and recognition, in particular, of his 'mission on Earth'. Through his deliriums — or, in Bispo's words, his 'visions' and 'voices' that ordered him to work — and the objects he produced, he found a way, at the same time, to survive and to stabilize his *madness*: he found a way, his own and singular way, to be in the world, that is, to construct a world for himself.

BISPO'S INVENTORY: WEATHERING THE END OF THE WORLD

Bispo do Rosário's objects speak about the asylum, his own history, about the people he met throughout life, lived with and talked to in the asylum and elsewhere. These objects are all part of a unique and rigorous system that aim at a 'representation of the existent material on Earth', as he often claimed himself.[21] I do not propose to read his work uniquely through a biographical lens, but the elements recalled above should help better situate his production and draw attention to the colonial and racial elements profoundly marked in his trajectory: from his childhood in Japartuba and later in a cacao plantation, from the Navy to footman, 'indigent', and to the oblivion in an asylum, *slave* of voices.

In order to produce his pieces, Bispo assembled everyday objects like tapes, forks, knives, fabric, shoes — everything he could put his hands on. More than eight hundred artistic objects were preserved over the years. After his death, in 1989, the asylum personnel wanted to dismantle the objects to return some of the everyday objects to their customary use. Thanks to the effort of several people, an association was created in 1989 and, in order to preserve his works, they were sent to the Nise da Silveira Museum, located at an old pavilion of the Colônia.[22] A first solo exhibition, *Registros de minha passage pela Terra*,

---

Segregation in the Brazilian Mental Health System', in *Democracy and Brazil: Collapse and Regression*, ed. by Bernardo Bianchi, Jorge Chaloub, Frieder Otto Wolf, and Patricia Rangel (London: Routledge, forthcoming 2020).

21   Bispo do Rosário in Hugo Denizart, *O prisioneiro da passagem*, at ca. 16min; my translation.

22   Later, in 2000, renamed Bispo do Rosário Museum, and in 2002, Bispo do Rosário Museum for Contemporary Art, located at the Colônia Juliano Moreira.

was then, at the end of the same year, curated by Frederico Morais at the Parque Lage Visual Arts School, comprising some five hundred objects.[23] Morais, along with the psychologist Denise Almeida Correa, responsible for the Nise da Silveira Museum, started to organize and classify Bispo's works. In particular, they classified the series of works giving them names as, for example, 'O.R.F.A.' (objects wrapped by blue threads, also called 'mummified' or 'embalmed' objects), 'banners', and 'assemblages'. Bispo himself called the latter 'showcases' or 'display windows' (*vitrines*) combining different sorts of items such as powdered milk tins, packages, cleaning products, shoes, miniature saints, and other religious items, but also sometimes organic elements, such as apples. By organizing, classifying, and naming Bispo's production, Morais's tried to inscribe Bispo's work within the context of modern and postmodern artistic production, an ambiguous gesture one might want to critique, yet has to also understand as strategic, a question that will not be my focus here.[24]

---

23   The work of Bispo was first exhibited in the 1982 collective exhibition *À margem da vida* at the Museum of Modern Art of Rio (MAM) thanks to the efforts of the artist Maria Amélia Mattei. The exhibition, made in a context of re-democratization process and movements for a psychiatric reform, reunited works from people living at penal and mental institutions. Bispo never visited the exhibition, but chose which works should be exhibited and how they should be displayed. Morais discovered the pieces at that exhibition and invited Bispo to go live and work at the MAM, offer that he refused. After the 1989 exhibition, Bispo became quickly recognized in the art world and had his work exhibited in different countries, in particular, at the 1995 Venice Biennale. Despite this worldwide recognition, most of his works, stored at the Bispo do Rosário Museum for Contemporary Art, lack of funding and interest to get the deserved attention and restoration work they need.

24   Transforming Bispo into a contemporary artist risks losing the *starting point* of his work, that is, the psychiatric institution. The danger is to lose the *situatedness* of his practice. This does not mean that his work would not have value in itself or that one has to make paternalistic concessions in order to see it as 'art'. On the contrary, Bispo engages in very complex conceptual and artistic procedures. But by situating them, one can better appreciate their critical quality. Indeed, as has often been pointed out, his work can be compared to (neo)dadaist work, Duchampian ready-mades, Warholian pop, Oitician *parangolé*, or a total work of art such as that of Kurt Schwitters. Bispo, however, never tried to question the codes of art history and did what he did for other reasons. At the same time, one must recognize the strategy implied in Morais's gesture: to give symbolic prestige by inscribing it into art history and hence to attract interest to his work. By doing this, he achieved recognition for a black 'madman's' work produced at the periphery of capitalism and, above all, he secured a chance of saving it from oblivion and destruction. Kaira Cabañas critically engages, but also in a nuanced way, this discussion in a chapter about Bispo's work in her book *Learning from Madness: Brazilian Modernism and Global Contemporary Art* (Chicago: Chicago

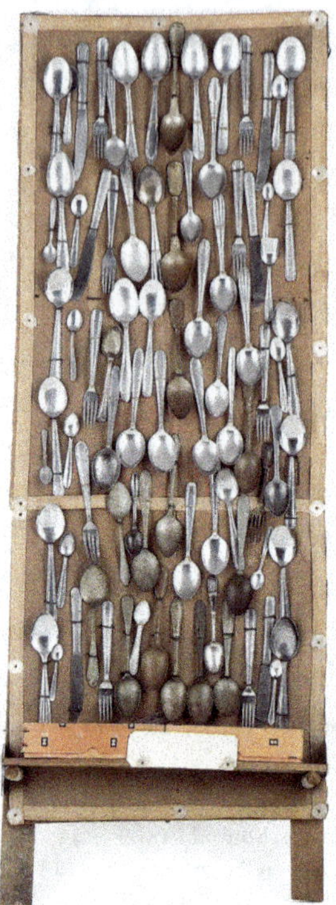

Figure 3. *Talheres* (Cutlery), Museu Bispo do Rosario Collection.
Photography: Rodrigo Lopes.

Bispo also created mantles and cloaks, sceptres, different kinds of
maps, small installations, miniature representations of things on Earth
(kites, carousels, ox carts, etc.), pieces, sashes, and tissues about Miss
World pageants and participants — that construct a 'Pop Geography',
according to curator and art critic Paulo Herkenhoff.[25] The works on
fabric constitute often very complex, detailed, and repetitive embroideries. Among the mantles, one can find the 'Exu cape' or the famous
'Mantle of presentation', which he worked on for several decades. On
the inside part of the latter, he inscribed the names of people he chose

University Press, 2018). This book gives a recent and very good account in English of
the Brazilian history of the relationship between art and madness.

25   Paulo Herkenhoff, 'The Longing for Art and Existing Material in the World of Men', in
Arthur Bispo do Rosário, ed. by Araújo, pp. 140–83 (p. 145).

for redemption. This mantle was the object of his final performance: he would wear it before dying and presenting himself before God.

Finally, Bispo produced also several kinds of ready-mades, such as the *Roda da fortuna* (Wheel of Fortune), of a stunning resemblance to Marcel Duchamp's *Roue de bicyclette*.

The O.R.F.A are particularly interesting in respect to Bispo's 'archive fever'. These three-dimensional objects are often related to the domestic sphere and labour. They constitute, as Frederico Morais first pointed out, a kind of 'total inventory of a certain stage of Brazilian society', a 'double or shadow' of objects that existed and will disappear after the end of times.[26] There are around five hundred objects of this type, all wrapped by a blue thread, which mostly came from patients' hospital gowns, the uniform of the hospital — when Bispo started making them, he would use his own uniform as source for the thread. He identified these objects by a number and its corresponding name: *Moinho de Cana* (Sugar Cane Mill, Figure 4), *Pá de Lixo* (Dustpan), *Pião* (Spinning Top), *Rolo de pintar* (Paint Roller Brush), etc. All of the objects were produced in the enclosed space of the asylum and 'embalmed' with the blue thread as a way to resist weathering — as a way to make them survive the end of times; to, in a certain sense, weather the weathering; to weather both the passing of time and the end of times.

Bispo's world is strongly and rigorously organized, and it is related to what he calls his 'mission', that is, of representing the 'existent materials on Earth'. By 'representing' them — and Bispo, as we saw earlier, makes use of the word — he means in fact the work of archiving these objects or creating an inventory in order to save them for Judgement Day. A significant amount of his objects also has text on them: letters, words, names, notes, fictional and biographical descriptions. The names often refer to the people Bispo met and who are also to be 'saved'. Several women's names are inscribed in his objects, women that he considered important and pictured in his religious imaginary as 'pure' and 'virgin' — in one famous banner, one can read how he welcomes the 'school of virgins', as one would talk of a 'school of fishes'.[27]

---

26 Corpas, *Arthur Bispo do Rosario*, p. 193 [my translation], paraphrasing Frederico Morais, *Registros de minha passagem pela Terra*, Catalogue (1989).

27 *Virgens em cardumes*, in Portuguese. This banner gave the name of an exhibition *Das virgens em cardumes e da cor das auras*, curated by Daniela Labra in 2016–17 at the

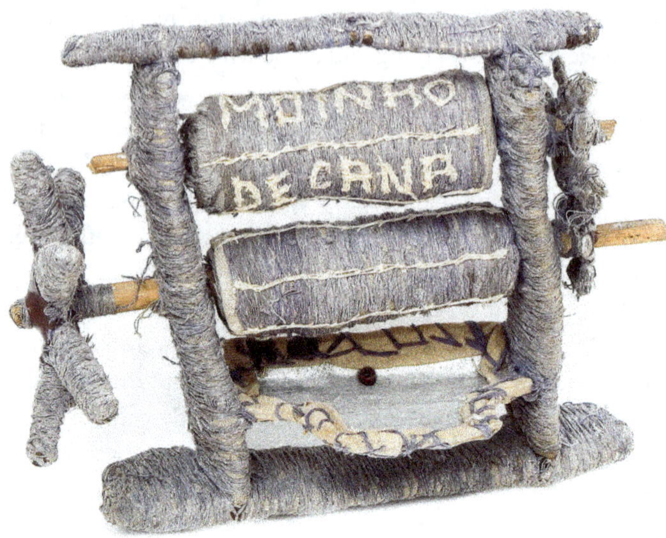

Figure 4. Example of an O.R.F.A (object wrapped by blue threads):
Moinho de Cana (*Sugar cane Mill*), Museu Bispo do Rosário Collection.
Photography: Rodrigo Lopes.

This task of creating an inventory of the world follows a logic of a 'poetic of accumulation' or of repetition through which he aims to repeat in order both 'to understand' and 'to include himself in history (which excluded him)'.[28] The inventory process is 'his way of rewriting the world'.[29] Flavia dos Santos Corpas identifies in Bispo's production three types of actions — 'extracting', 'reuniting', and 'registering'.[30] Through these actions, Bispo creates a very complex and coherent

---

Museu Bispo do Rosário. See Labra, ed., *Das virgens em cardumes*. The exhibition emphasized in particular the performative dimension of Bispo's works and a series of performances took place around the Museum during the exhibition.

28   Márcio Seligmann-Silva, 'Arthur Bispo do Rosário: a arte de "enloquecer" os signos', *ArteFilosofia*, 3 (2007), pp. 144–55 (p. 149; my translation) <https://periodicos.ufop. br:8082/pp/index.php/raf/article/view/761/717> [accessed 28 June 2020].

29   Ibid. See also Maria Esther Maciel, 'A enciclopédia de Arthur Bispo do Rosário', *Outra travessia*, 7 (2008), pp. 117–24 <https://doi.org/10.5007/2176-8552(0.7. 2008)(117-124)>, who emphasizes the (anti)encyclopedic dimension Bispo's work and the way he incorporates the 'registers of the margins'.

30   Corpas, *Arthur Bispo do Rosario*, p. 203; my translation.

work, through which at the same time he constructs his own world and takes position in it — or, perhaps more accurately, takes position in history. The accumulation of these everyday objects does not constitute a mere reproduction or reification, but present an artistic choice, removing them from their usual context, arranging, organizing, and displaying them in deliberate fashion. This way of taking a position in his delirium is a form of ordering his disorder, or how Louise Bourgeois puts it, 'he was looking for order in chaos, for the structure and rhythm in time and thought. One could say his was a pursuit for sanity, the very principle of organization behind all his work.'[31]

One could also add a fourth action to Corpas' list: that of performing. Indeed, Bispo also uses the word 'representing' in a performative sense and, as already noted above, his mantles are objects he wears and that convey a certain disposition or figure. Also, one knows how he chose precisely how pictures of him and his objects had to be taken — often capturing his shadows rather than his body, thus emphasizing the objects — how to arrange his objects in space, how to represent and perform actions during these shootings.

The Exu Cape (see Figure 5) is of particular importance in this context. It is not known how exactly Bispo imagined the spiritual entity of Exu — an orisha — how much the artist knew about him, and whether he also 'performed' Exu with this cape. In any case, not only does Bispo explicitly engage with the Afro-descendent tradition of the Candomblé — as he does also with other works, such as the display window *Macumba* (referring to a form of black witchcraft)[32] — but he chooses this very specific orisha: Exu, who is the messenger between the human and divinity realms, who has an important relationship

---

31 Louise Bourgeois, 'Arthur Bispo do Rosário', in *Arthur Bispo do Rosário*, ed. by Araújo, p. 27.

32 We can also mention here a work that remained unknown to the public until the exhibition *Quilombo do Rosário* at the Museu Bispo do Rosário Arte Contemporânea (August 2018–March 2019, curated by Roberto Conduru): an embroidery of the map of the African continent. Unfortunately, no catalogue was made for this exhibition. Conduru is also the author of a short entry on Bispo, written for *The Dictionary of Caribbean and Afro-Latin American Biography*, ed. by Franklin W. Knight and Henry Louis Gates, Jr. (Oxford: Oxford University Press, 2016) <https://doi.org/10.1093/acref/9780195301731.013.74989>.

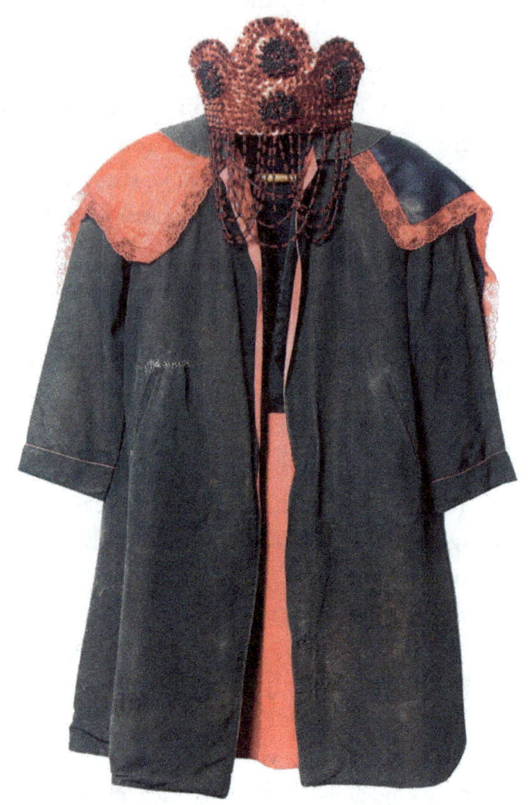

Figure 5. *Capa de Exu* (*Exu Cape*), Museu Bispo do Rosário Collection.
Photography: Rodrigo Lopes.

to word and language, as well as to time, travelling between past and present, and deeply connected to *ancestrality*.[33]

It is interesting to look at what Eleonora Fabião, referring to Bispo do Rosário, calls a 'performative historiography'. She has in mind a form of historiography performed by a body as it is traversed by past, present, and future, by individual, collective, imaginary, and sensorial

---

33   Cf. Florence Marie Dravet, 'Corpo, linguagem e real: o sopro de exu bará e seu lugar na comunicação', *Ilha Desterro*, 68.3 (2015) <https://doi.org/10.5007/2175-8026. 2015v68n3p15>.

marks; by a body that actualizes these dimensions through its movements and gestures. Building on Hélio Oiticica's *objectact* and Lygia Clark's *quasi-corporeal* objects, she proposes to look at Bispo's works as constituting an 'object-archive' to be thought as an 'open circuit of acts'.[34] What is at stake here, following Fabião's suggestion, is the very gesture of the inventory, but also how these objects, in a certain sense, ask to be performed and what they re-actualize through this performance. Furthermore, these objects engage, re-organize, and re-actualize the marks of the past, those traversing and constituting Bispo's body.

Like other mentally ill patients, Bispo (re)organizes his inner turmoil by producing objects.[35] That is the form he finds to weather his storms. And in this singular (re)construction of the world, *his* world, ships play indeed an important role. Drawings of boats were found scratched on the walls of his cells; he produced different sorts of rafts, ships, boats, vessels, arks (of Noah), frigates, sometimes complex structures consisting of several boats; he also embroidered many ships in his fabric works. In a certain sense, his cell had also become a boat. And even his bed, in his last years, became, as he claimed, a '(space)ship' taking part in his final performance,[36] and which would carry him, as he would also wear his mantle of presentation, to the Judgment Day. While a lot has been said about the metaphors of the passenger or of the adventure at sea, I propose to read these objects also as surfaces of re-inscription of histories, memories, marks that certainly belong to the subject 'Bispo', but that exceed his only personal and individual biography. These boats thus also reveal a form of dealing with the history of the Atlantic Ocean and the consequences that he himself, as a black poor man in Brazilian society, suffered. These boats can be read in a long series, inside a constellation of several ship-objects, constituting, thus, a certain ecology and his own way of traversing the

---

34 Eleonora Fabião, 'History and Precariousness: In Search of a Performative Historiography', in *Perform, Repeat, Record*, ed. by Amelia Jones and Adrian Heathfield (London: Thames & Hudson, 2012), pp. 121–36 (p. 126).

35 I should also add that even though Bispo spent most of his time at the asylum, he was not entirely cut off from the world. He kept reading newspapers and magazines, and his work contains several ironic references to politics and even mundane events — he was, for example, particularly obsessed with beauty pageants.

36 His bed was also the 'stage' of a 'performance' he did as a form to say goodbye to psychologist Rosangela Maria Grilo Magalhães at the end of her internship at the Colônia in 1983. It consisted in a kind of reenactment of Romeo and Juliet (Figure 6).

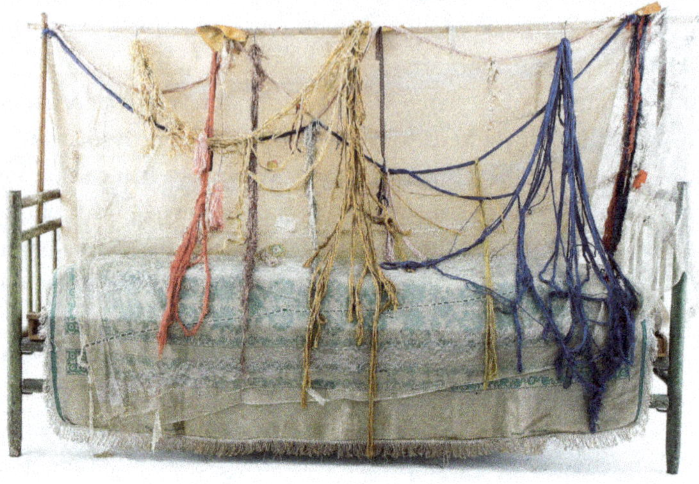

Figure 6. *Cama de Romeu e Julieta* (*Romeu and Juliet's bed*), Museu Bispo
do Rosario Collection. Photography: Rodrigo Lopes.

oceans of history. I think it is no mere coincidence that ships are so
recurrent in his artistic representations and productions — as well
as in those of the other artists who are part of the *Lugares do delírio*
exhibition.

Noah's ark, which appears in the film *O Bispo*, built with fabric
and cardboard, was destined to 'save the world'. One can imagine that
it would carry the inventoried objects chosen to weather the end of
times. Also, on the raft (Figure 7), one can see the word 'representation'
used once more: '[It] represents the maritime departments of all states.
Universe. Raft.' It is the *universe*, the totality — a certain totality chosen
by Bispo — which is represented and which will be saved. In his
eschatology, Bispo inverts established positions, he is the master of
representation, the redeemer, and chooses who and what will be saved.
This totality or whole certainly counters both the 'social death'[37] and

---

37   Cf. Orlando Patterson, *Slavery and Social Death: A Comparative Study* (Cambridge,
MA: Harvard University Press, 1982) as well as Fred Moten, *The Universal Machine*
(Durham, NC: Duke University Press, 2018), in particular chapter 3.

the psychotic dismantlement experienced by him as black, poor, mad subject.

ECOLOGIES OF THE SEA

Rather than advancing any further, I would like to digress before concluding with a proposal. If one wants to take Bispo's work seriously, one has to assume that there is no such thing as a 'mad artist' outside culture. In Bispo's case, this is especially evident, and his work deals with historical, social, geographical marks; his work takes position in, with, against them. It takes position in a very aggressive *climate*.

Christina Sharpe's book *In the Wake: On Blackness and Being* is entirely built around metaphors relating to the sea and to boats. To begin with the title: 'wake' means 'the track left on the water's surface by a ship.' She conceptualizes 'weather' in a specific pessimistic way as 'the totality of our environments', as 'the machine in which we live' and this weather-machine, this 'total climate' 'is antiblack', 'slavery undeniably became the total environment'.[38]

I find the way she relates 'memory', 'weather', and the 'sea' particularly interesting. In the beginning of the fourth chapter (*The weather*), Sharpe takes a passage from Toni Morrison's *Beloved* and constructs her argument around 'watered' images. Following Morrison's description, Sethe, the novel's protagonist and a former slave, tries to protect her daughter from the memories of the past. However, this past is not really a past, it persists in the present. As a consequence, Sethe has this 'thought picture', or, as she puts it, this 'picture *floating* around out here outside my head'.[39] Interestingly, this picture is, first of all, characterized as *floating* and, secondly, it is not in her head, but *out there*. Sharpe concludes: 'It is weather, and even if the country, every country, any country, tries to forget […], it is the atmosphere.'[40] Sharpe emphasizes that, despite the end of slavery, its logics persist, it constitutes the atmospheric condition where one lives — with its consequences constantly affecting black bodies. Even if the state or a conscious subject

---

38   Christina Sharpe, *In the Wake: On Blackness and Being* (Durham, NC: Duke University
        Press, 2016), p. 104.
39   Ibid., p. 105, my emphasis.
40   Ibid.

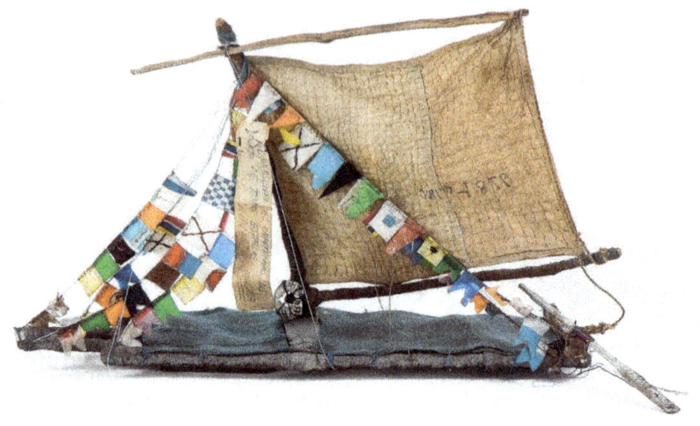

Figure 7. *Jangada* (*Raft*), Museu Bispo do Rosario Collection.
Photography: Rodrigo Lopes.

tries to obliterate the memory, there is such a thing as the *weather*, the atmosphere, where these questions and traces remain present. More than haunting, they structure the space, the world in which one lives; they give form to this 'one ecology of the ship that continues into the present'.[41]

*

The relationship between the sea and death is a recurrent one in contemporary black literature. The Angolan writer Agostinho Neto writes the following in his short story *Nausea* (1985):

> Mu'alunga. The sea. The death. This water! This salted water is perdition. The sea goes so far away, out there. Until it reaches the sky. It goes to America. Above, it's blue, below, it's very deep, black. [...] Cousin Xico died there, in the sea, when the raft sunk, there in the great sea. Died swallowing water. Kalunga. Afterwards, ships came, ships left. And the sea is always Kalunga. The death. The Sea took grandfather to other

---

41   Ibid., p. 106.

> continents. Slavery is Kalunga. The enemy is the sea. […]
> Kalunga chained people in the hold and the people only had
> fear. Kalunga whipped their backs and the people could only
> heal the wounds. Kalunga is fate. And why didn't the people
> flee the sea? Kalunga is really death. […] And Kalunga don't
> know Man. It does not know that people suffer. It only knows
> to make them suffer.[42]

Neto makes an interesting move in this text by introducing the word *Kalunga* and making it resonate. In Kimbundu, *ka'lunga*, means 'sea', but it is also used in the sense of 'immensity' and 'grandeur', both related to its cosmological connotation. Clyde Ford recalls that *Kalunga* is often associated with death, but also with a feminine creative force, relating to 'the cosmic waters [...], the yolk inside the egg, the amniotic fluid of the womb'.[43] The sea, in Yoruba myths, is also where Yemoja dies at the same time as her womb dilates due to the salty water — giving birth, in the process, to the other Orishas of the African pantheon.[44] Likewise, Édouard Glissant, in the opening pages of his *Poetics of Relation*, inevitably associates the sea with an abyss, but also makes it a principle of memory, knowledge, and shared history.[45]

While the sea is marked by the history of slavery and the trip to the hold, it also represents the connection to the homeland, the trace of a return or, in Martin Lienhard's words, the possibility of 'an archaeology of the discourse of slavery'.[46] Agostinho Neto is well aware of this and in his poem 'Havemos de voltar' (We shall return) describes the

---

42 Agostinho Neto, *Náusea* (Luanda: UEA, 2006), p. 25; my translation.

43 Clyde W. Ford, *The Hero with an African Face* (New York: Bantam, 2000), p. 197.

44 Cf. *Antologia do mar na poesia africana de língua portuguesa do Século xx*, ed. by Carmem Lucia Tindó Secco (Rio de Janeiro: Programa de Letras Vernáculas/UFRJ, 1996), i.

45 Édouard Glissant, *Poetics of Relation*, trans. by Betsy Wing (Ann Arbor: University of Michigan Press, 1997), pp. 8–9: 'For though this experience made you, original victim floating toward the sea's abysses, an exception, it became something shared and made us, the descendants, one people among others. Peoples do not live on exception. Relation is not made up of things that are foreign but of shared knowledge. This experience of the abyss can now be said to be the best element of exchange. […] And for this Relation made of storms and profound moments of peace in which we may honour our boats. [...] We cry our cry of poetry. Our boats are open, and we sail them for everyone.'

46 Martin Lienhard, 'O mato e o mar: apontamentos para uma arqueologia do discurso escravo', in *Brasil: um país de negros?*, ed. by Jéferson Bacelar and Carlos Cardoso (Rio de Janeiro/Salvador: Pallas/CEAO, 1999), pp. 113–23: 'For the enslaved Africans in America, the sea, which reminded them undoubtedly of the trip to the hold, appeared

coming back to the homeland through specific words that rematerialize the land: *mulemba* (a fig tree), *marimba* (a percussion instrument), *quissange* (also an instrument).[47]

The sea triggers what, in Portuguese, one calls *saudade* and, in Kimbundu, *banzo*, the affect of melancholia, nostalgia, homesickness, but also that which enables what the black Brazilian poet Conceição Evaristo names, with a neologism, *escrevivência* — writing to survive, writing to experience, writing to reconnect. '*The banzo stirs in me.* | From the *black ink of my oceans* | the pain, revisited, submerges | flaying my skin | that surges in suns | and lofty moons of a | *time that is now*', she writes in the first verses of 'Filhos na rua' (Children in the street).[48] Or her 'Recordar é preciso' (Remembering is a necessity):

> The sea wanders rolling beneath my thoughts.
> Turbulent memory sets sail:
> Remembering is a necessity.
> On the waters of recollection the to and fro
> of my weeping eyes crashes over my life,
> Curing my face and my taste. I am an eternal shipwreck.
> But the ocean depths do not frighten me or paralyze me.
> A profound passion is the buoy that rises before me.
> I know mystery lies beyond the waters.[49]

Conceição Evaristo does not succumb to the deadly attraction of the mysterious deep sea and, through her *passion*, she writes, making a

---

also as bond to the original land and to the utopic path of a "return"' (p. 118; my translation).

47 Agostinho Neto, 'Havemos de voltar', Fundação Dr. António Agostinho Neto (FAAN) <http://www.agostinhoneto.org/index.php?option=com_content&id=561: desterro> [accessed 28 June 2020].

48 Conceição Evaristo, 'Children in the Street', in Conceição Evaristo, 'Poems', trans. by Tamara Mitchell, *Hiedra Magazine*, 1 (2013), pp. 65–68 (p. 67; my emphasis) <https://www.hiedramagazine.com/conceicao-evaristo> [accessed 28 June 2020].

49 Conceição Evaristo, 'Remembering Is a Necessity', in Evaristo, 'Poems', p. 68. In the original: 'O mar vagueia onduloso sob os meus pensamentos. | A memória bravia lança o leme: | Recordar é preciso. | O movimento de vaivém nas águas-lembranças | dos meus marejados olhos transborda-me a vida, | salgando-me o rosto e o gosto. Sou eternamente náufraga. | Mas os fundos oceanos não me amedrontam nem me imobilizam. | Uma paixão profunda é a boia que me emerge. | Sei que o mistério subsiste além das águas.' See also Conceição Evaristo, *Poemas Malungos — Cânticos Irmãos* (doctoral thesis, Universidade Federal Fluminense, 2011) <https://app.uff.br/riuff/bitstream/1/7741/1/Tese_Dout.Concei%C3%A7%C3%A3oEvaristo_def.pdf> [accessed 28 June 2020].

twist inside a long history. She takes over the ancient prescription 'navegar é preciso, viver não é preciso' (sailing is necessary, living is not necessary) and subverts it by emphasizing life and memory. The prescription first conveyed, according to Plutarch, by the Roman consul Pompey (*'Navigare necesse est, vivere non est necesse'*), later immortalized by Petrarch, then commonly used by Portuguese sailors, immortalized by Fernando Pessoa, reworked by Caetano Veloso in the form of a Fado, finally becomes with Conceição Evaristo a matter of recollection, a question of survival — a struggle both for life and memory.

CONCLUSION: *ESCREVIVÊNCIA*

In the total climate of antiblackness that comprises Brazilian society, within which Bispo evolved as an artist,[50] he develops his weathering techniques in confinement; he performs his *escrivevência*, inscribing his name, through his works, in history, and searching to represent the world that should be saved.

Against the simplicity of very few words — thirteen, to be precise — defining Bispo in his medical record, he *writes*. His embroideries weave memories, reconnect constantly to (his) history, assemble and re-assemble mnemonic and historic marks. That is precisely what one realizes with the famous banner *Eu preciso destas palavras. Escrita*. One does not know if Bispo miswrites the last word and means 'I need these words *written*' or if he chooses to emphasize the noun *'writing'*: 'I need these words. *Writing*' (Figure 2). Among the series of words in the banner, one notes the strange sequence of words: 'In The Chest

---

50   I could not develop here the question of differences between the Brazilian, USA and other countries' contexts, but they exist and are crucial. One must remember that Brazil was the last country in the world to abolish slavery (in 1888) and the largest importer of slaves coming from Africa. Despite these facts, since the beginning of the twentieth century, the myth of 'racial democracy' — in a great extent derived from Gilberto Freyre's seminal work from 1933 *Casa grande e senzala*, in English as *The Masters and the Slaves: A Study in the Development of Brazilian Civilization* (New York: Knopf, 1964) — helped to, on the surface, soften racial tensions and, above all, to conceal, even to deny for a very long time structural racism. At the same time that whitening practices, hygienics and racist discourses shaped Brazilian institutions — psychiatry perfectly exemplifies this — there was little organized struggle against these same structures. And when there was, they were often brutally repressed.

Carries Water Is the Word' (*No Peito Traz Água É Nome*; transformed into an orderly syntax — but should it be? — it could read: 'In the chest, water is carried, that is the word'). And as Paulo Herkenhoff first noted, the word 'Africa' also appears in the banner along with 'tasks' (*afazeres*) and 'afflicted' (*aflito*) — one can also add that, in the same line, the word 'fogamento' appears (probably *'afogamento'* misspelled, i.e., drowning). Far from a mere association, the *need* of words, of writing, expresses a positioning charged with historical meaning.

> Here, the inexplicable list of ideas would not just be a sur-realistic 'free association' to trigger the unconscious. Bispo do Rosário is black. In that association, the artist needs words that can both build and synthesise the ultimate memory of slavery time. From the name Africa the following words are all read concurrently: origins, works (tasks such as slavery economic reasons) and punishment or suffering (afflicted). It is a triple incorporation — physical, spiritual, and political — in the anatomy with a body and a soul. [...] Black is another perception in Bispo do Rosário's anatomy, it is the designation of the non-colour, of the absence of colour or of slaves from Africa.[51]

The understanding of antiblackness as climate also explains how Bispo could spend so many years in confinement. And the Colônia Juliano Moreira was a typical psychiatric hospital designed according to the 'colony' model. Conceived at the beginning of the twentieth century and isolated from the urban centres, this sort of asylum constituted places where patients were meant to work as part of their treatment, in accord with the motto *Labor/Praxis Omnia Vincit* (work conquers all). Like many other institutions across Brazil, the 'colonies' were conceived as places not only for the mad, but for all those branded as undesirable: alcoholics, the mad, the retarded, delinquents, prostitutes, *indigents*, 'enemies' of the state or of powerful men, women pregnant as a result of rape — frequently by their bosses or lovers — or the daughters of influential landowners who had engaged in premarital sex. These spaces became very quickly over-populated over the course

---

51   Herkenhoff, 'The Longing for Art', p. 152. Bispo's words appearing in the banner, placed below and on the left side, are in fact, as indicated above, 'Africa', '*Afazeres*' (Tasks), '*Aflito*' (Afflicted), as well as 'Fogamento' (probably 'Drowning' misspelled) in the beginning of the same line.

of the twentieth century; they were characterized by the use of abusive disciplinary methods and they took part, particularly from the 1960s onward, in what has been called the 'industry of madness', a model for the reproduction of mental illness and 'chronification' based on long-term hospitalizations — a lucrative business for hospitals receiving money from the state for each patient hospitalized.[52]

The term 'colony' is even more brutal in the case of the Juliano Moreira asylum, as the institution was created in an area that had indeed decades before been a colonial plantation. The new pavilions coexisted with the other old buildings of the slave master's house (*casa grande*), the slaves' quarters (*senzala*), the church in the central square... The asylum, as a result, was grafted onto this essentially colonial topology.

Taking these elements into account, Bispo's works can be understood in a new light. The re-utilization of iconic items from the asylum (uniforms, syringes, blankets) signals resistance to the psychiatric order. His boats (some of them resemble caravels and also point towards the colonial 'age of discovery'), as well as the Exu cape, for example, signal an attempt to re-actualize the marks referring to his roots — marks that were constantly obliterated by his surrounding society. Representing the world in his own way, he invents a way of rewriting it, he (re)constructs reality. And, in a certain sense, despite his stated or not stated intentions, he seemed aware of this narrative power as a strategy to counter all the effects of social death. As he used to claim, 'one day I simply appeared'. Through this constructed (but vital) narrative and auto-fiction, Bispo anchors himself in the world, his works are marked by an attempt to rewrite his biography. His work weaves his own history, resists the forced obliteration of memory and *ancestrality* imposed upon racialized subjects in racist societies.

The several boats Bispo built over and over are therefore to be read inside this ever-expanding, indefinite and interminable marine ecology — it is curious, apropos, as some ships appear in series inside a single object (see, for example, Figures 1 and 8). Hence, under no condition, his work is to be interpreted as a sort of final reparation

---

52   See, for example, *Loucos pela vida: a trajetória da reforma psiquiátrica no Brasil*, ed. by Paulo Amarante (Rio de Janeiro: Fiocruz, 2000).

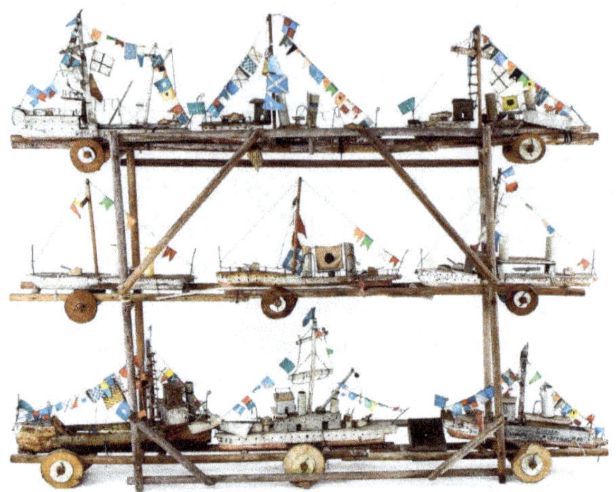

Figure 8. *Distroey — Rio Grande do Norte,* Museu Bispo do Rosário
Collection. Photography: Rodrigo Lopes.

or reconciliatory synthesis. Bispo until the very end does not present himself as artist, citizen or mad, but rather as, *at the same time,* 'slave' — this indelible mark — and 'redeemer'. It is this endless struggle and contradiction that is inscribed in and through his work. And if he names the 'universe', recreates a whole, it is only to counter the dismantlement, both social and psychic, of his body.

The *escrevivência* is neither in this sense a reparative narrative that could be absorbed into the easiness of cultural memory, but constitutes a gesture of suspension in order to survive and to persist. To be 'an eternal shipwreck', but, *at the same time,* to become apt to look at ocean's abyss and not getting paralyzed anymore. Buoy for Evaristo, ship for Bispo. In both cases, remaining in the sea, but finally attempting to navigate.

POST SCRIPTUM

During the years in which Bispo remained confined at the Colônia Juliano Moreira, another figure, another black 'indigent', was locked up there, as well, and wandered in those spaces, a woman by the name of

Stela do Patrocínio. Born in 1941, she was the daughter of a housemaid considered mad and sent to the Colônia, before she herself would suffer the same fate: she became a housemaid herself and was sent to the Colônia in 1966, remaining there until her death in 1992. The two figures, Bispo and Stela, probably never met since they lived in different pavilions.

Stela do Patrocínio kept erring in the asylum spaces and talking. She was known to practice a powerful way of talking, which she opposed to quotidian speech and defined as *fazendo falatório* (a very rough translation could be 'making chattering') or as *colocando o mundo para gozar* ('putting the world into jouissance'). Her speeches were ultimately recorded in 1991 and later transcribed and published as a book. They are poetic, ferocious, raw, powerful. They constantly play with language, can hardly be translated and give form to a life marked by continuous gendered and racialized violence. As with Bispo's objects, these speeches refer to a poetic form of reaction to the arbitrariness of a violent society that incessantly locked up people like them.

> Eu sou Stela do Patrocínio
> Bem patrocinada
> Estou sentada numa cadeira
> Pegada numa mesa negra preta e crioula
> Eu sou uma nega preta e crioula
> Que a Ana me disse
>
> (I am Stela do Patrocínio
> With a good patronage
> I am seated on a chair
> Attached to a table, black, negro, creole
> I am a black, a negro, a creole
> That's what Ana told me)[53]

*

---

53   Stela do Patrocínio, *Reino dos bichos e dos animais é o meu nome* (Rio de Janeiro: Azougue Editorial, 2001), p. 66; my tranlation.

É dito: pelo chão você não pode ficar
Porque lugar da cabeça é na cabeça
Lugar de corpo é no corpo
Pelas paredes você também não pode
Pelas camas também você não vai poder ficar
Pelo espaço vazio você também não vai poder ficar
Porque lugar da cabeça é na cabeça
Lugar de corpo é no corpo

(It is said: on the floor you cannot stay
For the head's place is in the head
The body's place is in the body
Around the walls you also cannot
Around the beds you also cannot stay
Around the empty space you also cannot stay
For the head's place is in the head
The body's place is in the body)[54]

---

54   Ibid., p. 52; my translation.

Enduring Rain
On Vajiko Chachkhiani's *Living Dog Among Dead Lions*
CLAUDIA PEPPEL

In bad weather, you can't be casual.

Martin Parr

A wooden hut in the rain. An unusual, weathered hut jacked up on bricks. The four sides have high filigree lattice windows. Small steps at the front and the back lead to closed doors with window panes, through which, like the windows on the sides, one can peep inside: A large front room with an enclosed porch, sparsely furnished. A single bed with a metal frame takes up a lot of space on one side, a portrait of a woman is hanging over the bed. The opposite wall has only a curtained window and a small framed picture. A dining table in the middle of the room with four different wooden chairs is covered with a plastic tablecloth. An oil lamp and a small pot are placed on top of it. A narrow daybed, a chair, and a side table are out on the porch, some kitchen utensils, plates, glasses, and enamel metal bowls are piled up on the chair as well as on the side table. The two rooms convey a certain frugality; their rustic decoration looks forlorn and from times past. Except for the two pictures and some bunches of dried herbs on the walls there is no decoration, no books. The hut is devoid of people, no residents in sight, though a dim yellow light, which illuminates

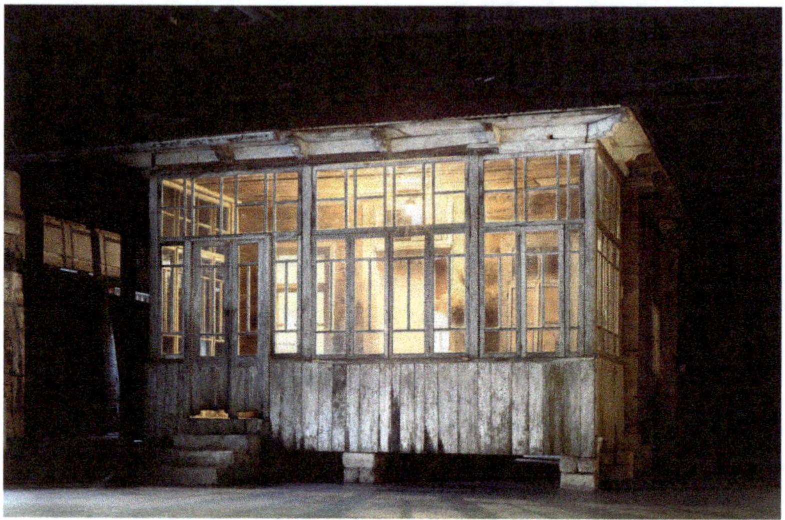

Figure 1. © Vajiko Chachkhiani, *Living Dog Among Dead Lions*,
57th Venice Biennale, Venice, 2017. Photo credit: Sandro Sulaberidze.

the gloomy and almost stage-like setting, suggests that something is anticipated, that at any given moment someone might arrive — or return — to animate the abandoned scenery.

Instead, bad weather has taken hold of the interior and the viewer witnesses heavy rain pouring *inside*. Over the six months in which Vajiko Chachkhiani's *Living Dog Among Dead Lions* was on display in the Georgian Pavilion at the 57th Venice Biennale in 2017, it was 'soaked in water and exposed to the elements'.[1] In Georgia, the Caucasus region of Eurasia, one still regularly encounters old wooden houses of this type (some nearly a hundred years old) made of greyish brown boards and prominent lattice windows. Originally located in the mountains, this particular abandoned hut was found in a village close to the manganese-mining town of Chiatura. It was purchased, taken apart, rebuilt in a factory hall in Tbilisi, and then had the irrigation system hidden in its ceiling. Apparently, the house came with

---

1   Text accompanying the official Biennale video, Vajiko Chachkhiani, 'Georgia — Vajiko Chachkhiani — *Living Dog Among Dead Lions* — Venice Biennale 2017', at 3:03 min, YouTube <https://www.youtube.com/watch?v=eryvtbZv5y0> [accessed 30 March 2020].

some basic furnishings, though it is not known what was kept, added, or taken away.[2] Both the hut and the rain were translocated, 'placed' in an unusual setting — Is this simultaneity intended? The idea of the 'natural' decay of materials is conjured in order to have the viewer wonder about the possible results of this performative deterioration. And although probably no visitor (nor any Biennale staff) recorded the exact appearance of the installation in all its different stages of decay over the course of the more than six months of the Biennale, this time span inevitably provokes the imagination, generating ideas on what would or might happen to the hut. However, there is no storm coming, no apocalyptic culmination, no tipping point, and an end of the weathering is nowhere in sight.[3] This work of art has no apparent beginning or end or rather the end is being transferred into the viewer's imagination.

At first sight, nothing moves, except for the jars and glasses that shiver while slowly filling with water. The dripping water creates a constant, evocative background noise. Strangely, while observing the unfamiliar scenery, the continuous rain is heard and then forgotten, heard, and then forgotten again. One's mind is wandering, recalling leakages in ceilings, water butts — distracting, frightening, or strangely soothing side effects of heavy rain fall.[4] How different places can look with a sudden, furious change in weather. The rain swamps the senses, the viewer feels sucked up and finds herself in a state of absorption, trying to keep all details in view. Some sodden lengths of wallpaper are peeling off the walls. And despite the floors being covered with plastic sheeting, the water seeps right through. Almost magically, nothing escapes, the floor of the exhibition hall stays dry. The viewer's gaze is lingering on the jars and bowls collecting the water. Does it ever change: the speed or shape of the drops? A delay, a subtle decoupling

---

2   Julian Heynen, 'Georgia — Vajiko Chachkhiani: *Living Dog Among Dead Lions*', in *Viva Arte Viva, 57th International Art Exhibition La Biennale di Venezia 2017: Catalogue, Participants, Countries, Collateral Events*, ed. by Flavia Fossa Margutti (Venice: SIAE, 2017), pp. 62–63.

3   Many thanks to Delfina Cabrera, Christoph Holzhey, Marlon Miguel, and Arnd Wedemeyer for their astute and generous comments on the subject.

4   I wish to thank Amelia Groom for suggesting the apocalyptic film *The Hole* (Dòng), dir. by Tsai Ming-Liang (Fox Lorber, 1998, 95 min) to me, which depicts the life of two neighbours in a rundown apartment block in Taiwan during times of a strange disease — while outside rain is pouring heavily.

of seeing and hearing takes place. Usually, during bad weather, one retreats indoors, but in this case, one is better off outside. The indoor space, the very definition of human shelter, is itself being exposed to weather and weathering, uniting contradictions and admitting the unexpected. Opposing impressions are evoked simultaneously and play out in different intensities: the steady pitter-patter of rain drops on the scattered pieces of furniture while the surroundings appear perfectly silent. There is a constant dampness that seeps through the entire hut while the beholder stays dry. There is also a dim expectation of the possible arrival of people or other creatures, coupled with the intuition that this house has been abandoned a long time ago. Sensing a kind of nostalgic coziness within its remains, blurry traces suggesting that '[c]ontemporary nostalgia is not so much about the past as about the vanishing present.'[5] A subtle relief and sense of comfort results from being located outside of the hut, yet is mingled with a discomfort at observing and witnessing its destruction. The pouring rain evokes pangs of longing. It intimately links the eerie strangeness of an atmospheric happening to the human condition in order to have the viewer sense the fictional dimension of the real or the real in its fictional dimension.[6]

Within this inversion, the outside turned inside, there is a moment of irritation — of something weird happening. The inverted normality of the house has a certain reality and persuasiveness and, at the same time, a dream-like fantasy to it. One feels caught between what one sees or hopes to see, between one's expectations of what may happen, and an exceptional time zone where 'natural' weathering is being performed as a subject of meditative observation. Eventually, the spaces and furniture exposed to rain and water stagnation will begin to rot and disintegrate, and mould and moss might grow over them. This artificially generated process provokes thoughts about the nature of the here and now as well as of the future appearance of the hut's water-sensitive insides. In a similar vein, Emanuela Zanon suggests,

> [T]he natural process of rotting of the materials exposed to
> moisture and water stagnation generated a sort of spontaneous

---

5   Svetlana Boym, *The Future of Nostalgia* (New York: Basic Books, 2001), p. 351.

6   In a similar vein, in the exhibit *The Last Day* nature invades human spaces. Helmut Wimmer at Kunsthistorisches Museum Wien in 2018/19 <http://www. helmutwimmer.net/the-last-day-galerie> [accessed 10 January 2020].

dramaturgy that led to meditate (or rather to perceive) the
existential implications of resistance and change.[7]

Assuming that nature informs and *'re-forms* the "finished" artwork',[8]
this installation 'cannot perform without the assistance of its environment',[9] involving spectators and forcing them to imagine or anticipate
what is going to happen. One recalls Marcel Broodthaers *La pluie
(Projet pour un texte)* [The Rain (Project for a Text)] from 1969,[10]
and similar to Hans Haacke's *Condensation Cube*[11] — an installation
from 1965 inviting viewers to discover 'the marvels that occur as water
inside the cube condenses'[12] — *Living Dog Among Dead Lions* is kept
from further human or external interference, hermetically sealed as in
a lab experiment. Visitors are kept outside and can only watch, wait,
and witness the changing state of disintegration. The work invites a
slow, obsessive kind of contemplation, a penetrating observation. A
gaze that adds and subtracts, a weathering gaze. Slowly, a relationship
between a firm object that sits passively, waiting to be destroyed and
the spectator, demanding some kind of damage to be observed, seems
to be forming. Suddenly, one thinks of crowds of gawkers who cannot
take their eyes from accidents, natural disasters, or acts of violence. The
space outside the house feels like a waiting room; and the steady gaze of
the audience suggests a kind of mastery of the situation: where nothing

---

7   Emanuela Zanon, 'Vajiko Chachkhiani: The Poet of Absence at the de' Foscherari
        Gallery', *Juliet*, 30 January 2019 <https://www.juliet-artmagazine.com/en/vajiko-
        chachkhiani-de-foscherari-gallery/> [accessed 3 January 2020].

8   Mohsen Mostafavi and David Leatherbarrow, *On Weathering: The Life of Buildings in
        Time* (Cambridge, MA: MIT Press, 1993), p. 64. For Mostafavi and Leatherbarrow the
        informing and reforming applies to buildings.

9   To quote Hans Haacke, for whom the concept of change proved to be the ideological
        basis of his work, *Untitled Statement*, in Linda Weintraub, *To Life! Eco Art in Pursuit
        of a Sustainable Planet* (Berkeley: University of California Press, 2012), p. 71. This
        statement stems from Haacke's exhibition manifesto for his exhibition in Cologne in
        1965.

10   *La pluie (Projet pour un texte)*, dir. by Marcel Broodthaers (Collection Centre Pom-
        pidou, inventory number: AM 1996-F1310, 1969, 2 min). A digitized replica of the
        16mm black and white, silent film was posted by Matthias Planitzer, 'La pluie', *Castor &
        Pollux* (5 December 2009) <http://www.castor-und-pollux.de/2009/12/la-pluie/>
        [accessed 20 December 2019].

11   Hans Haacke, *Condensation Cube*, 1963–65, perspex, steel, and water, 305 x 305 x 305
        mm, Tate Modern, London.

12   Linda Weintraub, *Eco Art in Pursuit of a Sustainable Planet* (Berkeley: University of
        California Press, 2012), p. 70.

will happen to me as long as I stand outside and observe the disaster that takes place at a distance — and not to me. Omer Fast has framed it as feeling safe 'as long as you are in the waiting room like in a womb, what happens outside is not what actually happens to you'.[13]

Once the scenery is observed more closely, it becomes clear that the beds are tightly wrapped in plastic sheeting, as are the floors and tables, perhaps to delay the weathering or to shield the wrapped objects from being worn out too quickly, from re-forming, and from any rampant deterioration by the rain.[14] A former life now vacuum-packed and preserved. The protective layers insert a distance, a shield against outside influences, and hint at the conservation of tradition.[15] At the same time, it feels as if these objects cannot breathe, as if obsessive precautions were taken against dirt or unwanted affection. Can the inside of the hut be seen 'as metaphor for the interior life of an individual, the rain as metaphor for a slowly nagging threat but also for an enduring ablution', as Christine Macel suggests?[16] An invocation of healing through ablution? Or rather a cage of domesticity weathered in order to 'transcend its core phoenix-like'?[17] The scenery refers to complex inter-relationships of past, actual, and anticipated events and to weathering as an inscriptive and imaginative force.

'The weather', to quote Christina Sharpe, 'necessitates changeability and improvisation: it is an atmospheric condition of time and space.'[18] How does rain invoke spheres of meaning? Rain is restless, all-permeating, and, by virtue of being liquid, 'flexible in form and embracing in scope', it comes with the 'extreme power for self-

---

13   Cristina Baldacci and Claudia Peppel, 'Zwischen den Wasserlilien. Ein Interview mit Omer Fast', in *Die Kunst des Wartens*, ed. by Brigitte Kölle and Claudia Peppel (Berlin: Wagenbach, 2019), pp. 98–107 (p. 105).

14   Mostafavi and Leatherbarrow, *On Weathering*, p. 64.

15   The wrapping of furniture in plastic sheeting is used in the Georgian countryside in order to protect objects. See Vajiko Chachkhiani and Claudia Peppel, 'Life Never Stops Being Violent. A Conversation', in this volume, pp. 293–94.

16   Christine Macel, director of the 2017 Venice Biennale, see Heynen, 'Georgia — Vajiko Chachkhiani', p. 62.

17   Gerhard Matzig, 'Geist aus der Asche. "Yakisugi" ist die Kunst des Verkohlens: Warum Architektur brennen muss, um zu leben', *Süddeutsche Zeitung*, 124, 30 May – 1 June 2020, p. 56; my translation of: 'Das Kunstwerk wird an der Oberfläche zerstört, um es im Kern phoenixhaft über sich hinauswachsen zu lassen.'

18   Christina Sharpe, *In the Wake: On Blackness and Being* (Durham, NC: Duke University Press, 2016), p. 205.

transformation and transformation of its resistant opponents.'[19] Rain — as weather in general is — is experienced as a 'highly affective phenomenon that can evoke a strong sense of wonder, delight, or terror, as well as a myriad of minor perceptions every moment'.[20] 'Memories of certain weather events are often nostalgically framed, they haunt and persist.'[21] Weather shapes the perception of people in their environment, it causes sensations, creates spaces of experience, triggers pain, and influences mental states: The rain orchestrates emotional reactions such as feelings of abandonment and loss of control as well as a general awareness that things are being worn down. A recent study referred to rain as being the 'background noise of human history', and its results suggest that the sound of rain can even improve people's memory, promoting relaxation as well as stimulating concentration. In fact, for those of us lacking sleep or having trouble concentrating, YouTube videos offer anywhere from three to ten hours of non-stop rain fall.[22]

Despite the impressive number of artworks in the past decades that involve rain as a fluid material and substantial weather element, art-historical research has hardly paid close attention to the atmospheric phenomenon.[23] In recent years, a new genre called 'weather art' or 'meteorological art' has appeared in art criticism. Works that

---

19   Chung-ying Cheng, 'Chinese Philosophy and Symbolic Reference', *Philosophy East and West*, 27.3 (July 1977), pp. 307–22 (p. 317) <https://doi.org/10.2307/1398001>.

20   Janine Randerson, *Weather as Medium: Toward a Meteorological Art* (Cambridge, MA: MIT Press, 2018), pp. xvi and xiv.

21   Georgina Endfield and Simon Naylor, 'Climate and Cultural Heritage: An Experiment with the 'Weather Memory Bank', in *The Future of Heritage as Climates Change: Loss, Adaptation and Creativity*, ed. by David C. Harvey and Jim Perry (London: Routledge, 2015), pp. 62–77 (p. 72).

22   One example is *Heavy Rain at Night*, a ten-hour video to reduce stress and/or insomnia as well as to improve concentration, Mermaid Waters, YouTube, 14 February 2020 <https://www.youtube.com/watch?v=9QneqUhCVtU> [accessed 20 June 2020]. For more information regarding the study see Alex Rühle, 'Flüssige Freude', *Süddeutsche Zeitung*, 140, 20–21 June 2020, p. 17.

23   Instead, disproportionately more art-related research was done on fluids, fog, and blur. See *State of Flux: Aesthetics of Fluid Materials*, ed. by Marcel Finke and Friedrich Weltzien (Berlin: Reimer, 2017); Markus Finke, 'Im Nebel. Fluide Materialien und die Kunst der Zerstreuung', in *Wessen Wissen? Materialität und Situiertheit in den Künsten*, ed. by Kathrin Busch, Kathrin Peters, Christina Dörfling, and Ildikó Szántó (Paderborn: Fink, 2018), pp. 97–114; *Einfluss, Strömung, Quelle: Aquatische Metaphern der Kunstgeschichte*, ed. by Ulrich Pfisterer and Christine Tauber (Bielefeld: transcript, 2018).

are classified under this (rather broad) term range from land art to recent eco-critical art forms and consist of, or include, meteorological elements and/or engage with environmental components and/or climate change and its consequences. Janine Randerson conceptualizes weather as a medium within these artworks in the two-fold sense of a constitutive 'material' as well as an operating force. On the one hand, weather is contained within the materiality of its conditions, which connect us 'to the world and to each other through the rain, wind, and sunlight that carry sensations to our human and machinic receptors.' When represented *in* the media, for example in the news or in forecasting, weather takes on a different quality, as nature and human technology meet and 'atmospheric phenomena are foregrounded and not a given'.[24] Randerson suggests that we 'treat the weather as a lively provocateur, collaborator, and catalyst for vital ecocritical conversations'.[25] For her, meteorological art refers to 'social encounters with live weather' and 'sustains an inter- and intradisciplinary perspective in which art is lately infused with atmospheric science and social politics'.[26] Perhaps too far-reaching a claim.

Although Randerson strives to delineate ecocritical tendencies as well as socio-political statements in weather art, Matthew Bower — in what he describes as 'curious obsession' — opts for a more playful approach: 'As far as aesthetic subject matters go, weather is just begging for interactivity, some movement and spectacle that don't just portray the elements, but actually imitate them.'[27] One example is Ryan Gander's *I Need Some Meaning I Can Memorise (The Invisible Pull)* at documenta (13) in 2012, which consisted of a light breeze in the large, completely empty room situated just after the entrance of the exhibition hall 'Fridericianum'. As far as rain installations are concerned, however, two types can be roughly distinguished, some — like *Living Dog Among Dead Lions* — keep the spectator observing at a distance, with no direct involvement. Others, building on the traditions of inter-

---

24   Randerson, *Weather as Medium*, p. xvii.

25   Ibid., p. xiv.

26   Ibid., pp. xvi and xvii.

27   Matthew Bower, 'A Storm in a Jar: 10 Very Cool Art Installations That Imitate Weather', *The Atlantic*, 9 November 2012 <https://www.theatlantic.com/entertainment/archive/2012/11/a-storm-in-a-jar-10-very-cool-art-installations-that-imitate-weather/265017/> [accessed 20 December 2019].

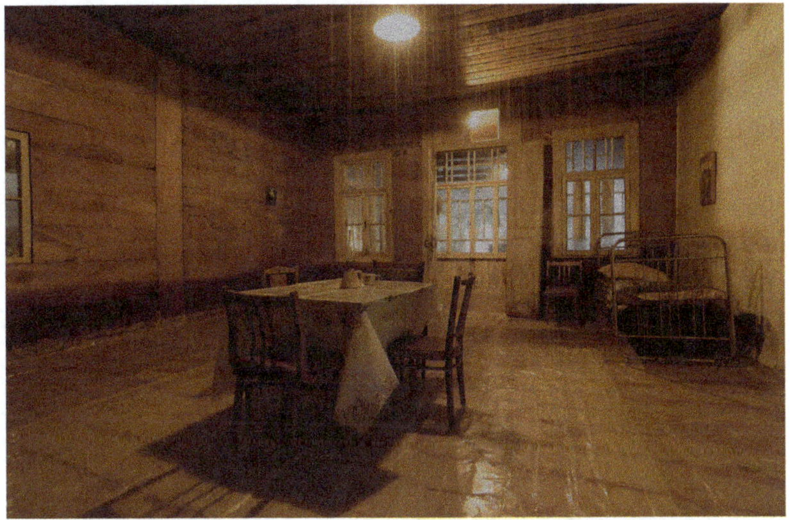

Figure 2. © Vajiko Chachkhiani, *Living Dog Among Dead Lions*,
57th Venice Biennale, Venice, 2017. Photo credit: Sandro Sulaberidze.

active art, create a situation in which the viewer physically enters the installation, moves around, and makes the artwork 'respond' to the human presence or movement. *Rain Room*, for instance, is an immersive artwork by Hannes Koch and Florian Ortkrass for Random International, in which visitors, upon entering the space, are given a sense of control over the weather, as the falling rain stops once a human body is detected. Viewers find themselves 'simultaneously exposed to and protected' from the heavy downpour.[28] Another example is *Symphony in D Minor*, a set of interactive hanging sculptures by Chris Klapper & Patrick Gallagher, which works in a similar way: 'the hanging cylinders respond to movement, intensifying the effects of heavy rain, lightning, and thunder as the audience leaps and flails beneath.'[29] Without referring to any particular event, existential 'weather' implications of fixity and change, of endurance and resistance are at play.

---

28   The first exhibit of *Rain Room* by Random International took place at Barbican, London in 2012 <https://www.random-international.com/rain-room-2012> [accessed 20 June 2020].

29   Bower, 'A Storm in a Jar'.

Living Dog Among Dead Lions — as will be explained in more detail in the following interview — stems from an idea for a film called *Heavy Metal Honey*, which Chachkhiani could realize only much later.[30] In *Heavy Metal Honey*, rain is falling *inside* a living room and disturbs a family's gathering at the table. The meal ends abruptly when the mother shows up with a gun and kills several members of the family.[31] Blood, wine, and rain are mixed on the table. Only once the rain stops, the violence ends. It remains unclear whether the family members are still alive or whether this is the fantasy of the female protagonist (who is herself obviously doomed to die). Both works refer to rain water damaging confined territories and allude to the devastating flood in Tbilisi in 2015, when torrential rainfall bloated the river and led to it bursting its banks, dragging nineteen people to their deaths and flooding many homes. The city zoo was destroyed, some three hundred animals escaped and found themselves enjoying an unexpected freedom, 'roaming the streets for the following days, seeking shelter between the ruins', until they drowned or were shot.[32] Only very few could be recaptured.[33] One might interpret the title of the work, *Living Dog Among Dead Lions*, a quote from the Bible (Ecclesiastes 9. 4), to be suggesting that it might be better to adapt and not to take risks rather than being exposed to the danger of wilderness and supposedly being killed. The title may imply that 'humble individuals [...] thanks to their meekness, manage to stay alive' in harsh living conditions.[34] 'A traumatic experience changes the interior life of a person', Chachkhiani said in a press release, and it seems that the confined heavy rain in the hut expresses the self-absorbed quality of the human psyche,

---

30   For his solo exhibition *Heavy Metal Honey* in 2018, see the interview with the curator Susanne Kleine at the opening at Bundeskunsthalle, YouTube, 28 June 2018 <https://www.youtube.com/watch?v=-naE2m5l89w> [accessed 20 December 2019].

31   Renate Puvogel, 'Bonn, Vajiko Chachkhiani, *Heavy Metal Honey*, 29 June – 7 October 2018 Bundeskunsthalle', *Kunstforum*, 256 (2018), pp. 260–62 (p. 260).

32   In Vajiko Chachkhiani's recent exhibition *Glass Ghosts*, the catastrophic flooding is again evoked, this time without rain but remnants of cages hanging from the ceiling populated with wooden animal figures (Zanon, 'Vajiko Chachkhiani').

33   Rein Wolfs, 'Preface', in *Vajiko Chachkhiani: Heavy Metal Honey*, ed. by Kunst- und Ausstellungshalle der Bundesrepublik Deutschland (Bonn: Kunst- und Ausstellungshalle der Bundesrepublik Deutschland, 2018), pp. 11–12.

34   Anna Battista, *Irenebrination: Notes on Architecture, Art, Fashion, Fashion Law & Technology*, 17 May 2017 <https://irenebrination.typepad.com/irenebrination_notes_on_a/2017/05/vajiko-chachkhiani-venice-biennale.html> [accessed 10 May 2020].

and reminds the viewer how traumatic incidents tend to constantly reappear, linger, and reshape the remains.[35] The performance captures both the nostalgic grip within the process and its ongoing endurance, a landscape of a former life, witness to moments of irrevocable dramatic action that is somehow, nonetheless, withstood. It puts the viewer in a state of quiet reflection, a state of a rare and fleeting exposure to psychic metamorphoses, in which what once was has to be related to the exhausting awareness of change. What remains and what weathers? In *Living Dog Among Dead Lions*, rain acts as a malleable agent to explore existential questions: Weathering is the desire for *re-covery* and the road to transformation.

---

35   Ibid.

Life Never Stops Being Violent
A Conversation
VAJIKO CHACHKHIANI AND CLAUDIA PEPPEL

The interview was supposed to take place in Berlin on the occasion of the ICI Workshop *On Weathering*. However, in the late summer of 2019, Vajiko Chachkhiani received a Villa Aurora fellowship and moved to Los Angeles. Therefore, the interview was conducted online. Vajiko Chachkhiani (born in 1985 in Tbilisi, USSR now Georgia) studied art at the Gerrit Rietveld Academie in Amsterdam and at the Universität der Künste Berlin. Chachkhiani received a DAAD scholarship in 2013 and the ISCP Residency Program in 2016. He was awarded the prestigious 7th Rubens Promotional Award of the Contemporary Art Museum Siegen in 2014. His latest exhibitions include *Heavy Metal Honey*, Bundeskunsthalle, Bonn (2018), *Moment in and out of time*, SCAI The Bathhouse gallery, Tokyo (2018), *Glass Ghost*, Galleria de'Foscherari, Bologna (2019), and *Winter which was not there*, Gallery Cork, Ireland (2019).

Claudia Peppel: In the context of the presentation of your work *Living Dog Among Dead Lions* at the 57th Biennale 'Viva Arte Viva' in 2017, you said that setting up this hut was driven by your personal experiences. How did you come up with the idea of reconstructing one of these typical Georgian wooden huts in Venice?

Vajiko Chachkhiani: It all started with an idea for a film called *Heavy Metal Honey*, which I could not make at the time. For the film, a family would gather in a living room, and eventually it would start to rain inside the room. And then some other things would happen. That was the idea. Then, when we applied for the Georgian Pavilion, I first had a different proposal in mind, but when I saw the space, I thought, 'ok, maybe it would be cool to have a kind of big sculpture.' And as my works often deal with history and somehow also psychology, I thought the best thing would be to come up with a house, which has its own history. Then, the idea of the rain came back, and I thought, there should also be rain inside that would deform the interior; the wooden hut in this context is important because it has this authentic aura and also has a very intense wooden smell when it gets wet.

CP: After a heavy rainfall in 2015, Tbilisi, the capital of Georgia, experienced a torrential flood; the river Vere overflowed its banks and the city's zoo was also inundated. Nineteen people and more than three hundred animals lost their lives. Because of the flood, several zoo animals experienced an unusual and unexpected freedom, like the white tiger that was eventually shot after assaulting and killing a man. Did this exceptional situation influence the outcome of this work or its title? I have read that you called the flood a mythical event?

VC: This flood affected me in a profound way. It was really tragic to see a worker eaten by a tiger. And as you mentioned, it was like a mythological encounter. There is no need to write mythologies any-more because they happen on their own. That flood really stayed with me for a long time. And I think unconsciously that could be the reason I brought rain into my work. After the piece, *Living Dog Among Dead Lions*, I did the solo show in the Bundeskunsthalle in Bonn, which was dedicated to the worker who was eaten by the tiger. It consisted of a different set of sculptural installations called *Heavy Metal Honey*, which is the same title as the film I mentioned above. The title of the piece I presented in Venice comes from the Bible. In the Old Testament, there is one section where it says that it is better to be a dog and live than a lion and die. When you are alive, you still have the possibilities to do things or change them. You have more potential, essentially.

CP: The rain pouring down inside the hut inverts our expecta-tions of how weather unfolds: Usually you would seek shelter indoors from pouring rain; here it is the opposite, outside one stays dry and everything remains intact, while inside everything gets wet and is slowly rotting. Within this inversion — the outside made inside — there is a moment of irritation. One knows it's not real, but it convinces you at the moment of the performance. What role does this reversal or inversion of reality play for you? Does the tension within the work arise from the fact that you know it is not real but pretend that it is?

VC: In my work, I often use open and direct metaphors. And I don't reflect upon what is fictional vs. what is real because I believe fiction turns into reality, like mythology or stories. When stories refer to real human problems or conflicts, that's when they have impact. The piece consists of two narrative strands, an outer, where the hut remains inaccessible and untouched, and an inner one, where things change with a lot of dynamics and eventually become deformed. When I developed the idea, I had a couple of things in mind: I was thinking about the way history creates tendencies and affects someone's psyche and the present-day life. It is generally inscribed in a certain way. The past can deform a person's interior but you don't perceive these effects on the exterior. I think mostly we consider the impact of history on society, while we neglect the personal inflictions. On a personal level, you never really know what's going on. And the piece is a metaphor of that duality of inner and outer narration. What we present to the world vs. how we are feeling on the inside, that's really a different story. The secret story of a person is the psyche, and in the end, that's what I'm trying to understand, and what I am really interested in: the psychic life, and the way it is affected by history. It could be political or social.

CP: Viewers cannot enter or interact, they literally remain outside and can only watch the pouring rain and wait to witness the destruction or state of disintegration. Even though little happens, it is very suspenseful. I felt this suggests an obsessive, almost intrusive kind of observation, which is gazing rather than looking. Slowly, a bond seems to form between an interior that passively sits there, waiting to be destroyed, and the gaze from the outside, demanding to see something. What role do you assign to the audience? Are the viewers an active ingredient merging gaze and destruction into a situation on a greater scale?

VC: Conceptually I thought of making a classic sculpture, one that you look at but you cannot walk through, a space you observe that refuses entry. Because metaphorically the house stands in for the interior of a human being. It is about looking at it from the outside, and yes, I think people really enjoy watching tragic things. They don't enjoy but are captivated by them. But as long as the tragedy is distant you aren't pulled in. But when you are involved in a disaster, you don't want to be observed. I think that is an interesting twist: to be watching while at the same time being immersed. In reality, if you watch the news and a tragic thing happens, that's a very different thing, but in this case, I wanted people to feel the tension and the subtle violence that happens to the interior, while at the same time the hut is almost sentimental and has this romantic appeal.

CP: *Living Dog Among Dead Lions* is a rather process- and time-based work, it is not a finite object. Does it address environmental concerns?

VC: I did not intend to address any environmental concerns, but somehow the work does. But this was not my intention, it happened independent of me. The work raises these concerns by itself.

CP: The weathering caused by the artificial rain accelerated a process that would have happened sooner or later without the rain: the hut would have eventually been destroyed 'by nature'. Why did you want to accelerate this process or make it so vividly perceptible? Can weathering be seen as a neutralizing destiny or as a 'romantic form of aging' like ruination, or rather as an act of inscription?

VC: What I find interesting about rain is that it is romantic. It can make the city very beautiful because of the reflections produced. Especially at night if you have wet streets. But on the other hand, it can also destroy or ruin everything, if there is a flood, for example. And that was the anchor. I have used the motif of water a lot in my work. Because it has this duality that it is beautiful, romantic, and sentimental, but on the other hand, in an instant it can become violent. And it also refers metaphorically to human nature. In the piece, the acceleration of decay adds an important dimension, the idea of the piece is based on the weathering process, without rain, it would be just a hut with just a history. Involving weathering aspects creates the drama of an interior human psyche.

CP: Weathering therefore adds to and subtracts from the 'finish': for example, it takes away colours, destroys the surfaces, but adds the finish of the environment.[1] In this sense, the rain or what grows out of it re-forms the artwork although it is artificially controlled by the artist. What was the idea behind this process and what did you think the hut would look like at the end of the performance, after six months on display at the Biennale? Many people imagined right from the beginning that moss and mould might grow.

VC: This piece is somehow a sculpture but at the same time a performative installation. And the role of weather is really important because it makes the work function. It is the inner life of the piece to deform, change, and transform. And that is also my observation of how history works. It is an authentic house, which was inhabited by people for a long time. It was my idea to use this duality of the rain to create romantic ambiance, while at the same time it deforms the interior. The whole idea of the sculpture is that it is performative.

CP: Atmosphere refers on the one hand to meteorological facts, on the other hand to the characteristics that a space or place radiates and to the immediate perception of these characteristics. In your piece these aspects seem to come together. Any thoughts about these 'atmospheric' dimensions?

VC: Previously, I made a piece called *Rite (Dog Days)* (2014), which was a kind of heat sculpture, an empty space filled with hot air. The humidity and heat were based on historical data from different geographical sites (two prison sites) and combining them created a corridor, a transitory experience, somehow a rite of passage. This passage was immaterial and intense and through the intensified atmosphere the piece tried to evoke empathy. In *Living Dog Among Dead Lions,* the atmospheric dimension is also important since the concept of the deformation of the interior stems from this intensified atmosphere.

CP: Your installation remained not only untouched from the outside and devoid of people but was also closed as if hermetically sealed in a kind of vacuum-packaging. Some of the furniture was actually wrapped in plastic sheeting as if to protect it from too much weathering or destruction. Why?**VC**: In houses in the countryside, people nor-

---

1   Mohsen Mostafavi and David Leatherbarrow, *On Weathering: The Life of Buildings in Time* (Cambridge, MA: MIT Press, 1993), p. 64.

mally put plastic sheeting on the furniture and on the ground because they don't want to wear it out. That's a very common thing they do there, a kind of preservation and conservation of the interior. Mostly in the living room and the porch. I used it to create more authenticity. That was the idea — to do a replica of what countryside people do in their houses.

CP: The German artist Hans Haacke once said that weather is a prototypical example of a system of interactive physical components with metaphorical significance, while Susanne Kleine, the curator at Bundeskunsthalle of *Heavy Metal Honey*, suggested that the permanent rain in the house can be read as a metaphorical condensation of living conditions or traumatic events and their consequences.[2] Can you tell me more about the metaphorical impact and about the role the artificial rain plays within this setting? Does it reflect an interplay or continuity of violence and vulnerability?

VC: The permanent rain is a reflection on nature and of the way life unfolds. Life never stops being violent; it never stops being vulnerable. It is always about motion, about transformation, about dynamics. The artificial rain somehow cleans up the environment, but on the other hand, it also can be violent in excess. But it depends also on the geography: in some places, you don't have so much rain, or you would like to have rain because there are a lot of fires. In other areas, you have cities with too much rain, and it could cause problems. Metaphorically, it suggests human psychic life is like a process of permanent inner salvation. It always runs. The rain represents the inner dynamics, the way it is in nature, and that history can be really traumatic and deform the interior. That is what the rain does in this piece.

---

2   Jack Burnham, 'Hans Haacke — Wind and Water Sculpture', in *Art in the Land: A Critical Anthology of Environmental Art*, ed. by Alan Sonfist (New York: Dutton, 1983), pp. 105–25 (p. 109). Susanne Kleine, 'Interior and Exterior Spaces', in *Vajiko Chachkhiani: Heavy Metal Honey*, ed. by Kunst- und Ausstellungshalle der Bundesrepublik Deutschland (Bonn: Kunst- und Ausstellungshalle der Bundesrepublik Deutschland, 2018), pp. 33–43 (p. 33).

Confined Weathers
Graciela Iturbide and Mario Bellatin's *The Bathroom of Frida Kahlo/Demerol without Expiration Date*
DELFINA CABRERA

WEATHERING AT WORK

The images evoked by the word 'weathering' rarely refer to interiors.[1] They are often accompanied by the belief that weathering must be fought, stopped, or controlled. But perhaps the only successful battles against this pervasive enemy are those that join forces with it. Many artists have understood this and rather than avoiding the supposed evils of weathering, they have copied them, turning the work of unseen powers and the feared passage of time into creative devices. Weathering, in this sense, is at the very heart of art. It dwells inside the work, in its most sheltered intimacy.

When in 1954 the Mexican painter Diego Rivera decreed that Frida Kahlo's bathroom should remain locked for fifteen years after his death, he could not foresee that this period would stretch into almost five decades. In 1958, the house where they had lived was turned into

---

1   I am grateful to Claudia Peppel, Marlon Miguel, Christoph Holzhey, Arnd Wedemeyer, and Graciela Goldchluk for their generous readings and insightful comments on this essay.

a museum, but the bathroom was made accessible to the public only in 2005 when the museum invited photographer Graciela Iturbide and writer Mario Bellatin to engage with it. Their excursions resulted in a double-sided book that read *The Bathroom of Frida Kahlo*, when turned in one direction, and *Demerol Without Expiration Date*, when turned in the other. The first title corresponds to a series of photographs by Iturbide and the second to a text by Bellatin.[2] Both, the photographs and the text, address the work of weathering on one of the most iconic artistic legacies of the twentieth century.

This book, at first touch, entails an altering gesture, a certain disorder: from the first bourgeois fortress of privacy, the ultimate architectural element, the bathroom, Iturbide and Bellatin extract and expose objects that had been concealed. Frida's dried corsets, the rusted enema pots, a box of Demerol painkillers, a poster of Stalin warped by humidity, an anatomy chart of intra-uterine life (intact), the metal crutches, the stained hospital gown, an orthopaedic leg leaned against the wall, two stuffed birds, and a turtle are some of those things, now part of the museum's permanent collection and protected under strict conservation rules. But *The Bathroom of Frida Kahlo/Demerol without Expiration Date* offers to the eye what the display cases cannot show. Within Iturbide and Bellatin's book, Kahlo's ambivalent presence bears witness to this effort and opens up questions about how art, improper bodies, and medicalization mingle, but also the relations between art, the process of weathering, and the art market.[3]

After her death, Frida Kahlo was captured in a continuous present. She became an international celebrity, a trademark — licensed by the Frida Kahlo Corporation — and since 2010, her portrait can be found on billions of five hundred Mexican peso banknotes.[4] Likewise,

---

2   Graciela Iturbide and Mario Bellatin, *El baño de Frida Kahlo/Demerol, sin fecha de caducidad* (Ciudad de México: Galería López Quiroga/Editorial RM, 2008).

3   For a pioneering analysis of Iturbide and Bellatin's book, see Paola Cortés-Rocca, 'La insoportable levedad del yo. Iturbide y Bellati en *El Baño de Frida Kahlo*', *Filología*, 44.1 (2012), pp. 121–38.

4   The Frida Kahlo Corporation owns the trademark rights and interests to the name Frida Kahlo worldwide <https://fridakahlocorporation.com/> [accessed 18 June 2020]. As to the five hundred peso banknote, it features a self-portrait of Diego Rivera on the reverse alongside a fragment of his painting *Desnudo con alcatraces* (Nude with Calla Lilies). The motif on the reverse is a self-portrait of Frida Kahlo accompanied by an image of her work *El abrazo de amor del Universo, la tierra (México), yo, Diego*

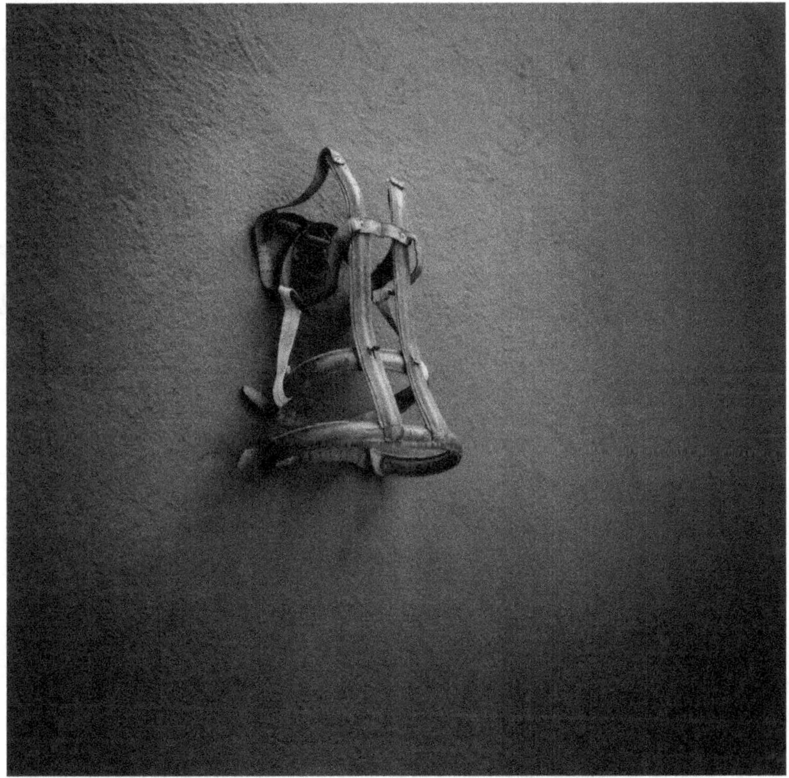

Figure 1. © Graciela Iturbide, *El baño de Frida* VII. Courtesy of the artist.

her personal belongings, including the ones that were found in her bathroom and that allegedly unveil her most guarded secrets, are spectacularly displayed and consumed.[5]

It could be then inferred that Diego Rivera's order to board up her bathroom was intended to protect his wife's intimacy from public view.

---

y el Señor Xólotl (Love's Embrace of the Universe, Earth (Mexico), I, Diego, and Mr. Xólotl). The banknote will soon be replaced by a new one featuring former Mexican president, Benito Juárez, on the front and a gray whale with its young on the back.

5   The 2018 exhibition, *Frida Kahlo: Making Her Self Up*, at the Victoria and Albert Museum in London is indicative of this way of presenting Kahlo's legacy: <https://www.vam.ac.uk/exhibitions/frida-kahlo-making-her-self-up> [accessed 25 May 2020]. For a thoughtful discussion on the 'Fridomanía', see Margo Glantz, 'Frida Kahlo. Diseminación y amplificación', *Revista de la Universidad de México*, 104 (2012), pp. 15–25.

Perhaps, but Iturbide and Bellatin seem to suggest otherwise. Instead of protection, Rivera was seeking exposure, and let weathering do the work. Changes in temperature, humidity, the lack or excess of light, the effects of microorganisms, among other natural agents, subjected the silent dwellers of the bathroom to a series of unpredictable, discrete, and continuous metamorphoses.

Who would have thought that with this intended closure and deferred opening, one of the fathers of Mexican muralism, the archetype of the committed Latin American artist, from the centre of Coyoacán — the centre of the periphery — would be more than two decades ahead of the pop art icon, Andy Warhol, who packed more than three hundred thousand items of his possessions — clothes, bounced checks, toys, letters, acne medicines, nail clippings, a mummified foot, used condoms — into some six hundred sealed cardboard boxes archived with rigorous compulsion during the last thirteen years of his life?

Once closed, Frida's bathroom and Warhol's *Time Capsules*, become acephalous laboratories of transformation and contingent interactions. Bacteria, humidity, mould, pests — the villains of art preservation — push the artist out of frame. Iturbide photographs the ragged corsets that once supported Frida's body and which now hang in the shower, on a rusted nail, on a coat rack. The hospital gown (are the stains on it paint or blood?) is held by a hanger. Three entangled enema hoses come out of the rusted enamel pots. A stuffed turtle whose shell is falling into pieces rises from the bathtub. Stalin, on a bent poster, sinks into it. The placements of the objects have been sensibly orchestrated and the photographer's attentiveness to the dryness of plastic, the stiffness of leather, the consumed paper and the stained fabric, together with the rather promiscuous arrangements, instead of pointing towards decay and death, infuse a breath of life into the weathered objects that, like the Demerol box, have 'no expiration date'.

Literary critic Paola Cortés-Rocca situates Iturbide's series within the history of still life painting, traditionally relegated to the lowest level in the hierarchy of art genres as it dealt with 'low forms of life' — inanimate or non-corporeal objects — and as it took private property as its main subject-matter.[6] Accordingly, Iturbide's photographs trans-

---

6   Norman Bryson, *Looking at the Overlooked: Four Essays on Still Life Painting* (London: Reaktion Books, 1990).

form the mundane things of Frida's bathroom into aesthetic objects, emphasizing in them the articulation between property, exhibition, and gaze:

> This articulation that the still life genre stages — a series of objects are exhibited as someone's property and, in turn, are contemplated as if they could be consumed or appropriated — is transferred to the figure of the artist. In other words: since an institution like the museum is wary of a rusty tin can, an old prosthesis or a worn poster [...], if a series of hoses for making enemas becomes aesthetic material, if they are worthy of occupying the photographic field it is because they once belonged to Frida Kahlo.[7]

But also, these photographs of weathered things locked up in 'the most psychosexually charged room in a building', as Beatriz Colomina and Mark Wigley name it,[8] might be mapping a cartography of desire that does not conform to the canonical image of the painter. Taking Cortés-Rocca insights one step further, it can be said that Iturbide's disturbing series subtly pay homage to Kahlo's overlooked *naturalezas muertas*.

Undoubtedly, there has always been a question of life or death at stake in the still life genre, and the ways of naming it in different languages and art traditions account for this tension. Instead of the English term 'still life' (derived from the Dutch *stilleven*) that connotes immobility but also survival; Romance languages such as French or Spanish adopted, later in time, the term *nature morte*, which brings immobility closer to death. Aware of this, Kahlo, who spent much of her life in beds, at hospitals and at home, named one of her *naturalezas muertas Naturaleza viva* (Living Nature or *Nature vivante*, 1952), and wrote on a slice of watermelon, in her last painting (a still life), *Viva la vida* (Long Live Life).

Kahlo began painting *naturalezas muertas* at an early age, the first, *Charola de amapolas* (Tray with Poppies), dating from 1924. None-

---

7   Cortés-Rocca, 'La insoportable levedad', p. 128; my translation.

8   In contrast to the generalized disregard that the bathroom has received in architectural thought, Beatriz Colomina and Mark Wigley go as far as to state that 'the history of Modern architecture could be written from the point of view of the toilet'. As an introduction to their original perspective on this topic, see 'Toilet Architecture: An Essay about the Most Psychosexually Charged Room in a Building', *PIN–UP Magazine*, 23 (Fall/Winter 2017/18), <https://pinupmagazine.org/articles/toilet-modern-architecture/> [accessed 17 July 2020].

theless, as art historian Nancy Deffebach notes, considering the large number of still lifes that Kahlo created over a period of thirty years (more than twenty-five out of a total of one hundred forty-four artworks) few studies have been done on these pieces, which comprise, in addition, many generic transgressions.[9] According to Deffebach, this omission is probably due to the fact that 'Kahlo's still lifes resist the predominant biographical interpretations that have been applied to her self-portraits'.[10] By the same token, the rare analyses devoted to these works disregard their pictorial specificities and privilege instead popular themes of Kahlo's biography such as her turbulent marriage with Rivera or her physical martyrdom.[11]

However, Kahlo's *naturalezas muertas* undermine the markers assigned to the artist's public figure: the betrayed wife, the restless rebel, the sufferer. In these works, the protagonists are the transformative affinities between diverse forms of life, as in the weathering process: in *Naturaleza muerta (tondo)* (Still Life (Round)), for instance, various vegetables and other species, such as mushrooms and flowers, open up to each other like the sliced squash in the middle, a butterfly, and a moth hovering over them; in *Naturaleza viva* (1952), a pigeon hatches into a sweet potato while some roots write 'Living Nature' on the ground; in *Tunas* (Prickly Pears, 1938), two half-cut cactus fruits ripe open like an open heart. Iturbide, in her photographical series, echoes the contagious force of these disregarded paintings. She withdraws from the widespread representations of Kahlo and by freeing the artist's objects from a pre-established meaning, she mobilizes new

---

9   For a detailed analysis of Kahlo's still lifes, see Nancy Deffebach, *María Izquierdo and Frida Kahlo: Challenging Visions in Modern Mexican Art* (Austin: University of Texas Press, 2015), pp. 135–39.

10   Ibid., p. 135.

11   Deffebach argues that this analytical framework predominates in the works of Helga Prignitz-Poda and Salomon Grimberg. To this respect, she notes: 'Prignitz-Poda literally sees Diego Rivera in the watermelons in *Viva la vida* (*Long Live Life*) of 1954 and asserts that in all the slices of melon he "turns around himself as if in a macabre dance of dismemberment", a vision that rather ingeniously facilitates her conclusion that "for Kahlo there is no more room in the world". In a 2004 article titled "Frida Kahlo's Still Lifes", Salomon Grimberg declares: "Kahlo's still lifes often read like pages in a diary." To illustrate his claim, he alleges that a small piggy bank represents Rivera while a figurine of a horse stands for Kahlo in *Still Life with Piggy Bank and Black Horse* of ca. 1928. Later in the article he sights Rivera in a slice of watermelon and a prickly pear' (p. 136).

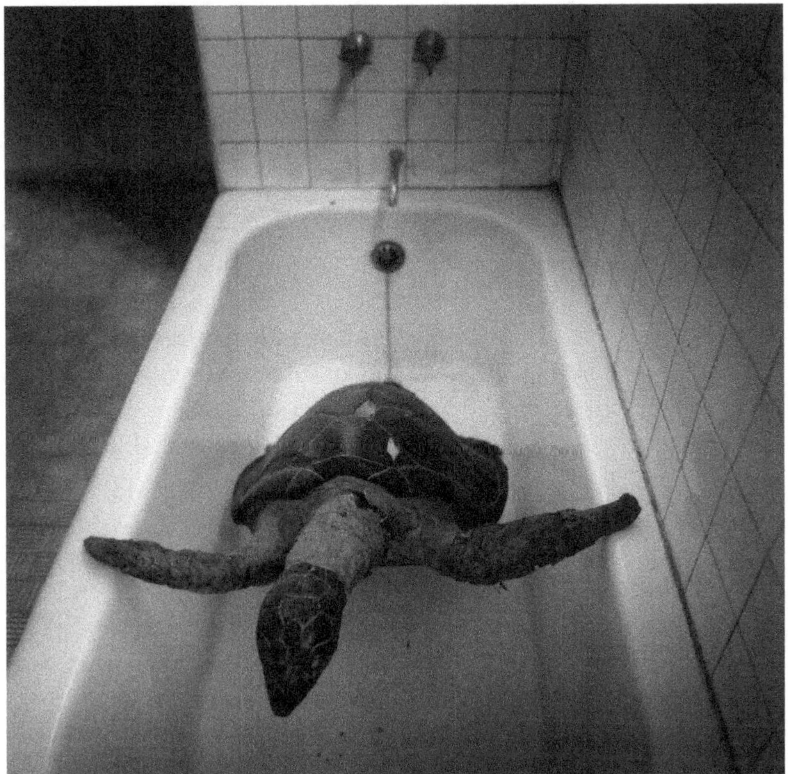

Figure 2. © Graciela Iturbide, *El baño de Frida* XIV. Courtesy of the artist.

lines of interpretation and interrogates the tragic immobility to which Kahlo's oeuvre has been subjected since her death.

At this point, one might suspect a certain archivist drive in *The Bathroom of Frida Kahlo*, a need to delve into a space where weathering has done its work, and to look for new constellations in what is left. Iturbide acutely reads in the sealed room the construction of a confined weather that would only preserve what matters. Sensitive as he was to the productive architecture of spaces, Rivera decided to make an archival one for Kahlo. He knew, like Warhol, that the archive guarantees the oeuvre's survival, emptying it of its many mystifications, even of the most resistant of all: the authority of the name of the author.

WEATHERED NAMES

Demerol without Expiration Date is the second text that Bellatin wrote about Kahlo — the first, which bears the title of one of the painter's most celebrated work, *Las dos Fridas*, tells the story of a writer who has been commissioned by the Mexican Council for Culture and the Arts (a request officially made to Bellatin) to write Kahlo's biography, and who searches, camera in hand, for a living Frida who is supposed to be working in a Mexican food market.

Las dos Fridas interrogates the mediations between reality and fiction, as well as the causal relationship between a single author-producer and her corresponding 'original' work. This problem is not new to Bellatin, but rather, it traverses all his texts and artistic interventions.[12] *Demerol without Expiration Date* is no exception. In it, Bellatin calls into question the artifices of originality and the figure of the author through another recurrent creative strategy in his writing: the re-utilization of his own texts. *Demerol*, as we shall see, combines fragments that have already appeared in many of his other books, replicated in such a way that it becomes almost impossible to determine which fragment came first. In this same vein, many of Bellatin's books are advertised as translations of non-existent texts or biographies of fictional characters that are presented as real ones. In other cases, the characters seem to be replicas of Bellatin himself — like the writer of *Flores*, who uses an orthopaedic leg — or become the authors of Bellatin's books, like frida kahlo who, in *Demerol*, is virtually alive and has painted three artworks (*Damas chinas, Salón de belleza* and *El jardín de la señora murakami*) that are indeed novels published by Bellatin in 1995, 1994, and 2000 respectively:

> Once a conference was organized where a teacher introduced himself with a singular didactic apparatus. It was an artefact supplied with a screen, through which a sort of film of reality was shown. [...] Suddenly, the screen began to show images, fragments, of the life of the artist frida kahlo, which was pre-

---

12   Bellatin is a writer who makes films (such as *Bola Negra. Ciudad Juárez's Musical*, co-directed with Marcela Rodríguez in 2012), works as a curator (as in dOCU-MENTA/13, where he exhibited the project *Die hunderttausend Bücher von Bellatin*), puts on performances (such as the famous *Writers' Doubles Congress* in Paris in 2003 and the ongoing *Cine vivo*). He is also involved in photography and theatre.

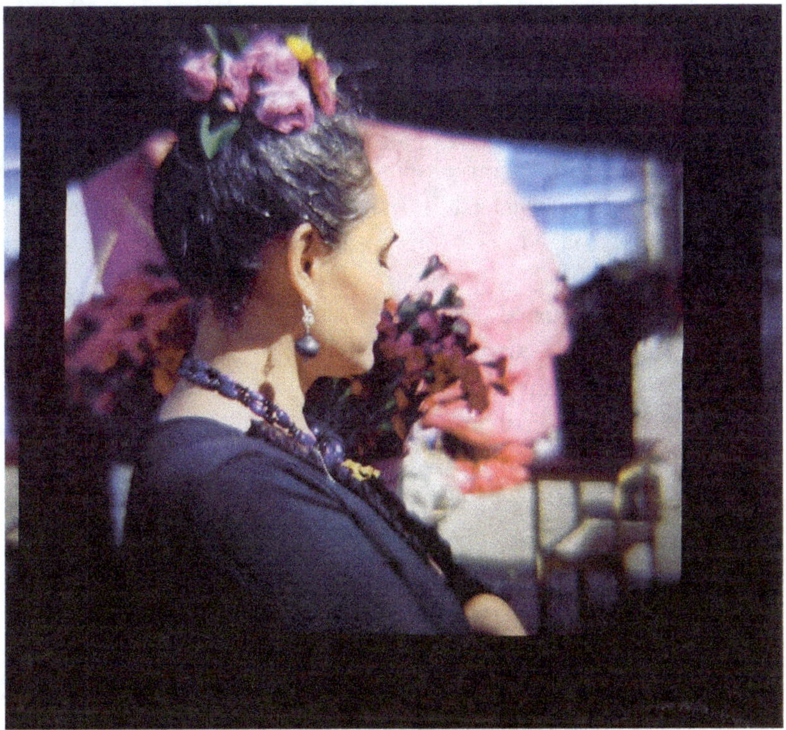

Figure 3. © Archivo Mario Bellatin, *Las dos Fridas* [The Two Fridas].
Image credit: Mario Bellatin.

cisely the theme that had gathered the public that night. The curious thing was that a rather old kahlo was shown, as if she had continued to live after her death. At a certain moment, always through the screen, the image of the Russian leader joseph stalin was seen, placed behind two pewter pots for clysters, and a very old demerol box. The rubber hoses necessary for the enema pots to perform their functions were detached from the receptacles. But the biggest surprise for those present at the conference occurred when three unknown pictorial works were seen through the apparatus. They were entitled *Damas chinas, Salón de belleza,* and *El jardín de la señora murakami.*[13]

---

13   Mario Bellatin, *Demerol, sin fecha de caducidad,* in Graciela Iturbide and Mario Bellatin, *El baño de Frida Kahlo/ Demerol, sin fecha de caducidad* (Ciudad de México: Galería López Quiroga/Editorial RM, 2008), p. 2; my translation.

During the conference, frida shares with the audience her thoughts
on the creative process, shows some of her most renowned works and
stresses her constant search for 'painting without painting', a phrase
that recalls Bellatin's guiding principle 'writing without writing'.[14] Following the pattern of many proper names in Bellatin's work, hers is
written in lowercase: frida kahlo. The author becomes a common noun
and an empty placeholder to be potentially occupied by any other
name.[15]

Bellatin, like Iturbide, always delves into what is left, and what
might seem a simple cut-and-paste exercise — the replacement of a
proper name by another, the repetitions of chunks of text over which
the reader stumbles again and again — is a complex weathering process. For instance, the cited fragment of *Demerol* also appears in an
undated manuscript, probably from the same period. It is named after
Malcolm Lowry's famous closing quote from *Under the Volcano*: 'Do
you like this garden that is yours? Don't let your children destroy it.'
Bellatin writes:

> Once a conference was organized where a teacher introduced
> himself with a singular didactic apparatus. It was an artefact

---

14   Paradoxical as it may seem, 'writing without writing' is the way in which Bellatin
has labelled his complex creative process, which he succinctly summarizes as follows: 'a constant concern for highlighting the voids, the omissions, rather than the
presences'. See Mario Bellatin, 'Escribir sin escribir', in *Obra reunida 2* (Barcelona:
Alfaguara, 2014), pp. 3–12. For a detailed analysis of Bellatin's writing strategies, see
Delfina Cabrera and Graciela Goldchluk, 'Una mortaja de papel: la emergencia del
archivo en la escritura de Mario Bellatin', in *Bellatin en su proceso: los gestos de una
escritura*, ed. by Palma Castro, and others (México-Buenos Aires, Benemérita Universidad de Puebla-Prometeo, 2018), pp. 121–46; Juan Pablo Cuartas, *Los comienzos
de Mario Bellatin: tiempo y consistencia en Efecto invernadero* (unpublished thesis,
Universidad Nacional de La Plata, Argentina, 2014) <http://www.memoria.fahce.
unlp.edu.ar/tesis/te.1044/te.1044.pdf> [accessed 14 April 2020]; Graciela Goldchluk, 'Lecciones de realismo para una liebre muerta (sobre la obra de Mario Bellatin)', I Simposio Internacional Imágenes y Realismos en América Latina, 29 de
septiembre al 1 de octubre de 2011, Leiden, Países Bajos, in *Actas online*, ed. by Miguel
Caballero Vázquez, Luz Rodríguez Carranza, and Christina Soto van der Plas <https://
imagenesyrealismosleiden.wordpress.com/> <http://www.memoria.fahce.unlp.edu.
ar/trab_eventos/ev.13717/ev.13717.pdf> [accessed 11 June 2020].

15   In *Demerol*, frida kahlo's paintings carry the titles of Bellatin's novels; she rewrites
Kafka's *The Metamorphosis* and awards samuel beckett the authorship of one of her
paintings (*La jornada de la mona y el paciente* (The Day of the Monkey and the
Patient)) which is named after a short story by Bellatin. She also stages a theatre piece
based on her painting *Beauty Salon*, which is the title of Bellatin's most famous novel,
published in Lima and later turned into a play in Mexico City.

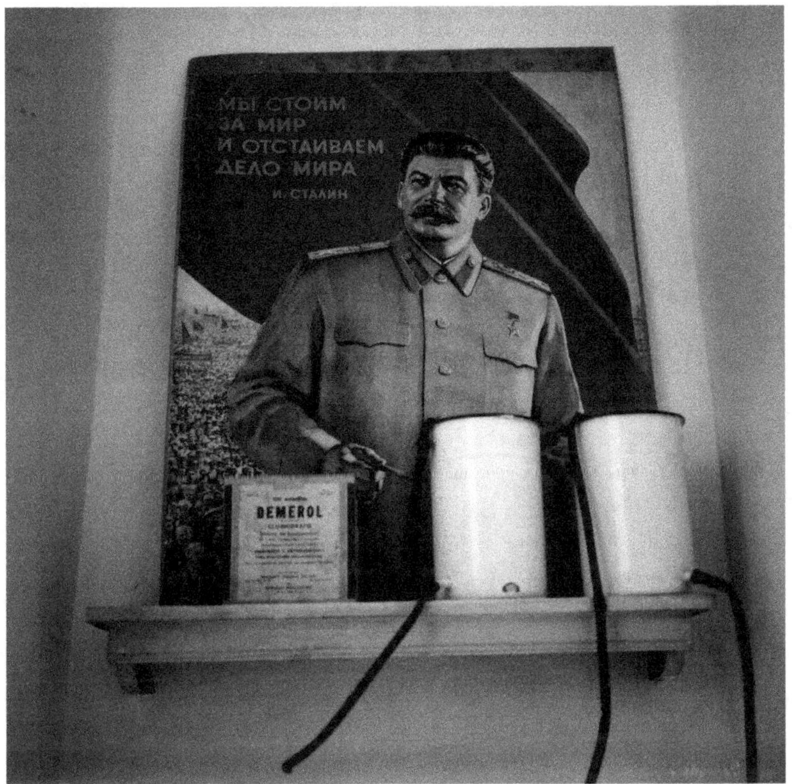

Figure 4. © Graciela Iturbide, *El baño de Frida XII*. Courtesy of the artist.

supplied with a screen, through which a sort of film of reality
was shown. [...] Suddenly, the screen began to show images,
fragments, of the life of the writer mario bellatin, which was
precisely the subject that had gathered the public that night.
The curious thing was that a rather old bellatin was shown, as if
he had continued to live after his death. At a certain moment,
always through the apparatus, the covers of three books were
seen: *Damas chinas*, *Salón de belleza* and *El jardín de la señora
murakami*.[16]

And again, in *Biografía ilustrada de Mishima*, a novel almost immediately following *Demerol*:

---

16 La Plata, Archivo Mario Bellatin, Universidad Nacional de La Plata, fol. 13; my
transcription and translation.

> [Mishima] is now in an educational institution where a lecture will be given on Yukio Mishima. [...] Suddenly a professor who gives the impression of being Japanese appears in the room. Mishima notices that he brings with him an apparatus through which, once installed, he begins to show a sort of film of reality. The attendees stare at the screen. The first image is of the schoolyard where we are gathered. It is a highly prestigious institution. [...] Mishima stays in the room showing a definite sense of superiority. He looks like a middle-aged man. He wears a military uniform and has no head.[17]

The correspondence of the texts is almost perfect, like a piece of tracing paper that reveals the one underneath, we can spot certain silhouettes that coincide, although this coincidence is never fully achieved. As we compare the fragments, we may think at first glance that they are almost the same, but no: Bellatin's project aims at setting in motion a weathering force capable of eroding any supposed origin or originality of writing. Through overexposure, Bellatin weathers the author's place in order to show the traces, not of a discourse, but of the movements of an improper body in writing, always in progress, errant, incomplete. In this sense, together with the notions of author and oeuvre, what is also challenged in *Demerol* is the fiction of the normal, organically whole body (even the textual body). Perhaps this explains why, in his more than forty published books, Bellatin has concentrated on creating worlds of his own, confined weathers that only respond to the fiction that sustains them.

CLAUSTROPHILIA

Since his first novel, *Efecto invernadero* (Greenhouse Effect), which takes place almost exclusively in one room, Bellatin has locked his characters in places of confinement that are somehow makeshift. Sometimes, one could even say that it is the characters who lock themselves in, perhaps as a counterbalance to the history of confinement of non-normative bodies: the transvestite hairdresser whose beauty salon, surrounded by aquariums, becomes a *moridero* (a place to die); the

---

17   Mario Bellatin, *Biografía ilustrada de Mishima* (Buenos Aires: Entropía, 2009), p. 4; my translation.

paralytic dog trainer of *Perros héroes* (Hero Dogs) who never leaves the house, or the deaf and blind twins locked up in the Colonia de Alienados Etchepare, the madhouse-school-asylum of his most recent book, *Carta sobre los ciegos para uso de los que ven* (Letter on the Blind for the Use of Those Who Can See). In *Demerol*, frida is locked into a 'singular didactic apparatus' or, at least, there is no clear indication that her life (her afterlife), can be detached from this machine.

For this reason, even if in *Demerol*, there are rather few direct references to Frida's bathroom (only the hoses for making enemas, the orthopaedic leg and Stalin's poster are mentioned in some passages), the text revolves around an atmospheric problem in its most basic sense: how is life possible in a closed space? Such a problem also intrigued Roland Barthes, who references it in his famous 1977 lecture series *How to Live Together*, which explores the tension between the individual and the common through several confined spaces, such as the monastery, the bourgeois house, the hotel room, or the desert.[18] Indeed, Barthes considers the desert to be the archetype of a closed space, precisely because it appears to be an open space, but one from which it is impossible to escape and which denotes, etymologically, extreme solitude (from the Greek *eremos* and from the Latin *eremus*: desert, solitary).

Hence, it is no coincidence that this space becomes the landscape of the last performance of frida in *Demerol*: while preparing an artistic presentation for a congress on cinema and mysticism to which she had been invited, frida recalled the column prop of Luis Buñuel's film *Simon of the Desert*:[19]

> frida remembered that someone had told her that the column of buñuel's film — a film she had not been able to appreciate in life — was abandoned in the desert. kahlo then set about the task of getting a recent image of the column. As one might imagine, she was not in a position to go personally to the place where the column was, but she asked for a picture of it. Finally, a perfect image arrived. [...] frida kahlo, after admiring it for a few days, had it framed as if it were a religious image. She

---

18 Roland Barthes, *How to Live Together: Novelistic Simulations of Some Everyday Spaces*, trans. by Kate Briggs (New York: Columbia University Press, 2012).

19 *Simón del desierto*, dir. by Luis Buñuel (Sindicato de Trabajadores de la Producción Cinematográfica, 1965).

also made a series of saint cards of the column and distributed them among her neighbours. The next day she photographed them one by one holding the saint cards. kahlo pretended that her neighbours were members of a brotherhood that had been created around the lost column. The text that accompanied the photos mentioned that a group of people had decided to flee the city in order to improve their living conditions. On the way to their pilgrimage they found the column from buñuel's film. These people decided to take this astonishing event as a sign and settled in the column's surroundings.[20]

Bellatin carried out a similar performance himself, using a picture that had been taken by Graciela Iturbide:

> I remembered that someone had told me that in the pachuca desert there was still the column from which Luis Buñuel had made his film *Simon of the Desert*. [...] *Simon of the Desert* is one of my favourite films and it perfectly fits into the category of cinema and mysticism. In the research I undertook, I found that the photographer Graciela Iturbide had images of the column that she herself had taken. I asked her to give me one as a present and had it framed as a religious picture. I printed out a series of those framed images and I distributed them among my neighbours. [...] Then, I photographed the people to whom I had given the images to pass them off as members of a brotherhood that had been created from the forgotten column.[21]

In the desert, the 'realm of weathering' par excellence, *Demerol* goes back to *The Bathroom of Frida Kahlo*. The survival of works of art, Bellatin and Iturbide suggest, depends not only on its display but on its opening up to a commons. Contrary to the logics of the museum, their archival operations contest aseptic protocols. Theirs is an invitation to a living archive that welcomes time and weather, and shelters what can be shared: 'Another tenant lives now in your house', such is the final line of *Simon of the Desert*. The devil's daughter speaks it to the son of God. In the column, writes Mario Bellatin, thousands of tenants now live.

---

20   Mario Bellatin, *Demerol*, p. 14.
21   Mario Bellatin, 'Escribir sin escribir', in Mario Bellatin, *Obra reunida 2* (Barcelona: Alfaguara, 2014), p. 11.

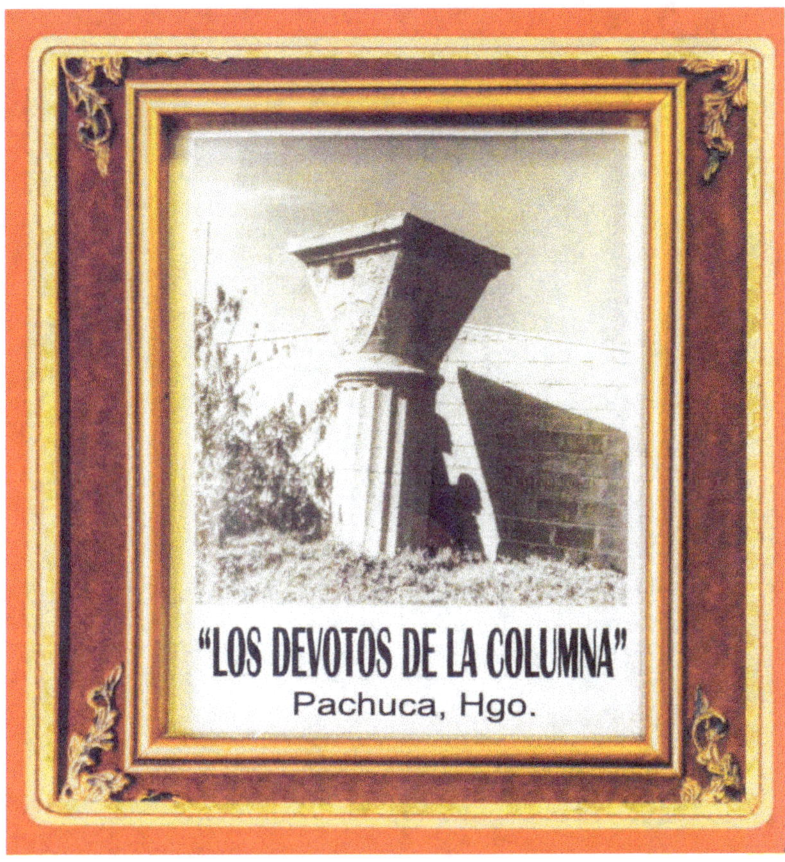

Figure 5. © Archivo Mario Bellatin, *Los devotos de la columna* [The Devotees of the Column]. Image credit: Mario Bellatin.

References

BIBLIOGRAPHY

Abel, Carl, *Über den Gegensinn der Urworte* (Leipzig: Verlag von Wilhelm Friedrich, 1884)

Abensour, Miguel, 'Contre la souveraineté de la philosophie sur la politique. La Lecture arendtienne du mythe de la caverne', in *Hannah Arendt. Crises de l'état-nation. Pensées alternatives*, ed. by Anne Kupiec, Martine Leibovici, Géraldine Muhlmann, and Etienne Tassin (Paris: Sens & Tonka), pp. 341–68

—— *Hannah Arendt contre la philosophie politique?* (Paris: Sens & Tonka, 2006)

Achbari, Azadeh, and Frans van Lunteren, 'Dutch Skies, Global Laws: The British Creation of "Buys Ballot's Law"', *Historical Studies in the Natural Sciences*, 46.1 (February 2016), pp. 1–43 <https://doi.org/10.1525/hsns.2016.46.1.1>

Agamben, Giorgio, *A che punto siamo? L'epidemia come politica* (Macerata: Quodlibet, 2020)

—— *Homo Sacer: Sovereign Power and Bare Life*, trans. by Daniel Heller-Roazen (Stanford, CA: Stanford University Press, 1998) <https://doi.org/10.1515/9780804764025>

—— 'The Idea of Language', in Agamben, *Potentialities*, pp. 39–47

—— *Language and Death: The Place of Negativity*, trans. by Karen E. Pinkus with Michael Hardt (Minneapolis: University of Minnesota Press, 1991)

—— '*Pardes*: The Writing of Potentiality', in Agamben, *Potentialities*, pp. 205–19

—— 'La parola e il sapere', *aut aut*, 179–80 (September–December 1980), pp. 155–66

—— 'Philosophy and Linguistics', in Agamben, *Potentialities*, pp. 62–76

—— *Potentialities*, ed. and trans. by Daniel Heller-Roazen (Stanford, CA: Stanford University Press, 1999)

—— *The Sacrament of Language: An Archaeology of the Oath*, trans. by Adam Kotsko (Stanford, CA: Stanford University Press, 2011)

—— 'The Thing Itself', in Agamben, *Potentialities*, pp. 27–38

—— 'Tradition of the Immemorial', in Agamben, *Potentialities*, pp. 104–15

—— *The Use of Bodies*, trans. by Adam Kotsko (Stanford, CA: Stanford University Press, 2016)

—— *What Is Philosophy?*, trans. by Lorenzo Chiesa (Stanford, CA: Stanford University Press, 2018) <https://doi.org/10.1515/9781503604056>

Ahuja, Neel, 'Intimate Atmospheres: Queer Theory in a Time of Extinctions',
    GLQ: A Journal of Lesbian and Gay Studies, 21.2–3 (2015), pp. 365–85
    <https://doi.org/10.1215/10642684-2843227>

Alaimo, Stacy, *Bodily Natures: Science, Environment, and the Material Self*
    (Bloomington: Indiana University Press, 2010)

—— *Exposed: Environmental Politics and Pleasures in Posthuman Times* (Min-
    neapolis: University of Minnesota Press, 2016) <https://doi.org/10.
    5749/minnesota/9780816621958.001.0001>

—— 'Insurgent Vulnerability and the Carbon Footprint of Gender', *Women,
    Gender, and Research* (Kvinder, Køn og Forskning, Denmark), 3–4
    (2009), pp. 22–35

Amarante, Paulo, ed., *Loucos pela vida: a trajetória da reforma psiquiátrica no
    Brasil* (Rio de Janeiro: Fiocruz, 2000)

Amin, Ash, 'Placing Globalization', *Theory, Culture & Society*, 14.2 (1997), pp.
    123–37 <https://doi.org/10.1177/026327697014002011>

Aquino, Ricardo, 'From Picturesque to Points in Time: A Biographical Image',
    in *Arthur Bispo do Rosário*, ed. by Araújo and others (Rio de Janeiro:
    Réptil, 2012), pp. 48–105

Araújo, Emanoel, and others, eds, *Arthur Bispo do Rosário*, curated by Wilson
    Lazaro; trans. by Regina Alfarano (Rio de Janeiro: Réptil, 2012)

Araújo, João Henrique Queiroz de, and Ana Maria Jacó-Vilela, 'The Ex-
    perience of Art at the Juliano Moreira Colony in the 1950s', trans. by
    Rebecca Atkinson, *História, Ciências, Saúde-Manguinhos*, 25.2 (2018)
    <https://doi.org/10.1590/s0104-59702018000200002>

Arendt, Hannah, 'Action and the Pursuit of Happiness', Paper delivered at
    the Meeting of the American Political Science Association, The Hannah
    Arendt Papers at the Library of Congress, MSS Box 61, 1960, pp. 1–21

—— *Between Past and Future: Eight Exercises in Political Thought* (New York:
    Penguin, 1993)

—— 'Concern with Politics in Recent European Philosophical Thought', in
    her *Essays in Understanding*, pp. 428–47

—— 'Concern with Politics in Recent European Philosophical Thought', in
    The Modern Challenge to Tradition: Fragmente eines Buchs, ed. by Barbara
    Hahn and James McFarland (Göttingen: Wallstein Verlag, 2018), pp.
    560–92

—— 'Concern with Politics in Recent European Philosophical Thought', in
    *Perspektiven politischen Denkens. Beiträge anläßlich des 100. Geburtstags
    von Hannah Arendt*, ed. by Antonia Grunenberg, Waltraud Meints,
    Oliver Bruns, and Christine Harckensee (Frankfurt a.M.: Peter Lang
    Verlag, 2008), pp. 11–31

—— *Denktagebuch: 1950 bis 1973*, ed. by Ursula Ludz and Ingeborg Nord-
    mann, 2 vols (Munich: Piper, 2002), I

—— *Elemente und Ursprünge totaler Herrschaft* (Frankfurt a.M.: Europäische
    Verlagsanstalt, 1955)

—— *Essays in Understanding: 1930–1974. Formation, Exile, and Totalitarianism*, ed. by Jerome Kohn (New York: Schocken, 2005)

—— 'Franz Kafka: A Revaluation. On the Occasion of the Twentieth Anniversary of his Death', in her *Essays in Understanding*, pp. 69–80

—— 'Franz Kafka', in her *Die verborgene Tradition. Essays* (Frankfurt a.M.: Suhrkamp, 1976), pp. 95–116

—— 'Franz Kafka, von neuem gewürdigt', *Die Wandlung*, 1.12 (1945/1946), pp. 1050–62

—— *Hannah Arendt–Karl Jaspers Briefwechsel. 1926–1969*, ed. by Lotte Köhler and Hans Saner (Munich: Piper, 1985)

—— *The Human Condition* (Chicago: Chicago University Press, 1998)

—— *Der Liebesbegriff bei Augustin. Versuch einer philosophischen Interpretation* (Hildesheim: Olms, 2006)

—— *The Life of the Mind*, ed. by Mary McCarthy, 2 vols (New York: Harcourt Brace Jovanovich, 1977–78), I: *Thinking* (1977)

—— 'Martin Heidegger ist achtzig Jahre alt', in *Antwort. Martin Heidegger im Gespräch*, ed. by Günther Neske and Emil Kettering (Tübingen: Neske, 1988), pp. 232–46

—— 'On the Nature of Totalitarianism: An Essay in Understanding', in her *Essays in Understanding*, pp. 328–60

—— *On Revolution* (London: Penguin, 1990)

—— *The Origins of Totalitarianism* (London: Hartcourt Brace Jovanovich, 1973)

—— *The Origins of Totalitarianism* (New York: Meridian, 1958)

—— 'Philosophie und Soziologie. Anläßlich Karl Mannheims *Ideologie und Utopie*', *Die Gesellschaft*, 7.1 (1930), pp. 163–76

—— 'Philosophy and Politics', *Social Research*, 57.1 (1990), pp. 73–103

—— *Wahrheit gibt es nur zu zweien. Briefe an die Freunde*, ed. by Ingeborg Nordmann (Munich: Piper, 2013)

—— *Was ist Politik? Fragmente aus dem Nachlaß*, ed. by Ursula Ludz and Kurt Sontheimer (Munich: Piper, 1993)

—— 'What Is Existenz Philosophy?', in her *Essays in Understanding*, pp. 163–87

Arendt, Hannah, and Martin Heidegger, *Hannah Arendt / Martin Heidegger. Briefe 1925 bis 1975 und andere Zeugnisse* (Frankfurt a.M.: Klostermann, 1998); English trans. as *Letters: 1925–1975*, ed. by Ursula Ludz (New York: Harcourt, 2004)

Aristotle, *Meteorologica*, ed. and trans. by Henry D. P. Lee, rev. edn, Loeb Classical Library, 397 (Cambridge, MA: Harvard University Press, 1952)

—— *Physics*, ed. by Francis Macdonald Cornford and trans. by Philip H. Wicksteed, rev. edn, 2 vols, Loeb Classical Library, 228 and 255 (Cambridge, MA: Harvard University Press, 1934–57) <https://doi.org/10.4159/DLCL.aristotle-physics.1957>

Auerbach, Erich, 'Dante and the Romantics', in *Time, History, and Literature: Selected Essays of Erich Auerbach*, ed. by James I. Porter, trans. by Jane O. Newman (Princeton, NJ: Princeton University Press, 2014)

Avelino, Jacques, Marco Cristancho, Selena Georgiou, and others, 'The Coffee Rust Crises in Colombia and Central America (2008–2013): Impacts, Plausible Causes and Proposed Solutions', *Food Security* 7 (2015), pp. 303–21 <https://doi.org/10.1007/s12571-015-0446-9>

Bacelar, Jéferson, and Carlos Cardoso, eds, *Brasil: um país de negros?* (Rio de Janeiro/Salvador: Pallas/CEAO, 1999)

Badiou, Alain, *Le Séminaire. Heidegger. L'Être 3 — Figure du retrait. 1986–1987* (Paris: Fayard, 2015)

—— 'Sur la situation épidémique', *Quartier général. Le Média libre* <https://qg.media/2020/03/26/sur-la-situation-epidemique-par-alain-badiou/> [accessed 30 March 2020]

Baldacci, Cristina, and Claudia Peppel, 'Zwischen den Wasserlilien. Ein Interview mit Omer Fast', in *Die Kunst des Wartens*, ed. by Brigitte Kölle and Claudia Peppel (Berlin: Wagenbach, 2019), pp. 98–107

Barad, Karen, *Meeting the Universe Halfway: Quantum Physics and the Entanglement of Matter and Meaning* (Durham, NC: Duke University Press, 2007) <https://doi.org/10.1215/9780822388128>

Barthes, Roland, *How to Live Together. Novelistic Simulations of Some Everyday Spaces* (New York: Columbia University Press, 2012)

Battista, Anna, *Irenebrination: Notes on Architecture, Art, Fashion, Fashion Law & Technology*, 17 May 2017 <https://irenebrination.typepad.com/irenebrination_notes_on_a/2017/05/vajiko-chachkhiani-venice-biennale.html> [accessed 10 May 2020]

BBC News, 'Greece suspends asylum applications as migrants seek to leave Turkey', 1 March 2020 <https://www.bbc.com/news/world-europe-51695468> [accessed 7 June 2020]

Beard, Mary, John North, and Simon Price, *Religions of Rome*, 2 vols (Cambridge: Cambridge University Press, 1998), ii: *A Sourcebook*

Bellatin, Mario, *Biografía ilustrada de Mishima* (Buenos Aires: Entropía, 2009)

—— *Carta sobre los ciegos para uso de los que ven* (Madrid: Alfaguara, 2017)

—— *Las dos Fridas* (Ciudad de México: Conaculta, 2008)

—— *Efecto invernadero* (Ciudad de México: Ediciones del Equilibrista, 1992)

—— '¿Le gusta este jardín que es suyo? No deje que sus hijos lo destruyan' (Archivo Mario Bellatin: Universidad Nacional de La Plata), fol. 13

—— *Obra reunida 2* (Barcelona: Alfaguara, 2014)

—— *Salón de belleza* (Lima: Jaime Campodónico Editor, 1994)

Benjamin, Walter, *The Arcades Project*, trans. by Howard Eiland and Kevin McLaughlin (Cambridge, MA: Harvard University Press, 1999)

Benso, Silvia, *The Face of Things: A Different Side of Ethics* (Albany: State University of New York Press, 2000)

Bernardo, Bianca, 'Quem você deixaria entrar em sua cela sem precisar acertar a cor da sua aura?', in *Das virgens em cardumes e da cor das auras*, ed. by Daniela Labra (São Paulo: WMF Martins Fontes, 2016), pp. 122–35

Berti, Enrico, 'De Meteoris (Meteorologica)', in *Enciclopedia Dantesca Italiana* (1970) <http://www.treccani.it/enciclopedia/de-meteoris_ (Enciclopedia-Dantesca)> [accessed 18 March 2020]

Birmingham, Peg, 'Heidegger and Arendt: The Birth of Political Action and Speech', in *Heidegger and Practical Philosophy*, ed. by François Raffoul and David Pettigrew (Albany: State University of New York Press, 2002), pp. 191–202

Blumenberg, Hans, *Das Lachen der Thrakerin. Eine Urgeschichte der Theorie* (Frankfurt a.M.: Suhrkamp, 1987)

—— *Shipwreck with Spectator: Paradigm of a Metaphor for Existence*, trans. by Steven Rendall (Cambridge, MA: MIT Press, 1996)

Bobbette, Adam, and Amy Donovan, 'Political Geology: An Introduction', in *Political Geology* (Springer, 2019), pp. 1–34 <https://doi.org/10.1007/978-3-319-98189-5_1>

Bolinger, Dwight, 'Ambient *It* Is Meaningful Too', *Journal of Linguistics*, 9.2 (1973), pp. 261–70 <https://doi.org/10.1017/S0022226700003789>

—— *Meaning and Form*, English Language Series, 11 (London: Longman, 1977)

Borges, Viviane Trindade, *Do esquecimento ao tombamento. A invenção de Arthur Bispo do Rosário* (doctoral dissertation, Universidade Federal do Rio Grande do Sul, 2010) <https://www.lume.ufrgs.br/handle/10183/22989>

Bovolo, C. Isabella, Thomas Wagner, Geoff Parkin, David Hein-Griggs, Ryan Pereira, and Richard Jones, 'The Guiana Shield Rainforests— Overlooked Guardians of South American Climate', *Environmental Research Letters*, 13.7 (2018), 074029 <https://doi.org/10.1088/1748-9326/aacf60>

Bower, Matthew, 'A Storm in a Jar: 10 Very Cool Art Installations That Imitate Weather', *The Atlantic*, 9 November 2012 <https://www.theatlantic.com/entertainment/archive/2012/11/a-storm-in-a-jar-10-very-cool-art-installations-that-imitate-weather/265017/> [accessed 20 December 2019].

Boyde, Patrick, *Dante Philomythes and Philosopher: Man in the Cosmos* (Cambridge: Cambridge University Press, 1981) <https://doi.org/10.1017/CBO9780511553882>

Boym, Svetlana, *The Future of Nostalgia* (New York: Basic Books, 2001)

Braidotti, Rosi, 'Intensive Genre and the Demise of Gender', *Angelaki*, 13.2 (2008), pp. 45–57 <https://doi.org/10.1080/09697250802432112>

Bryant, Raymond L., 'Political Ecology: An Emerging Research Agenda in Third-World Studies', *Political Geography*, 11.1 (1992), pp. 12–36 <https://doi.org/10.1016/0962-6298(92)90017-N>

—— 'Power, Knowledge and Political Ecology in the Third World: A Review', *Progress in Physical Geography*, 22.1 (1998), pp. 79–94

Bryson, Norman, *Looking at the Overlooked: Four Essays on Still Life Painting* (London: Reaktion Books, 1990)

Buck, Holly Jean, Andrea R. Gammon, and Christopher J. Preston, 'Gender and Geoengineering', *Hypatia*, 29.3 (2014), pp. 651–69 <https://doi.org/10.1111/hypa.12083>

Burnham, Jack, 'Hans Haacke — Wind and Water Sculpture', in *Art in the Land: A Critical Anthology of Environmental Art*, ed. by Alan Sonfist (New York: Dutton, 1983), pp. 105–25

Butler, Judith, *Precarious Life: The Powers of Mourning and Violence* (London: Verso, 2004)

Butler, Judith, Zeynep Gambetti, and Leticia Sabsay, eds, *Vulnerability in Resistance* (Durham, NC: Duke University Press, 2016) <https://doi.org/10.1215/9780822373490>

Bäckstrand, Karin, and Eva Lövbrand, 'Planting Trees to Mitigate Climate Change: Contested Discourses of Ecological Modernization, Green Governmentality and Civic Environmentalism', *Global Environmental Politics*, 6.1 (2006), pp. 50–75 <https://doi.org/10.1162/glep.2006.6.1.50>

Cabañas, Kaira Marie, *Learning from Madness: Brazilian Modernism and Global Contemporary Art* (Chicago: Chicago University Press, 2018) <https://doi.org/10.7208/chicago/9780226556314.001.0001>

Cabrera, Delfina, and Graciela Goldchluk, 'Una mortaja de papel: la emergencia del archivo en la escritura de Mario Bellatin', in *Bellatin en su proceso: los gestos de una escritura*, ed. by Palma Castro, and others (México-Buenos Aires: Benemérita Universidad de Puebla-Prometeo, 2018), pp. 121–46

Callender, Craig, 'Taking Thermodynamics Too Seriously', *Studies in History and Philosophy of Science Part B*, 32.4 (2001), pp. 539–53 <https://doi.org/10.1016/S1355-2198(01)00025-9>

Camprubí, Lino, and Philipp Lehmann, 'The Scales of Experience: Introduction to the Special Issue Experiencing the Global Environment', *Studies in History and Philosophy of Science Part A*, 70 (August 2018), pp. 1–5 <https://doi.org/10.1016/j.shpsa.2018.05.003>

Canales, Jimena, *A Tenth of a Second: A History* (Chicago: University of Chicago Press, 2009) <https://doi.org/10.7208/chicago/9780226093208.001.0001>

Cane, Lucy, 'Hannah Arendt on the Principles of Political Action', *European Journal of Political Theory*, 14.1 (2015), pp. 55–75 <https://doi.org/10.1177/1474885114523939>

Canovan, Margaret, *Hannah Arendt: A Reinterpretation of Her Political Thought* (Cambridge: Cambridge University Press, 1992) <https://doi.org/10.1017/CBO9780511521300>

—— 'Socrates or Heidegger? Hannah Arendt's Reflections on Philosophy and Politics', *Social Research*, 57.1 (1990), pp. 135–65

Cassin, Barbara, Emily Apter, Jacques Lezra, and Michael Wood, eds, *Dictionary of Untranslatables: A Philosophical Lexicon* (Princeton, NJ: Princeton University Press, 2014) <https://doi.org/10.1515/9781400849918>

Cavarero, Adriana, *Inclinations: A Critique of Rectitude*, trans. by Amanda Minervini and Adam Sitze (Stanford, CA: Stanford University Press, 2016) <https://doi.org/10.1515/9781503600416>

Cestaro, Gary, *Dante and the Grammar of the Nursing Body* (Notre Dame, IN: University of Notre Dame Press, 2003)

Chachkhiani, Vajiko, 'Georgia — Vajiko Chachkhiani — *Living Dog Among Dead Lions* — Venice Biennale 2017', YouTube <https://www.youtube.com/watch?v=eryvtbZv5y0> [accessed 30 March 2020]

Chafe, Wallace L., *Meaning and the Structure of Language* (Chicago: University of Chicago Press, 1970)

Chakrabarty, Dipesh, 'The Climate of History: Four Theses', *Critical Inquiry*, 35.2 (Winter 2009), pp. 197–222 <https://doi.org/10.1086/596640>

—— 'The Human Condition in the Anthropocene', in *The Tanner Lectures on Human Values, 35*, ed. by Mark Matheson (Salt Lake City: University of Utah Press, 2016), pp. 139–88, available online: <https://tannerlectures.utah.edu/Chakrabarty%20manuscript.pdf> [accessed 1 August 2020]

—— 'Postcolonial Studies and the Challenge of Climate Change', *New Literary History*, 43.1 (2012), pp. 1–18 <https://doi.org/10.1353/nlh.2012.0007>

Chave, Anna C., 'Minimalism and the Rhetoric of Power', *Arts Magazine*, 64.5 (January 1990), pp. 44–63

Cheng, Chung-ying, 'Chinese Philosophy and Symbolic Reference', *Philosophy East and West*, 27.3 (July 1977), pp. 307–22 <https://doi.org/10.2307/1398001>

'Chernobyl Wild Zone: Radioactive Rabies, Autumn Fruit and Foxes', online video recording, YouTube <https://www.youtube.com/watch?v=u_ZvHMGXdbE> [accessed 24 February 2020]

Chomsky, Noam, *Lectures on Government and Binding*, Studies in Generative Grammar, 9 (Dordrecht: Foris Publications, 1981)

Coen, Deborah R., 'Big Is a Thing of the Past: Climate Change and Methodology in the History of Ideas', *Journal of the History of Ideas*, 77.2 (April 2016), pp. 305–21 <https://doi.org/10.1353/jhi.2016.0019>

—— *Climate in Motion: Science, Empire, and the Problem of Scale* (Chicago: University of Chicago Press, 2018)

Cogan, Marc, *The Design in the Wax: The Structure of the 'Divine Comedy' and its Meaning* (South Bend, IN: Notre Dame University Press, 1999) <https://doi.org/10.2307/j.ctvpj7dm5>

Collins, Yolanda Ariadne, 'Colonial Residue: REDD+, Territorialisation and the Racialized Subject in Guyana and Suriname', *Geoforum*, 106 (2019), pp. 38–47 <https://doi.org/10.1016/j.geoforum.2019.07.019>

—— 'How REDD+ Governs: Multiple Forest Environmentalities in Guyana and Suriname', *Environment and Planning E: Nature and Space*, 3.2 (2020), pp. 323–45 <https://doi.org/10.1177/2514848619860748>

Colomina, Beatriz, and Mark Wigley, 'Toilet Architecture: An Essay about the Most Psychosexually Charged Room in a Building', *PIN–UP Magazine*, 23 (Fall/Winter 2017/18) <https://pinupmagazine.org/articles/toilet-modern-architecture/> [accessed 17 July 2020]

Conduru, Roberto, 'Rosário, Arthur Bispo do', in *The Dictionary of Caribbean and Afro-Latin American Biography*, ed. by Franklin W. Knight and Henry Louis Gates, Jr. (Oxford: Oxford University Press, 2016) <https://doi.org/10.1093/acref/9780195301731.013.74989>

Cork, Richard, *Breaking Down the Barriers: Art in the 1990s* (New Haven, CT: Yale University Press, 2003)

Cornish, Alison, 'The Vulgarization of Science: Dante's Meteorology in Context', in *Science and Literature in Italian Culture from Dante to Calvino: A Festschrift for Patrick Boyde*, ed. by Pierpaolo Antonello and Simon A. Gilson (Oxford: Legenda, 2004), pp. 53–71

Corpas, Flavia dos Santos, *Arthur Bispo do Rosario: Do claustro infinito à instalação de um nome* (doctoral thesis, Pontifícia Universidade Católica PUC-Rio, 2014) <https://www.maxwell.vrac.puc-rio.br/35039/35039.PDF> [accessed 28 June 2020]

Cortés-Rocca, Paola, 'La insoportable levedad del yo. Iturbide y Bellatin en el baño de Frida Kahlo', *Filología*, 41 (2012), pp. 121–38

Cuartas, Juan Pablo, *Los comienzos de Mario Bellatin: tiempo y consistencia en Efecto invernadero* (unpublished thesis, Universidad Nacional de La Plata, Argentina, 2014) <http://www.memoria.fahce.unlp.edu.ar/tesis/te.1044/te.1044.pdf> [accessed 14 April 2020]

Dante Alighieri, *Commedia*, trans. by Robert and Jean Hollander, 3 vols (New York: Doubleday/Anchor, 2000–07)

—— *Dante's 'Il Convivio'*, trans. by Richard H. Lansing, Garland Library of Medieval Literature, 65 (New York: Garland, 1990)

—— *De vulgari eloquentia*, trans. by Steven Botterill (Cambridge: Cambridge University Press, 1996) <https://doi.org/10.1017/CBO9780511519444>

—— *Monarchia*, trans. by Prue Shaw (Cambridge: Cambridge University Press, 1996)

—— *Quaestio de Aqua et Terra*, ed. by Francesco Mazzoni, in *Opere*, dir. by Marco Santagata, 2 vols (Milan: Mondadori, 2011–14)

Daston, Lorraine, and Peter Galison, 'The Image of Objectivity', *Representations*, 40 (1992), pp. 81–128 <https://doi.org/10.2307/2928741>

Davis, Mike, *Late Victorian Holocausts: El Niño Famines and the Making of the Third World* (London: Verso, 2002)

Debray, Cécile, Rémi Labrusse, and Maria Stavrinaki, eds, *Préhistoire. Une Énigme moderne* (Paris: Centre Pompidou, 2019)

Deffebach, Nancy, *María Izquierdo and Frida Kahlo: Challenging Visions in Modern Mexican Art* (Austin: University of Texas Press, 2015)

de Lutz, Christian, and Regine Rapp, 'Invisible Forces' exhibition text, ArtLaboratory Berlin (2019)

Derrida, Jacques, 'Before the Law', trans. by Avital Ronell and Christine Roulston, in his *Acts of Literature*, ed. by Derek Attridge (London: Routledge, 1992), pp. 181–220

—— *Dissemination*, trans. by Barbara Johnson (Chicago: University of Chicago Press, 1981)

—— *Heidegger: The Question of Being and History*, trans. by Geoffrey Bennington (Chicago: University of Chicago Press, 2016) <https://doi.org/10.7208/chicago/9780226355252.001.0001>

—— *On the Name*, trans. by David Wood, John P. Leavey, Jr., Ian McLeod (Stanford, CA: Stanford University Press, 1995)

—— *Specters of Marx: The State of the Debt, the Work of Mourning, and the New International*, trans. by Peggy Kamuf (New York: Routledge, 1994)

de Vet, Eliza, and Lesley Head, 'Everyday Weather-Ways: Negotiating the Temporalities of Home and Work in Melbourne, Australia', *Geoforum*, 108 (2020), pp. 267–74 <https://doi.org/10.1016/j.geoforum.2019.08.022>

Dixon, Robert M. W. and Alexandra Y. Aikhenvald, eds, *Changing Valency: Case Studies in Transitivity* (Cambridge: Cambridge University Press, 2000) <https://doi.org/10.1017/CBO9780511627750>

'Documenta 14-Arbeit "View from Above" von Hiwa K ist in das Stadtmuseum zurückgekehrt', Kassel.de, 27 May 2019 <https://www.kassel.de/pressemitteilungen/2019/mai/view-from-above-von-hiwa-k-ist-in-das-stadtmuseum-kassel-zurueckgekehrt.php> [accessed 7 June 2020]

Dooley, Kate, and Tom Griffiths, eds, *Indigenous Peoples' Rights, Forests and Climate Policies in Guyana — A Special Report* (Georgetown, Guyana: Amerindian Peoples Association, 2014)

Douglas, Elliot, 'Germany: New Accusations of Police Violence in Death of Asylum-Seeker', *Deutsche Welle*, 2 November 2019 <https://www.dw.com/en/germany-new-accusations-of-police-violence-in-death-of-asylum-seeker/a-51067499> [accessed 7 June 2020]

Douglass, Frederick, *The Life and Times of Frederick Douglass* (Boston: De Wolfe, Fiske & Co., 1892)

Dravet, Florence Marie, 'Corpo, linguagem e real: o sopro de exu bará e seu lugar na comunicação', *Ilha Desterro*, 68.3 (2015) <https://doi.org/10.5007/2175-8026.2015v68n3p15>

The Encyclopaedia Britannica: A Dictionary of Arts, Sciences, Literature and General Information, 11th edn, 29 vols (London: The Encyclopaedia Britannica Company, 1911), XVII

Endfield, Georgina, and Simon Naylor, 'Climate and Cultural Heritage: An Experiment with the 'Weather Memory Bank', in *The Future of Heritage as Climates Change: Loss, Adaptation and Creativity*, ed. by David C. Harvey and Jim Perry (London: Routledge, 2015), pp. 62–77

Esther Maciel, Maria, 'A enciclopédia de Arthur Bispo do Rosário', *Outra travessia*, 7 (2008), pp. 117–24 <https://doi.org/10.5007/2176-8552(0.7.2008)(117-124)>

Ettinger, Elzbieta, *Hannah Arendt/Martin Heidegger* (New Haven, CT: Yale University Press, 1995)

Evaristo, Conceição, *Poemas Malungos — Cânticos Irmãos* (doctoral thesis, Universidade Federal Fluminense, 2011) <https://app.uff.br/riuff/bitstream/1/7741/1/Tese_Dout.Concei%C3%A7%C3%A3oEvaristo_def.pdf> [accessed 28 June 2020]

—— 'Poems', trans. by Tamara Mitchell, *Hiedra Magazine*, 1 (2013), pp. 65–68 <https://www.hiedramagazine.com/conceicao-evaristo> [accessed 28 June 2020]

Fabian, Johannes, *Time and the Other: How Anthropology Makes its Object*, foreword by Matti Bunzl, new edn (New York: Columbia University Press, 2014) <https://doi.org/10.7312/fabi16926>

Fabião, Eleonora, 'History and Precariousness: In Search of a Performative Historiography', in *Perform, Repeat, Record*, ed. by Amelia Jones and Adrian Heathfield (London: Thames & Hudson, 2012), pp. 121–36

Faye, Emmanuel, *Arendt et Heidegger. Extermination nazie et destruction de la pensée* (Paris: Albin Michel, 2016)

—— *Heidegger, l'introduction du nazisme dans la philosophie. Autour des séminaires inédits de 1933–1935* (Paris: Albin Michel, 2005)

Ferrante, Joan, *The Political Vision of Dante's 'Comedy'* (Princeton, NJ: Princeton University Press, 1984)

Filipovic, Elena, *David Hammons: Bliz-aard Ball Sale* (London: Afterall Books, 2017)

Finke, Marcel, and Friedrich Weltzien, eds, *State of Flux: Aesthetics of Fluid Materials* (Berlin: Reimer, 2017)

Finke, Markus, 'Im Nebel. Fluide Materialien und die Kunst der Zerstreuung', in *Wessen Wissen? Materialität und Situiertheit in den Künsten*, ed. by Kathrin Busch, Kathrin Peters, Christina Dörfling, and Ildikó Szántó (Paderborn: Fink, 2018), pp. 97–114

Fletcher, Robert, 'Environmentality Unbound: Multiple Governmentalities in Environmental Politics', *Geoforum*, 85.Supplement C (2017), pp. 311–15 <https://doi.org/10.1016/j.geoforum.2017.06.009>

Ford, Clyde W., *The Hero with an African Face* (New York: Bantam, 2000)

Forti, Simona, *Vita della mente e tempo della polis* (Milano: Franco Angeli, 1996), pp. 43–87

Fortuna, Sara, and Manuele Gragnolati, 'Dante after Wittgenstein: "Aspetto", Language, and Subjectivity from *Convivio* to *Paradiso*', in *Dante's Plurilingualism: Authority, Knowledge, Subjectivity*, ed. by Sara Fortuna,

Manuele Gragnolati, and Jürgen Trabant (Oxford: Legenda, 2010), pp. 223–48

Foster, Hal, 'The Crux of Minimalism', in Hal Foster, *The Return of the Real: The Avant-Garde at the End of the Century* (Cambridge, MA: MIT Press, 1996), pp. 35–71

Foucault, Michel, *History of Madness*, ed. by Jean Khalfa, trans. by Jonathan Murphy (London: Routledge, 2006)

—— *The History of Sexuality* (New York: Pantheon Books, 1978), I: *An Introduction*

Fraser, Andrea, 'Isn't This a Wonderful Place? (A Tour of a Tour of the Guggenheim Bilbao)', in *Museum Highlights: The Writings of Andrea Fraser*, ed. by Alexander Alberro (Cambridge, MA: MIT Press, 2005), pp. 233–59

Freud, Sigmund, *The Standard Edition of the Complete Psychological Works of Sigmund Freud*, ed. and trans. by James Strachey, 24 vols (London: Hogarth, 1953–74), IV: The Interpretation of Dreams (1900) (1953)

—— 'Instincts and Their Vicissitudes', in *The Standard Edition*, ed. by Strachey, XIV: *On the History of the Psycho-Analytic Movement, Papers on Metapsychology, and Other Works (1914–1916)* (1957), pp. 109–40

—— 'Neurosis and Psychosis', in *The Standard Edition*, ed. by Strachey, XIX: *The Ego and the Id and Other Works (1923–25)* (1961), pp. 147–54

Freyre, Gilberto, *The Masters and the Slaves: A Study in the Development of Brazilian Civilization* [Portuguese orig., *Casa grande e senzala* (1933)] (New York: Knopf, 1964)

Frisinger, H. Howard, *The History of Meteorology: To 1800* (New York: Science History Publications, 1977)

Gammel, Irene, *Baroness Elsa: Gender, Dada* (Cambridge, MA: MIT Press, 2003) <https://doi.org/10.7551/mitpress/1517.001.0001>

Gaynor, Gloria, 'Texas Will Survive', Twitter, 31 August 2017 <https://twitter.com/gloriagaynor/status/903027825443254273> [accessed 5 July 2020]

Gibbs, Allan K., and Christopher Norman Barron, *The Geology of the Guiana Shield*, Oxford Monographs on Geology and Geophysics, 22 (Oxford: Oxford University Press, 1993)

Glantz, Margo, 'Frida Kahlo. Diseminación y amplificación', *Revista de la Universidad de México*, 104 (2012), pp. 15–25

Gleick, James, *Chaos: Making a New Science* (London: Cardinal, 1988)

Glissant, Édouard, *Poetics of Relation*, trans. by Betsy Wing (Ann Arbor: University of Michigan Press, 1997) <https://doi.org/10.3998/mpub.10257>

Goldchluk, Graciela, 'Lecciones de realismo para una liebre muerta (sobre la obra de Mario Bellatin)', I Simposio Internacional Imágenes y Realismos en América Latina, 29 de septiembre al 1 de octubre de 2011, Leiden, Países Bajos, in *Actas online*, ed. by Miguel Caballero

Vázquez, Luz Rodríguez Carranza, and Christina Soto van der Plas <https://imagenesyrealismosleiden.wordpress.com/> <http://www.memoria.fahce.unlp.edu.ar/trab_eventos/ev.13717/ev.13717.pdf> [accessed 11 June 2020]

Gordon, Avery, *Ghostly Matters: Haunting and the Sociological Imagination* (Minneapolis: University of Minnesota Press, 2008)

Gould, Stephen Jay, *Time's Arrow, Time's Cycle: Myth and Metaphor in the Discovery of Geological Time* (Cambridge, MA: Harvard University Press, 1988)

Gragnolati, Manuele, *Amor che move: Linguaggio del corpo e forma del desiderio in Dante, Pasolini e Morante* (Milan: Il Saggiatore, 2013)

—— 'Diffracting Dante's *Paradiso*: Transformation, Identity, and the Form of Desire', in *Reception, Translation, and Transformation of Italian Literature*, ed. by Brian Richardson, Guido Bonsaver, and Giuseppe Stellardi (Oxford: Legenda, 2017), pp. 352–66

—— *Experiencing the Afterlife: Soul and Body in Dante and Medieval Culture* (South Bend, IN: Notre Dame University Press, 2005)

—— 'Gluttony and the Anthropology of Pain in Dante's *Inferno* and *Purgatorio*', in *History in the Comic Mode: Medieval Communities and the Matter of Person*, ed. by Rachel Fulton and Bruce W. Holsinger (New York: Columbia University Press, 2007), pp. 238–50 <https://doi.org/10.7312/fult13368-022>

Graham, Stephen, 'Life Support: The Political Ecology of Urban Air', *City*, 19.2–3 (2015), pp. 192–215 <https://doi.org/10.1080/13604813.2015.1014710>

Greene, Thomas M., 'Dramas of Selfhood in the *Comedy*', in *From Time to Eternity: Essays on Dante's 'Divine Comedy'*, ed. by Thomas G. Bergin (New Haven, CT: Yale University Press, 1967), pp. 103–36

Groom, Amelia, *Beverly Buchanan: Marsh Ruins* (London: Afterall Books, forthcoming in 2021)

Grove, Richard, and George Adamson, *El Niño in World History*, Palgrave Studies in World Environmental History (London: Palgrave Macmillan, 2018) <https://doi.org/10.1057/978-1-137-45740-0>

Grunenberg, Antonia, *Hannah Arendt und Martin Heidegger. Geschichte einer Liebe* (Munich: Piper, 2006)

Haacke, Hans, *Condensation Cube*, 1963–65, perspex, steel, and water, 305 x 305 x 305 mm, Tate Modern, London

—— *Untitled Statement*, in Linda Weintraub, *To Life! Eco Art in Pursuit of a Sustainable Planet* (Berkeley: University of California Press, 2012)

Haden, Philippa, 'Forestry Issues in the Guiana Shield Region: A Perspective on Guyana and Suriname', 1999 <https://www.odi.org/sites/odi.org.uk/files/odi-assets/publications-opinion-files/5700.pdf> [accessed 1 July 2020]

Halpern, Orit, 'Hopeful Resilience', *e-flux*, 19 April 2017 <https://www.e-flux.com/architecture/accumulation/96421/hopeful-resilience/> [accessed 8 April 2020]

Hamacher, Werner, 'Intensive Languages', trans. by Ira Allen with Steven Tester, *MLN*, 127.3 (2012), pp. 485–541 <https://doi.org/10.1353/mln.2012.0084>

—— 'Position Exposed: Friedrich Schlegel's Poetological Transposition of Fichte's Absolute Proposition', in his *Premises: Essays on Philosophy and Literature from Kant to Celan,* trans. by Peter Fenves (Cambridge: Harvard University Press, 1996), pp. 222–60

—— 'Premises', in his *Premises: Essays on Philosophy and Literature from Kant to Celan,* trans. by Peter Fenves (Cambridge: Harvard University Press, 1996), pp. 1–43

David Hammons: Rousing the Rubble (New York: P. S. 1 Contemporary Art Center, 1991)

Hancock, Gary J., Stephen G. Tims, L. Keith Fifield, and Ian T. Webster, 'The Release and Persistence of Radioactive Anthropogenic Nuclides', *Geological Society, London, Special Publications*, 395.1 (2014), pp. 265–81 <https://doi.org/10.1144/SP395.15>

Haraway, Donna J., *Staying with the Trouble: Making Kin in the Chthulucene* (Durham, NC: Duke University Press, 2016) <https://doi.org/10.1215/9780822373780>

Haskell, Thomas L., 'Objectivity Is Not Neutrality: Rhetoric Vs. Practice in Peter Novick's *That Noble Dream*', *History and Theory*, 29.2 (May 1990), pp. 129–57 <https://doi.org/10.2307/2505222>

Hecht, Gabrielle, *Being Nuclear: Africans and the Global Uranium Trade* (Cambridge, MA: MIT Press, 2012)

Heemskerk, Marieke, *Rights to Land and Resources for Indigenous Peoples and Maroons in Suriname,* (Paramaribo: Amazon Conservation Team, 2005) <http://www.act-suriname.org/wp-content/uploads/2015/02/ACT_land-rights-report-2005.pdf> [accessed 2 August 2017]

Hegel, G. W. F., *Hegel's Aesthetics: Lectures on Fine Art*, ed. and trans. by Thomas Malcolm Knox, 2 vols (Oxford: Clarendon Press, 1975) <https://doi.org/10.1093/actrade/9780198244998.book.1>

—— *Hegel's Phenomenology of Spirit*, trans. by A. V. Miller (Oxford: Oxford University Press, 1977)

Heidegger, Martin, *Die Frage nach dem Ding. Zu Kants Lehre von den transzendentalen Grundsätzen* (Tübingen: Niemeyer, 1962)

—— *Gesamtausgabe*, 102 vols (Frankfurt a.M.: Klostermann, 1975–) (hereafter *GA*)

—— *GA*, xxxv: Der Anfang der abendländischen Philosophie. Auslegung des Anaximander und Parmenides, ed. by Peter Trawny (2012)

—— *GA*, xxxvi/xxxvii: *Sein und Wahrheit*, ed. by Hartmut Tietjen (2001)

—— *GA*, xxxviii: *Logik als die Frage nach dem Wesen der Sprache*, ed. by Günter Seubold (1998)

——— *GA*, XL: *Einführung in die Metaphysik*, ed. by Petra Jaeger (1983)

——— *GA*, LV: *Heraklit. Der Anfang des abendländischen Denkens. Logik. Heraklits Lehre vom Logos*, ed. by Manfred Frings (1987)

——— *GA*, LXV: *Beiträge zur Philosophie (Vom Ereignis)*, ed. by Friedrich-Wilhelm von Herrmann (1994)

——— *GA*, LXX: *Über den Anfang*, ed. by Paola-Ludovika Coriando (2005)

——— *GA*, LXXI: *Das Ereignis*, ed. by Friedrich-Wilhelm von Herrmann (2009)

——— *GA*, LXXIII.1–2: *Zum Ereignis-Denken*, ed. by Peter Trawny (2013)

——— *GA*, XCIV: *Überlegungen II-IV (Schwarze Hefte 1931–1938)*, ed. by Peter Trawny (2014)

——— *GA*, XCV: *Überlegungen VII-XI (Schwarze Hefte 1938/1939)*, ed. by Peter Trawny (2014)

——— *GA*, XCVI: *Überlegungen XII-XV (Schwarze Hefte 1939-1941)*, ed. by Peter Trawny (2014)

——— *GA*, XCVII: *Anmerkungen I-V (Schwarze Hefte 1942-1948)*, ed. by Peter Trawny (2015)

——— 'Hegel, "Rechtsphilosophie"', 'Hegel, Rechtsphilosophie. WS 34/35. Mitschrift Wilhelm Hallwachs', 'Hegel, Rechtsphilosophie. WS 34/35. Protokolle', in *GA*, LXXXVI: *Seminare. Hegel-Schelling*, ed. by Peter Trawny (2011), pp. 55–184, pp. 549–611, pp. 613–55

——— 'Über Wesen und Begriff von Natur, Geschichte und Staat. Übung aus dem Wintersemester 1933/34', in *Heidegger und der Nationalsozialismus. Dokumente*, ed. by Alfred Denker and Holger Zaborowski (Freiburg: Alber, 2009), pp. 53–88

Herkenhoff, Paulo, 'The Longing for Art and Existing Material in the World of Men', in *Arthur Bispo do Rosário*, pp. 140–83

Herrmann, Friedrich-Wilhelm von, and Francesco Alfieri, *Martin Heidegger. La verita' sui Quaderni Neri* (Brescia: Morcelliana Editrice, 2016)

Heynen, Julian, 'Georgia — Vajiko Chachkhiani: Living Dog Among Dead Lions', in *Viva Arte Viva: Biennale arte 2017: Catalogue, Participants, Countries, Collateral Events*, ed. by Flavia Fossa Margutti (Venice: SIAE, 2017), pp. 62–63

Hidalgo, Luciana, *Arthur Bispo do Rosário. O senhor do Labirinto* (Rio de Janeiro: Rocco, 2011)

Hilb, Claudia, 'El principio del *initium*', in *Revolución y violencia en la filosofía de Hannah Arendt*, ed. by Marco Estrada Saavedra and María Teresa Muñoz (México D.F.: El Colegio de México, 2015), pp. 67–102

Hilborn, Robert C., 'Sea Gulls, Butterflies, and Grasshoppers: A Brief History of the Butterfly Effect in Nonlinear Dynamics', *American Journal of Physics*, 72.4 (2004), pp. 425–27 <https://doi.org/10.1119/1.1636492>

Holzhey, Christoph F. E., 'Conatus Errans: Paradoxe Lust zwischen Teleologie und Mechanik', in *Conatus und Lebensnot: Schlüsselbegriffe der Medienanthropologie*, ed. by Astrid Deuber-Mankowsky and Anna Tuschling, Cultural Inquiry, 12 (Vienna: Turia + Kant, 2017), pp. 66–123

Honig, Bonnie, 'Declarations of Independence: Arendt and Derrida on the Problem of Founding a Republic', *The American Political Science Review*, 85.1 (1991), pp. 97–113 <https://doi.org/10.2307/1962880>

—— *Emergency Politics: Paradox, Law, Democracy* (Princeton, NJ: Princeton University Press, 2009) <https://doi.org/10.1515/9781400830961>

Hryhorczuk, Nicholas, 'Radioactive Heritage: The Universal Value of Chernobyl as a Dark Heritage Site', *Qualitative Inquiry*, 25.9–10 (2019), pp. 1047–55 <https://doi.org/10.1177/1077800418787553>

Ingold, Tim, *The Life of Lines* (Abingdon: Routledge, 2015) <https://doi.org/10.4324/9781315727240>

Isaac, Rami K., and Laurencija Budryte-Ausiejiene, 'Interpreting the Emotions of Visitors: A Study of Visitor Comment Books at the Grūtas Park Museum, Lithuania', *Scandinavian Journal of Hospitality and Tourism*, 15.4 (2015), pp. 400–24 <https://doi.org/10.1080/15022250.2015.1024818>

Iturbide, Graciela, and Mario Bellatin, *El baño de Frida Kahlo/Demerol, sin fecha de caducidad* (Ciudad de México: Galería López Quiroga/Editorial RM, 2008)

K, Hiwa, 'A View from Above' <http://www.hiwak.net/anecdotes/a-view-from-above/> [accessed 7 June 2020]

Kalyvas, Andreas, *Democracy and the Politics of the Extraordinary: Max Weber, Carl Schmitt, and Hannah Arendt* (Cambridge: Cambridge University Press, 2008) <https://doi.org/10.1017/CBO9780511755842>

Karaman, Burcu I., 'On Contronymy', *International Journal of Lexicography*, 21.2 (2008), pp. 173–92 <https://doi.org/10.1093/ijl/ecn011>

Keenan, Allan, 'Promises, Promises: The Abyss of Freedom and the Loss of the Political in the Work of Hannah Arendt', in his *Democracy in Question. Democratic Openness in a Time of Political Closure* (Stanford, CA: Stanford University Press, 2003), pp. 76–101

Klein, Ursula, *Humboldts Preussen: Wissenschaft und Technik im Aufbruch* (Darmstadt: Wissenschaftliche Buchgesellschaft, 2015)

Kleine, Susanne, 'Interior and Exterior Spaces', in *Vajiko Chachkhiani: Heavy Metal Honey*, ed. by Kunst- und Ausstellungshalle der Bundesrepublik Deutschland (Bonn: Kunst- und Ausstellungshalle der Bundesrepublik Deutschland, 2018), pp. 33–43

—— 'Interview with Vajiko Chachkhiani at the opening of *Heavy Metal Honey* at Bundeskunsthalle', YouTube, 28 June 2018 <https://www.youtube.com/watch?v=-naE2m5l89w> [accessed 20 December 2019]

Kunst- und Ausstellungshalle der Bundesrepublik Deutschland, ed., *Vajiko Chachkhiani: Heavy Metal Honey* (Bonn: Kunst- und Ausstellungshalle der Bundesrepublik Deutschland, 2018)

Kusukawa, Sachiko, *The Transformation of Natural Philosophy: The Case of Philip Melanchthon* (Cambridge: Cambridge University Press, 1995) <https://doi.org/10.1017/CBO9780511598524>

Labra, Daniela, ed., *Das virgens em cardumes e da cor das auras* (São Paulo: WMF Martins Fontes, 2016)

Langacker, Ronald W., *Foundations of Cognitive Grammar*, 2 vols (Stanford, CA: Stanford University Press, 1991), ii: *Descriptive Application*

Laplanche, Jean, *Life and Death in Psychoanalysis*, trans. by Jeffrey Mehlman (Baltimore, MD: Johns Hopkins University Press, 1976)

Laplanche, Jean, and Jean-Bertrand Pontalis, 'Fantasy and the Origins of Sexuality' [Fantasme originaire, fantasmes de origines, origines du fantasme], in *Formations of Fantasy*, ed. by Victor Burgin, James Donald, and Cora Kaplan (London: Routledge, 1989), pp. 5–34

—— *The Language of Psycho-Analysis* (London: Hogarth, 1973)

Latour, Bruno, *Facing Gaia: Eight Lectures on the New Climatic Regime*, trans. by Catherine Porter (Cambridge: Polity, 2017)

—— *Pandora's Hope: Essays on the Reality of Science Studies* (Cambridge, MA: Harvard University Press, 1999)

Le Goff, Jacques, *The Birth of Purgatory*, trans. by Arthur Goldhammer (Chicago, IL: University of Chicago Press, 1984)

Levin, Beth, and Bonnie Krejci, 'Talking about the Weather: Two Construals of Precipitation Events in English', *Glossa: A Journal of General Linguistics*, 4.1 (2019), Art. 58, pp. 1–29 (p. 1) <https://doi.org/10.5334/gjgl.794>

Levinas, Emmanuel, *Otherwise than Being, or Beyond Essence*, trans. by Alphonso Lingis (Dordrecht: Nijhoff, 1981)

—— *Totality and Infinity: An Essay on Exteriority*, trans. by Alphonso Lingis (The Hague: Nijhoff, 1979) <https://doi.org/10.1007/978-94-009-9342-6>

Lienhard, Martin, 'O mato e o mar: apontamentos para uma arqueologia do discurso escravo', in *Brasil: um país de negros?*, ed. by Jéferson Bacelar and Carlos Cardoso (Rio de Janeiro/Salvador: Pallas/CEAO, 1999), pp. 113–23

Lindberg, David C., *The Beginnings of Western Science*, 2nd edn (Chicago: University of Chicago Press, 2007)

—— *Theories of Vision from Al-Kindi to Kepler*, rev. edn (Chicago: University of Chicago Press 1996)

Lippit, Akira Mizuto, *Atomic Light (Shadow Optics)* (Minneapolis: University of Minnesota Press 2005)

Llewelyn, John, *The Middle Voice of Ecological Conscience: A Chiasmic Reading of Responsibility in the Neighborhood of Levinas, Heidegger and Others* (London: Macmillan, 1992)

Lombardi, Elena, *The Syntax of Desire: Love and Language in Augustine, the Modistae, Dante* (Toronto: University of Toronto Press, 2007)

—— *The Wings of the Doves: Love and Desire in Dante and Medieval Culture* (Montreal: McGill-Queen's University Press, 2012)

Lorenz, Edward N., 'Available Potential Energy and the Maintenance of the General Circulation', *Tellus* 7.2 (January 1955), pp. 157–67 <https://doi.org/10.3402/tellusa.v7i2.8796>

—— *The Essence of Chaos* (London: UCL Press, 1995)

—— *The Nature and Theory of the General Circulation of the Atmosphere* (Geneva: World Meteorological Organization, 1967)

Lütticken, Sven, 'Nuclear Aesthetics: Beyond Big Bangs', *kunstlicht: Journal for Visual Art, Visual Culture, and Architecture*, 39.3–4 (2018) pp. 13–19

Malm, Andreas, *Fossil Capital: The Rise of Steam Power and the Roots of Global Warming* (London: Verso, 2016)

Marchart, Oliver, *Die politische Differenz. Zum Denken des Politischen bei Nancy, Lefort, Badiou, Laclau und Agamben* (Berlin: Suhrkamp, 2010)

—— *Post-Foundational Political Thought: Political Difference in Nancy, Lefort, Badiou and Laclau* (Edinburgh: Edinburgh University Press, 2007) <https://doi.org/10.3366/edinburgh/9780748624973.001.0001>

Marder, Michael, and Anaïs Tondeur, *The Chernobyl Herbarium: Fragments of an Exploded Consciousness* (Open Humanities Press, 2016) <https://doi.org/10.26530/OAPEN_606220>

Margules, Max, 'On the Energy of Storms', in *The Mechanics of the Earth's Atmosphere*, trans. by Cleveland Abbe (Washington, DC: Smithsonian, 1910), pp. 533–95

Markell, Patchen, 'Anonymous Glory', *European Journal of Political Theory*, 16.1 (2017), pp. 77–99

—— 'The Rule of the People: Arendt, Archê, and Democracy', *The American Political Science Review*, 100.1 (2006), pp. 1–14 <https://doi.org/10.1017/S000305540606196X>

Masco, Joseph, *The Nuclear Borderlands: The Manhattan Project in Post Cold-War New Mexico* (Princeton, NJ: Princeton University Press, 2006) <https://doi.org/10.1515/9781400849680>

Matzig, Gerhard, 'Geist aus der Asche. "Yakisugi" ist die Kunst des Verkohlens: Warum Architektur brennen muss, um zu leben', *Süddeutsche Zeitung*, 124, 30 May – 1 June 2020, p. 56

Mavrokordopoulou, Kyveli, and Ruby de Vos, eds, *Nuclear Aesthetics* (=*kunstlicht: Journal for Visual Art, Visual Culture, and Architecture*, 39.3–4 (2018))

Mbembe, Achille, 'Necropolitics', *Public Culture*, 15.1 (2003), pp. 11–40 <https://doi.org/10.1215/08992363-15-1-11>

McCook, Stuart, *Coffee Is Not Forever: A Global History of the Coffee Leaf Rust* (Athens: Ohio University Press, 2019)

McDonough, Jimmy, *Shakey: Neil Young's Biography* (New York: Random House, 2010)

Merriam-Webster.com Dictionary (Springfield, MA: Merriam-Webster, 2020) <https://www.merriam-webster.com/dictionary/weather>

Miguel, Marlon, 'Psychiatric Power: Exclusion and Segregation in the Brazilian Mental Health System', in *Democracy and Brazil: Collapse and Regression*, ed. by Bernardo Bianchi, Jorge Chaloub, Frieder Otto Wolf, and Patricia Rangel (London: Routledge, forthcoming 2020)

Miles, Malcolm, 'Representing Nature: Art and Climate Change', *Cultural Geographies*, 17.1 (2010), pp. 19–35 <https://doi.org/10.1177/1474474009349997>

Mintz, Sidney Wilfred, *Sweetness and Power* (New York: Viking, 1985) <http://www.followthethings.com/sweetnessandpower.shtml> [accessed 8 February 2017]

Mitchell, Andrew, and Peter Trawny, eds, *Heidegger's Black Notebooks. Responses to Anti-Semitism* (New York: Columbia University Press, 2017) <https://doi.org/10.7312/mitc18044>

Morais, Frederico, *Arthur Bispo do Rosario: arte além da loucura* (Rio de Janeiro: Livre Galeria e Nau Editora, 2013)

Morton, Timothy, *Dark Ecology: For a Logic of Future Coexistence*, The Wellek Library Lectures in Critical Theory (New York: Columbia University Press, 2016)

—— *Hyperobjects: Philosophy and Ecology after the End of the World* (Minneapolis: University of Minnesota Press, 2010)

Mostafavi, Mohsen, and David Leatherbarrow, *On Weathering: The Life of Buildings in Time* (Cambridge, MA: MIT Press, 1993)

Moten, Fred, *The Universal Machine* (Durham, NC: Duke University Press, 2018) <https://doi.org/10.1215/9780822371977>

Moulier Boutang, Yann, 'No Longer Reserve Army: Theses on the Autonomy of Migration and the Necessary End of the Regime of Labour Migration', *Jungle World*, 3 April 2002 <https://jungle.world/artikel/2002/14/nicht-laenger-reservearmee> [accessed 7 June 2020]

Murphy, Michelle, 'Alterlife and Decolonial Chemical Relations', *Cultural Anthropology*, 32.4 (2017), pp. 494–503 <https://doi.org/10.14506/ca32.4.02>

Nancy, Jean-Luc, 'Abandoned Being', in his *The Birth to Presence*, trans. by Brian Holmes (Stanford, CA: Stanford University Press, 1993), pp. 36–47

—— *Banalité de Heidegger* (Paris: Éditions Galilée, 2015)

Nayeri, Dina, *The Ungrateful Refugee* (Edinburgh: Canongate, 2019)

Neimanis, Astrida, and Jennifer Mae Hamilton, 'Open Space Weathering', *Feminist Review*, 118.1 (2018), pp. 80–84 <https://doi.org/10.1057/s41305-018-0097-8>

Neimanis, Astrida, and Rachel Loewen Walker, 'Weathering: Climate Change and the "Thick Time" of Transcorporeality', *Hypatia*, 29.3 (2014), pp. 558–75 <https://doi.org/10.1111/hypa.12064>

Neto, Agostinho, 'Havemos de voltar', Fundação Dr. António Agostinho Neto (FAAN) <http://www.agostinhoneto.org/index.php?option=com_content&id=561:desterro> [accessed 28 June 2020]

—— *Náusea* (Luanda: UEA, 2006)

Nichol, Mark, '75 Contronyms (Words with Contradictory Meanings)' <https://www.dailywritingtips.com/75-contronyms-words-with-contradictory-meanings/> [accessed 15 June 2020]

Nietzsche, Friedrich Wilhelm, *Beyond Good and Evil / On the Genealogy of Morality*, trans. by Adrian Del Caro, The Complete Works of Friedrich Nietzsche, 8 (Stanford, CA: Stanford University Press, 2014)

—— *Beyond Good and Evil: Prelude to a Philosophy of the Future*, trans. by Walter Arnold Kaufmann (New York: Vintage Books, 1989)

Nosowitz, Dan, 'The Woman Who Ate Chernobyl's Apples', online video recording, Atlas Obscura, <https://www.atlasobscura.com/articles/the-woman-who-ate-chernobyl-s-apples> [accessed 4 March 2020]

Obruchev, Vladimir A., *Fundamentals of Geology: Popular Outline* (Moscow: Foreign Languages Publishing House, 1959)

OED Online (Oxford: Oxford University Press, 2020) <https://www.oed.com/>

Online Etymology Dictionary (2020) <https://www.etymonline.com/>

Oreskes, Naomi, and Erik M. Conway, *Merchants of Doubt: How a Handful of Scientists Obscured the Truth on Issues from Tobacco Smoke to Global Warming* (New York: Bloomsbury, 2010)

O'Brian, John, ed., *Camera Atomica*. Art Gallery of Toronto (London: Black Dog Publishing, 2014)

Parr, Martin, *Bad Weather* (New York: Valerie Sonnenthal, 2014) [1982]

Patrocínio, Stela do, *Reino dos bichos e dos animais é o meu nome* (Rio de Janeiro: Azougue Editorial, 2001)

Patterson, Orlando, *Slavery and Social Death: A Comparative Study* (Cambridge, MA: Harvard University Press, 1982)

Pertile, Lino, 'L'antica fiamma: La metamorfosi del fuoco nella *Commedia* di Dante', *The Italianist*, 11.1 (1991), pp. 29–60

Petrocchi, Giorgio, ed., *La Commedia secondo l'antica vulgata*, 2nd edn, 4 vols (Florence: Le Lettere, 1994)

Petryna, Adriana, *Life Exposed: Biological Citizens After Chernobyl* (Princeton: Princeton University Press, 2013) <https://doi.org/10.1515/9781400845095>

Pezzullo, Phaedra C., *Toxic Tourism: Rhetorics of Pollution, Travel, and Environmental Justice* (Tuscaloosa: University of Alabama Press, 2007)

Pfisterer, Ulrich, and Christine Tauber, eds, *Einfluss, Strömung, Quelle: Aquatische Metaphern der Kunstgeschichte* (Bielefeld: transcript, 2018) <https://doi.org/10.14361/9783839443880>

Pinheiro, Fatima, and Tania Rivera, 'In Situ | Lugares do Delírio — Entrevista com Tania Rivera', *Subversos* (2017) <http://subversos.com.br/in-situ-lugares-do-delirio-entrevista-com-tania-rivera/> [accessed 28 June 2020]

Plato, *Theaetetus*, ed. by Bernard Williams, M. J. Levett, and Myles Burnyeat (Indianapolis, IN: Hackett, 1992)

Pliny, *Natural History*, 10 vols (Cambridge, MA: Harvard University Press, 1938–62), ix: *Books 33–35*, trans. by H. Rackham, Loeb Classical Library, 394 (1952)

Polt, Richard, 'Self-Assertion as Founding', in Martin Heidegger, *On Hegel's Philosophy of Right: The 1934–35 Seminar and Interpretative Essays*, ed. by Peter Trawny, Marcia Sá Cavalcante Schuback, and Michael Marder (London: Bloomsbury, 2014), pp. 67–81

Porena, Manfredi, *La Divina Commedia di Dante Alighieri commentata da Manfredi Porena* (Bologna: Zanichelli, 1981), available online in the Dartmouth Dante Project <https://dante.dartmouth.edu/> [accessed 8 April 2020]

Porter, Theodore M., 'The Objective Self', *Victorian Studies*, 50.4 (2008), pp. 641–47 <https://doi.org/10.2979/VIC.2008.50.4.641>

Prigogine, Ilya, and Isabelle Stengers, *Order Out of Chaos: Man's New Dialogue with Nature* (London: Heinemann, 1984)

Puvogel, Renate, 'Bonn, Vajiko Chachkhiani, *Heavy Metal Honey*, 29 June – 7 October 2018 Bundeskunsthalle', *Kunstforum*, 256 (2018), pp. 260–62

Quijano, Anibal, 'Coloniality of Power and Eurocentrism in Latin America', *International Sociology*, 15.2 (2000), pp. 215–32 <https://doi.org/10.1177/0268580900015002005>

Randerson, Janine, *Weather as Medium: Toward a Meteorological Art* (Cambridge, MA: MIT Press, 2018) <https://doi.org/10.7551/mitpress/11081.001.0001>

Rivera, Tania, 'Museu dos delírios — notas sobre a exposição *Lugares do delírio*', *Ao Largo*, 6 (2018) <https://www.maxwell.vrac.puc-rio.br/33478/33478.PDF> [accessed 28 June 2020]

Rouphail, Robert M., 'Cyclonic Ecology: Sugar, Cyclone Science, and the Limits of Empire in Mauritius and the Indian Ocean World, 1870s–1930s', *Isis*, 110.1 (March 2019), pp. 48–67 <https://doi.org/10.1086/702729>

Rudwick, Martin J. S., *Bursting the Limits of Time: The Reconstruction of Geohistory in the Age of Revolution* (Chicago: University of Chicago Press, 2005) <https://doi.org/10.7208/chicago/9780226731148.001.0001>

—— *Earth's Deep History: How It Was Discovered and Why It Matters* (Chicago: University of Chicago Press, 2014) <https://doi.org/10.7208/chicago/9780226204093.001.0001>

—— *The Great Devonian Controversy: The Shaping of Scientific Knowledge Among Gentlemanly Specialists* (Chicago: University of Chicago Press, 1985) <https://doi.org/10.7208/chicago/9780226731001.001.0001>

—— *Worlds Before Adam: The Reconstruction of Geohistory in the Age of Reform* (Chicago: University of Chicago Press, 2008) <https://doi.org/10.7208/chicago/9780226731308.001.0001>

Ruskin, John, 'The Work of Iron in Nature, Art, and Policy', in *The Two Paths: Being Lectures on Art and its Application to Decoration and Manufacture Delivered in 1858–9*, ed. by Christine Roth (West Lafayette, IN: Parlor Press, 2004), pp. 91–119

Rühle, Alex, 'Flüssige Freude', *Süddeutsche Zeitung*, 140, 20–21 June 2020, p. 17

Sacco, Damiano, 'Highest Openness: On Agamben's Promise', in *Openness in Medieval Culture*, ed. by Manuele Gragnolati and Almut Suerbaum (Berlin: ICI Berlin Press, forthcoming)

—— 'Of *Apousia* and *Parousia*: The Correlation between Heidegger and Meillassoux', *Pli*, 30 (2019), pp. 141–63

Sanyal, Debarati, 'Humanitarian Detention and Figures of Persistence at the Border', *Critical Times*, 2.3 (December 2019), pp. 435–65 <https://doi.org/10.1215/26410478-7862552>

Schettini, Ariel, 'En el castillo de Barbazul. El caso Mario Bellatin', *Otra Parte*, 6 (Winter 2005), pp. 14–17

Schriber, Abbe, '"Those Who Know Don't Tell": David Hammons c. 1981', *Women & Performance: A Journal of Feminist Theory*, 29 (2019), pp. 41–61 <https://doi.org/10.1080/0740770X.2019.1571866>

Schrödinger, Erwin, *What Is Life? The Physical Aspect of the Living Cell with Mind and Matter and Autobiographical Sketches* (Cambridge: Cambridge University Press, 2013)

Schürmann, Reiner, *Le Principe d'anarchie. Heidegger et la question de l'agir* (Paris: Éditions du Seuil, 1982) <https://doi.org/10.7591/9781501744662-010>

—— 'Technicity, Topology, Tragedy: Heidegger on "That Which Saves" in the Global Reach', in *Technology in the Western Political Tradition*, ed. by Arthur M. Melzer, Jerry Weinberger, and M. Richard Zimman (Ithaca, NY: Cornell University Press, 1993), pp. 190–213

Secco, Carmem Lucia Tindó, ed., *Antologia do mar na poesia africana de língua portuguesa do Século xx* (Rio de Janeiro: Programa de Letras Vernáculas/UFRJ, 1996), I

Seligmann-Silva, Márcio, 'Arthur Bispo do Rosário: a arte de "enloquecer" os signos', *ArteFilosofia*, 3 (2007), pp. 144–55 <https://periodicos.ufop.br:8082/pp/index.php/raf/article/view/761/717> [accessed 28 June 2020]

Semprun, Jamie, *La Nucléarisation du monde* (France: IVREA Press, 1986)

Serra, Richard, *Writings/Interviews* (Chicago: University of Chicago Press, 1994)

Sharpe, Christina, *In the Wake: On Blackness and Being* (Durham, NC: Duke University Press, 2016) <https://doi.org/10.1215/9780822373452>

Shkuda, Aaron, *The Lofts of SoHo: Gentrification, Art, and Industry in New York, 1950–1980* (Chicago: University of Chicago Press, 2016)

Simondon, Gilbert, *On the Mode of Existence of Technological Objects*, trans. by Cécile Malaspina and John Rogove (Minneapolis: Univocal, 2017)

Slocum, Rachel, 'Polar Bears and Energy-Efficient Lightbulbs: Strategies to Bring Climate Change Home', *Environment and Planning D: Society and Space*, 22 (2004), pp. 1–26 <https://doi.org/10.1068/d378>

Smith, William, *Section of the Strata through Hampshire and Wiltshire to Bath, on the Road from Bath to Salisbury* (London: John Cary, 1819)

Solomon, Deborah, 'Richard Serra Is Carrying the Weight of the World', *The New York Times*, 28 August 2019

Stafford, Robert A., *Scientist of Empire: Sir Roderick Murchison, Scientific Exploration, and Victorian Imperialism* (Cambridge: Cambridge University Press, 1989)

Steinbach, Jörg, 'Kassel in Schutt und Asche: Trümmermodell wieder zu sehen', *Hessische Niedersächsische Allgemeine*, 2 March 2016 <https://www.hna.de/kassel/kassel-schutt-asche-6171148.html> [accessed 7 June 2020]

Stockhammer, Robert, 'Philology in the Anthropocene', in *Meteorologies of Modernity: Weather and Climate Discourses in the Anthropocene*, ed. by Sarah Fekadu, Hanna Straß-Senol, and Tobias Döring (=*REAL: Yearbook of Research in English and American Literature*, 33 (Tübingen: Narr Francke Attempto, 2017)), pp. 43–64

Stone, Philip, 'Dark Tourism — an Old Concept in a New World', *The Tourism Society Journal*, 125.20 (2005) <http://clok.uclan.ac.uk/29705/>

Sytas, Andrius, 'New Tours, Painful Reminders in Lithuania After Hit Chernobyl Show', *Reuters*, 31 July 2019, <https://www.reuters.com/article/us-lithuania-chernobyl/new-tours-painful-reminders-in-lithuania-after-hit-chernobyl-show-idUSKCN1UQ1WF> [accessed 19 July 2020]

Taminiaux, Jacques, 'La Déconstruction arendtienne des vues politiques de Heidegger', *Cahiers philosophiques*, 3.111 (2007), pp. 16–30 <https://doi.org/10.3917/caph.111.0016>

—— *La Fille de Thrace et le penseur professionnel. Arendt et Heidegger* (Paris: Payot, 1992)

Tassin, Étienne, 'Les Gloires ordinaires: Actualité du concept arendtien d'espace public', *Cahiers Sens Public*, 15–16 (2013), pp. 23–36 <https://doi.org/10.3917/csp.015.0023>

Terry, Don, 'A 16-Ton Sculpture Falls, Injuring 2', *The New York Times*, 27 October 1988, Section B, p. 6

Thomas, Julia Adeney, 'History and Biology in the Anthropocene: Problems of Scale, Problems of Value', *American Historical Review*, 119.5 (December 2014), pp. 1587–1607 <https://doi.org/10.1093/ahr/119.5.1587>

Thompson, Graham R., and Jonathan Turk, *Introduction to Physical Geology* (Fort Worth, TX: Brooks/Cole Publishing Company, 1998)

Thomä, Dieter, 'Hannah Arendt. Liebe zur Welt', in *Heidegger Handbuch. Leben-Werk-Wirkung*, ed. by Dieter Thomä (Stuttgart: Metzler, 2013), pp. 397–402

Tomkins, Calvin, 'Man of Steel', *The New Yorker*, 5 August 2002 <http://www.newyorker.com/magazine/2002/08/05/man-of-steel> [accessed 2 July 2020]

Trawny, Peter, and Andrew Mitchell, eds, *Heidegger, die Juden, noch einmal* (Frankfurt a.M.: Klostermann, 2015)

Tsing, Anna Lowenhaupt, *The Mushroom at the End of the World: On the Possibility of Life in Capitalist Ruins* (Princeton, NJ: Princeton University Press, 2015) <https://doi.org/10.2307/j.ctvc77bcc>

UNFCCC, Conference of the Parties, 'Adoption of the Paris Agreement. Proposal by the President' (Bonn: UNFCCC Secretariat, 2015) <https://unfccc.int/resource/docs/2015/cop21/eng/l09r01.pdf> [accessed 1 August 2020]

Vayda, Andrew P., and Bradley B. Walters, 'Against Political Ecology', *Human Ecology*, 27.1 (1999), pp. 167–79 <https://doi.org/10.1023/A:1018713502547>

Vetter, Jeremy, *Field Life: Science in the American West During the Railroad Era* (Pittsburgh, PA: University of Pittsburgh Press, 2016) <https://doi.org/10.2307/j.ctt1gxxqcp>

Villa, Dana, *Arendt and Heidegger: The Fate of the Political* (Princeton, NJ: Princeton University Press, 1996) <https://doi.org/10.1515/9781400821846>

Waldman, Jonathan, *Rust: The Longest War* (New York: Simon and Schuster, 2015)

Waters, Colin N., and others, 'Can Nuclear Weapons Fallout Mark the Beginning of the Anthropocene Epoch?', *Bulletin of the Atomic Scientists*, 71.3 (2015) <https://doi.org/10.1177/0096340215581357>

Webb, Heather, *Dante's Persons: An Ethics of the Transhuman* (Oxford: Oxford University Press, 2016) <https://doi.org/10.1093/acprof:oso/9780198733485.001.0001>

Webb, J. H., 'The Fogging of Photographic Film by Radioactive Contaminants in Cardboard Packaging Materials', *Physical Review*, 76.3 (1949), pp. 375–80 <https://doi.org/10.1103/PhysRev.76.375>

Weintraub, Linda, *Eco Art in Pursuit of a Sustainable Planet* (Berkeley: University of California Press, 2012)

Weyergraf-Serra, Clara, and Martha Buskirk, eds, *The Destruction of Tilted Arc: Documents* (Cambridge, MA: MIT Press, 1991)

Williams, David-Antoine, 'Poetic Antagonyms', *The Comparatist*, 37.1 (2013), pp. 169–85 <https://doi.org/10.1353/com.2013.0009>

Williams, Raymond, 'Structure of Feeling', in *Marxism and Literature* (Oxford: Oxford University Press, 1977), pp. 128–35

Wolfs, Rein, 'Preface', in *Vajiko Chachkhiani: Heavy Metal Honey*, ed. Kunst- und Ausstellungshalle der Bundesrepublik Deutschland (Bonn: Kunst- und Ausstellungshalle der Bundesrepublik Deutschland, 2018), pp. 11–12

Wolin, Richard, *Heidegger's Children. Hannah Arendt, Karl Löwith, Hans Jonas, and Herbert Marcuse* (Princeton, NJ: Princeton University Press, 2015) <https://doi.org/10.1515/9781400873692>

Yankovska, Ganna, and Kevin Hannam, 'Dark and Toxic Tourism in the Chernobyl Exclusion Zone,' *Current Issues in Tourism*, 17.10 (2014), pp. 929–39 <https://doi.org/10.1080/13683500.2013.820260>

Yusoff, Kathryn, *A Billion Black Anthropocenes or None* (Minneapolis: University of Minnesota Press, 2018) <https://doi.org/10.5749/9781452962054>

Zadoks, J. C., *On the Political Economy of Plant Disease Epidemics* (Wageningen: Wageningen Academic Publishers, 2008) <https://doi.org/10.3920/978-90-8686-653-3>

Zalasiewicz, Jan, and others, 'When Did the Anthropocene Begin? A Mid-Twentieth Century Boundary Level Is Stratigraphically Optimal', *Quaternary International* 383 (2015), pp. 196–203 <https://doi.org/10.1016/j.quaint.2014.11.045>

Zanon, Emanuela, 'Vajiko Chachkhiani: The Poet of Absence at the de' Foscherari Gallery', *Juliet*, 30 January 2019 <https://www.juliet-artmagazine.com/en/vajiko-chachkhiani-de-foscherari-gallery/> [accessed 3 January 2020]

Zerilli, Linda, 'Castoriadis, Arendt, and the Problem of the New', *Constellations*, 9.4 (2002), pp. 540–53 <https://doi.org/10.1111/1467-8675.00302>

FILMOGRAPHY

Aldona, dir. by Emilija Škarnulytė (2013)

Die Entscheider, dir. by Susanne Ofteringer (1992)

Forst, dir. by Ascan Breuer, Ursula Hansbauer, Wolfgang Konrad, in cooperation with The Voice Refugee Forum and others(2005) <http://www.forstfilm.com/> [accessed 7 June 2020]

La Forteresse, dir. by Fernand Melgar (2008)

The Hole (Dòng), dir. by Tsai Ming-Liang (Fox Lorber, 1998, 95 min)

Island of Hungry Ghosts, dir. by Gabrielle Brady (2018) <http://www.christmasislandfilm.com/> [accessed 7 June 2020]

O Bispo, dir. by Fernando Gabeira (Globo TV, 1985) <https://www.youtube.com/watch?v=x9wc-_XoCcw> [accessed 28 June 2020].

O prisioneiro da passagem: Arthur Bispo do Rosário, dir. by Hugo Denizart (Centro Nacional de Produção Independente, 1982) <https://www.youtube.com/watch?v=PjgP1LYLZOU> [accessed 28 June 2020]

La pluie (Projet pour un texte), dir. by Marcel Broodthaers (Collection Centre Pompidou, inventory number: AM 1996-F1310, 1969, 2 min)

Purple Sea, dir. by Amel Alzakout and Khaled Abdulwahed (2020) <https://purplesea.pong-berlin.de/> [accessed 7 June 2020]

Simón del desierto, dir. by Luis Buñuel (Sindicato de Trabajadores de la Producción Cinematográfica, 1965)

View from Above, dir. by Hiwa K (2017)

Zentralflughafen THF, dir. by Karim Aïnouz (2018) <https://www.zentralflughafen-thf.de/> [accessed 7 June 2020]

Contributors

Delfina Cabrera holds a BA in sociology from the Universidad de Buenos Aires and received her PhD in comparative literature from the Université de Perpignan via Domitia, in conjunction with the Università degli Studi di Bergamo. She works on contemporary Latin American literature and has specialized in literary archives and the analysis of writing processes. Her research engages a wide range of fields that includes translation studies, genetic criticism, gender theory, and the visual arts.

Yolanda Ariadne Collins is a lecturer in international relations at the University of St. Andrews in Scotland. She holds a PhD in environmental science and policy from Central European University in Budapest, Hungary. Trained as an interdisciplinary environmental social scientist, her work investigates the relationship between climate change, colonialism and market-based methods for conserving forests in the Guiana Shield.

Nicolò Crisafi is a retained lecturer in Italian at Pembroke College, Oxford and a former ICI Fellow 2018–2020. His monograph *Dante's Masterplot and Alternative Narratives in the 'Commedia'*, forthcoming with Oxford University Press in 2021, investigates paradoxes, detours, and representations of the future as alternatives to the dominant narrative of Dante Alighieri's *Commedia*: the teleological 'masterplot'.

Manuele Gragnolati is professor of Italian literature at Sorbonne Université, associate director of the ICI Berlin Institute for Cultural Inquiry, and senior research fellow at Somerville College, Oxford. He is the author of *Experiencing the Afterlife: Soul and Body in Dante and Medieval Culture* (2005), *Amor che move. Linguaggio del corpo e forma del desiderio in Dante, Pasolini e Morante* (2013), and *Possibilities of Lyric: Reading Petrarch in Dialogue* (with Francesca Southerden, forthcoming 2020), as well as the co-editor of several volumes on Dante and the Middle Ages.

Amelia Groom was a fellow at ICI Berlin from 2018 to 2020. She holds a PhD in art history and theory from the University of Sydney, and teaches theory and writing on the Critical Studies MA degree at the Sandberg Institute. Her writing has appeared in *Frieze, e-flux journal, Art-Agenda, Metropolis M*, and various artist monographs, exhibition catalogues, and academic volumes. She edited the Documents of Contemporary Art anthology on TIME, and her book *Beverly Buchanan: Marsh Ruins* is forthcoming as part of Afterall's One Work series.

Christoph F. E. Holzhey is the founding director of the ICI Berlin Institute for Cultural Inquiry, which he has led since 2007. He received a PhD in theoretical physics (1993) and another one in German literature (2001). He has run several projects at the ICI Berlin and (co-)edited several volumes, including *Tension/Spannung* (2010), *Multistable Figures* (2014), *De/Constituting Wholes* (2017), and *Re-* (2019).

Daniel Liu is a historian of the modern life and physical sciences. His recent publications include 'The Artificial Cell, the Semipermeable Membrane, and the Life That Never Was, 1864–1901' (*Historical Studies in the Natural Sciences*, 49.5), and 'The Cell and Protoplasm as Container, Object, and Substance, 1835–1861' (*Journal for the History of Biology*, 50.4), the latter of which received the *Journal of the History of Biology*'s Everett Mendelsohn Prize for 2020.

Anja Sunhyun Michaelsen is a researcher, writer, and an ICI affiliated fellow. She holds an MA in gender studies and German literature (Humboldt-Universität zu Berlin) and a PhD in media studies (Ruhr-Universität Bochum). Her work focuses on antiracist, postcolonial, and queer archives and (non-)relationality.

Marlon Miguel is a FCT — Fundação para a Ciência e a Tecnologia researcher at the Centre for Philosophy of Science of the University of Lisbon (CFCUL) and an ICI Berlin affiliated fellow. He holds a double PhD in philosophy (Federal University of Rio de Janeiro) and fine arts (Université Paris 8). His current research focuses on the intersection between art, philosophy, and psychiatry.

Claudia Peppel is the Academic Coordinator at the ICI Berlin. She studied Romance literature at the Freie Universität Berlin and at La Sapienza in Rome. Peppel's research focuses on literary and cultural studies as well as art history and food cultures. Her monograph explored the Metaphysical Art of Giorgio de Chirico. She has curated exhibitions of contemporary art, has taught at the Berlin University of the Arts, and recently co-edited the volume *Die Kunst des Wartens* (with Brigitte Kölle, 2019).

Damiano Sacco holds a PhD in theoretical physics from King's College London. Having published in both physics and philosophy, he currently works on modern and contemporary aspects of the continental philosophical tradition. His research focuses on twentieth-century European philosophy, and on the relationship between the history of physics and the history of metaphysics in the West.

Alison Sperling currently holds an International Postdoctoral Initiative (IPODI) Fellowship at Technische Universität Berlin in the Center for Interdisciplinary Women's and Gender Studies Research (Zentrum für Interdisziplinäre Frauen und Geschlechterforschung) and is an affiliated fellow at the ICI Berlin. She studies twentieth and twenty-first century science and weird fictions, contemporary ecological art, feminist and queer theory, and the Anthropocene.

M. Ty thinks of the sea even while not now in it — and is an assistant professor of literature at the University of Wisconsin, Madison.

Facundo Vega is an Assistant Professor of Philosophy at Universidad Adolfo Ibáñez. He received his PhD from Cornell University in 2018. Vega is currently completing his first book, titled *Extraordinary Matters: The Political after Martin Heidegger*. His articles have appeared or are forthcoming in, among other venues, *Philosophy Today*, *Cahier de L'Herne*, and *diacritics*. Vega has been a Research Scientist at CONICET as well as a Fellow at the ICI Berlin.

Arnd Wedemeyer is senior researcher at the ICI Berlin. He earned his PhD from the Humanities Center at Johns Hopkins University, and has taught at Princeton and Duke University. His research focuses on political and continental philosophy, comparative literature, and art and cultural history. He has published on Kant, Kafka, Jacob Taubes and Carl Schmitt, Borges and Salomo Friedländer, and Joseph Beuys. He has co-edited *Re-: An Errant Glossary* (2019).

Umut Yildirim's research interests lie at the intersection of the anthropology of the state and sovereignty, ecological anthropology, anarchist, decolonial, and indigenous resistance, and feminist and queer theories of affect and subjectivity. Her first anthropological articles on affective modes of political organizing are out and forthcoming in *Anthropological Theory* (2019) and *Current Anthropology* (2021). She is currently an Einstein Guest Researcher in the Institute for Social and Cultural Anthropology at Freie Universität Berlin (2021) and will teach graduate courses in the Center for Near Eastern Studies at UCLA in 2022.

Index

Cultural Inquiry

EDITED BY CHRISTOPH F. E. HOLZHEY
AND MANUELE GRAGNOLATI